The 20th Century in Poetry

The 20th Century in Poetry

EDITED BY

Michael Hulse and Simon Rae

PEGASUS BOOKS

NEW YORK LONDON

THE 20TH CENTURY IN POETRY

Pegasus Books LLC
80 Broad Street, 5th Floor
New York, NY 10004

ISBN: 978-1-60598-364-6

10 9 8 7 8 6 5 4 3 2 1

Printed in the United States of America
Distributed by W. W. Norton & Company, Inc.

CONTENTS

I

1900–1914 Never such innocence again

II

1915–1922 War to Waste Land

III
1923–1939 Danger and hope

IV
1940–1945 War

V
1946–1968 Peace and Cold War

VI
1969–1988 From the Moon to Berlin

VII

1989–2000 Endgames

The 20th Century
in Poetry

Introduction

THIS BOOK gathers over four hundred poems written in many parts of the English-speaking world in the twentieth century. They are arranged chronologically, as the poems appeared, rather than in bundles dictated by the birth dates of the poets. In many cases the poems appear under the date of first volume publication, or in some cases under the date of composition, if known (Larkin's 'The Whitsun Weddings' is one such). In other cases it is the event to which the poem relates that has determined the place it occupies in this book. In the relatively short opening section, for instance, there are already nine examples of this. Gibson's poem on the mystery of Flannan Isle was not written till 1912; Murray's on the hanging of Jimmy Governor, and Noël Coward's on the perceived watershed of 1901, were written long after the events, as was Linda Bierds' poem on the death of Tolstoy; so too were Stewart's meditation on Rutherford's work on the atom (dated here to the year in which the physicist developed the model of the atom that is known by his name), Tate's account of a lynching, and Pratt's magisterial poem on the loss of the *Titanic*, written in the mid-Thirties. Our last selections for this opening group of poems, which takes us to the outbreak of the First World War – Hill's lines on the armies of France 'reeling towards Verdun', and Larkin's 'MCMXIV', the very title of which recalls a lapidary inscription on a memorial – underscore the historically-minded inclusion of the past in the present. That sense of the long shadows events cast across after-years is an especially important strand in the fabric of this book. Our aim has been to allow the poems to tell the stories of the century, both public and private, that the poets wanted to tell, whether at the time or after the event.

The poems have been chosen because the editors believe they are richly rewarding, in the ways that worthwhile, living poems are richly rewarding, whatever their form or style, whatever the time in which they were written or the culture in which they originated. Some of the poems have long been familiar, and critics and readers have agreed on their value; others are still in the process of acquiring that weight of consent; others are well known in their own countries but have too little currency elsewhere; still others, we hope, will come as surprising discoveries or re-discoveries. Poems here by a Frost or Hardy, Eliot or Yeats, Auden or Lowell, are of the first kind; poems by a Moore or Bishop, Heaney or Mahon, Porter or Gray of the second; poems by virtually all the poets from New Zealand, Canada, India and Anglophone Africa are of the third kind, at least from the perspective of the UK and the US; and, as for the surprises, the less we say here, the better they will be.

These first opening remarks are couched in what we hope are uncontroversial terms. Our aim is to offer pleasures, both simple and complex, rather than to brew up a storm in poetry's tea-cup. But of course we recognise that all of the presuppositions underlying them might spark disagreement. Questions of value and consent, for example, have become steadily more contentious in recent decades, since they imply both the passing of critical judgement and the formation of a 'canon'. So it's right that we say a few words about our assumptions.

While it's not for us to speculate whether this book will play a part in the creation or reinforcement of a 'canon', it is in the nature of anthologies that they're read in the context of this process, and it is disingenuous of anthologists to pretend otherwise. But the 'canon' as imagined here is broad and generous in spirit. This book stands for a new understanding of the 'canon', an understanding that is all about co-presence. It recognises that different poetries in English existed side by side in the twentieth century, some of them 'old' and some of them 'new', drawing partly on common sources in the poetries of past centuries but also on the distinctive characters, traditions and agendas of the places in which poetry was now being written in English. In a world that has moved beyond the old-style empires, there are no longer any 'centres' in the sense in which London or New York were once thought to be the 'centres' of the English-speaking world. The centre is wherever the language is used with vitality, in poetry that comes from the heart of lived experience, pitched thought, vigorous engagement with the public and private life of the age.

This book has been several years in the making, and throughout we have devoted our attention to these fundamental questions: *What is the poem setting out to do?* and *How well has it done it?* Other criteria – of ideology, race, gender, membership of this or that aesthetic movement – were secondary at best, and of course we were guided by James Fenton's basic rule: 'when a line seems to be meaningless or untrue, it is not a bad idea to entertain the possibility that it is indeed meaningless or untrue'. We wanted to feel ourselves in the presence of poetry that was fully achieved, poetry that didn't require special pleading, poetry that respected the primacy of communication (since we are all creatures of language), poetry that had the courage of its convictions, poetry that would honour any 'canon' it finally ended up in, once the organic process of canon formation – by which generations of readers vote with their considered preferences – has run its course. We are convinced that many of the poems in this book will endure. What's more, our chronological arrangement not only comes up with some thought-provoking juxtapositions (the selections for 1958 or 1973 speak volumes) but also poses a continuous challenge to national self-preoccupation: British readers who haven't come across Yusef Komunyakaa or Yvette Christiansë, Americans who haven't read Judith Wright or R. A. K. Mason, Australians who haven't encountered Don Coles or Elizabeth Spires, can prepare for a discovery. Our regret, inevitably, is for the excellent poems and poets we were still unable to include.

★　★

It is a truism that poetry has undergone profound change since 1900. Early in the twentieth century, T. S. Eliot considered it 'likely that poets in our civilization, as it exists at present, must be *difficult*'. Late in the century, Geoffrey Hill told an interviewer: 'Poetry should, ideally, turn towards the people, but, the world being what it is, there's an ignorant expectation that one must succumb to a lowest common denominator of demand.' The two remarks map a key problem for modern poetry. The complexity Eliot experienced in a world that was seeing the collapse of old certainties could not be accounted for in simple terms, and the forms taken by his responses in poetry were complex. In Hill, in many ways Eliot's poetic kinsman, we see the converse of Eliot's dilemma: glad to acknowledge the man in the street as the arbiter in principle, Hill is anxious in practice not to sell poetry short by dumbing down. The gap that has seemingly widened between poets and readers over the past hundred years, and the distrust that has arguably weakened the age-old contract, could easily be discussed in terms derived from their respective positions.

But that would be a partial account. From Lawrence Ferlinghetti in the jazz clubs of the Fifties and Robert Lowell on the Pentagon march to the extraordinary popularity enjoyed by writers as different as Dylan Thomas, Allen Ginsberg, Sylvia Plath, Wendy Cope or Virginia Hamilton Adair, there has been no shortage of reminders that poetry possessed of intelligence and address, whether high or light, priestly or irreverent, can speak to a wide audience. In fact, the true story of poetry in English in the twentieth century is not told by tracing the line of communicative and conceptual intractability, a line which fetches up in the dead end of poetry fired by linguistic philosophy and designed to appeal to a coterie of initiates. It is a story of success in finding ways of dealing with the truly complex experience of modern life in language that is resonant yet down-to-earth. Berryman's *Dream Songs*, Mahon's 'A Disused Shed in County Wexford', Pinsky's 'Shirt', Bishop's 'At the Fishhouses', Mason's 'Lugete o veneres', Owen's 'Dulce et Decorum Est', Wright's 'At Cooloolah', Hardy's 'At Castle Boterel', have nothing in common – nothing, that is, but the most important thing of all, their determination to grasp in its fullness the experience or thought that they wish to tell of, and, having grasped it, to put what they have understood into the most arresting and abiding of words and forms. Many poems work to a low common denominator, faking intimacy, pumping up bogus moments of epiphany, or addressing the reader as if from an open microphone or an election poster. Many others work to an abstrusely high agenda, perhaps perceiving the need for an aesthetic corrective but mistaking the extent to which the common reader is willing or able to share the preoccupations of specialists. The poems we as editors believe have the potential to keep on winning readers are those that were written in the understanding that the common reader (the species still exists, though it may be endangered) possesses intelligence, sensitivity, experience of life and of literature, a familiarity with the past, and an openness to the new.

The superabundance of debates in twentieth-century poetics tells us a great deal about the self-perpetuating difficulties the art has got itself into, and the insecurities poets and critics now seem so deeply entrenched in. It is hard to think of any previous period that saw so many struggles for position, so many movements and avant-gardes and wars for influence, so much contemptuous or cantankerous dismissal of other writers by those with a line to push. And the watchwords of one battle have often been handed down, stripped of context and meaning, to be parroted by later combatants. 'Go in fear of abstractions,' warned Ezra Pound in the Imagist heyday, when it mattered to sweep away some of the lazier habits of early twentieth-century poets, and to this day, in poetry workshops the length and breadth of the English-speaking world, a ban on abstraction is enforced by those who are reluctant to consider that abstract language is at the heart of much of the century's finest poetry – one need only think of Eliot's *Four Quartets*. Another example: in Canto LXXXI, written in his Pisan detention in 1945, Pound reflected: 'to break the pentameter, that was the first heave'. Generations of critics have sagely nodded, agreeing that the pentameter was mercifully broken and that all manner of thing has been well in poetry since we swept the pieces into the dust-pan. But Glyn Maxwell's riposte is strong: 'The most positive poetic achievement of the twentieth century was not the breaking of the pentameter to serve contemporary discomfort, but the remastering of it to serve contemporary breath.' His example is striking: 'The true revolutionary is Frost, whose lines most closely approximate the meeting of breath and thought, and whose silences are beyond anyone's in kind and depth.' In our own book, we might point to the final line of the first of Baxter's *Jerusalem Sonnets* – 'His silent laugh still shakes the hills at dawn' – as an instance of a perfect and beautiful iambic pentameter implanted in a free verse context, making a quiet, uninsistent appeal to the reader's inner ear. Baxter had spent many years writing syllabics and free verse, but he had not forgotten that centuries of great poetry in English had hard-wired the pentameter's rhythm into the collective rhythmic subconscious of the language. That wonderful line radiates to enhance the free verse around it with a subtly energised music. Bishop shows the same deep awareness when she allows an occasional pentameter into 'At the Fishhouses'. The poem is of course written in a relaxed free verse *parlando*, but a little voice in our ear whispers 'blank verse' when we first see it on the page, and Bishop's metrical lines are gracefully allowed into the poem in recognition that the free and the metrical can flourish in the same hedgerow.

What does this mean? It means that the benefits of the century's upheavals in poetics have been gladly adopted by the poets, but they haven't seen the need to throw out everything that the past had given them. Thoughtful poets have understood the century's correctives – the greater emphasis on free forms, the speaking voice, and breath, the heightened attention to things rather than to ideas about things – as an enrichment of the means available to them. We believe our anthology demonstrates that they have reaped the harvest of the upheavals not in a spirit of *either . . . or* but in a spirit of *not only . . . but also.* And to those many, poets and critics, who have imagined it was possible or desirable to lay down the law, the poets have always made swift reply. When ink was being spilt on the rules imagined to govern free verse, D. H. Lawrence baldly observed: 'It is no use inventing fancy laws for free verse, no use drawing a melodic line which all the feet must toe. Free verse toes no melodic line, no matter what drill-sergeant.' The aesthetic debate on the nature of beauty, ongoing even now, was brushed aside in the Forties by Marianne Moore, in her poem 'In Distrust of Merits', when she briskly declared: 'Beauty is everlasting'. And when Bill Manhire in an interview approves of 'poets who produced work that sounded tidy and symmetrical on the page – yet inside the apparent tidiness all sorts of imaginative and emotional leaps were taking place' (his example is fellow New Zealander R. A. K. Mason), it is hard not to think of Sylvia Plath's long tussle with *terza rima*, easily followed through the pages of her *Collected Poems*, and the fruit that that formal engagement bore in the radical freedom of 'Lady Lazarus'. The one rule in poetry is that there are no rules. In the great vineyard, many kinds of labourer may go about their work.

We believe that the poems are what matters, not secondary comment on the poems, so the notes we have provided are light, and aim only to remove difficulties or to enhance the reading experience; and we've arranged the contents in 'chapters' that follow cut-off points given by history (1914, 1945, 1989), each chapter prefaced with a few user-friendly pointers. In arranging the poems in this book chronologically, we have found that a simple, familiar truth about poetry re-asserted itself. It is this: that the art finds its subjects wherever it wants. Poetry has always been public by nature, confronting the great political and military turning-points and traumas that station the collective experience of humanity, and the high achievement of poetry that tells of war is a signal accomplishment of the twentieth century. (It can be no coincidence that Homer's *Iliad* throws so dark a shadow over poetry since 1900.) Writing here by Owen, Gurney, Rosenberg and Sassoon, by Douglas, Jarrell, Manifold and Simpson, and others, speaks directly of the two global wars; poems by Auden, Hamburger, Hecht, Hill, Motion, Jorie Graham and Kit Wright live under the shadow of the genocide, atrocities and camps of the Nazi Reich; poems by Mason, Wilbur, Lowell, Nemerov, Forché, Fenton, White and Komunyakaa address the proxy, 'sideshow' wars fought around the world through the decades of the Cold War, while John Forbes observes the Gulf War of 1991 from the perspective most of us now share, that of the television viewer. (We have included an extract from Christopher Logue's *War Music* in the conviction, shared by George Steiner and others, that it is not so much a translation of Homer as a poem of twentieth century warfaring, in its own right.) Other strands that can be followed through the book deal with the British Empire and its aftermath, the nature of 'the West', questions of race, of national identities, of science, technology, and the environment. Equally, poetry has always been private by nature, and intimate lyrics, poems of love and grief and celebration, are here too. As medical advances enable us to live longer, the poetry of old age can be seen to become more substantial; aspects of ageing are broached in poems by Coles, Tony Harrison, Hugo Williams, Kleinzahler and Gray. The complex experience of living in modern communities, whether large cities or small villages, is examined from various angles in poems by Moore, Smithyman, Kinnell, Gray, Gustafson, Hofmann, Spires and Doty – the motto here, we feel, might be Forster's 'only connect'. And a still space is always preserved by the poets – by a Frances Cornford, Frost, Clarke, or R. S. Thomas, say – for those numinous moments in which self is glad to yield to the great other.

★　★

WE HAVE received help and support from many people during the compilation of this anthology, and would like to thank all those who contributed so generously to the project. These include Phil Errington of the John Masefield Society, Angus McIntyre of the Salamander/Oasis Trust, Caroline Ardrey, Siân Hughes, Tony Barnstone, librarians at the Bodleian, British and London libraries, and those at our mainstay, the Poetry Library in the Royal Festival Hall. We would like to thank our editor, Carey Smith, for her patience and commitment, and express similar gratitude to Roxanne Benson-Mackey, editorial assistant, and to the rest of the team at Ebury. This anthology would not exist without a generous commission from Felix Dennis in the first place, and we are extremely grateful to him for his unflagging enthusiasm. We also owe a considerable debt to his personal assistant, Caroline Rush, who undertook the gruelling task of clearing the permissions. Finally, we would both like to thank those closest to us for their support and forbearance: Kathrin Hulse and Susan Hitch.

MH
SR

I

1900—1914
Never such innocence again

RETIRED NOVELIST Thomas Hardy greeted the twentieth century with characteristic pessimism, and indeed there might seem 'little cause for carolings' to anyone taking a dispassionate view. Britain was embroiled in an increasingly frustrating war in South Africa, in which its professional army was regularly outwitted and humiliated by the Afrikaaners' resourceful guerrilla forces, and public impatience was growing at military incompetence and the mounting death toll with its 'hourly posted sheets of scheduled slaughter', as Hardy put it in another poem. The Boer War produced a plethora of patriotic verse, notably A. C. Benson's 'Land of Hope and Glory', to many even now the unofficial national anthem of England. But less strident voices could be heard through the bellicose din, as William Watson gently reminded his readers of uncomfortable parallels in 'Rome and Another', and Rudyard Kipling, who controversially canonised the imperialist project as 'the White man's burden', confronted the costs, especially those borne by the empire's humblest servants.

The war ended in 1902, with might winning, though many remained unconvinced that it was right. The year before, Queen Victoria had died (after a reign of sixty-four years), bringing to an end the age to which she gave her name. The sense of loss was genuine, but as the more than middle-aged Prince of Wales mounted the throne after his marathon wait to succeed, his subjects hoped for a breath of fresh air. The great glacier of Victorian social attitudes had been showing cracks for some years. The Labour Party, struggling into existence, had won its first two seats in the 1900 general election, and, while the Conservatives doggedly held on to age-old privileges, the Liberals fought to introduce the rudiments of a welfare system. Though Thomas Hardy had given up fiction after the outraged response to the emotional and sexual honesty of *Jude the Obscure* (1895), the 1890s had in fact seen a mounting challenge to stultifying conventions, especially in regard to relations between the sexes. Frances Cornford's 'Autumn Morning at Cambridge' captures the mood of optimism that assumed superiorities and ingrained inequalities could be challenged.

The road to equality for women was of course a long one. Dorothy Sayers, later famous as a crime writer, won a scholarship to Somerville College, Oxford, in 1912, but in spite of achieving a first class result (in 1915) could not yet be awarded a degree at the time, and had to wait. Today it requires a real effort of the imagination to comprehend the brutally repressive reaction to the suffragette movement. Protesters were dragged off to prison, where those who went on hunger strike were subjected to the painful indignities of force-feeding – all to deny women the simple right to vote (ceded almost without a murmur after they had kept the home fires burning, and the munitions factories going, during the First World War).

In Ireland, poetry was in robust shape. The leading figure was William Butler Yeats, who declared in 1909, following the deaths of Swinburne and George Meredith, 'And now I am king of the cats.' After years devoted to the heroes of Irish folklore, Yeats was forced into engagement with contemporary events by his involvement with (and unrequited love for) the beautiful and headstrong nationalist, Maude Gonne, whom he mythologised as a modern-day Helen of Troy while disapproving of her revolutionary agenda. Brilliant younger writers included James Joyce and the playwright J. M. Synge, who led the way in challenging the grip of the Roman Catholic Church on all aspects of life. Synge's play *The Playboy of the Western World* provoked a riot in Dublin, and Joyce opted for exile to escape censorship, but the heat of controversy forged an Irish literature of such quality that it achieved global recognition and influence.

Elsewhere in the English-speaking world, poetry was in the doldrums in the opening years of the century. The six Australian colonies had been federated into the Commonwealth of Australia in 1901, but no burst of poetic energy accompanied the new charge of socio-political life. The poetic achievements of Henry Lawson and A. B. 'Banjo' Paterson belonged chiefly to the 1890s, and in the pre-1914 years the lone figures of Christopher Brennan and Shaw Neilson stand out as writers engaged in the profound endeavour to forge their own voices in a land still imagined to be 'new'. In the United States of war veteran and hunter Theodore Roosevelt, poetry found no immediate succession either to the line of Walt Whitman (who had died in 1892) or to that of Emily Dickinson (whose posthumously published poems had proved a sensational success in the 1890s), and first Ezra Pound and then T. S. Eliot made their homes on the European side of the Atlantic. For many of the extraordinary events, on a larger or smaller scale, that have captured the imaginations of later generations – from the loss of the *Titanic* to the racism behind the stories of an aboriginal outlaw hanged for murder in Australia or a black victim lynched in Kentucky – poetry did not as yet have a language or vision. The long shadow cast across the twentieth century by the scientific work of Ernest Rutherford attracted no response from poets at the time, and William Watson's prophetic sonnet seemingly previsioning the spectre of destruction under which mankind has lived since 1945 was the exception, not the rule.

If the old dispensation was gradually giving way, it did not always seem to know it, not even when the great Russian novelist Leo Tolstoy died at a railway station, inspiring a wave of mourning that washed across the world and affected many with the sense that an era had ended. Despite individual horrors, the mass enslavements of mass production, and the growing awareness that social and political life was beginning to change, there was still, in the pre-war period, a deep and rich sense of untrammelled space. The train was a fact of life (and for many, a blessed escape from the towns), and the motor car was still the preserve of the tiny minority, and had yet to dominate the countryside. 'Driving' in Hardy's pre-war poems meant being drawn by horse; the open road was still a place where all might wander at will, as it had been throughout human history. Both W. H. Davies, the self-proclaimed Super Tramp, and John Masefield, in very early youth, spent years on the road in America. Shaw Neilson celebrated the peripatetic life of the 'sundowner' along

Australia's 'Tucker Track', while Ezra Pound tramped the roads of southern France in his quest for a cultural continuum that would fuel a lifetime's literary labour. G. K. Chesterton, Pound's opposite in almost every regard, put his trust in the rolling English road, and the rolling English drunkard (and, with his friend and fellow satirist Hilaire Belloc, made many a convivial journey from pub to pub down Sussex lanes). The walkers perhaps overlooked the fearful isolation of rural living. The American Robert Frost might be seen, amongst much else, as the laureate of loneliness, and in poem after poem he focused on slow lives lived in an unrelieved obscurity that was in sharp contrast to the increasingly hectic pace of the lives led by the majority.

So when Philip Larkin, in later times, wrote of the 'innocence' of the years before 1914, it was of that opportunity to walk blithely out among the 'flowering grasses' that he was thinking, among other things. His poem 'MCMXIV' knows of the hierarchy that stretched from kings and queens to servants, but its foregrounding of 'innocence' does not mean by that word the self-interested manoeuvres of the great powers, as they positioned themselves for advantage while maintaining the ball-room niceties of diplomacy, nor does it mean the Anglo-German arms race. From the forging of alliances and the drawing-up of war plans to the whipping-up of jingoistic sentiment by the popular press, the pre-1914 years were of course anything but innocent. But Britain had fought its wars as imperial sideshows for so long, in faraway places with faraway names like Afghanistan, Egypt or South Africa, that it imagined it had been at peace, and war, when it came, could seem rather an exciting prospect – an attitude Larkin captures brilliantly in his reference to the lines of young men queuing to volunteer as though waiting to get into a football or cricket match. The eager anticipation was such that many boys lied about their age to get a uniform. Cambridge golden boy Rupert Brooke rose to national prominence with a series of sonnets embracing the conflict, claiming his generation were as 'swimmers into cleanness leaping', and imagining a patriotic hero's death for himself in 'The Soldier'. The terrible unheroic truths about the First World War were left to an Owen, a Rosenberg or a Sassoon to write.

1900

The Darkling Thrush

Thomas Hardy

I leant upon a coppice gate
    When Frost was spectre-gray,
And Winter's dregs made desolate
    The weakening eye of day.
The tangled bine-stems scored the sky
    Like strings of broken lyres,
And all mankind that haunted nigh
    Had sought their household fires.

The land's sharp features seemed to be
    The Century's corpse outleant,
His crypt the cloudy canopy,
    The wind his death-lament.
The ancient pulse of germ and birth
    Was shrunken hard and dry,
And every spirit upon earth
    Seemed fervourless as I.

At once a voice arose among
    The bleak twigs overhead
In a full-hearted evensong
    Of joy illimited;
An aged thrush, frail, gaunt, and small,
    In blast-beruffled plume,
Had chosen thus to fling his soul
    Upon the growing gloom.

So little cause for carolings
　　Of such ecstatic sound
Was written on terrestrial things
　　Afar or nigh around,
That I could think there trembled through
　　His happy good-night air
Some blessed Hope, whereof he knew
　　And I was unaware.

31 December 1900

The Victorians regarded 31 December 1900 as the end of the nineteenth century. To some there seemed little to celebrate as they looked toward the twentieth, with the country fighting a costly imperial war in South Africa. The Boer War ended in 1902.

1900

Flannan Isle

WILFRID WILSON GIBSON

Though three men dwell on Flannan Isle
To keep the lamp alight,
As we steer'd under the lee, we caught
No glimmer through the night!

A passing ship at dawn had brought
The news; and quickly we set sail,
To find out what strange thing might ail
The keepers of the deep-sea light.

The winter day broke blue and bright,
With glancing sun and glancing spray,
As o'er the swell our boat made way,
As gallant as a gull in flight.

But, as we near'd the lonely Isle;
And look'd up at the naked height;
And saw the lighthouse towering white,
With blinded lantern, that all night
Had never shot a spark
Of comfort through the dark,
So ghastly in the cold sunlight
It seem'd, that we were struck the while
With wonder all too dread for words.

And, as into the tiny creek
We stole beneath the hanging crag,
We saw three queer, black, ugly, birds –
Too big, by far, in my belief,
For guillemot or shag –
Like seamen sitting bold upright
Upon a half-tide reef:
But, as we near'd, they plunged from sight,
Without a sound, or spurt of white.

And still too mazed to speak,
We landed; and made fast the boat;
And climb'd the track in single file,
Each wishing he was safe afloat,
On any sea, however far,
So it be far from Flannan Isle:
And still we seem'd to climb, and climb,
As though we'd lost all count of time,
And so must climb for evermore.
Yet, all too soon, we reached the door –
The black, sun-blister'd lighthouse door,
That gaped for us ajar.

As, on the threshold, for a spell,
We paused, we seem'd to breathe the smell
Of limewash and of tar,
Familiar as our daily breath,
As though 'twere some strange scent of death:
And so, yet wondering, side by side,
We stood a moment, still tongue-tied:
And each with black foreboding eyed
The door, ere we should fling it wide,
To leave the sunlight for the gloom:
Till, plucking courage up, at last,
Hard on each other's heels we pass'd
Into the living-room.

Yet, as we crowded through the door,
We only saw a table, spread
For dinner, meat and cheese and bread;
But all untouch'd; and no one there:
As though, when they sat down to eat,
Ere they could even taste,
Alarm had come; and they in haste
Had risen and left the bread and meat:
For on the table-head a chair
Lay tumbled on the floor.
We listen'd; but we only heard
The feeble cheeping of a bird

That starved upon its perch:
And, listening still, without a word,
We set about our hopeless search.

We hunted high, we hunted low,
And soon ransack'd the empty house;
Then o'er the Island, to and fro,
We ranged, to listen and to look
In every cranny, cleft or nook
That might have hid a bird or mouse:
But, though we searched from shore to shore,
We found no sign in any place:
And soon again stood face to face
Before the gaping door:
And stole into the room once more
As frighten'd children steal.

Aye: though we hunted high and low,
And hunted everywhere,
Of the three men's fate we found no trace
Of any kind in any place,
But a door ajar, and an untouch'd meal,
And an overtoppled chair.

And, as we listen'd in the gloom
Of that forsaken living-room –
O chill clutch on our breath –
We thought how ill-chance came to all
Who kept the Flannan Light:
And how the rock had been the death
Of many a likely lad:
How six had come to a sudden end
And three had gone stark mad:
And one whom we'd all known as friend
Had leapt from the lantern one still night,
And fallen dead by the lighthouse wall:
And long we thought
On the three we sought,
And of what might yet befall.

Like curs a glance has brought to heel,
We listen'd, flinching there:
And look'd, and look'd, on the untouch'd meal
And the overtoppled chair.

We seem'd to stand for an endless while,
Though still no word was said,
Three men alive on Flannan Isle,
Who thought on three men dead.

The Flannan Isles are a group of uninhabited islands in the Outer Hebrides, off the coast of Scotland. The lighthouse on Eilean Mòr, designed by David Alan Stevenson (cousin of the writer Robert Louis Stevenson), was taken into service in December 1899, and a year later, ten days before Christmas 1900, was the scene of a mystery that remains unsolved to this day, when the three lighthouse keepers vanished without trace (presumably swept into the sea by freak waves). Gibson's ballad-like narrative poem, written in 1912, is apparently mistaken in suggesting that the men were interrupted at their meal, but is otherwise marvellously (and accurately) evocative of the scene that met those who first investigated the extinction of the light. The story also inspired Peter Maxwell Davies's chamber opera *The Lighthouse* (1979).

1901

The Ballad of Jimmy Governor

LES MURRAY

HM Prison, Darlinghurst, 18 January 1901

You can send for my breakfast now, Governor.
The colt from Black Velvet's awake
and the ladies all down from the country
are gathered outside for my sake.

Soon be all finished, the running.
No tracks of mine lead out of here.
Today, I take that big step
on the bottom rung of the air
and be in Heaven for dinner.
Might be the first jimbera there.

The Old People don't go to Heaven,
good thing. My mother might meet
that stockman feller my father
and him cut her dead in the street.
Mother, today I'll be dancing
your way and his way on numb feet.

But a man's not a rag to wipe snot on,
I got that much into their heads,
them hard white sunbonnet ladies
that turned up their short lips and said
my wife had a slut's eye for colour.
I got that into their head

and the cow-cockies' kids plant up chimneys
they got horse soldiers out with the Law
after Joe and lame Jack and tan Jimmy –
but who learnt us how to make war
on women, old men, babies?
It ain't all one way any more.

The papers, they call us bushrangers:
That would be our style, I daresay,
bushrangers on foot with our axes.
It sweetens the truth, anyway.
They don't like us killing their women.
Their women kill us every day.

And the squatters are peeing their moleskins,
that's more than a calf in the wheat,
it's Jimmy the fencer, running
along the top rail in the night,
it's the Breelong mob crossing the ranges
with rabbitskins soft on their feet.

But now Jack in his Empire brickyard
has already give back his shoes
and entered the cleanliness kingdom,
the Commonwealth drums through the walls
and I'm weary of news.

I'm sorry, old Jack, I discharged you,
you might have enjoyed running free
of plonk and wet cornbags and colour
with us pair of outlaws. But see,
you can't trust even half a whitefeller.
You died of White Lady through me.

They tried me once running, once standing:
one time ought to do for the drop.
It's more trial than you got, I hear, Joe,
your tommyhawk's chipped her last chop.
I hope you don't mind I got lazy
when the leaks in my back made me stop.

If any gin stands in my print
I'll give her womb sorrow and dread,
if a buck finds our shape in the tussocks
I'll whiten the hair in his head,
but a man's not a rag to wipe boots on
and I got that wrote up, bright red,

where even fine ladies can read it
who never look at the ground
for a man that ain't fit to breed from
may make a terrible bound
before the knacker's knife gets him.
Good night to you, father. Sleep sound.

Fetch in my breakfast, Governor,
I have my journey to make
and the ladies all down from the country
are howling outside for my sake.

Jimmy Governor, a part-aboriginal man in his mid-twenties, was hanged at Darlinghurst gaol, Sydney, in January 1901 for a string of murders committed together with his brother Joe and a third man, Jacky Underwood. His motive is taken to have been the racist contempt to which he was routinely exposed. The story was fictionalised in a celebrated novel by Thomas Kenneally, *The Chant of Jimmie Blacksmith* (1972), which in turn was made into a highly-praised film (1978) directed by Fred Schepisi.

1901

1901

NOËL COWARD

When Queen Victoria died
The whole of England mourned
Not for a so recently breathing old woman
A wife and a mother and a widow,
Not for a staunch upholder of Christendom,
A stickler for etiquette
A vigilant of moral values
But for a symbol.
A symbol of security and prosperity
Of 'My Country Right or Wrong'
Of 'God is good and Bad is bad'
And 'What was good enough for your father
Ought to be good enough for you'
And 'If you don't eat your tapioca pudding
You will be locked in your bedroom
And given nothing but bread and water
Over and over again until you come to your senses
And are weak and pale and famished and say
Breathlessly, hopelessly and with hate in your heart
"Please Papa I would now like some tapioca pudding very
    much indeed"'
A symbol too of proper elegance
Not the flaunting, bejewelled kind
That became so popular
But a truly proper elegance,
An elegance of the spirit,
Of withdrawal from unpleasant subjects
Such as Sex and Poverty and Pit Ponies
And Little Children working in the Mines
And Rude Words and Divorce and Socialism
And numberless other inadmissible horrors.

When Queen Victoria died
They brought her little body from the Isle of Wight
Closed up in a black coffin, finished and done for,
With no longer any feelings and regrets and Memories of Albert
And no more blood pumping through the feeble veins
And no more heart beating away
As it had beaten for so many tiring years.
The coffin was placed upon a gun-carriage
And drawn along sadly and slowly by English sailors.

But long before this the people had mourned
And walked about the streets and the Parks and Kensington
   Gardens
Silently, solemnly and dressed in black.
Now, with the news already a few days old
The immediate shock had faded.
The business of the funeral was less poignant than the first
   realization of death,
This was a pageant, right and fitting, but adjustments were
   already beginning to be made.
This was something we were all used to,
This slow solemnity
This measured progress to the grave.

If it hadn't been for the gun-carriage
And the crowds and all the flags at half mast
And all the shops being closed
It might just as well have been Aunt Cordelia
Who died a few months earlier in Torquay
And had to be brought up to London by the Great Western
In a rather large coffin
And driven slowly, oh so slowly
To the family burial ground at Esher
With all the relatives driving behind
Wearing black black black and peering furtively out of the
   carriage windows
To note for a moment that life was going on as usual.
For Aunt Cordelia was no symbol really
And her small death was of little account.

She was, after all, very old indeed
Although not quite so old as Queen Victoria
But on the other hand she didn't have so much prestige
Except of course in her own personal mind
And that was snuffed out at the same moment as everything else.
Also, unlike Queen Victoria, she had few mourners
Just the family and Mrs Stokes who had been fond of her
And Miss Esme Banks who had looked after her in Torquay
And two remote cousins
Who couldn't rightly be classed as family
Because they were so very far removed
And only came to the cemetery because it was a sign of respect,
Respect, what is more, without hope
For there was little or no likelihood of their being mentioned in
    the will
But there they were all the same
Both tall and bent, in black toques with veils,
And both crying.

When Queen Victoria died
And was buried and the gun-carriage was dragged empty away
    again
The shops reopened and so did the theatres
Although business was none too good.
But still it improved after a while
And everyone began to make plans for the Coronation
And it looked as if nothing much had happened
And perhaps nothing much had really
Except that an era, an epoch, an attitude of mind, was ended.

There would be other eras and epochs and attitudes of mind.
But never quite the same.

Queen Victoria died on 2 February 1901 after a reign of sixty-four years which gave a name to imperial ambitions, entrepreneurial achievements and moral certainties still reverberating through British culture today. Best known for his brilliant (if brittle) plays about the idle rich and his satirical lyrics about the Englishman abroad, Noël Coward was a leading light of the generation that gleefully mocked Victorian attitudes, but there is perhaps a hint of fondness for a lost world of security and stability beneath the surface of his impish sketch of the old queen's passing.

1901

Bridge-Guard in the Karroo

◄◊►

RUDYARD KIPLING

'. . . and will supply details of the Blood River Bridge.'
District Orders: Lines of Communication –
South African War

Sudden the desert changes,
　The raw glare softens and clings,
Till the aching Oudtshoorn ranges
　Stand up like the thrones of Kings –

Ramparts of slaughter and peril –
　Blazing, amazing, aglow –
'Twixt the sky-line's belting beryl
　And the wine-dark flats below.

Royal the pageant closes,
　Lit by the last of the sun –
Opal and ash-of-roses,
　Cinnamon, umber, and dun.

The twilight swallows the thicket,
　The starlight reveals the ridge.
The whistle shrills to the picket –
　We are changing guard on the bridge.

(Few, forgotten and lonely,
　Where the empty metals shine –
No, not combatants – only
　Details guarding the line.)

We slip through the broken panel
　Of fence by the ganger's shed;
We drop to the waterless channel
　And the lean track overhead;

We stumble on refuse of rations,
　　The beef and the biscuit-tins;
We take our appointed stations,
　　And the endless night begins.

We hear the Hottentot herders
　　As the sheep click past to the fold –
And the click of the restless girders
　　As the steel contracts in the cold –

Voices of jackals calling
　　And, loud in the hush between,
A morsel of dry earth falling
　　From the flanks of the scarred ravine.

And the solemn firmament marches,
　　And the hosts of heaven rise
Framed through the iron arches –
　　Banded and barred by the ties,

Till we feel the far track humming,
　　And we see her headlight plain,
And we gather and wait her coming –
　　The wonderful north-bound train.

(Few, forgotten and lonely,
　　Where the white car-windows shine –
No, not combatants – only
　　Details guarding the line.)

Quick, ere the gift escape us!
　　Out of the darkness we reach
For a handful of week-old papers
　　And a mouthful of human speech.

And the monstrous heaven rejoices,
　　And the earth allows again
Meetings, greetings, and voices
　　Of women talking with men.

So we return to our places,
   As out on the bridge she rolls;
And the darkness covers our faces,
   And the darkness re-enters our souls.

More than a little lonely
   Where the lessening tail-lights shine.
No – not combatants – only
   Details guarding the line!

The Karroo is a semi-arid plateau region of southwest South Africa. Oudtshoorn, with mountain ranges to the north and south, is the main town of the Klein Karroo. Blood River, referred to in the epigraph, was the site of a much earlier Boer victory over a greatly superior Zulu force (in 1838). Kipling's point in referring to this seems to have been to remind his countrymen that it is not always the bigger battalions that win. Despite being cast as the chief drum-beater for Empire, Kipling was by no means blind to the shortcomings of the imperial project, and never lost sympathy for those on the front line.

1901

Story of Lilavanti

— ‹o› —

LAURENCE HOPE (ADELA FLORENCE NICOLSON)

They lay the slender body down
  With all its wealth of wetted hair,
Only a daughter of the town,
  But very young and slight and fair.

The eyes, whose light one cannot see,
  Are sombre doubtless, like the tresses,
The mouth's soft curvings seem to be
  A roseate series of caresses.

And where the skin has all but dried
  (The air is sultry in the room)
Upon her breast and either side,
  It shows a soft and amber bloom.

By women here, who knew her life,
  A leper husband, I am told,
Took all this loveliness to wife
  When it was barely ten years old.

And when the child in shocked dismay
  Fled from the hated husband's care
He caught and tied her, so they say,
  Down to his bedside by her hair.

To some low quarter of the town,
  Escaped a second time, she flew;
Her beauty brought her great renown
  And many lovers here she knew,

When, as the mystic Eastern night
  With purple shadow filled the air,
Behind her window framed in light,
  She sat with jasmin in her hair.

At last she loved a youth, who chose
　　To keep this wild flower for his own,
He in his garden set his rose
　　Where it might bloom for him alone.

Cholera came; her lover died,
　　Want drove her to the streets again,
And women found her there, who tried
　　To turn her beauty into gain.

But she who in those garden ways
　　Had learnt of Love, would now no more
Be bartered in the market place
　　For silver, as in days before.

That former life she strove to change;
　　She sold the silver off her arms,
While all the world grew cold and strange
　　To broken health and fading charms.

Till, finding lovers, but no friend,
　　Nor any place to rest or hide,
She grew despairing at the end,
　　Slipped softly down a well and died.

And yet, how short, when all is said,
　　This little life of love and tears!
Her age, they say, beside her bed,
　　To-day is only fifteen years.

Adela Nicolson offered her poems as translations, and in many of them traded on an orientalist taste that ran high among British readers when the Indian Raj was at its peak, but in the 'Story of Lilavanti' she shows a firm-minded willingness to tell a shocking story in plain language.

1902

Sea-Fever

◄○►

JOHN MASEFIELD

I must go down to the seas again, to the lonely sea and the
   sky,
And all I ask is a tall ship and a star to steer her by,
And the wheel's kick and the wind's song and the white sail's
   shaking,
And a grey mist on the sea's face and a grey dawn breaking.

I must go down to the seas again, for the call of the running
   tide
Is a wild call and a clear call that may not be denied;
And all I ask is a windy day with the white clouds flying,
And the flung spray and the blown spume, and the sea-gulls
   crying.

I must go down to the seas again, to the vagrant gypsy life,
To the gull's way and the whale's way where the wind's like a
   whetted knife;
And all I ask is a merry yarn from a laughing fellow-rover,
And quiet sleep and a sweet dream when the long trick's
   over.

1902

Autumn Morning at Cambridge

FRANCES CORNFORD

I ran out in the morning, when the air was clean and new
And all the grass was glittering and grey with autumn dew,
I ran out to an apple-tree and pulled an apple down,
And all the bells were ringing in the old grey town.

Down in the town off the bridges and the grass,
They are sweeping up the leaves to let the people pass,
Sweeping up the old leaves, golden-reds and browns,
Whilst the men go to lecture with the wind in their gowns.

1902

The Olive

A. E. HOUSMAN

The olive in its orchard
  Should now be rooted sure,
To cast abroad its branches
  And flourish and endure.

Aloft amid the trenches
  Its dressers dug and died
The olive in its orchard
  Should prosper and abide.

Close should the fruit be clustered
  And light the leaf should wave,
So deep the root is planted
  In the corrupting grave.

1902

'I did not lose my heart in summer's even'

A. E. HOUSMAN

I did not lose my heart in summer's even,
   When roses to the moonrise burst apart:
When plumes were under heel and lead was flying,
   In blood and smoke and flame I lost my heart.

I lost it to a soldier and a foeman,
   A chap that did not kill me, but he tried;
That took the sabre straight and took it striking
   And laughed and kissed his hand to me and died.

1903

Cargoes

<o>

JOHN MASEFIELD

Quinquireme of Nineveh from distant Ophir
Rowing home to haven in sunny Palestine,
With a cargo of ivory,
And apes and peacocks,
Sandalwood, cedarwood, and sweet white wine.

Stately Spanish galleon coming from the Isthmus,
Dipping through the Tropics by the palm-green shores,
With a cargo of diamonds,
Emeralds, amethysts,
Topazes, and cinnamon, and gold moidores.

Dirty British coaster with a salt-caked smoke stack
Butting through the channel in the mad March days,
With a cargo of Tyne coal,
Road-rail, pig-lead,
Firewood, iron-ware, and cheap tin trays.

A quinquireme was a Roman galley ship, with five sets of oars on either side.
Nineveh was one of the great cities of ancient Assyria, on the banks of the
Tigris, and Ophir – a port mentioned in the Bible – was famous for its wealth.
Masefield's deceptively simple poem intriguingly has it both ways, associating the
'dirty British coaster' with the drab, mundane trade on which Britain's economic
power was founded, but also with the heroic romance of its predecessors on the
old trade routes.

1903

Rome and Another

WILLIAM WATSON

She asked for all things, and dominion such
    As never man had known,
The gods first gave; then lightly, touch by touch,
    O'erthrew her seven-hilled throne.

Imperial Power, that hungerest for the globe,
    Restrain thy conquering feet,
Lest the same Fates that spun thy purple robe
    Should weave thy winding-sheet.

In 1902, the new King, Edward VII, had instituted Empire Day to honour Queen Victoria's memory. Generally, imperialism was popular, and much self-congratulatory verse was produced. This poem was Watson's quiet reminder that no empire lasts for ever.

1904

Tilly

JAMES JOYCE

He travels after a winter sun,
Urging the cattle along a cold red road,
Calling to them, a voice they know,
He drives his beasts above Cabra.

The voice tells them home is warm.
They moo and make brute music with their hoofs.
He drives them with a flowering branch before him,
Smoke pluming their foreheads.

Boor, bond of the herd,
Tonight stretch full by the fire!
I bleed by the black stream
For my torn bough!

Dublin, 1904

1904

'Because your voice was at my side'

JAMES JOYCE

Because your voice was at my side
   I gave him pain,
Because within my hand I held
   Your hand again.

There is no word nor any sign
   Can make amend –
He is a stranger to me now
   Who was my friend.

1905

A Runnable Stag

JOHN DAVIDSON

When the pods went pop on the broom, green broom,
  And apples began to be golden-skinned,
We harboured a stag in the Priory coomb,
  And we feathered his trail up-wind, up-wind,
  We feathered his trail up-wind –
    A stag of warrant, a stag, a stag,
    A runnable stag, a kingly crop,
    Brow, bay and tray and three on top,
    A stag, a runnable stag.

Then the huntsman's horn rang yap, yap, yap,
  And 'Forwards' we heard the harbourer shout;
But 'twas only a brocket that broke a gap
  In the beechen underwood, driven out,
  From the underwood antlered out
    By warrant and might of the stag, the stag,
    The runnable stag, whose lordly mind
    Was bent on sleep, though beamed and tined
    He stood, a runnable stag.

So we tufted the covert till afternoon
  With Tinkerman's Pup and Bell-of-the-North;
And hunters were sulky and hounds out of tune
  Before we tufted the right stag forth,
  Before we tufted him forth,
    The stag of warrant, the wily stag,
    The runnable stag with his kingly crop,
    Brow, bay and tray and three on top,
    The royal and runnable stag.

It was Bell-of-the-North and Tinkerman's Pup
 That stuck to the scent till the copse was drawn.
'Tally ho! tally ho!' and the hunt was up,
 The tufters whipped and the pack laid on,
 The resolute pack laid on,
  And the stag of warrant away at last,
  The runnable stag, the same, the same,
  His hoofs on fire, his horns like flame,
  A stag, a runnable stag.

'Let your gelding be: if you check or chide,
 He stumbles at once and you're out of the hunt;
For three hundred gentlemen, able to ride,
 On hunters accustomed to bear the brunt,
 Accustomed to bear the brunt,
  And after the runnable stag, the stag,
  The runnable stag with his kingly crop,
  Brow, bay and tray and three on top,
  The right, the runnable stag.'

By perilous path in coomb and dell,
 The heather, the rocks, and the river-bed,
The pace grew hot, for the scent lay well,
 And a runnable stag goes right ahead,
 The quarry went right ahead —
  Ahead, ahead, and fast and far;
  His antlered crest, his cloven hoof,
  Brow, bay and tray and three aloof,
  The stag, the runnable stag.

For a matter of twenty miles and more,
 By the densest hedge and the highest wall,
Through herds of bullocks he baffled the lore
 Of harbourer, huntsman, hounds and all,
 Of harbourer, hounds and all —
  The stag of warrant, the wily stag,
  For twenty miles, and five and five,
  He ran, and he never was caught alive,
  This stag, this runnable stag.

When he turned at bay in the leafy gloom,
 In the emerald gloom where the brook ran deep,
He heard in the distance the rollers boom,
 And he saw in a vision of peaceful sleep,
 In a wonderful vision of sleep,
  A stag of warrant, a stag, a stag,
  A runnable stag in a jewelled bed,
  Under the sheltering ocean dead,
  A stag, a runnable stag.

So a fateful hope lit up his eye,
 And he opened his nostrils wide again,
And he tossed his branching antlers high
 As he headed the hunt down the Charlock glen,
 As he raced down the echoing glen
  For five miles more, the stag, the stag,
  For twenty miles, and five and five,
  Not to be caught now, dead or alive,
  The stag, the runnable stag.

Three hundred gentlemen, able to ride,
 Three hundred horses as gallant and free,
Beheld him escape on the evening tide,
 Far out till he sank in the Severn Sea,
 Till he sank in the depths of the sea –
  The stag, the buoyant stag, the stag
  That slept at last in a jewelled bed
  Under the sheltering ocean spread
  The stag, the runnable stag.

John Davidson, a prolific Scottish writer, of plays, essays and long philosophical poems, had a more positive view of British imperialism than Hardy or Watson, and threw his formidable rhetorical talent into the jingoistic fervour preceding the First World War. Patriotism, however, wasn't enough to save him from depression, and he drowned himself off the Cornish coast in 1909 – a fate prefigured in this, his metrical masterpiece.

1905

To the Mikado, Portsmouth, USA

◄◦►

H. D. RAWNSLEY

August 29, 1905

Because you fenced not for your rights, but stood
For Peace – a solid thing – no hollow name;
Because more dear than gold or conqueror's fame
You held the ties of human brotherhood;
Because you would not wade through seas of blood
To one last move in battle's desperate game;
Therefore we hold you honoured, and acclaim
You kingliest leader of the wise and good.

For in degenerate days when every throne
Unreverenced quakes, and lust, not life, is free,
There in your sea-girt isle of Old Japan
You teach how virtue lives from man to man,
How self-restraint, self-sacrifice must be
The bonds that make and keep a nation one.

In 1904, coincidentally the year of Puccini's *Madame Butterfly*, the Japanese attacked a Russian base, and a brief war ensued, with the Russians defeated at sea in the battle of Tsushima and on land in the battle of Mukden in Manchuria. US President Theodore Roosevelt mediated, and a peace treaty was signed at Portsmouth, New Hampshire, in September 1905. Many in England were sympathetic to 'old Japan', with which Britain had agreed an alliance in 1902 – one poet, George Barlow, ending a sonnet on Tsushima with the claim that 'Nelson's land is glad at Togo's fame'. Rawnsley celebrated the launch of an English-built Japanese battleship in July 1905 with the words that this 'child of England' was made of 'English iron' in an 'English home'. This sonnet lauding the Mikado (Emperor Meiji the Great) reflects the widespread perception at the time that Japan had exercised restraint in its conduct of the war and the treaty negotiations; in truth, Russian cessions to Japan were substantial.

1905

from The Apparition

STEPHEN PHILLIPS

My dear love came to me, and said:
  'God gives me one hour's rest
To spend with thee on earth again:
  How shall we spend it best?'

'Why, as of old,' I said; and so
  We quarrelled, as of old:
But, when I turned to make my peace,
  That one short hour was told.

1906

Beg-Innish

J. M. SYNGE

BRING Kateen-beug and Maurya Jude
To dance in Beg-Innish,
And when the lads (they're in Dunquin)
Have sold their crabs and fish,
Wave fawny shawls and call them in,
And call the little girls who spin,
And seven weavers from Dunquin,
To dance in Beg-Innish.

I'll play you jigs, and Maurice Kean,
Where nets are laid to dry,
I've silken strings would draw a dance
From girls are lame or shy;
Four strings I've brought from Spain and France
To make your long men skip and prance,
Till stars look out to see the dance
Where nets are laid to dry.

We'll have no priest or peeler in
To dance in Beg-Innish;
But we'll have drink from M'riarty Jim
Rowed round while gannets fish,
A keg with porter to the brim,
That every lad may have his whim,
Till we up sails with M'riarty Jim
And sail from Beg-Innish.

Dunquin (Gaelic: Dún Chaoin, meaning 'Caon's stronghold') is a Gaeltacht
village in west County Kerry, Ireland. Synge's rejection of the nay-saying 'priest
or peeler' rings out in this celebratory jig of a poem.

1907

The Sundowner

SHAW NEILSON

I know not when this tiresome man
With his shrewd, sable billy-can
  And his unwashed Democracy
His boomed-up Pilgrimage began.

Sometimes he wandered far outback
On a precarious Tucker Track;
  Sometimes he lacked Necessities
No gentleman would like to lack.

Tall was the grass, I understand,
When the old Squatter ruled the land.
  Why were the Conquerors kind to him?
Ah, the Wax Matches in his hand!

Where bullockies with oaths intense
Made of the dragged-up trees a fence,
  Gambling with scorpions he rolled
His Swag, conspicuous, immense.

In the full splendour of his power
Rarely he touched one mile an hour,
  Dawdling at sundown, History says,
For the Pint Pannikin of flour.

Seldom he worked; he was, I fear,
Unreasonably slow and dear;
  Little he earned, and that he spent
Deliberately drinking Beer.

Cheerful, sorefooted child of chance,
Swiftly we knew him at a glance;
  Boastful and self-compassionate,
Australia's Interstate Romance.

Shall he not live in Robust Rhyme,
Soliloquies and Odes Sublime?
    Strictly between ourselves, he was
A rare old Humbug all the time.

In many a Book of Bushland dim
Mopokes shall give him greeting grim;
    The old swans pottering in the reeds
Shall pass the time of day to him.

On many a page our Friend shall take
Small sticks his evening fire to make;
    Shedding his waistcoat, he shall mix
On its smooth back his Johnny-Cake.

’Mid the dry leaves and silvery bark
Often at nightfall will he park
    Close to a homeless creek, and hear
The Bunyip paddling in the dark.

The mopoke, in Australia, is the tawny frogmouth bird. (The Australian boobook owl is also sometimes referred to as a mopoke.) Johnny-cake is a quick bread, made with flour and baked in hot ashes, or fried in a skillet. The bunyip, in aboriginal mythology, is a large swamp-dwelling creature.

1908

A Beggar's Life

W. H. DAVIES

When farmers sweat and toil at ploughs,
　The wives give me cool milk and sweet;
When merchants in their office brood,
　Their ladies give me cakes to eat,
And hot tea for my happy blood;
　This is a jolly life indeed,
　To do no work and get my need.

I have no child for future thought,
　I feed no belly but my own,
And I can sleep when toilers fail;
　Content, though sober, sleeps on stone,
But Care can't sleep with down and ale;
　This is a happy life indeed,
　To do no work and get my need.

I trouble not for pauper's grave,
　There is no feeling after death;
The king will be as deaf to praise
　As I to blame – when this world saith
A word of us in after days;
　It is a jolly life indeed,
　To do no work and get my need.

1908

Dread

J. M. SYNGE

Beside a chapel I'd a room looked down,
Where all the women from the farms and town,
On Holy-days, and Sundays used to pass
To marriages, and Christenings and to Mass.

Then I sat lonely watching score and score,
Till I turned jealous of the Lord next door . . .
Now by this window, where there's none can see,
The Lord God's jealous of yourself and me.

In other drafts Synge titled this poem 'In Desolate Humour' or 'Beside a Chapel'.

1909

from Sonnets to Miranda

◄○►

WILLIAM WATSON

What if that fieriest Substance found of late –
That cousin to the uranium of the sun –
Should be a cause of all that we have done
And dreamed and been? A source of Love and Hate,
Virtue and Valour – yea, and Beauty great
As yours? – And could all this be hid in one
Impassioned seed through aeons, – known to none, –
Hid in one God-sown seed of Life and Fate?

Thus was the genie of the Arabian tale
Sealed in a vial for a thousand years
Under the ocean, till a fisher's net
Drew forth the vial, and the fisher set
The captive free, – but shrank amazed and pale,
When the loosed Afreet towered against the Spheres.

Marie Curie discovered radium in 1898 by removing the uranium component
from north Bohemian pitchblende and realizing that the remaining substance
also had radioactive properties.

1910

No Second Troy

⊲◦▻

W. B. YEATS

Why should I blame her that she filled my days
With misery, or that she would of late
Have taught to ignorant men most violent ways,
Or hurled the little streets upon the great,
Had they but courage equal to desire?
What could have made her peaceful with a mind
That nobleness made simple as a fire,
With beauty like a tightened bow, a kind
That is not natural in an age like this,
Being high and solitary and most stern?
Why, what could she have done, being what she is?
Was there another Troy for her to burn?

Yeats was obsessed with questions of Irish identity and nationality, and through
his own poetry and plays contributed strongly to the forging of a modern Irish
literature. His unrequited passion for the beautiful revolutionary Maude Gonne
inspired many poems, and his disagreements with her helped define his own less
radical, but equally fervent, politics. 'No Second Troy' demonstrates the myth-
making nature of Yeats's genius, though his likening Maude Gonne to Helen of
Troy reflects the power she had over his imagination rather than her actual ability
to influence events.

1910

White Bears: Tolstoy at Astapovo

◄○►

LINDA BIERDS

The wheels of the train were a runner's heartbeat –
systole, diastole, the hiss-tic of stasis –
as they flipped through the scrub trees and autumn grasses,
slowing at last at the station lamps.
And perhaps the fever had carried this memory,
or the journey, or, just ahead in the darkness,
the white, plump columns of lamplight.

He is five, six, locked at the center
of the evening's first parlor game:
Go stand in a corner, Lyova, until you stop thinking
of a white bear. To his left
there is pipe smoke. Behind him
a little laughter from the handkerchiefs.
And in his mind, white fur
like the blizzards of Tula! He studies the wall cloth
of vernal grass and asters, a buff stocking, trouser cuff,
but just at the rescue of a spinet bench
two claws scratch back. A tooth. Then
the lavender palate of polar bears.

I cannot forget it, he whispers. And would not,
through the decades that followed –
the white, cumbersome shape
swelling back, settling, at the rustling close
of an orchard gate, or the close
of a thousand pen-stroked pages,

white bear, in the swirls of warm mare's milk,
at the side of the eye. White bear,
when his listless, blustery, aristocratic life
disentangled itself, landlord to
shoemaker, on his back a tunic, in his lap

a boot, white bear, just then,
when his last, awl-steered, hammer-tapped peg
bit the last quarter sole.

In the gaps between curtains. And now,
in the lamp-brightened gaps between fence slats,
there and there, as if the bear
were lurching at the train's slow pace,
and behind it – he was certain – the stifling life he fled
rushing to meet him: family, servants, copyrights,
just over the hill in the birch trees.
Simplicity. He sighed. Dispossession.
A monastery, perhaps. Kasha in oil. At eighty-two
his body erased to the leaf-scrape of sandals.
And even the room near the station, the small bed
with its white haunch of pillow,

even the mattress, where he shivered
with fever or a train's slow crossing, and whispered,
and, just before morning, died,
was better. Deep autumn. Already the snows
had begun in the foothills, erasing
the furrows and scrub trunks, erasing at last
the trees themselves, and the brooks,
and the V-shaped canyons the brooks whittled.

There and there, the landscape no more
than an outreach of sky, a swelling, perhaps,
where an orchard waited, then boundary posts, fence wire,
then, below, the lavender grin of the clover.

The great Russian novelist spent his last days in the stationmaster's apartment at the remote station of Astapovo, where he had alighted after falling ill. Tolstoy's death was universally felt to mark the passing of an era, and became 'a media event in a surprisingly modern sense', according to William Nickell in *The Death of Tolstoy* (2010), with telegraphs and telephones, films and phonographs all used to convey the very latest news to the waiting world. Roy Fuller also wrote a poem about Tolstoy's death at Astapovo, and Jay Parini's 1990 novel *The Last Station* was made into a film starring Christopher Plummer and Helen Mirren, directed by Michael Hoffman.

1910

Uncle Ananias

EDWIN ARLINGTON ROBINSON

His words were magic and his heart was true,
    And everywhere he wandered he was blessed.
Out of all ancient men my childhood knew
    I choose him and I mark him for the best.
Of all authoritative liars, too,
    I crown him loveliest.

How fondly I remember the delight
    That always glorified him in the spring;
The joyous courage and the benedight
    Profusion of his faith in everything!
He was a good old man, and it was right
    That he should have his fling.

And often, underneath the apple-trees,
    When we surprised him in the summer time,
With what superb magnificence and ease
    He sinned enough to make the day sublime!
And if he liked us there about his knees,
    Truly it was no crime.

All summer long we loved him for the same
    Perennial inspiration of his lies;
And when the russet wealth of autumn came,
    There flew but fairer visions to our eyes –
Multiple, tropical, winged with a feathery flame,
    Like birds of paradise.

So to the sheltered end of many a year
    He charmed the seasons out with pageantry
Wearing upon his forehead, with no fear,
    The laurel of approved iniquity.
And every child who knew him, far or near,
    Did love him faithfully.

1910

Guards

D. H. LAWRENCE

A review in Hyde Park, 1910:
The crowd watches

Where the trees rise like cliffs, proud and blue-tinted
    in the distance,
Between the cliffs of the trees, on the grey-green park
Rests a still line of soldiers, red, motionless range
    of guards
Smouldering with darkened busbies beneath the
    bayonets' slant rain.

Colossal in nearness a blue police sits still on his horse
Guarding the path; his hand relaxed at his thigh,
And skywards his face is immobile, eyelids aslant
In tedium, and mouth relaxed as if smiling – ineffable
    tedium!

So! So! Gaily a general canters across the space,
With white plumes blinking under the evening grey
    sky.
And suddenly, as if the ground moved,
The red range heaves in slow, magnetic reply.

1910

The Ballad of Camden Town

JAMES ELROY FLECKER

I walked with Maisie long years back
    The streets of Camden Town,
I splendid in my suit of black,
    And she divine in brown.

Hers was a proud and noble face,
    A secret heart, and eyes
Like water in a lonely place
    Beneath unclouded skies.

A bed, a chest, a faded mat,
    And broken chairs a few,
Were all we had to grace our flat
    In Hazel Avenue.

But I could walk to Hampstead Heath,
    And crown her head with daisies,
And watch the streaming world beneath,
    And men with other Maisies.

When I was ill and she was pale
    And empty stood our store,
She left the latchkey on its nail,
    And saw me nevermore.

Perhaps she cast herself away
    Lest both of us should drown:
Perhaps she feared to die, as they
    Who die in Camden Town.

What came of her? The bitter nights
    Destroy the rose and lily,
And souls are lost among the lights
    Of painted Piccadilly.

What came of her? The river flows
   So deep and wide and stilly,
And waits to catch the fallen rose
   And clasp the broken lily.

I dream she dwells in London still
   And breathes the evening air,
And often walk to Primrose Hill,
   And hope to meet her there.

Once more together we will live,
   For I will find her yet:
I have so little to forgive;
   So much, I can't forget.

1911

Lord Finchley

HILAIRE BELLOC

Lord Finchley tried to mend the Electric Light
Himself. It struck him dead: And serve him right!
It is the business of the wealthy man
To give employment to the artisan.

1911

Last Lesson of the Afternoon

◄◊►

D. H. LAWRENCE

When will the bell ring, and end this weariness?
How long have they tugged the leash, and strained apart,
My pack of unruly hounds! I cannot start
Them again on a quarry of knowledge they hate to hunt,
I can haul them and urge them no more.

No longer now can I endure the brunt
Of the books that lie out on the desks; a full threescore
Of several insults of blotted pages, and scrawl
Of slovenly work that they have offered me.
I am sick, and what on earth is the good of it all?
What good to them or me, I cannot see!

                              So, shall I take
My last dear fuel of life to heap on my soul
And kindle my will to a flame that shall consume
Their dross of indifference; and take the toll
Of their insults in punishment? – I will not! –

I will not waste my soul and my strength for this.
What do I care for all that they do amiss!
What is the point of this teaching of mine, and of this
Learning of theirs? It all goes down the same abyss.

What does it matter to me, if they can write
A description of a dog, or if they can't?
What is the point? To us both, it is all my aunt!
And yet I'm supposed to care, with all my might.

I do not, and will not; they won't and they don't; and
    that's all!
I shall keep my strength for myself; they can keep theirs as
    well.
Why should we beat our heads against the wall
Of each other? I shall sit and wait for the bell.

1911

from Rutherford

DOUGLAS STEWART

Look at it this way, that way, face the thing squarely.
Could some fool in a laboratory, he'd asked his assistants,
Blow up the world with this? You could pay dearly
For probing too deeply into that dark resistance
Where light lay coiled in stone. He had seen clearly
In flashes of the mind each atom exploding the next
To the end of the world, and the light came out of the
     distance
Like a wave upon him, towering . . . They were perplexed,

Whether he was joking or not. Well, he was joking.
There was no need to cower, and what was more,
Though sometimes he touched these things with his hands
     shaking,
He did not propose to; he'd carry the load he bore,
Which was no light one, till his broad shoulders were
     aching.
But need not, except as precaution, think the unthinkable:
There was no chain-reaction could go so far;
The force must die out; the good old world was unsinkable.

So let his atoms be used to do man good
And nothing but good – pierce to the cancer cell
As the Curies were doing, bring him more health, more
     food,
Drive the turbine, the dynamo, turn the wheel,
Blow a mountain up if it got in his road.
Let him be master of air and earth and ocean,
The whole wide world and the stars if he liked as well.
He had not given his lifetime's skill and devotion

To bring man harm. And yet this thing was force;
And when could you give poor man and his five wits
Any new force but he would use it in his wars
And blow himself if not the whole world to bits?
Take off his trappings and, naked, hungry and fierce,
All over the earth, in jungle or civilized city,
Men were but savages yet; God help the poor brutes,
For this new power, appalling to love and pity,

Was force that no savage yet had dreamed of wielding.
Dare he release it? Alone in this still room
With those uncanny electrons whirling and shielding
The inviolable core, he felt he was living in a dream
And he saw towers falling and skyscrapers melting –
Fantastic, inconceivable; yet must be conceived.
Then you could turn away, pack up and go home,
Dismantling the apparatus. And he half believed

This moment that he could do it; get hold of a farm
Snug under snowy Egmont, beside the river,
And there where the frost melted and morning was warm
Stroll down to look at the pigs; there was much in favour
Of pigs, taken as pigs, life's earthiest form;
And in those paddocks there, starry with daisies,
Golden with dandelions, purple with clover,
(How rich was the land!) he'd have his herd of Jerseys,

And up in the dawn to milk them, hitch up the cart,
Off to the factory to yarn with others of his type
(Looked like a farmer, always a farmer at heart,
Corpulent, bushy-moustached, smoking his pipe)
Then feed the skim-dick to the pigs – it was a part
He had played in dreams, planted on that green shelf
With the cows and the oats and the turnips till he grew
    ripe
And simple and stolid as the good black earth
    itself . . .

Too stolid, perhaps. Well, you could hire labour,
A sharefarmer, say, and still find plenty worth doing:
Get on the County Council, do good to your neighbour,
Fix up the roads and bridges. And once you got going,
Why not keep on? Be Pungarehu's member
For Parliament, eh? Minister for Agriculture,
Prime Minister then, why not? There was no knowing
Where he would get to in that rustic future,

Who now had got to this room. And there already
That powerful body, that restless mind of his,
As soon as he looked forward with his hand steady
Were driving him still . . . On just such a journey as this
Where he had climbed as high as anybody
And liked it, too, although at times it shook him.
He had enjoyed so much the work, the success,
Discoveries sparkling like jewels wherever it took him.

'I'll dig no more potatoes!' so he had vowed
That day the telegram from Cambridge came,
And dug no more indeed, nor milked nor ploughed
Except in the great seas of thought and fame;
And where the surf broke high and white and loud
In wonder watched as island after island
Rose in his mind's eye with their dazzling gleam.
So he stood now, Earl Rutherford of Nelson,

The great sea-farer of science. But the room was silent.
Space, so it seemed, looked in upon him like eyes
And it seemed possible in that shattering moment
That just to be a schoolboy winning a prize
He had ended or nearly ended man's life on this planet.
Then no and no and no, he could only assert,
That was not true! Impossible to disguise
That what he had found could do mankind grave hurt,

None graver; true, too, he could never go back
And share the old simplicities with his father.
Let them live on! But he had grown to like
This life of power where scientists met together
And felt they were priests and rulers. He liked to talk
With his great peers that language wrapped in mystery —
But he'd be plain if he could. No, it was rather
He liked the thought that what he touched was history,

As in truth it was; he'd have his personal pride.
A man alive must show what he could do.
But that was irrelevant, nothing; something outside
That final, inner truth so well he knew,
Always with that chill in the blood, when hands that had
    died,
Or hands not human at all, beyond his seeking,
Hands not his own, like a mist, came creeping through
His own at their work and made what he was making.

He was so clumsy and blind, beyond all patience:
But out of the dark, from nowhere, flashed the conception
Like force in the atom and filled him with its radiance;
And steadily, patiently, always in the right direction
Despite his stumblings it moved in him in silence
Until at last what it wanted to do was done.
All things, it seemed, moved through time to perfection,
Through earth and wood and flesh, through the mind of
    man.

But whether it was some quite unknowable powers
Dark and divine, or simply the spirit of the race
That moved in him and grew these hot small flowers
That bloomed behind lead for safety, when could you trace
Though you sat here watching and watching all the dark
    hours
Such an imponderable, such an unprovable process?
It was the solid facts he had to face.
Yes, but they gave the same clear answer of progress:

And it was not merely the hand upon the wheel
That led to this, but the whole drive of the mind
Since first that restless radiance tore at its veil,
Rock, flesh and sky, to seek what lay behind.
And what did lie, as the Greeks guessed so well,
Was the whirling atoms; and what was the implication
Of that, God alone knew; but here, combined,
Thought and the hand had lit our civilization

With what it had dreamed of: not just his own ambition
But all mankind's, Lord knows what power beside,
Came here to some great moment of fruition
And into the future cast its glittering seed.
So now in God's name, thinking of nuclear fission
And looking out of the window into the dark
Where lay the whole teeming world that man had made,
London, Paris, Berlin, Moscow, New York,

How stop mankind destroying it? Easy to say
That only science could turn this force to destruction
And science must not; but fierily though it lay
On each man's conscience, there was such soft seduction
In science itself, and power and place and pay,
You could do evil or fall into taking a bribe
Almost without your knowing; and, clear of corruption,
Still you could make your conscience that of the tribe

And do its bidding without one trace of guilt
But rather, as he knew well, with a clear ardour.
And when the old passions were roused and blood was
    spilt
And the enemy hordes came swarming over the border
Like Gaul and the Hun again, like Scythian or Celt,
Civilized men in Europe killing and ravaging,
What else could man do but stand against the marauder?
That was the thing that must change, this pattern of
    savaging.

It was an old habit men had got into
Far back in the forest, grasping more food for the clan,
And served its purpose in quickening mind and sinew;
But now since it threatened the whole existence of man
We must not, could not, dare not let it continue.
And there was the crux, perhaps, in that word 'dare';
For never had there been such a weapon since time began
And men who would stop at nothing might stop at fear.

But this was the great high tide of power and thought
And not all men were savages – that was the certainty
That buoyed him up against these winds of doubt:
Think of such colleagues now as Hahn in Germany –
Good God, could he cross the Channel and cut his throat?
Men had outgrown such horror. He put his trust,
Despite the whole long course of human barbarity,
In what must supplant it, the rule of the strong and the
    just.

There would be place enough still for all the old chivalry
While half the world was savage; but now began,
Now must begin, a clear new turn in history,
And there in his atoms, cramped in so small a span,
It glittered before him and rayed away out to infinity.
How perilous and dark, how enigmatic a course
It seemed to set whirling there for the race of man
Now bound to the inmost force of the universe –

And yet as he looked at the sky so dark with warning
Vast over earth and its towers, the night heaved over
Close and familiar as a waterwheel turning
And shed its stars like drops of crystal water
And radiant over the world lay the clear morning.
Men moved in darkness truly, but also in the sun
And on that huge bright wheel that turned for ever
He left his thought, for there was work to be done.

Ernest Rutherford (1871–1937), later Baron Rutherford of Nelson (1931), was the son of first-generation immigrants to New Zealand, where he was born to a Scottish father and English mother. In 1898, after postgraduate work in Cambridge, he was appointed to a chair at McGill University in Montreal, where he did the work on radioactivity (following on from Marie and Pierre Curie) that brought him the Nobel Prize for chemistry in 1908. Returning to England, Rutherford worked (in Manchester, then in Cambridge) on the atom, devising in 1911 the planetary model which is named after him. Viewed now as the father of nuclear physics, Rutherford nurtured other Nobel laureates, among them John Cockcroft and Ernest Walton, who split the atom in 1932. Stewart's poem, which we have placed in the year of Rutherford's own first major breakthrough, imagines the cogitations that might have gone through his mind in the Thirties, when the German chemist and physicist Otto Hahn (1879–1968), with whom he had worked at McGill in earlier years, was working towards his discovery of nuclear fission in 1938.

1911

The Swimmers

ALLEN TATE

SCENE: *Montgomery County,*
Kentucky, July 1911

Kentucky water, clear springs: a boy fleeing
    To water under the dry Kentucky sun,
    His four little friends in tandem with him, seeing

Long shadows of grapevine wriggle and run
    Over the green swirl; mullein under the ear
    Soft as Nausicaä's palm; sullen fun

Savage as childhood's thin harmonious tear:
    O fountain, bosom source undying-dead
    Replenish me the spring of love and fear

And give me back the eye that looked and fled
    When a thrush idling in the tulip tree
    Unwound the cold dream of the copperhead.

– Along the creek the road was winding; we
    Felt the quicksilver sky. I see again
    The shrill companions of that odyssey:

Bill Eaton, Charlie Watson, 'Nigger' Layne
    The doctor's son, Harry Duèsler who played
    The flute; and Tate, with water on the brain.

Dog-days: the dusty leaves where rain delayed
    Hung low on poison-oak and scuppernong,
    And we were following the active shade

Of water, that bells and bickers all night long.
    'No more'n a mile,' Layne said. All five stood still.
    Listening, I heard what seemed at first a song;

Peering, I heard the hooves come down the hill.
  The posse passed, twelve horse; the leader's face
  Was worn as limestone on an ancient sill.

Then, as sleepwalkers shift from a hard place
  In bed, and rising to keep a formal pledge
  Descend a ladder into empty space,

We scuttled down the bank below a ledge
  And marched stiff-legged in our common fright
  Along a hog-track by the riffle's edge:

Into a world where sound shaded the sight
  Dropped the dull hooves again; the horsemen came
  Again, all but the leader. It was night

Momently and I feared: eleven same
  Jesus-Christers unmembered and unmade,
  Whose Corpse had died again in dirty shame.

The bank then levelling in a speckled glade,
  We stopped to breathe above the swimming-hole;
  I gazed at its reticulated shade

Recoiling in blue fear, and felt it roll
  Over my ears and eyes and lift my hair
  Like seaweed tossing on a sunk atoll.

I rose again. Borne on the copper air
  A distant voice green as a funeral wreath
  Against a grave: 'That dead nigger there.'

The melancholy sheriff slouched beneath
  A giant sycamore; shaking his head
  He plucked a sassafras twig and picked his teeth:

'We come too late.' He spoke to the tired dead
  Whose ragged shirt soaked up the viscous flow
  Of blood in which It lay discomfited.

A butting horse-fly gave one ear a blow
  And glanced off, as the sheriff kicked the rope
  Loose from the neck and hooked it with his toe

Away from the blood. – I looked back down the slope:
    The friends were gone that I had hoped to greet. –
    A single horseman came at a slow lope

And pulled up at the hanged man's horny feet;
    The sheriff noosed the feet, the other end
    The stranger tied to his pommel in a neat

Slip-knot. I saw the Negro's body bend
    And straighten, as a fish-line cast transverse
    Yields to the current that it must subtend.

The sheriff's Goddamn was a murmured curse
    Not for the dead but for the blinding dust
    That boxed the cortège in a cloudy hearse.

And dragged it towards our town. I knew I must
    Not stay till twilight in that silent road;
    Sliding my bare feet into the warm crust,

I hopped the stonecrop like a panting toad
    Mouth open, following the heaving cloud
    That floated to the court-house square its load

Of limber corpse that took the sun for shroud.
    There were three figures in the dying sun
    Whose light were company where three was crowd.

My breath crackled the dead air like a shotgun
    As, sheriff and the stranger disappearing,
    The faceless head lay still. I could not run

Or walk, but stood. Alone in the public clearing
    This private thing was owned by all the town,
    Though never claimed by us within my hearing.

Allen Tate drew heavily on his Southern upbringing, and his allegiance to the values and traditions of the Old South runs through many of his poems, the best-known of which is 'Ode to the Confederate Dead'. However, this powerful account of a lynching is a chilling reminder of the stark inhumanity festering beneath the surface of life in the southern states.

1912

'Oh! who are these in scant array?'

KATHLEEN EMERSON

Oh! who are these in scant array
Whom we behold at break of day;
Strange their attire! oh, who are they?
 The Suffragettes in Holloway.

And who are these when chapel's done
Stream out beneath an April sun,
To laugh and jump or shout and run?
 The Suffragettes in Holloway.

Who is it say in tones which freeze,
'Pass on this way, convicted, please;
Don't dare to think or breathe or sneeze'?
 The Wardresses in Holloway.

And who is he, tho' grand his air,
Doffs not his hat to ladies fair?
Is it because he has no hair?
 The Governor in Holloway.

Then whilst we eat our frugal food,
Who breaks upon our solitude,
And says, 'You're all so beastly rude'?
 Why 'Mother's own' in Holloway.

And who, with sanctimonious drone,
Tells tales of highly moral tone,
Whilst gazing upwards at the dome?
 The Chaplain, sure, in Holloway.

Hark! who is this with stealthy tread,
Comes round each day to count his dead,
And scalps his victims, so 'tis said?
    The Doctor, in grim Holloway.

The question of women's right to vote became ever more fiercely contested in the years prior to the First World War. Under the leadership of Emmeline Pankhurst, the suffragette movement took to the streets, provoking a brutally repressive response from the police and the prison service. Many women were incarcerated – and those who went on hunger strike were subjected to the indignities of force-feeding. But as this poem, from a suffragette pamphlet, *Holloway Jingles*, shows, the women remained indomitable through all their ill-treatment. Women were given the vote in the UK in 1918 (in New Zealand in 1893, in Australia in 1902, in Canada in 1917, and in the US in 1920).

1912

The Farmer's Bride

CHARLOTTE MEW

Three Summers since I chose a maid,
Too young maybe – but more's to do
At harvest-time than bide and woo.
    When us was wed she turned afraid
Of love and me and all things human;
Like the shut of a winter's day
Her smile went out, and 'twadn't a woman –
    More like a little frightened fay.
    One night, in the Fall, she runned away.

'Out 'mong the sheep, her be,' they said,
'Should properly have been abed;
But sure enough she wadn't there
Lying awake with her wide brown stare.
So over seven-acre field and up-along across the down
We chased her, flying like a hare
Before our lanterns. To Church-Town
    All in a shiver and a scare
We caught her, fetched her home at last
    And turned the key upon her, fast.

She does the work about the house
As well as most, but like a mouse:
    Happy enough to chat and play
    With birds and rabbits and such as they,
    So long as men-folk keep away.

'Not near, not near!' her eyes beseech
When one of us comes within reach.
    The women say that beasts in stall
    Look round like children at her call.
    I've hardly heard her speak at all.

Shy as a leveret, swift as he,
Straight and slight as a young larch tree,
Sweet as the first wild violets, she,
To her wild self. But what to me?

The short days shorten and the oaks are brown,
    The blue smoke rises to the low grey sky,
One leaf in the still air falls slowly down,
    A magpie's spotted feathers lie
On the black earth spread white with rime,
The berries redden up to Christmas-time.
    What's Christmas-time without there be
    Some other in the house than we!

    She sleeps up in the attic there
    Alone, poor maid. 'Tis but a stair
Betwixt us. Oh! my God! the down,
The soft young down of her, the brown,
The brown of her – her eyes, her hair, her hair!

1912

To God the Father

◄○►

KATHERINE MANSFIELD

To the little, pitiful God I make my prayer,
The God with the long grey beard
And flowing robe fastened with a hempen girdle
Who sits nodding and muttering on the all-too-big throne of
    Heaven.
What a long, long time, dear God, since you set the stars in
    their places,
Girded the earth with the sea, and invented the day and night.
And longer the time since you looked through the blue
    window of Heaven
To see your children at play in a garden . . .
Now we are all stronger than you and wiser and more arrogant,
In swift procession we pass you by.
'Who is that marionette nodding and muttering
On the all-too-big throne of Heaven?
Come down from your place, Grey Beard,
We have had enough of your play-acting!'
It is centuries since I believed in you,
But to-day my need of you has come back.
I want no rose-coloured future,
No books of learning, no protestations and denials –
I am sick of this ugly scramble,
I am tired of being pulled about –
O God, I want to sit on your knees
On the all-too-big throne of Heaven,
And fall asleep with my hands tangled in your grey beard.

Mansfield published this as a translation from the Russian of an imaginary poet,
Boris Petrovsky.

1912

The Old Vicarage, Grantchester

Rupert Brooke

Café des Westens, Berlin, May 1912

Just now the lilac is in bloom,
All before my little room;
And in my flower-beds, I think,
Smile the carnation and the pink;
And down the borders, well I know,
The poppy and the pansy blow . . .
Oh! there the chestnuts, summer through,
Beside the river make for you
A tunnel of green gloom, and sleep
Deeply above; and green and deep
The stream mysterious glides beneath,
Green as a dream and deep as death.
– Oh, damn! I know it! and I know
How the May fields all golden show,
And when the day is young and sweet,
Gild gloriously the bare feet
That run to bathe . . .
                              Du lieber Gott!

Here am I, sweating, sick, and hot,
And there the shadowed waters fresh
Lean up to embrace the naked flesh.
Temperamentvoll German Jews
Drink beer around; – and *there* the dews
Are soft beneath a morn of gold.
Here tulips bloom as they are told;
Unkempt about those hedges blows
An English unofficial rose;

And there the unregulated sun
Slopes down to rest when day is done,
And wakes a vague unpunctual star,
A slippered Hesper; and there are
Meads towards Haslingfield and Coton
Where *das Betreten*'s not *verboten*.
εἴθε γενοίμην . . . would I were
In Grantchester, in Grantchester! –
Some, it may be, can get in touch
With Nature there, or Earth, or such.
And clever modern men have seen
A Faun a-peeping through the green,
And felt the Classics were not dead,
To glimpse a Naiad's reedy head,
Or hear the Goat-foot piping low: . . .
But these are things I do not know.
I only know that you may lie
Day-long and watch the Cambridge sky,
And, flower-lulled in sleepy grass,
Hear the cool lapse of hours pass,
Until the centuries blend and blur
In Grantchester, in Grantchester . . .
Still in the dawnlit waters cool
His ghostly Lordship swims his pool,
And tries the strokes, essays the tricks,
Long learnt on Hellespont, or Styx.

Dan Chaucer hears his river still
Chatter beneath a phantom mill.
Tennyson notes, with studious eye,
How Cambridge waters hurry by . . .
And in that garden, black and white,
Creep whispers through the grass all night;
And spectral dance, before the dawn,
A hundred Vicars down the lawn;
Curates, long dust, will come and go
On lissom, clerical, printless toe;

And oft between the boughs is seen
The sly shade of a Rural Dean . . .
Till, at a shiver in the skies,
Vanishing with Satanic cries,
The prim ecclesiastic rout
Leaves but a startled sleeper-out,
Grey heavens, the first bird's drowsy calls,
The falling house that never falls.

God! I will pack, and take a train,
And get me to England once again!
For England's the one land, I know,
Where men with Splendid Hearts may go;
And Cambridgeshire, of all England,
The shire for Men who Understand;
And of *that* district I prefer
The lovely hamlet Grantchester.
For Cambridge people rarely smile,
Being urban, squat, and packed with guile;
And Royston men in the far South
Are black and fierce and strange of mouth;
At Over they fling oaths at one,
And worse than oaths at Trumpington,
And Ditton girls are mean and dirty,
And there's none in Harston under thirty,
And folks in Shelford and those parts
Have twisted lips and twisted hearts,
And Barton men make Cockney rhymes,
And Coton's full of nameless crimes,
And things are done you'd not believe
At Madingley, on Christmas Eve.
Strong men have run for miles and miles,
When one from Cherry Hinton smiles;
Strong men have blanched, and shot their wives,
Rather than send them to St Ives;

Strong men have cried like babes, bydam,
To hear what happened at Babraham.
But Grantchester! ah, Grantchester!
There's peace and holy quiet there,
Great clouds along pacific skies,
And men and women with straight eyes,
Lithe children lovelier than a dream,
A bosky wood, a slumbrous stream,
And little kindly winds that creep
Round twilight corners, half asleep.
In Grantchester their skins are white;
They bathe by day, they bathe by night;
The women there do all they ought;
The men observe the Rules of Thought.
They love the Good; they worship Truth;
They laugh uproariously in youth;
(And when they get to feeling old,
They up and shoot themselves, I'm told) . . .
    Ah God! to see the branches stir
Across the moon at Grantchester!
To smell the thrilling-sweet and rotten
Unforgettable, unforgotten
River-smell, and hear the breeze
Sobbing in the little trees.
Say, do the elm-clumps greatly stand
Still guardians of that holy land?
The chestnuts shade, in reverend dream,
The yet unacademic stream?
Is dawn a secret shy and cold
Anadyomene, silver-gold?
And sunset still a golden sea
From Haslingfield to Madingley?
And after, ere the night is born,
Do hares come out about the corn?

Oh, is the water sweet and cool,
Gentle and brown, above the pool?
And laughs the immortal river still
Under the mill, under the mill?
Say, is there Beauty yet to find?
And Certainty? and Quiet kind?
Deep meadows yet, for to forget
The lies, and truths, and pain? . . . Oh! yet
Stands the Church clock at ten to three?
And is there honey still for tea?

The Café des Westens, located in a fine 1890s building on the Kurfürstendamm in Berlin, was the meeting place of Berlin's arts intelligentsia before the First World War, till it moved in 1913. Composer Richard Strauss, painter Max Liebermann, dramatists Frank Wedekind and Carl Sternheim, poet Christian Morgenstern, and critics Herbert Ihering and Alfred Kerr were among the regulars. (The building was destroyed in April 1945.) Brooke's home thoughts from abroad trade on the line taken towards Germany by writers from Thackeray to Katherine Mansfield, and have behind them the acute pre-war rivalry of the uncomfortable cousins, England and Germany.

1912

from The Titanic

E. J. PRATT

ISIDOR AND IDA STRAUS

At the sixteenth – a woman wrapped her coat
Around her maid and placed her in the boat;
Was ordered in but seen to hesitate
At the gunwale, and more conscious of her pride
Than of her danger swiftly took her fate
With open hands, and without show of tears
Returned unmurmuring to her husband's side;
'We've been together now for forty years,
Whither you go, I go.'

              A boy of ten,
Ranking himself within the class of men,
Though given a seat, made up his mind to waive
The privilege of his youth and size, and piled
The inches on his stature as he gave
Place to a Magyar woman and her child.

And men who had in the world's run of trade,
Or in pursuit of the professions, made
Their reputation, looked upon the scene
Merely as drama in a life's routine:
Millet was studying eyes as he would draw them
Upon a canvas; Butt, as though he saw them
In the ranks; Astor, social, debonair,
Waved '*Good-bye*' to his bride – '*See you to-morrow*',
And tapped a cigarette on a silver case;
Men came to Guggenheim as he stood there
In evening suit, coming this time to borrow
Nothing but courage from his calm, cool face.

And others unobserved, of unknown name
And race, just stood behind, pressing no claim
Upon priority but rendering proof
Of their oblation, quiet and aloof
Within the maelstrom towards the rails. And some
Wavered a moment with the panic urge,
But rallied to attention on the verge
Of flight as if the rattle of a drum
From quarters faint but unmistakable
Had put the stiffening in the blood to check
The impulse of the feet, leaving the will
No choice between the lifeboats and the deck.

*

Out on the water was the same display
Of fear and self-control as on the deck –
Challenge and hesitation and delay,
The quick return, the will to save, the race
Of snapping oars to put the realm of space
Between the half-filled lifeboats and the wreck.
The swimmers whom the waters did not take
With their instant death-chill struck out for the wake
Of the nearer boats, gained on them, hailed
The steersmen and were saved: the weaker failed
And fagged and sank. A man clutched at the rim
Of a gunwale, and a woman's jewelled fist
Struck at his face: two others seized his wrist,
As he released his hold, and gathering him
Over the side, they staunched the cut from the ring.
And there were many deeds envisaging
Volitions where self-preservation fought
Its red primordial struggle with the 'ought',
In those high moments when the gambler tossed
Upon the chance and uncomplaining lost.

Aboard the ship, whatever hope of dawn
Gleamed from the *Carpathia*'s riding lights was gone,
For every knot was matched by each degree
Of list. The stern was lifted bodily

When the bow had sunk three hundred feet, and set
Against the horizon stars in silhouette
Were the blade curves of the screws, hump of the rudder.
The downward pull and after buoyancy
Held her a minute poised but for a shudder
That caught her frame as with the upward stroke
Of the sea a boiler or a bulkhead broke.

Climbing the ladders, gripping shroud and stay,
Storm-rail, ringbolt or fairlead, every place
That might befriend the clutch of hand or brace
Of foot, the fourteen hundred made their way
To the heights of the aft decks, crowding the inches
Around the docking, bridge and cargo winches.
And now that last salt tonic which had kept
The valour of the heart alive – the bows
Of the immortal seven that had swept
The strings to outplay, outdie their orders, ceased.
Five minutes more, the angle had increased
From eighty on to ninety when the rows
Of deck and port-hole lights went out, flashed back
A brilliant second and again went black.
Another bulkhead crashed, then following
The passage of the engines as they tore
From their foundations, taking everything
Clean through the bows from 'midships with a roar
Which drowned all cries upon the deck and shook
The watchers in the boats, the liner took
Her thousand fathoms journey to her grave.

★

And out there in the starlight, with no trace
Upon it of its deed but the last wave
From the *Titanic* fretting at its base,
Silent, composed, ringed by its icy broods,
The grey shape with the palaeolithic face
Was still the master of the longitudes.

Touted as unsinkable, the *Titanic* was the largest passenger steamship in the world when she set off on her maiden voyage from Southampton to New York on 10 April 1912. Four days into the crossing, at twenty minutes to midnight on 14 April, she struck an iceberg and sank at shortly after two the following morning, with a loss of 1,517 lives. Among those on board whom Pratt mentions by name were Isidor Straus, co-owner of Macy's department store in New York, and his wife Ida; American painter Francis Davis Millet; millionaire John Jacob Astor; and businessman Benjamin Guggenheim. The *Carpathia* rescued 705 survivors from the waters around the *Titanic*.

1912

The Listeners

WALTER DE LA MARE

'Is there anybody there?' said the Traveller,
   Knocking on the moonlit door;
And his horse in the silence champed the grasses
   Of the forest's ferny floor.
And a bird flew up out of the turret,
   Above the Traveller's head:
And he smote upon the door again a second time;
   'Is there anybody there?' he said.
But no one descended to the Traveller;
   No head from the leaf-fringed sill
Leaned over and looked into his grey eyes,
   Where he stood perplexed and still.
But only a host of phantom listeners
   That dwelt in the lone house then
Stood listening in the quiet of the moonlight
   To that voice from the world of men:
Stood thronging the faint moonbeams on the dark stair
   That goes down to the empty hall,
Hearkening in an air stirred and shaken
   By the lonely Traveller's call.
And he felt in his heart their strangeness,
   Their stillness answering his cry,
While his horse moved, cropping the dark turf,
   'Neath the starred and leafy sky;
For he suddenly smote on the door, even
   Louder, and lifted his head: –
'Tell them I came, and no one answered,
   That I kept my word,' he said.
Never the least stir made the listeners,
   Though every word he spake
Fell echoing through the shadowiness of the still house
   From the one man left awake:

Aye, they heard his foot upon the stirrup,
   And the sound of iron on stone,
And how the silence surged softly backward,
   When the plunging hoofs were gone.

1912

The Gypsy

—◄○►—

Ezra Pound

'Est-ce que vous avez vu des autres – des camarades –
avec des singes ou des ours?'
A Stray Gipsy – A.D.*1912*

That was the top of the walk, when he said:
'Have you seen any others, any of our lot,
With apes or bears?'
    – A brown upstanding fellow
Not like the half-castes,
    up on the wet road near Clermont.
The wind came, and the rain,
And mist clotted about the trees in the valley,
And I'd the long ways behind me,
    gray Arles and Biaucaire,
And he said, 'Have you seen any of our lot?'
I'd seen a lot of his lot . . .
    ever since Rhodez,
Coming down from the fair
    of St John,
With caravans, but never an ape or a bear.

The locations mentioned in Pound's anecdote of a walking tour (undertaken out
of his enthusiasm for mediaeval French poetry) are all in southern France.

1912

Your Last Drive

THOMAS HARDY

Here by the moorway you returned,
And saw the borough lights ahead
That lit your face – all undiscerned
To be in a week the face of the dead,
And you told of the charm of that haloed view
That never again would beam on you.

And on your left you passed the spot
Where eight days later you were to lie,
And be spoken of as one who was not;
Beholding it with a heedless eye
As alien from you, though under its tree
You soon would halt everlastingly.

I drove not with you . . . Yet had I sat
At your side that eve I should not have seen
That the countenance I was glancing at
Had a last-time look in the flickering sheen,
Nor have read the writing upon your face,
'I go hence soon to my resting-place;

'You may miss me then. But I shall not know
How many times you visit me there,
Or what your thoughts are, or if you go
There never at all. And I shall not care.
Should you censure me I shall take no heed,
And even your praises no more shall need.'

True: never you'll know. And you will not mind.
But shall I then slight you because of such?
Dear ghost, in the past did you ever find
The thought 'What profit,' move me much?
Yet abides the fact, indeed, the same, –
You are past love, praise, indifference, blame.

December 1912

Hardy's first wife, Emma, died in November 1912. Though they had been estranged for some time, Hardy was grief-stricken, and the poems he wrote in her memory, included as 'Poems of 1912–13' in *Satires of Circumstance* (1914), are widely considered to be among his finest.

1913

At Castle Boterel

—◄◦►—

THOMAS HARDY

As I drive to the junction of lane and highway,
   And the drizzle bedrenches the waggonette,
I look behind at the fading byway,
   And see on its slope, now glistening wet,
     Distinctly yet

Myself and a girlish form benighted
   In dry March weather. We climb the road
Beside a chaise. We had just alighted
   To ease the sturdy pony's load
     When he sighed and slowed.

What we did as we climbed, and what we talked of
   Matters not much, nor to what it led, –
Something that life will not be balked of
   Without rude reason till hope is dead,
     And feeling fled.

It filled but a minute. But was there ever
   A time of such quality, since or before,
In that hill's story? To one mind never,
   Though it has been climbed, foot-swift, foot-sore,
     By thousands more.

Primaeval rocks form the road's steep border,
   And much have they faced there, first and last,
Of the transitory in Earth's long order;
   But what they record in colour and cast
     Is – that we two passed.

And to me, though Time's unflinching rigour,
In mindless rote, has ruled from sight
The substance now, one phantom figure
Remains on the slope, as when that night
Saw us alight.

I look and see it there, shrinking, shrinking,
I look back at it amid the rain
For the very last time; for my sand is sinking,
And I shall traverse old love's domain
Never again.

March 1913

1913

'I said, This misery must end'

CHRISTOPHER BRENNAN

I said, This misery must end:
Shall I, that am a man and know
that sky and wind are yet my friend,
sit huddled under any blow?
so speaking left the dismal room
and stepped into the mother-night
all filled with sacred quickening gloom
where the few stars burned low and bright,
and darkling on my darkling hill
heard thro' the beaches' sullen boom
heroic note of living will
ring trumpet-clear against the fight;
so stood and heard, and raised my eyes
erect, that they might drink of space,
and took the night upon my face,
till time and trouble fell away
and all my soul sprang up to feel
as one among the stars that reel
in rhyme on their rejoicing way,
breaking the elder dark, nor stay
but speed beyond each trammelling gyre
till time and sorrow fall away
and night be withered up, and fire
consume the sickness of desire.

1914

Home Burial

ROBERT FROST

He saw her from the bottom of the stairs
Before she saw him. She was starting down.
Looking back over her shoulder at some fear.
She took a doubtful step and then undid it
To raise herself and look again. He spoke
Advancing toward her: 'What is it you see
From up there always – for I want to know.'
She turned and sank upon her skirts at that,
And her face changed from terrified to dull.
He said to gain time: 'What is it you see,'
Mounting until she cowered under him.
'I will find out now – you must tell me, dear.'
She, in her place, refused him any help
With the least stiffening of her neck and silence.
She let him look, sure that he wouldn't see,
Blind creature; and a while he didn't see,
But at last he murmured, 'Oh,' and again, 'Oh.'

'What is it – what?' she said.

                                   'Just that I see.'

'You don't,' she challenged. 'Tell me what it is.'

'The wonder is I didn't see at once.
I never noticed it from here before.
I must be wonted to it – that's the reason.
The little graveyard where my people are!
So small the window frames the whole of it.
Not so much larger than a bedroom, is it?

There are three stones of slate and one of marble,
Broad-shouldered little slabs there in the sunlight
On the sidehill. We haven't to mind *those*.
But I understand: it is not the stones,
But the child's mound—'

           'Don't, don't, don't, don't,' she cried.

She withdrew shrinking from beneath his arm
That rested on the banister, and slid downstairs;
And turned on him with such a daunting look,
He said twice over before he knew himself:
'Can't a man speak of his own child he's lost?'
'Not you! Oh, where's my hat? Oh, I don't need it!
I must get out of here. I must get air.
I don't know rightly whether any man can.'

'Amy! Don't go to some one else this time.
Listen to me. I won't come down the stairs.'
He sat and fixed his chin between his fists.
'There's something I should like to ask you, dear.'

'You don't know how to ask it.'
               'Help me, then.'

Her fingers moved the latch for all reply.

'My words are nearly always an offence.
I don't know how to speak of anything
So as to please you. But I might be taught,
I should suppose. I can't say I see how.
A man must partly give up being a man
With womenfolk. We could have some arrangement
By which I'd bind myself to keep hands off
Anything special you're a-mind to name.
Though I don't like such things 'twixt those that love.
Two that don't love can't live together without them.
But two that do can't live together with them.'
She moved the latch a little. 'Don't – don't go.
Don't carry it to some one else this time.
Tell me about it if it's something human.

Let me into your grief. I'm not so much
Unlike other folks as your standing there
Apart would make me out. Give me my chance.
I do think though, you overdo it a little.
What was it brought you up to think it the thing
To take your mother-loss of a first child
So inconsolably – in the face of love.
You'd think his memory might be satisfied –'

'There you go sneering now!'

                                    'I'm not, I'm not!
You make me angry. I'll come down to you.
God, what a woman! And it's come to this,
A man can't speak of his own child that's dead.'

'You can't because you don't know how to speak.
If you had any feelings, you that dug
With your own hand – how could you? – his little grave;
I saw you from that very window there,
Making the gravel leap and leap in air,
Leap up, like that, like that, and land so lightly
And roll back down the mound beside the hole.
I thought, Who is that man? I didn't know you.
And I crept down the stairs and up the stairs
To look again, and still your spade kept lifting.
Then you came in. I heard your rumbling voice
Out in the kitchen, and I don't know why,
But I went near to see with my own eyes.
You could sit there with the stains on your shoes
Of the fresh earth from your own baby's grave
And talk about your everyday concerns.
You had stood the spade up against the wall
Outside there in the entry, for I saw it.'

'I shall laugh the worst laugh I ever laughed.
I'm cursed. God, if I don't believe I'm cursed.'

'I can repeat the very words you were saying.
"Three foggy mornings and one rainy day
Will rot the best birch fence a man can build."

Think of it, talk like that at such a time!
What had how long it takes a birch to rot
To do with what was in the darkened parlour.
You *couldn't* care! The nearest friends can go
With any one to death, comes so far short
They might as well not try to go at all.
No, from the time when one is sick to death,
One is alone, and he dies more alone.
Friends make pretence of following to the grave,
But before one is in it, their minds are turned
And making the best of their way back to life
And living people, and things they understand.
But the world's evil. I won't have grief so
If I can change it. Oh, I won't, I won't!'

'There, you have said it all and you feel better.
You won't go now, you're crying. Close the door.
The heart's gone out of it: why keep it up.
Amy! There's some one coming down the road!'

'You – oh, you think the talk is all. I must go –
Somewhere out of this house. How can I make you –'

'If – you – do!' She was opening the door wider.
'Where do you mean to go? First tell me that.
I'll follow and bring you back by force. I will! –'

1914

Abu Salammamm – A Song of Empire

EZRA POUND

Being the sort of poem I would write if King George V should have me chained to the fountain before Buckingham Palace, and should give me all the food and women I wanted.

To my brother in chains Bonga-Bonga.

Great is King George the Fifth,
    for he has chained me to this fountain;
He feeds me with beef-bones and wine.
Great is King George the Fifth –
His palace is white like marble,
His palace has ninety-eight windows,
His palace is like a cube cut in thirds,
It is he who has slain the Dragon
    and released the maiden Andromeda.
Great is King George the Fifth;
For his army is legion,
His army is a thousand and forty-eight soldiers
    with red cloths about their buttocks,
And they have red faces like bricks.
Great is the King of England and greatly to be feared,
    For he has chained me to this fountain;
He provides me with women and drinks.
Great is King George the Fifth
    and very resplendent is this fountain.
It is adorned with young gods riding upon dolphins
And its waters are white like silk.
Great and Lofty is this fountain;
And seated upon it is the late Queen, Victoria,
The Mother of the great king, in a hoop-skirt,
    Like a woman heavy with child.

Oh may the king live forever!
Oh may the king live for a thousand years!
For the young prince is foolish and headstrong;
He plagues me with jibes and sticks,
And when he comes into power
He will undoubtedly chain someone else to this fountain,
And my glory will
Be at an end.

(*Poetry, 1914*)

1914

The Rolling English Road

G. K. CHESTERTON

Before the Roman came to Rye or out to Severn
  strode,
The rolling English drunkard made the rolling English
  road.
A reeling road, a rolling road, that rambles round the
  shire,
And after him the parson ran, the sexton and the squire;
A merry road, a mazy road, and such as we did tread
The night we went to Birmingham by way of Beachy
  Head.

I knew no harm of Bonaparte and plenty of the Squire,
And for to fight the Frenchman I did not much desire;
But I did bash their baggonets because they came
  arrayed
To straighten out the crooked road an English drunkard
  made,
Where you and I went down the lane with ale-mugs in
  our hands,
The night we went to Glastonbury by way of Goodwin
  Sands.

His sins they were forgiven him; or why do flowers run
Behind him; and the hedges all strengthening in the
  sun?
The wild thing went from left to right and knew not
  which was which,
But the wild rose was above him when they found him
  in the ditch.
God pardon us, nor harden us; we did not see so clear
The night we went to Bannockburn by way of
  Brighton Pier.

My friends, we will not go again or ape an ancient rage,
Or stretch the folly of our youth to be the shame of
  age,
But walk with clearer eyes and ears this path that
  wandereth,
And see undrugged in evening light the decent inn of
  death;
For there is good news yet to hear and fine things to be
  seen,
Before we go to Paradise by way of Kensal Green.

1914

Adlestrop

EDWARD THOMAS

Yes. I remember Adlestrop –
The name, because one afternoon
Of heat the express-train drew up there
Unwontedly. It was late June.

The steam hissed. Someone cleared his throat.
No one left and no one came
On the bare platform. What I saw
Was Adlestrop – only the name.

And willows, willow-herb, and grass,
And meadowsweet, and haycocks dry,
No whit less still and lonely fair
Than the high cloudlets in the sky.

And for that minute a blackbird sang
Close by, and round him, mistier,
Farther and farther, all the birds
Of Oxfordshire and Gloucestershire.

The railway station where Thomas's train made its unscheduled stop (on 23 June 1914) was closed in 1966.

1914

The Soldier

———◄○►———

RUPERT BROOKE

If I should die, think only this of me:
　That there's some corner of a foreign field
That is for ever England. There shall be
　In that rich earth a richer dust concealed;
A dust whom England bore, shaped, made aware,
　Gave, once, her flowers to love, her ways to roam,
A body of England's, breathing English air,
　Washed by the rivers, blest by suns of home.

And think, this heart, all evil shed away,
　A pulse in the eternal mind, no less
　　Gives somewhere back the thoughts by England
　　　　　　　　　　　　　　　　　given;
Her sights and sounds; dreams happy as her day;
　And laughter, learnt of friends; and gentleness,
　　In hearts at peace, under an English heaven.

1914

from The Mystery of the Charity of Charles Péguy

—◀◎▶—

GEOFFREY HILL

Crack of a starting-pistol. Jean Jaurès
dies in a wine-puddle. Who or what stares
through the café-window crêped in powder-smoke?
The bill for the new farce reads *Sleepers Awake*.

History commands the stage wielding a toy gun,
rehearsing another scene. It has raged so before,
countless times; and will do, countless times more,
in the guise of supreme clown, dire tragedian.

In Brutus' name martyr and mountebank
ghost Caesar's ghost, his wounds of air and ink
painlessly spouting. Jaurès' blood lies stiff
on menu-card, shirt-front and handkerchief.

Did Péguy kill Jaurès? Did he incite
the assassin? Must men stand by what they write
as by their camp-beds or their weaponry
or shell-shocked comrades while they sag and cry?

Would Péguy answer – stubbornly on guard
among the *Cahiers*, with his army cape
and steely pince-nez and his hermit's beard,
brooding on conscience and embattled hope?

Truth's pedagogue, braving an entrenched class
of fools and scoundrels, children of the world,
his eyes caged and hostile behind glass –
still Péguy said that Hope is a little child.

Violent contrariety of men and days; calm
juddery bombardment of a silent film
showing such things: its canvas slashed with rain
and St Elmo's fire. Victory of the machine!

The brisk celluloid clatters through the gate;
the cortège of the century dances in the street;
and over and over the jolly cartoon
armies of France go reeling towards Verdun.

French writer Charles Péguy (1873–1914), socialist, nationalist and Catholic, edited *Les Cahiers de la quinzaine* and was himself the influential fortnightly periodical's chief contributor. He increasingly turned against Jean Jaurès in the period before the First World War, denouncing him as a traitor to socialism and the French nation. Jaurès (1859–1914) was the leader of the French Socialist Party from its foundation in 1902 until the unification of the socialist movements in 1906. Well-known for his pacifist convictions, he was assassinated by a young French nationalist when the war broke out. Péguy was killed in combat on the day before the Battle of the Marne, in September 1914. The Battle of Verdun, which lasted for much of 1916, was to be one of the bloodiest engagements on the Western Front in the entire First World War.

1914

MCMXIV

◄◦►

PHILIP LARKIN

Those long uneven lines
Standing as patiently
As if they were stretched outside
The Oval or Villa Park,
The crowns of hats, the sun
On moustached archaic faces
Grinning as if it were all
An August Bank Holiday lark;

And the shut shops, the bleached
Established names on the sunblinds,
The farthings and sovereigns,
And dark-clothed children at play
Called after kings and queens,
The tin advertisements
For cocoa and twist, and the pubs
Wide open all day;

And the countryside not caring:
The place-names all hazed over
With flowering grasses, and fields
Shadowing Domesday lines
Under wheat's restless silence;
The differently-dressed servants
With tiny rooms in huge houses,
The dust behind limousines;

Never such innocence,
Never before or since,
As changed itself to past
Without a word – the men
Leaving the gardens tidy,

The thousands of marriages
Lasting a little while longer:
Never such innocence again.

Larkin's allusion in 'Domesday' is to the Domesday Book, the survey of England made by the Normans in 1086 under William the Conqueror, and suggests those ancient, vanished settlements, not a stone of which now remains, which can be 'seen' in shadowy outline when crops grow.

II

1915–1922

War to Waste Land

THOSE YOUNG men jostling to join up were soon disabused. Working to the unforgiving timetable of their Schlieffen Plan, the German army swept through Belgium towards the west of Paris, aiming to cut the French capital off from any help their British allies could offer. The British Expeditionary Force was thrown into battle to hold the Belgian town of Mons but was no match for a vastly superior force which had rehearsed every detail of the invasion, and the retreat soon saw the French and British pulling back to the Somme and then to within a very few miles of Paris. There, thanks in part to fleets of Parisian taxis rushing reinforcements to the front, the line was held. Casualties were high, and any hopes that the war would be over by Christmas were shown up as ludicrously optimistic. Both sides dug in and, by the end of the autumn, two unbroken lines of trenches stretched from the French coast to the Swiss border. By 1915, the true horror of modern warfare fought by vast forces armed with machine guns and backed up by artillery batteries was becoming apparent.

If the unofficial truce of the first wartime Christmas gave a spark of hope that sanity would assert itself, it was quickly snuffed out, and both sides faced each other for hundreds of miles in trenches often barely fifty yards apart. Isaac Rosenberg conveys the mundane routine of life in the trenches, while David Jones, achingly reminded by the green gentle slopes of places known in peacetime, describes with cinematic vividness the minute particulars of battle. 1916 was the year of the battle of the Somme, which saw the worst losses ever suffered by the

British army. There were 60,000 casualties on the first day of battle, with line after line of soldiers mown down by the German machine gunners who had survived the ten-day long artillery barrage. This was the flower of Kitchener's volunteer army, and the battle marked a turning point in the public's reaction to the war.

For the civilian population back home, war became the backdrop to all aspects of life. Edward Thomas's 'As the Team's Head-Brass' demonstrates how the most peaceful occupation was overshadowed by reflections on the war. Almost its companion piece, Thomas Hardy's 'In Time of "The Breaking of Nations"' attempts a lofty, dispassionate overview of human existence, with the rhythms of ploughing and the regenerative cycle of human sexuality outlasting the disruptiveness of war. Not everyone could adopt such a position. For Katherine Mansfield, the loss of her brother came as a sharp, bitter grief. And across the ocean in America, Carl Sandburg evinced a real and sympathetic understanding of the terrible reality of the grinding war machine and the fearful human sacrifice required to achieve any military objective, however insignificant.

The depressing conclusion that a generation of young men was being needlessly sent to the slaughter was given powerful voice by Siegfried Sassoon, whose repeated examples of personal bravery gave him licence to describe the war as he saw it and to castigate the attitudinising and sanctimonious rhetoric of those who stirred up pro-war sentiment at home. By 1917 Wilfred Owen, Sassoon's younger friend and protégé – they met while recuperating at Craiglockhart hospital in Edinburgh – was finding his own poetic voice, and developing the extraordinary blend of lush romanticism and unblinking realism which produced the most powerful and haunting evocation of the hell of trench warfare we have. While sharing his mentor's consuming fury at the senseless slaughter, Owen could convey, as Sassoon could not, the infernal landscape of the Western Front and, against this lurid backdrop, the individual soldier's despair, terror and astonishing courage.

Not every wartime thought was of the war, of course. Those in Ireland who had no reason to love British rule seized their opportunity, and 1916 finally saw tensions climax with the Easter Rising in Dublin. Though he disapproved of the revolutionary action, Yeats was nevertheless taken with the heroism of the uprising and immortalised the 'terrible beauty' of their tragic failure in his great poem, 'Easter, 1916', while Padraic Colum commemorated the execution of Roger Casement. Anna Wickham's poem of a woman's selfhood is a poem born of wartime, as also, in their different ways, are two great poems of the religious spirit, Wallace Stevens's 'Sunday Morning' and Hardy's 'The Oxen'. And in 1917 T. S. Eliot announced a radical new poetic with his elevation of urban drabness to something akin to pastoral in 'The Love Song of J. Alfred Prufrock'. The young American intellectual, who had married an English-woman two years earlier and was now working in a bank in London, was to emerge as the leader of the Modernist movement and aesthetic in poetry. The most deliberate of poets, he differed from his energetic compatriot Ezra Pound in being incapable of the spontaneous response to an event, a passing emotion, a visual image. Each Eliot poem is a finished work of art. With the publication of *The Love Song of J. Alfred Prufrock and Other Poems*, Eliot signalled the end of the fallow period stretching back to the Victorian heyday of Tennyson, Browning, Arnold and Clough. And the poem with which he in due course responded to the war would give the modern movement its greatest poetic masterpiece.

1918 saw the bloody final act of the Great War. Having made a separate peace with Russia following the Bolshevik revolution of October 1917, Germany made a last push for victory on the Western Front. The conflict had by this time become a war of attrition, but the entry of the Americans had tipped the scales in favour of the Allies. The sheer weight of numbers eventually told, and the Germans sued for an Armistice in November 1918. Wilfred Owen, the greatest poet of the war, was killed a week before it ended, leaving, amongst the last of the poems he wrote, an almost unbearable poem about the countdown to going over the top.

When the bloodletting was over at last, there was rejoicing first of all. Writing decades later, New Zealander Allen Curnow remembered the celebrations in his own boyhood, at the return of those who fought and survived. But after the rejoicing came the more considered, critical responses. Siegfried Sassoon, who had taunted the authorities by writing a pacifist letter to *The Times* and throwing his Military Cross into the Thames, bade farewell to the conflict in a poem tellingly titled 'Recon-ciliation', which must doubtless have touched the hearts of many thousands of bereaved parents – although, like so much of his writing, it includes withering words for the civilian population who had 'nourished hatred harsh and blind'. It is impossible to read the word 'hero', after Sassoon's poetry, without a radical sense of unsettlement. Rudyard Kipling, who had lost his own son and who had repeatedly criticised those who were responsible for the military disasters of the war, took the view that the lies told by the ruling classes were the root of the war's evils. Yeats's apocalyptic poem, 'The Second Coming', was written at a time when war and revolution appeared to have become the normal condition of human existence. And at a later date, writing with the benefit of hindsight but also with a socialist understanding of the origins of the First World War (and taking his title, 'Common Sense', from Tom Paine), Alan Brownjohn inscribed the statistics of wartime casualties into a context of other statistics, implying a critique and indictment of capitalism itself.

The two great Americans who had chosen European exile proved the most scathing. For Pound, the war dead had been sacrificed for 'an old bitch gone in the teeth', for 'a botched civilization', for 'two gross of broken statues' and 'a few thousand battered books'. And for Eliot, thousands of years of human life and endeavour had left nothing but the heap of fragments he swept together in his masterpiece, *The Waste Land*. Published in 1922, this Modernist classic (prepared for the press with editorial assistance from Pound) used a range of techniques – abstruse quotation, jarring rhythmical variation, cinematic jumps from one scene to another – to demonstrate the void at the heart of modern civilisation. It threw down an artistic gauntlet to the times. And the times responded by partying.

1915

In Time of 'The Breaking of Nations'

―◇―

THOMAS HARDY

I

Only a man harrowing clods
  In a slow silent walk
With an old horse that stumbles and nods
  Half asleep as they stalk.

II

Only thin smoke without flame
  From the heaps of couch-grass;
Yet this will go onward the same
  Though Dynasties pass.

III

Yonder a maid and her wight
  Come whispering by:
War's annals will cloud into night
  Ere their story die.

1915

Hardy's title alludes to Jeremiah 51:20.

1915

To L. H. B. (1894–1915)

‹◊›

KATHERINE MANSFIELD

Last night for the first time since you were dead
I walked with you, my brother, in a dream.
We were at home again beside the stream
Fringed with tall berry bushes, white and red.
'Don't touch them: they are poisonous,' I said.
But your hand hovered, and I saw a beam
Of strange bright laughter flying round your head
And as you stooped I saw the berries gleam –
'Don't you remember? We called them Dead Man's
    Bread!'
I woke and heard the wind moan and the roar
Of the dark water tumbling on the shore.
Where – where is the path of my dream for my eager
    feet?
By the remembered stream my brother stands
Waiting for me with berries in his hands . . .
'These are my body. Sister, take and eat.'

Mansfield's sonnet was written in memory of her brother, Leslie Heron Beau-
champ, killed in action near Armentières in France on 7 October 1915 while
serving in the South Lancashire Regiment. 'I never see anything that I like, or
hear anything, without the longing that he should see and hear, too,' she wrote
in a letter of 19 November, and in her journal she wrote in the same month: 'Yes,
though he is lying in the middle of a little wood in France and I am still walking
upright and feeling the sun and the wind from the sea, I am just as much dead
as he is.'

1915

Buttons

<o>

Carl Sandburg

I have been watching the war map slammed up for
  advertising in front of the newspaper office.
Buttons – red and yellow buttons – blue and black
  buttons – are shoved back and forth across the map.

A laughing young man, sunny with freckles,
Climbs a ladder, yells a joke to somebody in the crowd,
And then fixes a yellow button one inch west
And follows the yellow button with a black button one
  inch west.

(Ten thousand men and boys twist on their bodies in a
  red soak along a river edge,
Gasping of wounds, calling for water, some rattling death
  in their throats.)
Who would guess what it cost to move two buttons one
  inch on the war map here in front of the newspaper
  office where the freckle-faced young man is laughing
  to us?

The US did not enter the First World War until January 1917.

1915

Mrs Kessler

◄◦►

EDGAR LEE MASTERS

Mr Kessler, you know, was in the army,
And he drew six dollars a month as a pension,
And stood on the corner talking politics,
Or sat at home reading Grant's Memoirs;
And I supported the family by washing,
Learning the secrets of all the people
From their curtains, counterpanes, shirts and skirts.
For things that are new grow old at length,
They're replaced with better or none at all:
People are prospering or falling back.
And rents and patches widen with time;
No thread or needle can pace decay,
And there are stains that baffle soap,
And there are colors that run in spite of you,
Blamed though you are for spoiling a dress.
Handkerchiefs, napery, have their secrets —
The laundress, Life, knows all about it.
And I, who went to all the funerals
Held in Spoon River, swear I never
Saw a dead face without thinking it looked
Like something washed and ironed.

The memoirs Mr Kessler read were the *Personal Memoirs* of Ulysses S. Grant,
who commanded the Union forces in the American Civil War and later became
eighteenth President of the United States.

1915

Sunday Morning

⎯⎯⎯⎯◦⎯⎯⎯⎯

WALLACE STEVENS

I

Complacencies of the peignoir, and late
Coffee and oranges in a sunny chair,
And the green freedom of a cockatoo
Upon a rug mingle to dissipate
The holy hush of ancient sacrifice.
She dreams a little, and she feels the dark
Encroachment of that old catastrophe,
As a calm darkens among water-lights.
The pungent oranges and bright, green wings
Seem things in some procession of the dead,
Winding across wide water, without sound.
The day is like wide water, without sound,
Stilled for the passing of her dreaming feet
Over the seas, to silent Palestine,
Dominion of the blood and sepulchre.

II

Why should she give her bounty to the dead?
What is divinity if it can come
Only in silent shadows and in dreams?
Shall she not find in comforts of the sun,
In pungent fruit and bright, green wings, or else
In any balm or beauty of the earth,
Things to be cherished like the thought of heaven?
Divinity must live within herself:
Passions of rain, or moods in falling snow;
Grievings in loneliness, or unsubdued
Elations when the forest blooms; gusty

Emotions on wet roads on autumn nights;
All pleasures and all pains, remembering
The bough of summer and the winter branch.
These are the measures destined for her soul.

III

Jove in the clouds had his inhuman birth.
No mother suckled him, no sweet land gave
Large-mannered motions to his mythy mind
He moved among us, as a muttering king,
Magnificent, would move among his hinds,
Until our blood, commingling, virginal,
With heaven, brought such requital to desire
The very hinds discerned it, in a star.
Shall our blood fail? Or shall it come to be
The blood of paradise? And shall the earth
Seem all of paradise that we shall know?
The sky will be much friendlier then than now,
A part of labor and a part of pain,
And next in glory to enduring love,
Not this dividing and indifferent blue.

IV

She says, 'I am content when wakened birds,
Before they fly, test the reality
Of misty fields, by their sweet questionings;
But when the birds are gone, and their warm fields
Return no more, where, then, is paradise?'
There is not any haunt of prophecy,
Nor any old chimera of the grave,
Neither the golden underground, nor isle
Melodious, where spirits gat them home,
Nor visionary south, nor cloudy palm
Remote on heaven's hill, that has endured
As April's green endures; or will endure
Like her remembrance of awakened birds,

Or her desire for June and evening, tipped
By the consummation of the swallow's wings.

V

She says, 'But in contentment I still feel
The need of some imperishable bliss.'
Death is the mother of beauty; hence from her,
Alone, shall come fulfilment to our dreams
And our desires. Although she strews the leaves
Of sure obliteration on our paths,
The path sick sorrow took, the many paths
Where triumph rang its brassy phrase, or love
Whispered a little out of tenderness,
She makes the willow shiver in the sun
For maidens who were wont to sit and gaze
Upon the grass, relinquished to their feet.
She causes boys to pile new plums and pears
On disregarded plate. The maidens taste
And stray impassioned in the littering leaves.

VI

Is there no change of death in paradise?
Does ripe fruit never fall? Or do the boughs
Hang always heavy in that perfect sky,
Unchanging, yet so like our perishing earth,
With rivers like our own that seek for seas
They never find, the same receding shores
That never touch with inarticulate pang?
Why set the pear upon those river-banks
Or spice the shores with odors of the plum?
Alas, that they should wear our colors there,
The silken weavings of our afternoons,
And pick the strings of our insipid lutes!
Death is the mother of beauty, mystical,
Within whose burning bosom we devise
Our earthly mothers waiting, sleeplessly.

VII

Supple and turbulent, a ring of men
Shall chant in orgy on a summer morn
Their boisterous devotion to the sun,
Not as a god, but as a god might be,
Naked among them, like a savage source.
Their chant shall be a chant of paradise,
Out of their blood, returning to the sky;
And in their chant shall enter, voice by voice,
The windy lake wherein their lord delights,
The trees, like serafin, and echoing hills,
That choir among themselves long afterward.
They shall know well the heavenly fellowship
Of men that perish and of summer morn.
And whence they came and whither they shall go
The dew upon their feet shall manifest.

VIII

She hears, upon that water without sound,
A voice that cries, 'The tomb in Palestine
Is not the porch of spirits lingering.
It is the grave of Jesus, where he lay.'
We live in an old chaos of the sun,
Or old dependency of day and night,
Or island solitude, unsponsored, free,
Of that wide water, inescapable.
Deer walk upon our mountains, and the quail
Whistle about us their spontaneous cries;
Sweet berries ripen in the wilderness;
And, in the isolation of the sky,
At evening, casual flocks of pigeons make
Ambiguous undulations as they sink,
Downward to darkness, on extended wings.

1915

The Oxen

THOMAS HARDY

Christmas Eve, and twelve of the clock.
   'Now they are all on their knees,'
An elder said as we sat in a flock
   By the embers in hearthside ease.

We pictured the meek mild creatures where
   They dwelt in their strawy pen,
Nor did it occur to one of us there
   To doubt they were kneeling then.

So fair a fancy few would weave
   In these years! Yet, I feel,
If someone said on Christmas Eve,
   'Come; see the oxen kneel

'In the lonely barton by yonder coomb
   Our childhood used to know,'
I should go with him in the gloom,
   Hoping it might be so.

1916

Break of Day in the Trenches

Isaac Rosenberg

The darkness crumbles away.
It is the same old druid Time as ever,
Only a live thing leaps my hand,
A queer sardonic rat,
As I pull the parapet's poppy
To stick behind my ear.
Droll rat, they would shoot you if they knew
Your cosmopolitan sympathies.
Now you have touched this English hand
You will do the same to a German
Soon, no doubt, if it be your pleasure
To cross the sleeping green between.
It seems you inwardly grin as you pass
Strong eyes, fine limbs, haughty athletes,
Less chanced than you for life,
Bonds to the whims of murder,
Sprawled in the bowels of the earth,
The torn fields of France.
What do you see in our eyes
At the shrieking iron and flame
Hurled through still heavens?
What quaver – what heart aghast?
Poppies whose roots are in man's veins
Drop, and are ever dropping;

But mine in my ear is safe –
Just a little white with the dust.

1916

from In Parenthesis

—◄◦►—

DAVID JONES

The gentle slopes are green to remind you
of South English places, only far wider and flatter spread
    and
grooved and harrowed criss-cross whitely and the
    disturbed
subsoil heaped up albescent.

Across upon this undulated board of verdure chequered
bright
when you look to left and right
small, drab, bundled pawns severally make effort
moved in tenuous line
and if you looked behind – the next wave came slowly,
    as successive surfs creep in to dissipate on flat shore;
and to your front, stretched long laterally,
and receded deeply,
the dark wood.

And now the gradient runs more flatly toward the
    separate
scared saplings, where they make fringe for the interior
    thicket
and you take notice.
    There between the thinning uprights
at the margin
straggle tangled oak and flayed sheeny beech-bole, and
    fragile
birch whose silver queenery is draggled and ungraced
and June shoots lopt
and fresh stalks bled
    runs the Jerry trench.
And cork-screw stapled trip-wire
to snare among the briars

and iron warp with bramble weft
with meadow-sweet and lady-smock
for a fair camouflage.

Mr Jenkins half inclined his head to them – he walked
just barely in advance of his platoon and immediately
to the left of Private Ball.
He makes the conventional sign
and there is the deeply inward effort of spent men who
    would
make response for him,
and take it at the double.
He sinks on one knee
and now on the other,
his upper body tilts in rigid inclination
this way and back;
weighted lanyard runs out to full tether,
        swings like a pendulum
        and the clock run down.
Lurched over, jerked iron saucer over tilted brow,
clampt unkindly over lip and chin
nor no ventaille to this darkening
    and masked face lifts to grope the air
and so disconsolate;
enfeebled fingering at a paltry strap –
buckle holds,
holds him blind against the morning.
    Then stretch still where weeds pattern the chalk predella
– where it rises to his wire – and Sergeant T. Quilter
    takes over.

1916

Easter 1916

W. B. Yeats

I have met them at close of day
Coming with vivid faces
From counter or desk among grey
Eighteenth-century houses.
I have passed with a nod of the head
Or polite meaningless words,
Or have lingered awhile and said
Polite meaningless words,
And thought before I had done
Of a mocking tale or a gibe
To please a companion
Around the fire at the club,
Being certain that they and I
But lived where motley is worn:
All changed, changed utterly:
A terrible beauty is born.

That woman's days were spent
In ignorant good-will,
Her nights in argument
Until her voice grew shrill.
What voice more sweet than hers
When, young and beautiful,
She rode to harriers?
This man had kept a school
And rode our wingèd horse;
This other his helper and friend
Was coming into his force;
He might have won fame in the end,
So sensitive his nature seemed,
So daring and sweet his thought.
This other man I had dreamed

A drunken, vainglorious lout.
He had done most bitter wrong
To some who are near my heart,
Yet I number him in the song;
He, too, has resigned his part
In the casual comedy;
He, too, has been changed in his turn,
Transformed utterly:
A terrible beauty is born.

Hearts with one purpose alone
Through summer and winter seem
Enchanted to a stone
To trouble the living stream.
The horse that comes from the road,
The rider, the birds that range
From cloud to tumbling cloud,
Minute by minute they change;
A shadow of cloud on the stream
Changes minute by minute;
A horse-hoof slides on the brim,
And a horse plashes within it;
The long-legged moor-hens dive,
And hens to moor-cocks call;
Minute by minute they live:
The stone's in the midst of all.

Too long a sacrifice
Can make a stone of the heart.
O when may it suffice?
That is Heaven's part, our part
To murmur name upon name,
As a mother names her child
When sleep at last has come
On limbs that had run wild.
What is it but nightfall?
No, no, not night but death;
Was it needless death after all?
For England may keep faith

For all that is done and said.
We know their dream; enough
To know they dreamed and are dead;
And what if excess of love
Bewildered them till they died?
I write it out in a verse –
MacDonagh and MacBride
And Connolly and Pearse
Now and in time to be,
Wherever green is worn,
Are changed, changed utterly:
A terrible beauty is born.

September 25, 1916

On Easter Monday, 24 April 1916, Irish Republicans mounted an unsuccessful rising against British rule. Thomas MacDonagh, John MacBride, James Connolly and Patrick Pearse, referred to in the closing lines of the poem, played a leading part in the rising and were all executed for their role.

1916

Roger Casement

◄○►

PADRAIC COLUM

They have hanged Roger Casement to the tolling of a bell,
Ochone, och, ochone, ochone!
And their Smiths, and their Murrays, and their Cecils say it's
    well,
Ochone, och, ochone, ochone!
But there are outcast peoples to lift that spirit high,
Flayed men and breastless women who laboured fearfully,
And they will lift him, lift him, for the eyes of God to see,
And it's well, after all, Roger Casement!

They've ta'en his strangled body from the gallows to the pit,
Ochone, och, ochone, ochone!
And the flame that eats into it, the quicklime, brought to it,
Ochone, och, ochone, ochone!
To waste that noble stature, the grave and brightening face,
In which courtesy and kindliness had eminence of place,
But they – they'll die to dust which the wind will take
    a-pace,
While 'twas yours to die to fire, Roger Casement!

Roger Casement had a distinguished career in the British consular service but
in 1916 seized the opportunity to negotiate the supply of German arms to assist
Irish rebels. He was tried for treason and hanged at Pentonville prison, London,
on 3 August 1916.

1916

Beside the Bed

<o>

CHARLOTTE MEW

Some one has shut the shining eyes, straightened and folded
  The wandering hands quietly covering the unquiet breast:
So, smoothed and silenced you lie, like a child, not again to
  be questioned or scolded:
  But, for you, not one of us believes that this is rest.

Not so to close the windows down can cloud and deaden
  The blue beyond: or to screen the wavering flame subdue
  its breath:
Why, if I lay my cheek to your cheek, your grey lips, like
  dawn, would quiver and redden,
  Breaking into the old, odd smile at this fraud of death.

Because all night you have not turned to us or spoken
  It is time for you to wake; your dreams were never very
  deep:
I, for one, have seen the thin bright, twisted threads of them
  dimmed suddenly and broken.
  This is only a most piteous pretence of sleep!

1916

The Fired Pot

ANNA WICKHAM

In our town, people live in rows.
The only irregular thing in a street is the steeple;
And where that points to, God only knows,
And not the poor disciplined people!

And I have watched the women growing old,
Passionate about pins, and pence, and soap,
Till the heart within my wedded breast grew cold,
And I lost hope.

But a young soldier came to our town,
He spoke his mind most candidly.
He asked me quickly to lie down,
And that was very good for me.

For though I gave him no embrace –
Remembering my duty –
He altered the expression of my face,
And gave me back my beauty.

1916

As the Team's Head-Brass

EDWARD THOMAS

As the team's head-brass flashed out on the turn
The lovers disappeared into the wood.
I sat among the boughs of the fallen elm
That strewed the angle of the fallow, and
Watched the plough narrowing a yellow square
Of charlock. Every time the horses turned
Instead of treading me down, the ploughman leaned
Upon the handles to say or ask a word,
About the weather, next about the war.
Scraping the share he faced towards the wood,
And screwed along the furrow till the brass flashed
Once more.
          The blizzard felled the elm whose crest
I sat in, by a woodpecker's round hole,
The ploughman said. 'When will they take it away?'
'When the war's over.' So the talk began –
One minute and an interval of ten,
A minute more and the same interval.
'Have you been out?' 'No.' 'And don't want to, perhaps?'
'If I could only come back again, I should.
I could spare an arm. I shouldn't want to lose
A leg. If I should lose my head, why, so,
I should want nothing more . . . Have many gone
From here?' 'Yes.' 'Many lost?' 'Yes, a good few.
Only two teams work on the farm this year.
One of my mates is dead. The second day
In France they killed him. It was back in March,
The very night of the blizzard, too. Now if
He had stayed here we should have moved the tree.'
'And I should not have sat here. Everything
Would have been different. For it would have been
Another world.' 'Ay, and a better, though

If we could see all all might seem good.' Then
The lovers came out of the wood again:
The horses started and for the last time
I watched the clods crumble and topple over
After the ploughshare and the stumbling team.

1916

The Hero

◄○►

SIEGFRIED SASSOON

'Jack fell as he'd have wished,' the Mother said,
And folded up the letter that she'd read.
'The Colonel writes so nicely.' Something broke
In the tired voice that quavered to a choke.
She half looked up. 'We mothers are so proud
Of our dead soldiers.' Then her face was bowed.

Quietly the Brother Officer went out.
He'd told the poor old dear some gallant lies
That she would nourish all her days, no doubt.
For while he coughed and mumbled, her weak eyes
Had shone with gentle triumph, brimmed with joy,
Because he'd been so brave, her glorious boy.

He thought how 'Jack', cold-footed, useless swine,
Had panicked down the trench that night the mine
Went up at Wicked Corner; how he'd tried
To get sent home, and how, at last, he died,
Blown to small bits. And no one seemed to care
Except that lonely woman with white hair.

August 1916

Does not refer to anyone I have known. But it is pathetically true. And of course
the 'average Englishman' will hate it. This, and 'The Tombstone-Maker', 'The
One-Legged Man' and 'Arms and the Man', show a resemblance to Hardy's *Satires
of Circumstance*, which I read with amusement in 1914, but now find unworthy of
his greatness. (Sassoon's note.)

1916

'They'

<o>

SIEGFRIED SASSOON

The Bishop tells us: 'When the boys come back
They will not be the same; for they'll have fought
In a just cause: they lead the last attack
On Anti-Christ; their comrades' blood has bought
New right to breed an honourable race,
They have challenged Death and dared him face to face.'

'We're none of us the same!' the boys reply.
'For George lost both his legs; and Bill's stone blind;
Poor Jim's shot through the lungs and like to die;
And Bert's gone syphilitic: you'll not find
A chap who's served that hasn't found *some* change.'
And the Bishop said: 'The ways of God are strange!'

31 October 1916

Written at 40 Half Moon Street about 1 a.m. after a long evening with Robbie
Ross, More Adey and Roderick Meiklejohn. I was so sleepy I could hardly keep
my eyes open, but the thing just wrote itself. And Eddie Marsh, when I showed it
to him one wet morning (at 10 Downing Street!), said: 'It's *too* horrible.' As I was
walking back I actually met 'the Bishop' (of London) and he turned a mild shining
gaze on me and my M. C. (Sassoon's note.)

Like Graves and Jones, Sassoon was in the Royal Welch Fusiliers, and in 1916 was
awarded a Military Cross 'for conspicuous gallantry'. But in 1917 he refused to
return to the front, arguing in a public letter that the war had become one of
aggression. His scathing poems about the war often take civilian attitudes as their
targets. Eddie Marsh, referred to in Sassoon's note above, was Sir Edward Marsh
(1872–1953), known to the literary world as the editor of successive antholo-
gies of 'Georgian' poetry, but in political life, at the date of the Downing Street
encounter referred to by Sassoon, assistant private secretary to Prime Minister
Henry Asquith.

1917

Before Action

LEON GELLERT

We always had to do our work at night.
I wondered why we had to be so sly.
I wondered why we couldn't have our fight
Under the open sky.

I wondered why I always felt so cold.
I wondered why the orders seemed so slow,
So slow to come, so whisperingly told,
So whisperingly low.

I wondered if my packing-straps were tight,
And wondered why I wondered. Sound went wild . . .
An order came . . . I ran into the night
Wondering why I smiled.

1917

Dulce et Decorum Est

WILFRED OWEN

Bent double, like old beggars under sacks,
Knock-kneed, coughing like hags, we cursed through sludge,
Till on the haunting flares we turned our backs
And towards our distant rest began to trudge.
Men marched asleep. Many had lost their boots
But limped on, blood-shod. All went lame; all blind;
Drunk with fatigue; deaf even to the hoots
Of tired, outstripped Five-Nines that dropped behind.

Gas! GAS! Quick, boys! – An ecstasy of fumbling,
Fitting the clumsy helmets just in time;
But someone still was yelling out and stumbling
And flound'ring like a man in fire or lime . . .
Dim, through the misty panes and thick green light,
As under a green sea, I saw him drowning.

In all my dreams, before my helpless sight,
He plunges at me, guttering, choking, drowning.

If in some smothering dreams you too could pace
Behind the wagon that we flung him in,
And watch the white eyes writhing in his face,
His hanging face, like a devil's sick of sin;
If you could hear, at every jolt, the blood
Come gargling from the froth-corrupted lungs,
Obscene as cancer, bitter as the cud
Of vile, incurable sores on innocent tongues, –
My friend, you would not tell with such high zest
To children ardent for some desperate glory,
The old Lie: Dulce et decorum est
Pro patria mori.

The words 'dulce et decorum est pro patria mori' ('it is a sweet and seemly thing
to die for one's country') occur in one of Horace's Odes (III, 2).

1917

Strange Meeting

—◦—

WILFRED OWEN

It seemed that out of battle I escaped
Down some profound dull tunnel, long since scooped
Through granites which titanic wars had groined.
Yet also there encumbered sleepers groaned,
Too fast in thought or death to be bestirred.
Then, as I probed them, one sprang up, and stared
With piteous recognition in fixed eyes,
Lifting distressful hands as if to bless.
And by his smile, I knew that sullen hall,
By his dead smile I knew we stood in Hell.
With a thousand pains that vision's face was grained;
Yet no blood reached there from the upper ground,
And no guns thumped, or down the flues made moan,
'Strange friend,' I said, 'here is no cause to mourn.'
'None,' said that other, 'save the undone years,
The hopelessness. Whatever hope is yours,
Was my life also; I went hunting wild
After the wildest beauty in the world,
Which lies not calm in eyes, or braided hair,
But mocks the steady running of the hour,
And if it grieves, grieves richlier than here.
For of my glee might many men have laughed,
And of my weeping something had been left,
Which must die now. I mean the truth untold,
The pity of war, the pity war distilled.
Now men will go content with what we spoiled,
Or, discontent, boil bloody, and be spilled.
They will be swift with swiftness of the tigress.
None will break ranks, though nations trek from progress.
Courage was mine, and I had mystery.
Wisdom was mine, and I had mastery:
To miss the march of this retreating world

Into vain citadels that are not walled.
Then, when much blood had clogged their chariot-wheels,
I would go up and wash them from sweet wells,
Even with truths that lie too deep for taint.
I would have poured my spirit without stint
But not through wounds; not on the cess of war.
Foreheads of men have bled where no wounds were.
I am the enemy you killed, my friend.
I knew you in this dark: for so you frowned
Yesterday through me as you jabbed and killed.
I parried; but my hands were loath and cold.
Let us sleep now . . .'

1917

Anthem for Doomed Youth

WILFRED OWEN

What passing-bells for these who die as cattle?
   Only the monstrous anger of the guns.
   Only the stuttering rifles' rapid rattle
Can patter out their hasty orisons.
No mockeries now for them; no prayers nor bells,
   Nor any voice of mourning save the choirs, –
The shrill, demented choirs of wailing shells;
   And bugles calling for them from sad shires.

What candles may be held to speed them all?
   Not in the hands of boys, but in their eyes
Shall shine the holy glimmers of good-byes.
   The pallor of girls' brows shall be their pall;
Their flowers the tenderness of patient minds,
And each slow dusk a drawing-down of blinds.

1917

Bach and the Sentry

IVOR GURNEY

Watching the dark my spirit rose in flood
  On that most dearest Prelude of my delight.
The low-lying mist lifted its hood,
  The October stars showed nobly in clear night.

When I return, and to real music-making,
  And play that Prelude, how will it happen then?
Shall I feel as I felt, a sentry hardly waking,
  With a dull sense of No Man's Land again?

1917

Mesopotamia

◄◊►

RUDYARD KIPLING

1917

They shall not return to us, the resolute, the young,
  The eager and whole-hearted whom we gave:
But the men who left them thriftily to die in their own
  dung,
  Shall they come with years and honour to the grave?

They shall not return to us, the strong men coldly slain
  In sight of help denied from day to day:
But the men who edged their agonies and chid them in
  their pain,
  Are they too strong and wise to put away?

Our dead shall not return to us while Day and Night
  divide —
  Never while the bars of sunset hold.
But the idle-minded overlings who quibbled while they
  died,
  Shall they thrust for high employments as of old?

Shall we only threaten and be angry for an hour?
  When the storm is ended shall we find
How softly but how swiftly they have sidled back to
  power
  By the favour and contrivance of their kind?

Even while they soothe us, while they promise large
  amends,
  Even while they make a show of fear,
Do they call upon their debtors, and take counsel with
  their friends,
  To confirm and re-establish each career?

Their lives cannot repay us – their death could not
   undo –
The shame that they have laid upon our race.
But the slothfulness that wasted and the arrogance that
   slew,
Shall we leave it unabated in its place?

The British campaign against the Ottoman Turks in Mesopotamia, managed by
the government of India, had seen serious incompetence and reverses, though in
1917, when Kipling's poem was written, the military position was changing as
Kut was retaken and Baghdad liberated. During the course of the war, Kipling
published a number of attacks on military incompetence in *The Times*.

1917

The Love Song of J. Alfred Prufrock

T. S. ELIOT

S'io credessi che mia risposta fosse
a persona che mai tornasse al mondo,
questa fiamma staria senza più scosse.
Ma per ciò che giammai di questo fondo
non torno vivo alcun, s'i' odo il vero,
senza tema d'infamia ti rispondo.

Let us go then, you and I,
When the evening is spread out against the sky
Like a patient etherised upon a table;
Let us go, through certain half-deserted streets,
The muttering retreats
Of restless nights in one-night cheap hotels
And sawdust restaurants with oyster-shells:
Streets that follow like a tedious argument
Of insidious intent
To lead you to an overwhelming question . . .
Oh, do not ask, 'What is it?'
Let us go and make our visit.

In the room the women come and go
Talking of Michelangelo.

The yellow fog that rubs its back upon the window-
    panes,
The yellow smoke that rubs its muzzle on the window-
    panes,
Licked its tongue into the corners of the evening,
Lingered upon the pools that stand in drains,
Let fall upon its back the soot that falls from chimneys,
Slipped by the terrace, made a sudden leap,
And seeing that it was a soft October night,
Curled once about the house, and fell asleep.

And indeed there will be time
For the yellow smoke that slides along the street
Rubbing its back upon the window-panes;
There will be time, there will be time
To prepare a face to meet the faces that you meet;
There will be time to murder and create,
And time for all the works and days of hands
That lift and drop a question on your plate;
Time for you and time for me,
And time yet for a hundred indecisions,
And for a hundred visions and revisions,
Before the taking of a toast and tea.

In the room the women come and go
Talking of Michelangelo.

And indeed there will be time
To wonder, 'Do I dare?' and, 'Do I dare?'
Time to turn back and descend the stair,
With a bald spot in the middle of my hair –
(They will say: 'How his hair is growing thin!')
My morning coat, my collar mounting firmly to the
    chin,
My necktie rich and modest, but asserted by a simple
    pin –
(They will say: 'But how his arms and legs are thin!')
Do I dare
Disturb the universe?
In a minute there is time
For decisions and revisions which a minute will reverse.

For I have known them all already, known them
    all –
Have known the evenings, mornings, afternoons,
I have measured out my life with coffee spoons;
I know the voices dying with a dying fall
Beneath the music from a farther room.
    So how should I presume?

And I have known, the eyes already, known them all –
The eyes that fix you in a formulated phrase,
And when I am formulated, sprawling on a pin,
When I am pinned and wriggling on the wall,
Then how should I begin
To spit out all the butt-ends of my days and ways?
    And how should I presume?

    And I have known the eyes already, known them all –
Arms that are braceleted and white and bare
(But in the lamplight, downed with light brown hair!)
Is it perfume from a dress
That makes me so digress?
Arms that lie along a table, or wrap about a shawl.
    And should I then presume?
    And how should I begin?

                . . . . .

    Shall I say, I have gone at dusk through narrow streets
And watched the smoke that rises from the pipes
Of lonely men in shirt-sleeves, leaning out of windows? . . .

    I should have been a pair of ragged claws
Scuttling across the floors of silent seas.

                . . . . .

    And the afternoon, the evening, sleeps so peacefully!
Smoothed by long fingers,
Asleep . . . tired . . . or it malingers,
Stretched on the floor, here beside you and me.
Should I, after tea and cakes and ices,
Have the strength to force the moment to its crisis?
But though I have wept and fasted, wept and prayed,
Though I have seen my head (grown slightly bald)
    brought in upon a platter,
I am no prophet – and here's no great matter;
I have seen the moment of my greatness flicker,
And I have seen the eternal Footman hold my coat, and
    snicker,
And in short, I was afraid.

And would it have been worth it, after all,
After the cups, the marmalade, the tea,
Among the porcelain, among some talk of you and me,
Would it have been worth while,
To have bitten off the matter with a smile,
To have squeezed the universe into a ball
To roll it towards some overwhelming question,
To say: 'I am Lazarus, come from the dead,
Come back to tell you all, I shall tell you all' –
If one, settling a pillow by her head,
Should say: 'That is not what I meant at all.
That is not it, at all.'

And would it have been worth it, after all,
Would it have been worth while,
After the sunsets and the dooryards and the sprinkled
streets,
After the novels, after the teacups, after the skirts that
trail along the floor –
And this, and so much more? –
It is impossible to say just what I mean!
But as if a magic lantern threw the nerves in patterns
on a screen:
Would it have been worth while
If one, settling a pillow or throwing off a shawl,
And turning toward the window, should say:
'That is not it at all,
That is not what I meant, at all.'

.....

No! I am not Prince Hamlet, nor was meant to be;
Am an attendant lord, one that will do
To swell a progress, start a scene or two,
Advise the prince; no doubt, an easy tool,
Deferential, glad to be of use,
Politic, cautious, and meticulous;
Full of high sentence, but a bit obtuse;
At times, indeed, almost ridiculous –
Almost, at times, the Fool.

I grow old . . . I grow old . . .
I shall wear the bottoms of my trousers rolled.

Shall I part my hair behind? Do I dare to eat a
  peach?
I shall wear white flannel trousers, and walk upon the
  beach.
I have heard the mermaids singing, each to each.

I do not think that they will sing to me.

I have seen them riding seaward on the waves
Combing the white hair of the waves blown back
When the wind blows the water white and black.

We have lingered in the chambers of the sea
By sea-girls wreathed with seaweed red and brown
Till human voices wake us, and we drown.

The lines quoted in Eliot's epigraph are from Dante's *Divine Comedy* and occur in the *Inferno*, Canto XXVII, ll. 61–66. In the translation by Melville B. Anderson they read, 'If I supposed myself as answer making / to one who ever could return on high / into the world, this flame should stand unshaking: / but since none from this yawning cavity / ever returned alive, if truth I hear, / fearless of infamy, do I reply.'

1917

Common Sense

◄○►

ALAN BROWNJOHN

An agricultural labourer, who has
A wife and four children, receives 20s a week.
¾ buys food, and the members of the family
Have three meals a day.
How much is that per person per meal?
> – *From Pitman's Common Sense Arithmetic, 1917*

A gardener, paid 24s a week, is
Fined 1/3 if he comes to work late.
At the end of 26 weeks, he receives
£30.5.3. How
Often was he late?
> – *From Pitman's Common Sense Arithmetic, 1917*

A milk dealer buys milk at 3d a quart. He
Dilutes it with 3% water and sells
124 gallons of the mixture at
4d per quart. How much of his profit is made by
Adulterating the milk?
> —*From Pitman's Common Sense Arithmetic, 1917*

The table printed below gives the number
Of paupers in the United Kingdom, and
The total cost of poor relief.
Find the average number
Of paupers per ten thousand people.
> –*From Pitman's Common Sense Arithmetic, 1917*

An army had to march to the relief of
A besieged town, 500 miles away, which
Had telegraphed that it could hold out for 18 days.
The army made forced marches at the rate of 18
Miles a day. Would it be there in time?
> – *From Pitman's Common Sense Arithmetic, 1917*

Out of an army of 28,000 men,
15% were
Killed, 25% were
Wounded. Calculate
How many men there were left to fight.
        – From Pitman's Common Sense Arithmetic, 1917

These sums are offered to
That host of young people in our Elementary Schools,
    who
Are so ardently desirous of setting
Foot upon the first rung of the
Educational ladder . . .
        – From Pitman's Common Sense Arithmetic, 1917

1918

The Send-Off

WILFRED OWEN

Down the close darkening lanes they sang their way
To the siding-shed,
And lined the train with faces grimly gay.

Their breasts were stuck all white with wreath and spray
As men's are, dead.

Dull porters watched them, and a casual tramp
Stood staring hard,
Sorry to miss them from the upland camp.

Then, unmoved, signals nodded, and a lamp
Winked to the guard.

So secretly, like wrongs hushed-up, they went.
They were not ours:
We never heard to which front these were sent;

Nor there if they yet mock what women meant
Who gave them flowers.

Shall they return to beating of great bells
In wild train-loads?
A few, a few, too few for drums and yells,

May creep back, silent, to village wells,
Up half-known roads.

1918

Survivors

ALLEN CURNOW

Night falls on an unusual scene of public
rejoicing. A whole head taller than the crowd,

astride my father's nape, I can see the *jets
d'eau* the fire brigade pumps across the lake,

ebulliently spouted, illuminated.
Rose-coloured spectaculars blown to waterdrops

float off briskly, lifted into the dark
as the land-breeze variably puffs. Up above

searchlights find nothing but weather and themselves
(a dustier glare is where I see those headlamps

juddering for ever and all the way home
and hear the motor fire steadily) because

it's the end of the war, these are survivors
by the long wash of Australasian seas

a diminuendo of bells, guns, and prayers and
all these people simply enjoying themselves.

A wind freshens across the park, the crowd begins
thinning towards tomorrow. Climb up and see.

In Curnow's poem recalling celebrations (in New Zealand) to mark the end of the
First World War, published in later life in *Continuum* (1988), he remembers himself
as a boy of seven. The *jets d'eau* (fountains) may be referred to in French to bring
to mind poems such as Verlaine's 'Clair de lune'. The phrase 'by the long wash of
Australasian seas' is from Tennyson's 'The Brook'.

1918

Reconciliation

SIEGFRIED SASSOON

When you are standing at your hero's grave,
Or near some homeless village where he died,
Remember, through your heart's rekindling pride,
The German soldiers who were loyal and brave.

Men fought like brutes; and hideous things were done;
And you have nourished hatred harsh and blind.
But in that Golgotha perhaps you'll find
The mothers of the men who killed your son.

1918

Piano

<o>

D. H. LAWRENCE

Softly, in the dusk, a woman is singing to me;
Taking me back down the vista of years, till I see
A child sitting under the piano, in the boom of the
     tingling strings
And pressing the small, poised feet of a mother who smiles
     as she sings.

In spite of myself, the insidious mastery of song
Betrays me back, till the heart of me weeps to belong
To the old Sunday evenings at home, with winter outside
And hymns in the cosy parlour, the tinkling piano our
     guide.

So now it is vain for the singer to burst into clamour
With the great black piano appassionato. The glamour
Of childish days is upon me, my manhood is cast
Down in the flood of remembrance, I weep like a child
     for the past.

1919

from Epitaphs of the War
1914–18

RUDYARD KIPLING

COMMON FORM
If any question why we died,
Tell them, because our fathers lied.

A DEAD STATESMAN
I could not dig: I dared not rob:
Therefore I lied to please the mob.
Now all my lies are proved untrue
And I must face the men I slew.
What tale shall serve me here among
Mine angry and defrauded young?

1920

E. P. Ode Pour L'Election de son Sepulchre

EZRA POUND

I

For three years, out of key with his time,
He strove to resuscitate the dead art
Of poetry; to maintain 'the sublime'
In the old sense. Wrong from the start —

No, hardly, but seeing he had been born
In a half savage country, out of date;
Bent resolutely on wringing lilies from the acorn;
Capaneus; trout for factitious bait;

Ἴδμεν γάϐ τοι πάνθ ὅϲὲνὶ Τϐοίη
Caught in the unstopped ear;
Giving the rocks small lee-way
The chopped seas held him, therefore, that year.

His true Penelope was Flaubert,
He fished by obstinate isles;
Observed the elegance of Circe's hair
Rather than the mottoes on sun-dials.

Unaffected by 'the march of events',
He passed from men's memory in *l'an trentuniesme*
De son eage; the case presents
No adjunct to the Muses' diadem.

II

The age demanded an image
Of its accelerated grimace,
Something for the modern stage,
Not, at any rate, an Attic grace;

Not, not certainly, the obscure reveries
Of the inward gaze;
Better mendacities
Than the classics in paraphrase!

The 'age demanded' chiefly a mould in plaster,
Made with no loss of time,
A prose kinema, not, not assuredly, alabaster
Or the 'sculpture' of rhyme.

III

The tea-rose tea-gown, etc.
Supplants the mousseline of Cos,
The pianola 'replaces'
Sappho's barbitos.

Christ follows Dionysus,
Phallic and ambrosial
Made way for macerations;
Caliban casts out Ariel.

All things are a flowing,
Sage Heracleitus says;
But a tawdry cheapness
Shall outlast our days.

Even the Christian beauty
Defects – after Samothrace;
We see τὸ καλόν
Decreed in the market place.

Faun's flesh is not to us,
Nor the saint's vision.
We have the press for wafer;
Franchise for circumcision.

All men, in law, are equals.
Free of Pisistratus,
We choose a knave or an eunuch
To rule over us.

O bright Apollo,
τίν᾽ ἄνδρα, τίν᾽ ἥρωα, τινα θεόν,
What god, man, or hero
Shall I place a tin wreath upon!

IV

These fought in any case,
and some believing,

           pro domo, in any case . . .

Some quick to arm,
some for adventure,
some from fear of weakness,
some from fear of censure,
some for love of slaughter, in imagination,
learning later . . .
some in fear, learning love of slaughter;

Died some, pro patria,

             non 'dulce' non 'et decor' . . .
walked eye-deep in hell
believing in old men's lies, then unbelieving
came home, home to a lie,
home to many deceits,
home to old lies and new infamy;
usury age-old and age-thick
and liars in public places.

Daring as never before, wastage as never before.
Young blood and high blood,
fair cheeks, and fine bodies;

fortitude as never before

frankness as never before,
disillusions as never told in the old days,
hysterias, trench confessions,
laughter out of dead bellies.

V

There died a myriad,
And of the best, among them,
For an old bitch gone in the teeth,
For a botched civilization,

Charm, smiling at the good mouth,
Quick eyes gone under earth's lid,

For two gross of broken statues,
For a few thousand battered books.

Pound's title, 'for the choice of his tomb', suggests that the poem is to be read as we read funerary inscriptions on monumental tombs. The images in the first part liken the subject, E. P., to heroes of antiquity – Capaneus (one of the *Seven Against Thebes* in Aeschylus' play) and, chiefly, Odysseus, whose homeward travels to the faithful Penelope take him past the Sirens (the Greek quotation is from their song in the twelfth book of Homer's *Odyssey*, and means, 'because we know all things suffered in Troy'). The French novelist Gustave Flaubert (1821–80) served Pound as an exemplar of attentive, lapidary prose style. The French phrase 'l'an trentuniesme de son eage' means 'in his thirty-first year'. In the second and third parts of the poem, the perceived gracelessness and tawdriness of the modern era are contrasted with ancient Greece, with Athenian (Attic) grace sacrificed to the scoring of rapid effects and the pianola's sound preferred to that of the harp-like barbitos, an instrument associated with Sappho. What is decreed in the market place is 'the beautiful'; the second Greek phrase in the third part, in the invocation to Apollo, is translated by Pound in the next line. Pisistratus was an Athenian tyrant of the sixth century BC; Pound's view here appears to be that political mores have now become as debased as aesthetic taste. The fourth and fifth parts of the poem see the carnage of the First World War as the final outcome of, and verdict on, the 'botched civilization' that made it possible.

1920

Mohammed Bek Hadjetlache

‹o›

CARL SANDBURG

This Mohammedan colonel from the Caucasus yells with his
voice and wigwags with his arms.
The interpreter translates, 'I was a friend of Kornilov, he asks me
what to do and I tell him.'
A stub of a man, this Mohammedan colonel . . . a projectile
shape . . . a bald head hammered . . .
'Does he fight or do they put him in a cannon and shoot him
at the enemy?'
This fly-by-night, this bull-roarer who knows everybody.
'I write forty books, history of Islam, history of Europe, true
religion, scientific farming, I am the Roosevelt of the
Caucasus, I go to America and ride horses in the moving
pictures for $500,000, you get $50,000 . . .'
'I have 30,000 acres in the Caucasus, I have a stove factory in
Petrograd the bolsheviks take from me, I am an old friend of
the Czar, I am an old family friend of Clemenceau . . .'
These hands strangled three fellow workers for the czarist
restoration, took their money, sent them in sacks to a river
bottom . . . and scandalized Stockholm with his gang of
strangler women.
Mid-sea strangler hands rise before me illustrating a wish, 'I ride
horses for the moving pictures in America, $500,000, and you
get ten per cent . . .'
This rider of fugitive dawns . . .

Lavr Kornilov, a senior Russian general in the First World War, fought Lenin's
Bolsheviks after the separate peace took Russia out of the war with Germany,
and was killed in April 1918. Georges Clemenceau served for a second time as
French prime minister from 1917 to 1920. Sandburg's portrait of the Caucasian
'bull-roarer who knows everybody' is an eloquent sketch of the larger-than-life
characters who might be encountered in the social and political turmoil that
followed the war.

1920

Buffalo Dusk

CARL SANDBURG

The buffaloes are gone.
And those who saw the buffaloes are gone.
Those who saw the buffaloes by thousands and how they
  pawed the prairie sod into dust with their hoofs, their
  great heads down pawing on in a great pageant of dusk,
Those who saw the buffaloes are gone.
And the buffaloes are gone.

1920

The Rat

EDWIN ARLINGTON ROBINSON

As often as he let himself be seen
We pitied him, or scorned him, or deplored
The inscrutable profusion of the Lord
Who shaped as one of us a thing so mean –
Who made him human when he might have been
A rat, and so been wholly in accord
With any other creature we abhorred
As always useless and not always clean.

Now he is hiding all alone somewhere,
And in a final hole not ready then;
For now he is among those over there
Who are not coming back to us again.
And we who do the fiction of our share
Say less of rats and rather more of men.

1920

The Second Coming

W. B. YEATS

Turning and turning in the widening gyre
The falcon cannot hear the falconer;
Things fall apart; the centre cannot hold;
Mere anarchy is loosed upon the world,
The blood-dimmed tide is loosed, and everywhere
The ceremony of innocence is drowned;
The best lack all conviction, while the worst
Are full of passionate intensity.

Surely some revelation is at hand;
Surely the Second Coming is at hand.
The Second Coming! Hardly are those words out
When a vast image out of *Spiritus Mundi*
Troubles my sight: somewhere in sands of the desert
A shape with lion body and the head of a man,
A gaze blank and pitiless as the sun,
Is moving its slow thighs; while all about it
Reel shadows of the indignant desert birds.
The darkness drops again, but now I know
That twenty centuries of stony sleep
Were vexed to nightmare by a rocking cradle,
And what rough beast, its hour come round at last,
Slouches towards Bethlehem to be born?

1921

The Snow Man

<o>

WALLACE STEVENS

One must have a mind of winter
To regard the frost and the boughs
Of the pine-trees crusted with snow;

And have been cold a long time
To behold the junipers shagged with ice,
The spruces rough in the distant glitter

Of the January sun; and not to think
Of any misery in the sound of the wind,
In the sound of a few leaves,

Which is the sound of the land
Full of the same wind
That is blowing in the same bare place

For the listener, who listens in the snow,
And, nothing himself, beholds
Nothing that is not there and the nothing that is.

1921

The Census-Taker

ROBERT FROST

I came an errand one cloud-blowing evening
To a slab-built, black-paper-covered house
Of one room and one window and one door,
The only dwelling in a waste cut over
A hundred square miles round it in the mountains:
And that not dwelt in now by men or women.
(It never had been dwelt in, though, by women,
So what is this I make a sorrow of?)
I came as census-taker to the waste
To count the people in it and found none,
None in the hundred miles, none in the house,
Where I came last with some hope, but not much,
After hours' overlooking from the cliffs
An emptiness flayed to the very stone.
I found no people that dared show themselves,
None not in hiding from the outward eye.
The time was autumn, but how anyone
Could tell the time of year when every tree
That could have dropped a leaf was down itself
And nothing but the stump of it was left
Now bringing out its rings in sugar of pitch;
And every tree up stood a rotting trunk
Without a single leaf to spend on autumn,
Or branch to whistle after what was spent.
Perhaps the wind the more without the help
Of breathing trees said something of the time
Of year or day the way it swung a door
Forever off the latch, as if rude men
Passed in and slammed it shut each one behind him
For the next one to open for himself.
I counted nine I had no right to count
(But this was dreamy unofficial counting)

Before I made the tenth across the threshold.
Where was my supper? Where was anyone's?
No lamp was lit. Nothing was on the table.
The stove was cold – the stove was off the chimney –
And down by one side where it lacked a leg.
The people that had loudly passed the door
Were people to the ear but not the eye.
They were not on the table with their elbows.
They were not sleeping in the shelves of bunks.
I saw no men there and no bones of men there.
I armed myself against such bones as might be
With the pitch-blackened stub of an ax-handle
I picked up off the straw-dust-covered floor.
Not bones, but the ill-fitted window rattled.
The door was still because I held it shut
While I thought what to do that could be done –
About the house – about the people not there.
This house in one year fallen to decay
Filled me with no less sorrow than the houses
Fallen to ruin in ten thousand years
Where Asia wedges Africa from Europe.
Nothing was left to do that I could see
Unless to find that there was no one there
And declare to the cliffs too far for echo,
'The place is desert, and let whoso lurks
In silence, if in this he is aggrieved,
Break silence now or be forever silent.
Let him say why it should not be declared so.'
The melancholy of having to count souls
Where they grow fewer and fewer every year
Is extreme where they shrink to none at all.
It must be I want life to go on living.

The most recent US census, in 1920, had shown a clear drift of the American population from rural areas to the cities. 'New Hampshire's population was growing very slowly in the early twentieth century, and the rural population of the state was declining absolutely.' (Margo Anderson, *Social Science History* 32:1, spring 2008.)

1921

The Negro Speaks of Rivers

—◅◦▻—

LANGSTON HUGHES

To W. E. B. DuBois

I've known rivers:
I've known rivers ancient as the world and older than the
flow of human blood in human veins.

My soul has grown deep like the rivers.

I bathed in the Euphrates when dawns were young.
I built my hut near the Congo and it lulled me to sleep.
I looked upon the Nile and raised the pyramids above it.
I heard the singing of the Mississippi when Abe Lincoln
went down to New Orleans, and I've seen its muddy
bosom turn all golden in the sunset.

I've known rivers:
Ancient, dusky rivers.

My soul has grown deep like the rivers.

Hughes's poem is dedicated to the Massachusetts-born civil rights activist William
Edward Burghardt DuBois (1868–1963), who campaigned tirelessly on behalf
of America's black population. Abraham Lincoln (1809–65), sixteenth American
president, who oversaw the abolition of slavery in the US, had seen slave auctions
in New Orleans on visits in the 1820s and 1830s.

1921

Full Moon

VICTORIA SACKVILLE-WEST

She was wearing the coral taffeta trousers
Someone had brought her from Ispahan,
And the little gold coat with pomegranate blossoms,
And the coral-hafted feather fan;
But she ran down a Kentish lane in the moonlight,
And skipped in the pool of the moon as she ran.

She cared not a rap for all the big planets,
For Betelgeuse or Aldebaran,
And all the big planets cared nothing for her,
That small impertinent charlatan;
But she climbed on a Kentish stile in the moonlight,
And laughed at the sky through the sticks of her fan.

Ispahan (or Isfahan) is a great Persian (Iranian) city. Betelgeuse and Aldebaran are among the brightest stars in the night sky.

1922

from The Waste Land
———◄◊►———
T. S. ELIOT

III. The Fire Sermon

The river's tent is broken; the last fingers of leaf
Clutch and sink into the wet bank. The wind
Crosses the brown land, unheard. The nymphs are departed.
Sweet Thames, run softly, till I end my song.
The river bears no empty bottles, sandwich papers,
Silk handkerchiefs, cardboard boxes, cigarette ends
Or other testimony of summer nights. The nymphs are
  departed.
And their friends, the loitering heirs of City directors;
Departed, have left no addresses.
By the waters of Leman I sat down and wept . . .
Sweet Thames, run softly till I end my song,
Sweet Thames, run softly, for I speak not loud or long.
But at my back in a cold blast I hear
The rattle of the bones, and chuckle spread from ear to
  ear.

A rat crept softly through the vegetation
Dragging its slimy belly on the bank
While I was fishing in the dull canal
On a winter evening round behind the gashouse
Musing upon the king my brother's wreck
And on the king my father's death before him.
White bodies naked on the low damp ground
And bones cast in a little low dry garret,
Rattled by the rat's foot only, year to year.
But at my back from time to time I hear
The sound of horns and motors, which shall bring
Sweeney to Mrs Porter in the spring.
O the moon shone bright on Mrs Porter

And on her daughter
They wash their feet in soda water
Et O ces voix d'enfants, chantant dans la coupole!

Twit twit twit
Jug jug jug jug jug jug
So rudely forc'd.
Tereu

    Unreal City
Under the brown fog of a winter noon
Mr Eugenides, the Smyrna merchant
Unshaven, with a pocket full of currants
C.i.f. London: documents at sight,
Asked me in demotic French
To luncheon at the Cannon Street Hotel
Followed by a weekend at the Metropole.

    At the violet hour, when the eyes and back
Turn upward from the desk, when the human engine waits
Like a taxi throbbing waiting,
I Tiresias, though blind, throbbing between two lives,
Old man with wrinkled female breasts, can see
At the violet hour, the evening hour that strives
Homeward, and brings the sailor home from sea,
The typist home at teatime, clears her breakfast, lights
Her stove, and lays out food in tins.
Out of the window perilously spread
Her drying combinations touched by the sun's
    last rays,
On the divan are piled (at night her bed)
Stockings, slippers, camisoles, and stays.
I Tiresias, old man with wrinkled dugs
Perceived the scene, and foretold the rest –
I too awaited the expected guest.
He, the young man carbuncular, arrives,
A small house agent's clerk, with one bold stare,
One of the low on whom assurance sits
As a silk hat on a Bradford millionaire.
The time is now propitious, as he guesses,

The meal is ended, she is bored and tired,
Endeavours to engage her in caresses
Which still are unreproved, if undesired.
Flushed and decided, he assaults at once;
Exploring hands encounter no defence;
His vanity requires no response,
And makes a welcome of indifference.

(And I Tiresias have foresuffered all
Enacted on this same divan or bed;
I who have sat by Thebes below the wall
And walked among the lowest of the dead.)
Bestows one final patronising kiss,
And gropes his way, finding the stairs unlit . . .

    She turns and looks a moment in the glass,
Hardly aware of her departed lover;
Her brain allows one half-formed thought to pass:
'Well now that's done: and I'm glad it's over.'
When lovely woman stoops to folly and
Paces about her room again, alone,
She smoothes her hair with automatic hand,
And puts a record on the gramophone.

    'This music crept by me upon the waters'
And along the Strand, up Queen Victoria Street.
O City city, I can sometimes hear
Beside a public bar in Lower Thames Street,
The pleasant whining of a mandoline
And a clatter and a chatter from within
Where fishmen lounge at noon: where the walls
Of Magnus Martyr hold
Inexplicable splendour of Ionian white and gold.

    The river sweats
    Oil and tar
    The barges drift
    With the turning tide
    Red sails
    Wide
    To leeward, swing on the heavy spar.

The barges wash
Drifting logs
Down Greenwich reach
Past the Isle of Dogs.
             Weialala leia
             Wallala leialala

Elizabeth and Leicester
Beating oars
The stern was formed
A gilded shell
Red and gold
The brisk swell
Rippled both shores
Southwest wind
Carried down stream
The peal of bells
White towers
             Weialala leia
             Wallala leialala

'Trams and dusty trees.
Highbury bore me. Richmond and Kew
Undid me. By Richmond I raised my knees
Supine on the floor of a narrow canoe.'

'My feet are at Moorgate, and my heart
Under my feet. After the event
He wept. He promised "a new start."
I made no comment. What should I resent?'

'On Margate Sands.
I can connect
Nothing with nothing.
The broken fingernails of dirty hands.
My people humble people who expect
Nothing.'
             la la

To Carthage then I came

Burning burning burning burning
O Lord Thou pluckest me out
O Lord Thou pluckest

burning

The central third section of Eliot's great poem centres upon sensuality and seduction, with the celebrated 'hidden' sonnet at its heart (beginning with the line 'The time is now propitious, as he guesses'). All the more ironic, perhaps, that the title of the section should point readers to the Buddha's fire sermon, in which he instructed followers to avoid the flames of passion and sensuality, thus achieving release from the cycle of rebirth to gain Nirvana. A wide variety of sources lie behind this part of 'The Waste Land', and Eliot provided notes to some of his allusions. Thus 'By the waters of Leman I sat down and wept' recalls Psalm 137; 'Sweet Thames, run softly, till I end my song' is the refrain from Edmund Spenser's marriage song, 'Prothalamion'; 'But at my back in a cold blast I hear' echoes Marvell's 'To His Coy Mistress' – 'But at my back I always hear / Time's winged chariot hurrying near'; 'Musing upon the king my brother's wreck' takes us to *The Tempest* I, ii (Eliot's note – he refers us to the same play and scene for 'This music crept by me upon the waters'); the lines on Mrs Porter combine Day's 'Parliament of Bees' – 'When of the sudden, listening, you shall hear, / A noise of horns and hunting, which shall bring, / Actaeon to Diana in the spring, / Where all shall see her naked skin . . .' (Eliot's note) – with a song sung by Australian troops in the Dardanelles: 'O the moon shone bright on Mrs Porter / And on the daughter / Of Mrs Porter. / They wash their feet in soda water / And so they oughter / To keep them clean.' A Wagnerian note is sounded in '*Et O ces voix d'enfants, chantant dans la coupole!*' (And O those children's voices singing in the dome!) This exclamation, from Verlaine's 'Parsifal', evokes Wagner's opera about the Grail quest. The opera ends with a children's chorus praising Christ. Eliot sounds another Wagnerian note in his comment on the passage beginning 'The river sweats': 'The Song of the (three) Thames-daughters begins here,' writes Eliot. 'From line 292 to 306 inclusive they speak in turn.' Eliot refers us to *Götterdämmerung* (*Twilight of the Gods*) III, i: the three Rhine-maidens try to persuade Siegfried to give back their gold, which confers both power and death on its possessor. Its theft has deprived their river of its beauty. 'Weialala . . .' is the refrain of their song. After the seduction sonnet, Eliot alludes to a song from Oliver Goldsmith's *The Vicar of Wakefield*: 'When lovely woman stoops to folly / And finds too late that men betray, / What charm can soothe her melancholy, / What art can wash her guilt away?' Other glances at Ovid and Dante underpin the large mythic structure of this part of Eliot's poem, which culminates in the juxtaposition of fragments from the Buddha and from St Augustine's *Confessions*. Of the figure of Tiresias, Eliot noted: 'Tiresias, although a mere spectator and not indeed a "character", is yet the most important personage in the poem, uniting all the rest. Just as the one-eyed merchant, seller of currants, melts into the Phoenician Sailor, and the latter is not wholly distinct from Ferdinand Prince of Naples [in *The Tempest*], so all the women are one woman, and the two sexes meet in Tiresias. What Tiresias *sees*, in fact, is the substance of the poem . . .'

III

❦

1923–1939
Danger and hope

F OR SOME, they were the Roaring Twenties. The Jazz Age was fast-paced and thrilling, from New York to Paris and Berlin – the decade of the flapper, the foxtrot, the Charleston and the Lindy Hop, the decade of talking pictures, Charles Lindbergh's solo trans-Atlantic flight, and the triumph of the radio and the automobile. If the 'return to normalcy' proclaimed to post-War America by Warren Harding meant Prohibition and speakeasies, that seemed a price Americans were willing to pay, for a while at least. 'The business of America is business' was the famous watch-word of his successor as president, Calvin Coolidge, and for some years, before the Wall Street Crash of October 1929 and the ensuing global depression, it seemed possible to dance and drink away the post-War blues.

But a different story could be told of the 1920s. In the UK, disen-chantment with the ruling classes, seen in innocuous guise in Hilaire Belloc's 'On a General Election' and A. A. Milne's 'Buckingham Palace', was accompanied by a widespread experience of poverty: the itinerant tinkers in Hardy's 'No Buyers' are defeated by hard economic times, and the hungry marchers voiced by Idris Davies note the roses in the gentle-men's gardens even as they themselves beg for bread. Though Britain returned to the gold standard in 1925, the semblance of prosperity meant little to the many unemployed, and the General Strike of 1926 pointed to an underlying malaise. Edgell Rickword's distrust of commercial palaces is a reminder that the 'land fit for heroes' promised by David Lloyd George had proved a disappointment.

The disappointment of Americans was experienced in various ways.

America's black population were terribly accustomed to violence and discrimination, and the Ku Klux Klan went through a post-War boom, claiming four million members by 1924. Poems here by Jean Toomer, Countee Cullen and Langston Hughes are a stark reminder of the racial tensions that continued to trouble the US. Liberal American opinion was outraged by the execution of alleged anarchists Sacco and Vanzetti in 1927, at the peak of the post-War wave of xenophobic feeling that had entered the statute books in the Immigration Act of 1924. Numerous American writers elected to live outside the country: as well as the Lost Generation of Ernest Hemingway, F. Scott Fitzgerald and Gertrude Stein, other European exiles included T. S. Eliot and Ezra Pound. Emigration abroad was matched by emigration within. When William Carlos Williams contemplated his celebrated red wheelbarrow, or Eliot voiced a poem of spiritual anxiety for one of the old-order Magi, their poems appeared to turn away from the immediate concerns of the time, to those inward places of the self that become all the more important in times of upheaval. As the Thirties began, it was perhaps Marianne Moore in 'The Steeple-Jack', with its precarious balance of danger and hope, who wrote the poem most uncannily apt to the mood.

With hindsight the Thirties would strike W. H. Auden, in his poem 'September 1, 1939', as 'a low dishonest decade', and its 'hopes' would look no more than 'clever'. As economies collapsed and unemployment soared worldwide, the hopes and dishonesties alike were focused on the ideological stand-off of Left and Right. *The Decline of the West* and *Ten Days that Shook the World* had cast their shadow across debate throughout the Twenties, and now the Thirties in Britain belonged to Marx and Freud, the Left Book Club, and MacSpaunday (Roy Campbell's contemptuous collective name for the four left-wing poets who set the agenda: W. H. Auden, Louis MacNeice, Stephen Spender and C. Day Lewis). With Mussolini's Fascists in power in Italy since 1922, and Hitler's National Socialists in power in Germany from 1933, the danger from the extreme wing of capitalism and imperialism was understood to be as acute as that from Soviet-style Communism. The confrontation of the two sides came in the place that presently denoted (in the words of MacNeice, recalling a visit shortly before the outbreak of hostilities) 'our grief, our aspirations': Spain.

The Spanish Civil War, which began in July 1936 and raged till the fall of Madrid to General Franco's forces in March 1939, became in effect a proxy war, a rehearsal for the conflagration that Hitler would soon unleash. The Italian and German governments quickly recognised the nationalist regime that had seized power under Franco, and sent troops and arms. Volunteer opponents of Fascism, chiefly from Britain, France, Germany and Russia, swelled the International Brigade that supported the ousted republican Popular Front. South African-born Roy Campbell, often as pugnacious in his life as in his poetry, took Franco's side. John Cornford, who describes his first experience of combat in the Communist POUM in August 1936 in 'A Letter from Aragon', returned to Spain for a second time that December and was killed near Córdoba on the 28th. Another casualty of the war was the great Spanish poet Federico García Lorca, murdered at the age of thirty-eight in August 1936. Geoffrey Parsons' poem 'Lorca' raises a heroic Communist monument to the dead writer, mythologising him as a lone, unafraid figure outfacing his enemies, one with 'the people of Spain'. Spender visited Spain as an observer, and 'Port Bou' is evocative of a place and time but also poignantly anticipates the importance of the Pyrenees border, for countless refugees attempting to flee Europe, in the world war that was to come.

But overtowering these poems is W. H. Auden's 'Spain'. It is a poem in which political passion and rhetorical authority are seamlessly interwoven. It is also a poem that has remained controversial ever since its first publication – indeed, Auden felt obliged to revise the poem, cutting some material and substituting "the fact of murder", in its third-to-last stanza, for "the necessary murder" in the original version (which we have used here), a phrase that caused deep moral offence. George Orwell, who conceded that it was "one of the few decent things that have been written about the Spanish war", put the case against the poem in his essay 'Inside the Whale': "Nearly all the dominant writers of the thirties belonged to the soft-boiled emancipated middle class [. . .] To people of that kind such things as purges, secret police, summary executions, imprisonment without trial, etc. etc. are too remote to be terrifying [. . .] notice the phrase 'necessary murder' [. . .] The Hitlers and Stalins find murder necessary [. . .] Mr. Auden's brand of amoralism is only possible if you are the kind of person who is always somewhere else when the trigger is pulled."

Meanwhile, in the apolitical somewhere-else that is the usual experience of peacetime, poets were considering other, private matters. Sex was one. Basil Bunting, in later life the bearded sage of Northumbria, cuts a comical figure on a cinema date in wicked Berlin, failing to see Pudowkin's majestic Russian silent epic *Sturm über Asien* and settling for 'some other flicker', the obligatory box of chocolates, and glimpses of a screen actress's breasts when she leans towards the camera. The First World War had paradoxically brought greater freedoms for women. From Josephine Baker at the Folies Bergères to Hedy Lamarr in *Ecstasy*, women changed the erotic agenda. And in reporting the stirring of the mainly male audience, and his own preference of the screen blonde to his brunette companion, Bunting matched them by bringing a new candour about sexual feelings to poetry. So too, in the *faux naïf* manner that was his trademark, did e. e. cummings in 'may I feel said he'. But both poems arguably pale beside R. A. K. Mason's account of masturbation, daring at the time for its subject, its unapologetic use of the words 'penis' and 'arse', and even its sardonic appropriation of Catullus for its title.

It was also a period rich in elegy, from Edna St Vincent Millay's 'Dirge without Music' to Auden's public lament for Yeats to Kenneth Slessor's great 'Five Bells' – so rich in elegy, indeed, that we hear even in private grief an apprehension of the coming collective tragedy. Pound's magnificent 'usura' canto, though a somewhat idiosyncratic engagement with socio-economics lay in the background, puts its accusing finger unerringly on the corrosive, destructive power of capitalism, and in its image of corpses set to banquet seems to predict apocalypse. The whirling caper of MacNeice's 'Bagpipe Music' may appear to tell a different story, but perhaps it is only its music that is different – the shrill jig down the slope to oblivion wears a rictus of a grin. This is the Dance of Death. David Gascoyne's vision of red melting snow and loud drums, and Auden's of ten thousand soldiers 'looking for you and me, my dear, looking for you and me', are in terrible agreement. For now, danger has won over hope.

1923

The Red Wheelbarrow

WILLIAM CARLOS WILLIAMS

So much depends
upon

a red wheel
barrow

glazed with rain
water

beside the white
chickens

1923

Snake

D. H. LAWRENCE

A snake came to my water-trough
On a hot, hot day, and I in pyjamas for the heat,
To drink there.

In the deep, strange-scented shade of the great dark carob-
tree
I came down the steps with my pitcher
And must wait, must stand and wait, for there he was at the
trough before me.

He reached down from a fissure in the earth-wall in the
gloom
And trailed his yellow-brown slackness soft-bellied down, over
the edge of the stone trough
And rested his throat upon the stone bottom,
And where the water had dripped from the tap, in a small
clearness,
He sipped with his straight mouth,
Softly drank through his straight gums, into his slack long
body,
Silently.

Someone was before me at my water-trough,
And I, like a second comer, waiting.

He lifted his head from his drinking, as cattle do,
And looked at me vaguely, as drinking cattle do,
And flickered his two-forked tongue from his lips, and mused
a moment,
And stooped and drank a little more,
Being earth-brown, earth-golden from the burning bowels of
the earth
On the day of Sicilian July, with Etna smoking.

The voice of my education said to me
He must be killed,
For in Sicily the black, black snakes are innocent, the gold are
  venomous.

And voices in me said, If you were a man
You would take a stick and break him now, and finish him off.

But must I confess how I liked him,
How glad I was he had come like a guest in quiet, to drink
  at my water-trough
And depart peaceful, pacified, and thankless,
Into the burning bowels of this earth?

Was it cowardice, that I dared not kill him?
Was it perversity, that I longed to talk to him?
Was it humility, to feel so honoured?
I felt so honoured.

And yet those voices:
If you were not afraid, you would kill him!

And truly I was afraid, I was most afraid,
But even so, honoured still more
That he should seek my hospitality
From out the dark door of the secret earth.

He drank enough
And lifted his head, dreamily, as one who has drunken,
And flickered his tongue like a forked night on the air, so
  black;
Seeming to lick his lips,
And looked around like a god, unseeing, into the air,
And slowly turned his head,
And slowly, very slowly, as if thrice adream,
Proceeded to draw his slow length curving round
And climb again the broken bank of my wall-face.

And as he put his head into that dreadful hole,
And as he slowy drew up, snake-easing his shoulders, and
  entered farther,

A sort of horror, a sort of protest against his withdrawing into
  that horrid black hole,
Deliberately going into the blackness, and slowly drawing
  himself after,
Overcame me now his back was turned.

I looked round, I put down my pitcher,
I picked up a clumsy log
And threw it at the water-trough with a clatter.

I think it did not hit him,
But suddenly that part of him that was left behind convulsed
  in undignified haste,
Writhed like lightning, and was gone
Into the black hole, the earth-lipped fissure in the wall front,
At which, in the intense still noon, I stared with fascination.

And immediately I regretted it.
I thought how paltry, how vulgar, what a mean act!
I despised myself and the voices of my accursed human
  education.

And I thought of the albatross,
And I wished he would come back, my snake.

For he seemed to me again like a king,
Like a king in exile, uncrowned in the underworld,
Now due to be crowned again.

And so, I missed my chance with one of the lords
Of life.
And I have something to expiate;
A pettiness.

1923

Portrait in Georgia

JEAN TOOMER

Hair – braided chestnut,
coiled like a lyncher's rope,
Eyes – fagots,
Lips – old scars, or the first red blisters,
Breath – the last sweet scent of cane,
And her slim body, white as the ash
     of black flesh after flame.

1923

The Leaden-Eyed

◄◇►

NICHOLAS VACHEL LINDSAY

Let not young souls be smothered out before
They do quaint deeds and fully flaunt their pride.
It is the world's one crime its babes grow dull,
Its poor are ox-like, limp and leaden-eyed.

Not that they starve, but starve so dreamlessly;
Not that they sow, but that they seldom reap;
Not that they serve, but have no gods to serve;
Not that they die, but that they die like sheep.

1923

Stopping by Woods on a Snowy Evening

ROBERT FROST

Whose woods these are I think I know.
His house is in the village, though;
He will not see me stopping here
To watch his woods fill up with snow.

My little horse must think it queer
To stop without a farmhouse near
Between the woods and frozen lake
The darkest evening of the year.

He gives his harness bells a shake
To ask if there is some mistake.
The only other sound's the sweep
Of easy wind and downy flake.

The woods are lovely, dark, and deep,
But I have promises to keep,
And miles to go before I sleep,
And miles to go before I sleep.

1923

On a General Election

————◄◦►————

HILAIRE BELLOC

THE accursèd power which stands on Privilege
(And goes with Women, and Champagne and Bridge)
Broke – and Democracy resumed her reign:
(Which goes with Bridge, and Women and Champagne).

1924

Buckingham Palace

A. A. MILNE

They're changing guard at Buckingham Palace –
Christopher Robin went down with Alice.
Alice is marrying one of the guard.
'A soldier's life is terrible hard,'
  Says Alice.

They're changing guard at Buckingham Palace –
Christopher Robin went down with Alice.
We saw a guard in a sentry-box.
'One of the sergeants looks after their socks,'
  Says Alice.

They're changing guard at Buckingham Palace –
Christopher Robin went down with Alice.
We looked for the King, but he never came.
'Well, God take care of him, all the same,'
  Says Alice.

They're changing guard at Buckingham Palace –
Christopher Robin went down with Alice.
They've great big parties inside the grounds.
'I wouldn't be King for a hundred pounds,'
  Says Alice.

They're changing guard at Buckingham Palace –
Christopher Robin went down with Alice.
A face looked out, but it wasn't the King's.
'He's much too busy a-signing things,'
  Says Alice.

They're changing guard at Buckingham Palace –
Christopher Robin went down with Alice.
'Do you think the King knows all about *me*?'
'Sure to, dear, but it's time for tea,'
  Says Alice.

1924

To a Lady Friend

W. H. DAVIES

Since you have turned unkind,
  Then let the truth be known:
We poets give our praise
  To any weed or stone,
Or sulking bird that in
  The cold, sharp wind is dumb;
To this, or that, or you —
  Whatever's first to come.

You came my way the first,
  When the life-force in my blood —
Coming from none knows where —
  Had reached its highest flood;
A time when anything,
  No matter old or new,
Could bring my song to birth —
  Sticks, bones, or rags, or you!

1925

The Old Wives Sat at the Table

SHAW NEILSON

Black was the night where the wind went,
And blue and black the rain.
They said, 'Poor thing, she was pretty,
But aw – her shroud is plain.'

The old wives sat at the table;
They said their hearts were sore.
The pennies were on her eyelids
That moved so fine before.

These old wives all had daughters,
But none so fair as she,
And the bitterest thing in the bitter
Is a woman's jealousy.

She had craved for the sweet colours,
So many flowers she wore.
She had laughed in many a garden
And cried at her own door.

She spoke of Love to the roses,
So mad a maid was she;
She lived so long with the lilies
And the plaintive rosemary.

Her lips were the clean crimson;
Of love, wet was her tongue;
On the velvet of her white shoulders
All night the glory hung.

She had as fair a bosom
As ever fired a man;
The sunbeams of her sweet spirit
A-down her forehead ran.

The old wives by the table sat
And sourly did they pray.
They envied her no more, for now
Her beauty slipped away.

Blue was the night on the wind's walk
And blue and black the rain.
They said her love was finery,
But aw – her shroud was plain.

1925

No Buyers
A Street Scene

————◄◊►————

THOMAS HARDY

A load of brushes and baskets and cradles and chairs
    Labours along the street in the rain:
With it a man, a woman, a pony with whiteybrown hairs. –
    The man foots in front of the horse with a shambling sway
        At a slower tread than a funeral train,
      While to a dirge-like tune he chants his wares,
Swinging a Turk's-head brush (in a drum-major's way
        When the bandsmen march and play).

A yard from the back of the man is the whiteybrown pony's nose:
He mirrors his master in every item of pace and pose:
      He stops when the man stops, without being told,
    And seems to be eased by a pause; too plainly he's old,
        Indeed, not strength enough shows
      To steer the disjointed waggon straight,
    Which wriggles left and right in a rambling line,
    Deflected thus by its own warp and weight,
    And pushing the pony with it in each incline.

      The woman walks on the pavement verge,
        Parallel to the man:
She wears an apron white and wide in span,
And carries a like Turk's-head, but more in nursing-wise:
      Now and then she joins in his dirge,
      But as if her thoughts were on distant things.
      The rain clams her apron till it clings. –
So, step by step, they move with their merchandize,
      And nobody buys.

1925

Incident

◄○►

COUNTEE CULLEN

For Eric Walrond

Once riding in old Baltimore,
  Heart-filled, head-filled with glee,
I saw a Baltimorean
  Keep looking straight at me.

Now I was eight and very small,
  And he was no whit bigger,
And so I smiled, but he poked out
  His tongue, and called me, 'Nigger.'

I saw the whole of Baltimore
  From May until December;
Of all the things that happened there
  That's all that I remember.

Eric Derwent Walrond (1898–1966), Cullen's dedicatee, was born in what was then British Guiana, and after a childhood in Barbados and Panama made a career in fiction during the Twenties heyday of the Harlem Renaissance in the US, before settling in England for the rest of his life. His 1921 prizewinning story 'A Senator's Memoirs', a utopian sketch of a united Africa, gained him wide attention.

1926

Low Barometer

ROBERT BRIDGES

The south-wind strengthens to a gale,
Across the moon the clouds fly fast,
The house is smitten as with a flail,
The chimney shudders to the blast.

On such a night, when Air has loosed
Its guardian grasp on blood and brain,
Old terrors then of god or ghost
Creep from their caves to life again;

And Reason kens he herits in
A haunted house. Tenants unknown
Assert their squalid lease of sin
With earlier title than his own.

Unbodied presences, the pack'd
Pollution and remorse of Time,
Slipp'd from oblivion reënact
The horrors of unhouseld crime.

Some men would quell the thing with prayer
Whose sightless footsteps pad the floor,
Whose fearful trespass mounts the stair
Or bursts the lock'd forbidden door.

Some have seen corpses long interr'd
Escape from hallowing control,
Pale charnel forms – nay ev'n have heard
The shrilling of a troubled soul,

That wanders till the dawn hath cross'd
The dolorous dark, or Earth hath wound
Closer her storm-spredd cloke, and thrust
The baleful phantoms underground.

1926

The Sisters
<>

ROY CAMPBELL

After hot loveless nights, when cold winds stream
Sprinkling the frost and dew, before the light,
Bored with the foolish things that girls must dream
Because their beds are empty of delight,

Two sisters rise and strip. Out from the night
Their horses run to their low-whistled pleas –
Vast phantom shapes with eyeballs rolling white
That sneeze a fiery steam about their knees:

Through the crisp manes their stealthy prowling hands,
Stronger than curbs, in slow caresses rove,
They gallop down across the milk-white sands
And wade far out into the sleeping cove:

The frost stings sweetly with a burning kiss
As intimate as love, as cold as death:
Their lips, whereon delicious tremors hiss,
Fume with the ghostly pollen of their breath.

Far out on the grey silence of the flood
They watch the dawn in smouldering gyres expand
Beyond them: and the day burns through their blood
Like a white candle through a shuttered hand.

1926

'Cow-parsley and hawthorn blossom'

IDRIS DAVIES

Cow-parsley and hawthorn blossom
And a cottage among trees,
A thrush and a skylark singing,
And a gipsy lying at ease.

Roses in gentlemen's gardens
Smile as we pass by the way,
And the swans of my lord are sleeping
Out of the heat of the day.

And here we come tramping and singing
Out of the valleys of strife,
Into the sunlit cornlands,
Begging the bread of life.

1926

An Epilogue

<o>

JOHN MASEFIELD

I have seen flowers come in stony places;
And kindness done by men with ugly faces;
And the gold cup won by the worst horse at the races;
So I trust, too.

This poem, to which Masefield later gave the title it bears here, was called 'The Meditation of Highworth Ridden' when it first appeared in his novel *Odtaa* in 1926.

1926

Cross

<o>

LANGSTON HUGHES

My old man's a white old man
And my old mother's black.
If ever I cursed my white old man
I take my curses back.

If ever I cursed my black old mother
And wished she were in hell,
I'm sorry for that evil wish
And now I wish her well.

My old man died in a fine big house.
My ma died in a shack.
I wonder where I'm gonna die,
Being neither white nor black?

1927

Vision by Sweetwater

<o>

JOHN CROWE RANSOM

Go and ask Robin to bring the girls over
To Sweetwater, said my Aunt; and that was why
It was like a dream of ladies sweeping by
The willows, clouds, deep meadowgrass, and river.

Robin's sisters and my Aunt's lily daughter
Laughed and talked, and tinkled light as wrens
If there were a little colony all hens
To go walking by the steep turn of Sweetwater.

Let them alone, dear Aunt, just for one minute
Till I go fishing in the dark of my mind:
Where have I seen before, against the wind,
These bright virgins, robed and bare of bonnet,

Flowing with music of their strange quick tongue
And adventuring with delicate paces by the stream, –
Myself a child, old suddenly at the scream
From one of the white throats which it hid among?

Sweetwater is in Ransom's native state of Tennessee, where he was teaching, at Vanderbilt University, when he wrote this poem.

1927

Journey of the Magi

T. S. Eliot

'A cold coming we had of it,
Just the worst time of the year
For a journey, and such a long journey:
The ways deep and the weather sharp,
The very dead of winter.'
And the camels galled, sore-footed, refractory,
Lying down in the melting snow.
There were times we regretted
The summer palaces on slopes, the terraces,
And the silken girls bringing sherbet.
Then the camel men cursing and grumbling
And running away, and wanting their liquor and women,
And the night-fires going out, and the lack of shelters,
And the cities hostile and the towns unfriendly
And the villages dirty and charging high prices:
A hard time we had of it.
At the end we preferred to travel all night,
Sleeping in snatches,
With the voices singing in our ears, saying
That this was all folly.

Then at dawn we came down to a temperate valley,
Wet, below the snow line, smelling of vegetation,
With a running stream and a water-mill beating the
    darkness,
And three trees on the low sky.
And an old white horse galloped away in the meadow.
Then we came to a tavern with vine-leaves over the lintel,
Six hands at an open door dicing for pieces of silver,
And feet kicking the empty wine-skins.
But there was no information, so we continued
And arrived at evening, not a moment too soon
Finding the place; it was (you may say) satisfactory.

All this was a long time ago, I remember,
And I would do it again, but set down
This set down
This: were we led all that way for
Birth or Death? There was a Birth, certainly,
We had evidence and no doubt. I had seen birth and
    death,
But had thought they were different; this Birth was
Hard and bitter agony for us, like Death, our death.
We returned to our places, these Kingdoms,
But no longer at ease here, in the old dispensation,
With an alien people clutching their gods.
I should be glad of another death.

1928

Dirge without Music

<o>

EDNA ST VINCENT MILLAY

I am not resigned to the shutting away of loving hearts in
the hard ground.
So it is, and so it will be, for so it has been, time out of
mind:
Into the darkness they go, the wise and the lovely. Crowned
With lilies and with laurel they go; but I am not resigned.

Lovers and thinkers, into the earth with you.
Be one with the dull, the indiscriminate dust.
A fragment of what you felt, of what you knew,
A formula, a phrase remains, — but the best is lost.

The answers quick and keen, the honest look, the laughter,
the love, —
They are gone. They are gone to feed the roses. Elegant and
curled
Is the blossom. Fragrant is the blossom. I know. But I do not
approve.
More precious was the light in your eyes than all the roses in
the world.

Down, down, down into the darkness of the grave
Gently they go, the beautiful, the tender, the kind;
Quietly they go, the intelligent, the witty, the brave.
I know. But I do not approve. And I am not resigned.

1928

Acquainted with the Night

ROBERT FROST

I have been one acquainted with the night.
I have walked out in rain – and back in rain.
I have outwalked the furthest city light.

I have looked down the saddest city lane.
I have passed by the watchman on his beat
And dropped my eyes, unwilling to explain.

I have stood still and stopped the sound of feet
When far away an interrupted cry
Came over houses from another street,

But not to call me back or say good-by;
And further still at an unearthly height
One luminary clock against the sky

Proclaimed the time was neither wrong nor right.
I have been one acquainted with the night.

1928

Luxury

EDGELL RICKWORD

The long, sleek cars rasp softly on the kerb
and chattering women rise from cushioned nests,
flamingo-tall, whose coral legs disturb
the mirror-surface where creation rests.

Aconite, Opium, Mandragora, Girl!
Essential phials exquisite array!
Poisons whose frail, consumptive fervours whirl
the stony city to a fierce decay.

The churches' sun-dried clay crumbles at last,
the Courts of Justice wither like a stink
and honourable statues melt as fast
as greasy garbage down a kitchen-sink.

Commercial palaces, hotels de luxe
and Banks in white, immutable ravines,
life's skeleton unfleshed by cynic rooks,
remain to warn the traveller what it means.

The shady universe, once haunt of play,
in leafless winter bares its ways of stone;
the paths we shared, the mounds on which we lay
were ruled by Time and lifted by old bone.

Time has no pity for this world of graves
nor for its dead decked out in feathery shrouds.
The ghoul must perish with the flesh he craves
when stars' hoarse bells of doom toll in the clouds.

1929

A Name for All

HART CRANE

Moonmoth and grasshopper that flee our page
And still wing on, untarnished of the name
We pinion to your bodies to assuage
Our envy of your freedom — we must maim

Because we are usurpers, and chagrined —
And take the wing and scar it in the hand.
Names we have, even, to clap on the wind;
But we must die, as you, to understand.

I dreamed that all men dropped their names, and sang
As only they can praise, who build their days
With fin and hoof, with wing and sweetened fang
Struck free and holy in one Name always.

1930

Consider

W. H. AUDEN

Consider this and in our time
As the hawk sees it or the helmeted airman:
The clouds rift suddenly – look there
At cigarette-end smouldering on a border
At the first garden party of the year.
Pass on, admire the view of the massif
Through plate-glass windows of the Sport Hotel;
Join there the insufficient units
Dangerous, easy, in furs, in uniform,
And constellated at reserved tables,
Supplied with feelings by an efficient band,
Relayed elsewhere to farmers and their dogs
Sitting in kitchens in the stormy fens.

Long ago, supreme Antagonist,
More powerful than the great northern whale,
Ancient and sorry at life's limiting defect,
In Cornwall, Mendip, or the Pennine moor
Your comments on the highborn mining-captains,
Found they no answer, made them wish to die
– Lie since in barrows out of harm.
You talk to your admirers every day
By silted harbours, derelict works,
In strangled orchards, and a silent comb
Where dogs have worried or a bird was shot.

Order the ill that they attack at once:
Visit the ports and, interrupting
The leisurely conversation in the bar
Within a stone's throw of the sunlit water,
Beckon your chosen out. Summon
Those handsome and diseased youngsters, those women
Your solitary agents in the country parishes;

And mobilize the powerful forces latent
In soils that make the farmer brutal
In the infected sinus, and the eyes of stoats.
Then, ready, start your rumour, soft
But horrifying in its capacity to disgust
Which, spreading magnified, shall come to be
A polar peril, a prodigious alarm,
Scattering the people, as torn-up paper
Rags and utensils in a sudden gust,
Seized with immeasurable neurotic dread.

Seekers after happiness, all who follow
The convolutions of your simple wish,
It is later than you think; nearer that day
Far other than that distant afternoon
Amid rustle of frocks and stamping feet
They gave the prizes to the ruined boys.
You cannot be away, then, no
Not though you pack to leave within an hour,
Escaping humming down arterial roads:
The date was yours; the prey to fugues,
Irregular breathing and alternate ascendancies
After some haunted migratory years
To disintegrate on an instant in the explosion of mania
Or lapse for ever into a classic fatigue.

1930

Song: Lift-Boy

ROBERT GRAVES

Let me tell you the story of how I began:
I began as the boot-boy and ended as the boot-man,
With nothing in my pockets but a jack-knife and a button,
With nothing in my pockets but a jack-knife and a button,
With nothing in my pockets.

Let me tell you the story of how I went on:
I began as the lift-boy and ended as the lift-man,
With nothing in my pockets but a jack-knife and a button,
With nothing in my pockets but a jack-knife and a button,
With nothing in my pockets.

I found it very easy to whistle and play
With nothing in my head or my pockets all day,
With nothing in my pockets.

But along came Old Eagle, like Moses or David;
He stopped at the fourth floor and preached me
    Damnation:
'Not a soul shall be savèd, not one shall be savèd.
The whole First Creation shall forfeit salvation:
From knife-boy to lift-boy, from ragged to regal,
Not one shall be savèd, not you, not Old Eagle,
No soul on earth escapeth, even if all repent –'
So I cut the cords of the lift and down we went,
With nothing in our pockets.

1931

Aus dem Zweiten Reich

<o>

BASIL BUNTING

I

Women swarm in Tauentsienstrasse.
Clients of Nollendorferplatz cafés,
shadows on sweaty glass,
hum, drum on the table
        to the negerband's faint jazz.
Humdrum at the table.

Hour and hour
meeting against me,
efficiently whipped cream,
efficiently metropolitan chatter and snap,
transparent glistening wrapper
        for a candy pack.

Automatic, somewhat too clean,
body and soul similarly scented,
on time,
rapid, dogmatic, automatic and efficient,
ganz modern.

'Sturm über Asien' is off, some other flicker . . .
Kiss me in the taxi, twist fingers in the dark.
A box of chocolates is necessary.
I am preoccupied with Sie and Du.
        The person on the screen,
divorced and twenty-five, must pass for fourteen
for the story's sake, an insipidity
contrived to dress her in shorts
and a widenecked shirt with nothing underneath
so that you see her small breasts when she
often bends towards the camera.

Audience mainly male stirs,
    I am teased too,
I like this public blonde better than my brunette,
    but that will never do.
– Let's go,
arm in arm on foot over gleaming snow
past the Gedächtnis Kirche
to the loud crowded cafés near the Bahnhof Zoo.

Better hugged together ('to keep warm')
under street trees whimpering to the keen wind
over snow whispering to many feet,
find out a consolingly mediocre
neighbourhood without music, varnished faces
bright and sagacious against varnished walls,
youngsters red from skating,
businessmen reading the papers:
no need to talk – much:
what indolence supplies.
'If, smoothing this silk skirt, you pinch my thighs,
that will be fabelhaft.'

II

Herr Lignitz knows Old Berlin. It is near the Post Office
with several rather disorderly public houses.
'You have no naked pictures in your English magazines.
It is shocking. Berlin is very shocking to the English. Are
    you shocked?
Would you like to see the naked cabarets
in Jaegerstrasse? I think there is
nothing like that in Paris.
Or a department store? They are said to be
almost equal to Macy's in America.'

III

The renowned author of
more plays than Shakespeare
stopped and did his hair
with a pocket glass
before entering the village,
afraid they wouldnt recognize
caricature and picturepostcard,
that windswept chevelure.

Who talked about poetry,
and he said nothing at all;
plays,
and he said nothing at all;
politics,
and he stirred as if a flea
bit him
but wouldnt let on in company;
and the frost in Berlin,
muttered: 𝔖𝔠𝔥𝔯𝔢𝔠𝔨𝔩𝔦𝔠𝔥

Viennese bow from the hips,
notorieties
contorted laudatory lips,
wreaths and bouquets surround
the mindless menopause.
Stillborn fecundities,
frostbound applause.

Bunting's title means 'from the second empire', which is perplexing since
Germany's second empire came to an end with the abdication of Kaiser Wilhelm
II in November 1918, and Bunting's snapshot of Berlin dates from the Weimar
Republic. The first line of the poem misspells one of Berlin's fashionable
shopping streets, Tauentzienstrasse. A 'negerband' (negro band) would have been
usual in jazz-crazy inter-war Berlin. The Gedächtnis Kirche is the Kaiser Wilhelm
Memorial Church, built under Wilhelm II in honour of his grandfather, Kaiser
Wilhelm I, consecrated in 1895, and largely destroyed in 1943. The 'renowned
author of / more plays than Shakespeare' with the windswept mane of hair is
probably Gerhart Hauptmann (1862–1946), Nobel laureate of 1912.

1932

The Steeple-Jack

MARIANNE MOORE

Dürer would have seen a reason for living
    in a town like this, with eight stranded whales
to look at; with the sweet sea air coming into your house
on a fine day, from water etched
    with waves as formal as the scales
on a fish.

One by one in two's and three's, the seagulls keep
    flying back and forth over the town clock,
or sailing around the lighthouse without moving their wings –
rising steadily with a slight
    quiver of the body – or flock
mewing where

a sea the purple of the peacock's neck is
    paled to greenish azure as Dürer changed
the pine green of the Tyrol to peacock blue and guinea
gray. You can see a twenty-five-
    pound lobster; and fish nets arranged
to dry. The

whirlwind fife-and-drum of the storm bends the salt
    marsh grass, disturbs stars in the sky and the
star on the steeple; it is a privilege to see so
much confusion. Disguised by what
    might seem the opposite, the sea-
side flowers and

trees are favored by the fog so that you have
    the tropics at first hand: the trumpet-vine,
fox-glove, giant snap-dragon, a salpiglossis that has
spots and stripes; morning-glories, gourds,
    or moon-vines trained on fishing-twine
at the back door;

cat-tails, flags, blueberries and spiderwort,
    striped grass, lichens, sunflowers, asters, daisies –
yellow and crab-claw ragged sailors with green bracts –
    toad-plant,
petunias, ferns; pink lilies, blue
    ones, tigers; poppies; black sweet-peas.
The climate

is not right for the banyan, frangipani, or
    jack-fruit trees; or for exotic serpent
life. Ring lizard and snake-skin for the foot, if you see fit;
but here they've cats, not cobras, to
    keep down the rats. The diffident
little newt

with white pin-dots on black horizontal spaced-
    out bands lives here; yet there is nothing that
ambition can buy or take away. The college student
named Ambrose sits on the hillside
    with his not-native books and hat
and sees boats

at sea progress white and rigid as if in
    a groove. Liking an elegance of which
the source is not bravado, he knows by heart the antique
sugar-bowl shaped summer-house of
    interlacing slats, and the pitch
of the church

spire, not true, from which a man in scarlet lets
    down a rope as a spider spins a thread;
he might be part of a novel, but on the sidewalk a
sign says C. J. Poole, Steeple-Jack,
    in black and white; and one in red
and white says

Danger. The church portico has four fluted
   columns, each a single piece of stone, made
modester by white-wash. This would be a fit haven for
waifs, children, animals, prisoners,
   and presidents who have repaid
sin-driven

senators by not thinking about them. The
   place has a school-house, a post-office in a
store, fish-houses, hen-houses, a three-masted
schooner on
the stocks. The hero, the student,
   the steeple-jack, each in his way,
is at home.

It could not be dangerous to be living
   in a town like this, of simple people,
who have a steeple-jack placing danger-signs by the church
while he is gilding the solid-
   pointed star, which on a steeple
stands for hope.

1933

Aubade

◄◊►

WILLIAM EMPSON

Hours before dawn we were woken by the quake.
My house was on a cliff. The thing could take
Bookloads off shelves, break bottles in a row.
Then the long pause and then the bigger shake.
It seemed the best thing to be up and go.

And far too large for my feet to step by.
I hoped that various buildings were brought low.
The heart of standing is you cannot fly.

It seemed quite safe till she got up and dressed.
The guarded tourist makes the guide the test.
Then I said The Garden? Laughing she said No.
Taxi for her and for me healthy rest.
It seemed the best thing to be up and go.

The language problem but you have to try.
Some solid ground for lying could she show?
The heart of standing is you cannot fly.

None of these deaths were her point at all.
The thing was that being woken he would bawl
And finding her not in earshot he would know.
I tried saying Half an Hour to pay this call.
It seemed the best thing to be up and go.

I slept, and blank as that I would yet lie.
Till you have seen what a threat holds below,
The heart of standing is you cannot fly.

Tell me again about Europe and her pains,
Who's tortured by the drought, who by the rains.
Glut me with floods where only the swine can row
Who cuts his throat and let him count his gains.
It seemed the best thing to be up and go.

A bedshift flight to a Far Eastern sky.
Only the same war on a stronger toe.
The heart of standing is you cannot fly.

Tell me more quickly what I lost by this,
Or tell me with less drama what they miss
Who call no die a god for a good throw,
Who say after two aliens had one kiss
It seemed the best thing to be up and go.

But as to risings, I can tell you why.
It is on contradiction that they grow.
It seemed the best thing to be up and go.
Up was the heartening and the strong reply.
The heart of standing is we cannot fly.

1934

from Jerusalem the Golden
⟨o⟩

CHARLES REZNIKOFF

16

Going to work in the subway
this bright May morning
you have put on red slippers;
do they dance behind the counters
in the store, or about the machines
in the shop where you work?

20

In steel clouds
to the sound of thunder
like the ancient gods:
our sky, cement;
the earth, cement;
our trees, steel;
instead of sunshine,
a light that has no twilight,
neither morning nor evening,
only noon.

Coming up the subway stairs, I thought the moon
only another street-light —
a little crooked.

57

It was in my heart to give her wine and dainties,
silken gowns, furs against the wind;
a woolen scarf,
coffee and bread was all that I could buy:
It is enough, she said.

It was in my heart to show her foreign lands,
at least the fields beyond the city:
I could not pay our way;
when she would see a row of street-lamps shining,
How beautiful, she would say.

1934

mehitabel s morals

◄◦►

DON MARQUIS

boss i got
a message from
mehitabel the cat
the other day
brought me by
a cockroach
she asks for our help
it seems she is being
held at ellis
island while an
investigation is made
of her morals

Don Marquis is best known for Archy, a cockroach reincarnation of a free-verse poet whose work was supposedly tapped out on Marquis's typewriter, and which satirised American mores through reporting the scandalous life of Mehitabel, an alley cat. In the years after the 1924 Immigration Act, the immigration facility on Ellis Island in New York harbour was chiefly used as a detention centre prior to possible deportation.

1934

Lugete o veneres

R. A. K. MASON

With his penis swollen for the girl on the next farm and rigid
    here he lies on his bed
motionless dumb and his naked corpse goose-fleshed and as
    frigid
        as if he were dead:

Only at times a great sob rises up in his drawn aching throttle
    and dies like his hope
or the tear of his anguish drips down on his arm cold and
    mottled
        like a bar of blue soap.

For the people next door have packed up their pots and their
    table
    and their mats and their ploughs
they have brought up their pigs from the sty their steeds from
the stable
    and driven off the cows.

Tomorrow strange people will reign there tomorrow the
    stranger
    will inherit their places
other cows know the shed where they milk, new horses the
    manger
    and dogs with unknown faces.

Mark how dejected tormented he lies poor lad while shivers
    run and shake his fat arse:
for a space let us mourn here this tortured boy's slobbering
    quivers
        as we laugh at the farce.

Mason's title quotes 'Lugete o veneres cupidinesque', the first line of a poem by
Catullus that notes the grief of the speaker's girl at the death of her sparrow, and
translates as 'Mourn, O Venuses and Cupids!'

1935

'may i feel said he'

E. E. CUMMINGS

may i feel said he
(i'll squeal said she
just once said he)
it's fun said she

(may i touch said he
how much said she
a lot said he)
why not said she

(let's go said he
not too far said she
what's too far said he
where you are said she)

may i stay said he
(which way said she
like this said he
if you kiss said she

may i move said he
is it love said she)
if you're willing said he
(but you're killing said she

but it's life said he
but your wife said she
now said he)
ow said she

(tiptop said he
don't stop said she
oh no said he)
go slow said she

(cccome? said he
ummm said she)
you're divine! said he
(you are Mine said she)

1935

Canto XLV

Ezra Pound

With *Usura*

With usura hath no man a house of good stone
each block cut smooth and well fitting
that design might cover their face,
with usura
hath no man a painted paradise on his church wall
harpes et luz
or where virgin receiveth message
and halo projects from incision,
with usura
seeth no man Gonzaga his heirs and his concubines
no picture is made to endure nor to live with
but it is made to sell and sell quickly
with usura, sin against nature,
is thy bread ever more of stale rags
is thy bread dry as paper,
with no mountain wheat, no strong flour
with usura the line grows thick
with usura is no clear demarcation
and no man can find site for his dwelling.
Stonecutter is kept from his stone
weaver is kept from his loom
WITH USURA
wool comes not to market
sheep bringeth no gain with usura
Usura is a murrain, usura
blunteth the needle in the maid's hand
and stoppeth the spinner's cunning. Pietro Lombardo
came not by usura
Duccio came not by usura
nor Pier della Francesca; Zuan Bellin' not by usura
nor was 'La Calunnia' painted.

Came not by usura Angelico; came not Ambrogio Praedis,
Came no church of cut stone signed: *Adamo me fecit.*
Not by usura St Trophime
Not by usura Saint Hilaire,
Usura rusteth the chisel
It rusteth the craft and the craftsman
It gnaweth the thread in the loom
None learneth to weave gold in her pattern;
Azure hath a canker by usura; cramoisi is unbroidered
Emerald findeth no Memling
Usura slayeth the child in the womb
It stayeth the young man's courting
It hath brought palsey to bed, lyeth
between the young bride and her bridegroom
                    CONTRA NATURAM
They have brought whores for Eleusis
Corpses are set to banquet
at behest of usura.

N.B. Usury: A charge for the use of purchasing power, levied without regard to production; often without regard to the possibilities of production. (Hence the failure of the Medici bank.) (Pound's note.)

For much of the Thirties, living in Rapallo and filled with admiration for Italian fascism and Mussolini, Pound devoted substantial amounts of time to economics. In this canto he gives eloquent rein to his furiously impassioned conviction that greedy banking levies spelled the end of healthy cultural life and creation. Italian artists Lombardo, Duccio, della Francesca, Bellini, Botticelli (who painted 'La Calunnia'), Fra Angelico and Ambrogio de Predis, and Flemish Hans Memling, together with two French churches, the culture supported by the Gonzagas (the dynasty that ruled a duchy centred upon Mantua in northern Italy), and the church of San Zeno in Verona (where Pound saw the inscription '*Adamo me fecit*', or 'Adam made me'), are the poet's personal catalogue of the great achievements humanity is capable of, if the practice of charging excessive interest does not nip their efforts in the bud. The phrase '*harpes et luz*' means 'harps and lutes'. Eleusis was the site of sacred rituals in ancient Greece, and is used by Pound to clinch his argument.

1936

The Idea of Order at Key West

◄○►

WALLACE STEVENS

She sang beyond the genius of the sea.
The water never formed to mind or voice,
Like a body wholly body, fluttering
Its empty sleeves; and yet its mimic motion
Made constant cry, caused constantly a cry,
That was not ours although we understood,
Inhuman, of the veritable ocean.

The sea was not a mask. No more was she.
The song and water were not medleyed sound
Even if what she sang was what she heard,
Since what she sang was uttered word by word.
It may be that in all her phrases stirred
The grinding water and the gasping wind;
But it was she and not the sea we heard.
For she was the maker of the song she sang.
The ever-hooded, tragic-gestured sea
Was merely a place by which she walked to sing.
Whose spirit is this? we said, because we knew
It was the spirit that we sought and knew
That we should ask this often as she sang.

If it was only the dark voice of the sea
That rose, or even coloured by many waves;
If it was only the outer voice of sky
And cloud, of the sunken coral water-walled,
However clear, it would have been deep air,
The heaving speech of air, a summer sound
Repeated in a summer without end
And sound alone. But it was more than that,
More even than her voice, and ours, among
The meaningless plungings of water and the wind,
Theatrical distances, bronze shadows heaped

On high horizons, mountainous atmospheres
Of sky and sea.

                  It was her voice that made
The sky acutest at its vanishing.
She measured to the hour its solitude.
She was the single artificer of the world
In which she sang. And when she sang, the sea,
Whatever self it had, became the self
That was her song, for she was the maker. Then we,
As we beheld her striding there alone,
Knew that there never was a world for her
Except the one she sang and, singing, made.

Ramon Fernandez, tell me, if you know,
Why, when the singing ended and we turned
Toward the town, tell why the glassy lights,
The lights in the fishing boats at anchor there,
As the night descended, tilting in the air,
Mastered the night and portioned out the sea,
Fixing emblazoned zones and fiery poles,
Arranging, deepening, enchanting night.

Oh! Blessed rage for order, pale Ramon,
The maker's rage to order words of the sea,
Words of the fragrant portals, dimly-starred,
And of ourselves and of our origins,
In ghostlier demarcations, keener sounds.

1936

The Ghost of Roger Casement

W. B. YEATS

O what has made that sudden noise?
What on the threshold stands?
It never crossed the sea because
John Bull and the sea are friends;
But this is not the old sea
Nor this the old seashore.
What gave that roar of mockery,
That roar in the sea's roar?
The ghost of Roger Casement
Is beating on the door.

John Bull has stood for Parliament,
A dog must have his day,
The country thinks no end of him,
For he knows how to say,
At a beanfeast or a banquet,
That all must hang their trust
Upon the British Empire,
Upon the Church of Christ.
The ghost of Roger Casement
Is beating on the door.

John Bull has gone to India
And all must pay him heed,
For histories are there to prove
That none of another breed
Has had a like inheritance,
Or sucked such milk as he,
And there's no luck about a house
If it lack honesty.
The ghost of Roger Casement
Is beating on the door.

I poked about a village church
And found his family tomb
And copied out what I could read
In that religious gloom;
Found many a famous man there;
But fame and virtue rot.
Draw round, beloved and bitter men,
Draw round and raise a shout;
The ghost of Roger Casement
Is beating on the door.

For Roger Casement, see note to Padraic Colum's poem, p. 124. John Bull has been the traditional stereotypical Englishman since the early eighteenth century.

1936

On Seeing the Leni Riefenstahl Film of the 1936 Olympic Games

◄○►

ROY FULLER

The nation's face above the human shape,
Sunlight on leaf, gloved skin and water pearled
– No art can hide the shocking gulfs that gape
Even between such bodies and their world.

Art merely lets these tenants of a star
Run once again with legendary ease
Across the screen and years towards that war
Which lay in wait for them like a disease.

Leni Riefenstahl declared that she became a confirmed National Socialist after reading the first page of Hitler's *Mein Kampf*. It was Hitler who, impressed by her propaganda work filming Nazi rallies, invited her to film the 1936 Berlin Olympic Games. The resulting film, *Olympia*, is now seen as technically innovative (Riefenstahl pioneered tracking shots and slow motion shots, for example) but remains inseparable from the Nazi propaganda machine and the war which was already in preparation.

1936

from Autumn Journal

LOUIS MacNEICE

VI

And I remember Spain
  At Easter ripe as an egg for revolt and ruin
Though for a tripper the rain
  Was worse than the surly or the worried or the haunted
  faces
With writings on the walls –
  Hammer and sickle, Boicot, Viva, Muerra;
With café-au-lait brimming the waterfalls,
  With sherry, shellfish, omelettes.
With fretted stone the Moor
  Had chiselled for effects of sun and shadow;
With shadows of the poor,
  The begging cripples and the children begging.
The churches full of saints
  Tortured on racks of marble –
The old complaints
  Covered with gilt and dimly lit with candles.
With powerful or banal
  Monuments of riches or repression
And the Escorial
  Cold for ever within like the heart of Philip.
With ranks of dominoes
  Deployed on café tables the whole of Sunday;
With cabarets that call the tourist, shows
  Of thighs and eyes and nipples.
With slovenly soldiers, nuns,
  And peeling posters from the last elections
Promising bread or guns
  Or an amnesty or another
Order or else the old

Glory veneered and varnished
As if veneer could hold
The rotten guts and crumbled bones together.
And a vulture hung in air
Below the cliffs of Ronda and below him
His hook-winged shadow wavered like despair
Across the chequered vineyards.
And the boot-blacks in Madrid
Kept us half an hour with polish and pincers
And all we did
In that city was drink and think and loiter.
And in the Prado half-
wit princes looked from the canvas they had paid for
(Goya had the laugh –
But can what is corrupt be cured by laughter?)
And the day at Aranjuez
When the sun came out for once on the yellow river
With Valdepeñas burdening the breath
We slept a royal sleep in the royal gardens;
And at Toledo walked
Around the ramparts where they throw the garbage
And glibly talked
Of how the Spaniards lack all sense of business.
And Avila was cold
And Segovia was picturesque and smelly
And a goat on the road seemed old
As the rocks or the Roman arches.
And Easter was wet and full
In Seville and in the ring on Easter Sunday
A clumsy bull and then a clumsy bull
Nodding his banderillas died of boredom.
And the standard of living was low
But that, we thought to ourselves, was not our business;
All that the tripper wants is the *status quo*
Cut and dried for trippers.
And we thought the papers a lark
With their party politics and blank invective;
And we thought the dark

Women who dyed their hair should have it dyed more often.
  And we sat in trains all night
  With the windows shut among civil guards and peasants
And tried to play piquet by a tiny light
  And tried to sleep bolt upright;
And cursed the Spanish rain
  And cursed their cigarettes which came to pieces
And caught heavy colds in Cordova and in vain
  Waited for the right light for taking photos.
And we met a Cambridge don who said with an air
  'There's going to be trouble shortly in this country,'
And ordered anis, pudgy and debonair,
  Glad to show off his mastery of the language.
But only an inch behind
  This map of olive and ilex, this painted hoarding,
Careless of visitors the people's mind
  Was tunnelling like a mole to day and danger.
And the day before we left
  We saw the mob in flower at Algeciras
Outside a toothless door, a church bereft
  Of its images and its aura.
And at La Linea while
  The night put miles between us and Gibraltar
We heard the blood-lust of a drunkard pile
  His heaven high with curses;
And next day took the boat
  For home, forgetting Spain, not realising
That Spain would soon denote
  Our grief, our aspirations;
Not knowing that our blunt
  Ideals would find their whetstone, that our spirit
Would find its frontier on the Spanish front,
  Its body in a rag-tag army.

The Escorial, north of Madrid, was the residence and final resting-place of the kings of Spain, among them Philip II, who died there in 1598. The Museo del Prado is Madrid's great museum and art gallery. This part of MacNeice's *Autumn Journal* recalls his visit to Spain in the spring of 1936, just three months before the Civil War broke out and the hammer-and-sickle graffiti he saw on the walls, with slogans proclaiming boycott, life and death, became part of a terrible reality.

1936

A Letter from Aragon
◄◦►

JOHN CORNFORD

This is a quiet sector of a quiet front.

We buried Ruiz in a new pine coffin,
But the shroud was too small and his washed feet stuck
out.
The stink of his corpse came through the clean pine
boards
And some of the bearers wrapped handkerchiefs round
their faces.
Death was not dignified.
We hacked a ragged grave in the unfriendly earth
And fired a ragged volley over the grave.

You could tell from our listlessness, no one much missed
him.

This is a quiet sector of a quiet front.
There is no poison gas and no H. E.

But when they shelled the other end of the village
And the streets were choked with dust
Women came screaming out of the crumbling houses,
Clutched under one arm the naked rump of an infant.
I thought: how ugly fear is.

This is a quiet sector of a quiet front.
Our nerves are steady; we all sleep soundly.

In the clean hospital bed, my eyes were so heavy
Sleep easily blotted out one ugly picture,
A wounded militiaman moaning on a stretcher,
Now out of danger, but still crying for water,
Strong against death, but unprepared for such pain.

This on a quiet front.

But when I shook hands to leave, an Anarchist worker
Said: 'Tell the workers of England
This was a war not of our own making
We did not seek it.
But if ever the Fascists again rule Barcelona
It will be as a heap of ruins with us workers beneath it.'

Cornford fought on the Aragon front with the POUM (Partido Obrero Unificación Marxista) militia. H.E. is high explosive.

1936

LORCA

◄○►

GEOFFREY PARSONS

The Fascists have only one answer for a poet –
Their stuttering lead syllables prevent repartee
Putting an end to his stanzas and fancy speech.

And the poet dies easily, his human flesh
Parts easily as a babe's for the bullets to enter
And all his words are done and there's an end to him.

And for Lorca the civil guard had a special hatred
A personal spite: there were certain deeds in the past
Had been pilloried, had been whistled through Spain in a
    ballad.

So they smelt him out and marched through the town, to
    the trees,
He walking straight as a tree, and knowing to what end:
While others behind piled his books on the Plaza del
    Carmen.

They halted to take their stance: Lorca alone
Continued away from Granada. How many steps
Would they let him take towards freedom? A flutter of
    capes

Raising of rifles. They would let him take all but the last
    one,
Hoping that he would run for it, hoping for fear.
But the bullfighter's friend was not afraid of their hate.

And he stopped and turned and faced them, standing still;
He stared at their aiming eyes, his imminent murder;
He was one with the people of Spain and he stood as they
    stand.

What is the power of words against flight of bullets?
A puff of articulate air, no deflector of death;
But they dared not listen, they burst the bubble of speech.

And a volley was heard in Granada. Lorca fell.
His books, a billow of smoke, rose over the Plaza.
The civil guard marched back, and there was an end of
    him.

A poet dies easily, easily as a babe.
So Lorca merges with Spain, and over the city
In ashes his writings disperse, disappear like a shell burst.

And they in the city drink to that easy death,
The generals and colonels who feared to be put in a
    ballad:
The foul-mouthed general in Seville announces an end to
    him.

But this side of the line, and secretly that side
His friends, the people, the peasants, remember his songs
And chant them through Spain. And to them there will be
    no end.

Federico García Lorca (1898–1936), the most formidable Spanish poet and play-wright of the twentieth century, was murdered on 19 August 1936. The exact circumstances remain unclear, and Parsons' account exemplifies the triumph of rhetoric over fact.

1937

Spain

—◆◇◆—

W. H. AUDEN

Yesterday all the past. The language of size
Spreading to China along the trade-routes; the diffusion
    Of the counting-frame and the cromlech;
Yesterday the shadow-reckoning in the sunny climates.

Yesterday the assessment of insurance by cards,
The divination of water; yesterday the invention
    Of cartwheels and clocks, the taming of
Horses. Yesterday the bustling world of the navigators.

Yesterday the abolition of fairies and giants,
The fortress like a motionless eagle eyeing the valley,
    The chapel built in the forest;
Yesterday the carving of angels and alarming gargoyles.

The trial of heretics among the columns of stone;
Yesterday the theological feuds in the taverns
    And the miraculous cure at the fountain;
Yesterday the Sabbath of witches; but to-day the struggle.

Yesterday the installation of dynamos and turbines,
The construction of railways in the colonial desert;
    Yesterday the classic lecture
On the origin of Mankind. But to-day the struggle.

Yesterday the belief in the absolute value of Greece,
The fall of the curtain upon the death of a hero;
    Yesterday the prayer to the sunset
And the adoration of madmen. But to-day the struggle.

As the poet whispers, startled among the pines,
Or where the loose waterfall sings compact, or upright
    On the crag by the leaning tower:
'O my vision. O send me the luck of the sailor.'

And the investigator peers through his instruments
At the inhuman provinces, the virile bacillus
    Or enormous Jupiter finished:
'But the lives of my friends. I inquire. I inquire.'

And the poor in their fireless lodgings, dropping the sheets
Of the evening paper: 'Our day is our loss, O show us
    History the operator, the
Organizer, Time the refreshing river.'

And the nations combine each cry, invoking the life
That shapes the individual belly and orders
    The private nocturnal terror:
'Did you not found the city state of the sponge,

'Raise the vast military empires of the shark
And the tiger, establish the robin's plucky canton?
    Intervene. O descend as a dove or
A furious papa or a mild engineer, but descend.'

And the life, if it answers at all, replies from the heart
And the eyes and the lungs, from the shops and squares of
    the city:
    'O no, I am not the mover;
Not to-day; not to you. To you, I'm the

'Yes-man, the bar-companion, the easily-duped;
I am whatever you do. I am your vow to be
    Good, your humorous story.
I am your business voice. I am your marriage.

'What's your proposal? To build the just city? I will.
I agree. Or is it the suicide pact, the romantic
    Death? Very well, I accept, for
I am your choice, your decision. Yes, I am Spain.'

Many have heard it on remote peninsulas,
On sleepy plains, in the aberrant fisherman's islands
    Or the corrupt heart of the city,
Have heard and migrated like gulls or the seeds of a flower.

They clung like birds to the long expresses that lurch
Through the unjust lands, through the night, through the
   alpine tunnel;
     They floated over the oceans;
They walked the passes. All presented their lives.

On that arid square, that fragment nipped off from hot
Africa, soldered so crudely to inventive Europe;
     On that tableland scored by rivers,
Our thoughts have bodies; the menacing shapes of our fever

Are precise and alive. For the fears which made us respond
To the medicine ad, and the brochure of winter cruises
     Have become invading battalions;
And our faces, the institute-face, the chain-store, the ruin

Are projecting their greed as the firing squad and the bomb.
Madrid is the heart. Our moments of tenderness blossom
     As the ambulance and the sandbag;
Our hours of friendship into a people's army.

To-morrow, perhaps the future. The research on fatigue
And the movement of packers; the gradual exploring of all
   the
     Octaves of radiation;
To-morrow the enlarging of consciousness by diet and
   breathing.

To-morrow the rediscovery of romantic love,
The photographing of ravens; all the fun under
     Liberty's masterful shadow;
To-morrow the hour of the pageant-master and the musician,

The beautiful roar of the chorus under the dome;
To-morrow the exchanging of tips on the breeding of
   terriers,
     The eager election of chairmen
By the sudden forest of hands. But to-day the struggle.

To-morrow for the young poets exploding like bombs,
The walks by the lake, the weeks of perfect communion;
    To-morrow the bicycle races
Through the suburbs on summer evenings. But to-day the
    struggle.

To-day the deliberate increase in the chances of death,
The conscious acceptance of guilt in the necessary murder;
    To-day the expending of powers
On the flat ephemeral pamphlet and the boring meeting.

To-day the makeshift consolations: the shared cigarette,
The cards in the candlelit barn, and the scraping concert,
    The masculine jokes; to-day the
Fumbled and unsatisfactory embrace before hurting.

The stars are dead. The animals will not look.
We are left alone with our day, and the time is short, and
    History to the defeated
May say alas but cannot help or pardon.

1937

Thoughts during an Air Raid

STEPHEN SPENDER

Of course, the entire effort is to put oneself
Outside the ordinary range
Of what are called statistics. A hundred are killed
In the outer suburbs. Well, well, one carries on.
So long as this thing 'I' is propped up on
The girdered bed which seems so like a hearse,
In the hotel bedroom with the wall-paper
Blowing smoke-wreaths of roses, one can ignore
The pressure of those names under the fingers
Indented by lead type on newsprint,
In the bar, the marginal wailing wireless.
Yet supposing that a bomb should dive
Its nose right through this bed, with one upon it?
The thought's obscene. Still, there are many
For whom one's loss would illustrate
The 'impersonal' use indeed. The essential is
That every 'one' should remain separate
Propped up under roses, and no one suffer
For his neighbour. Then horror is postponed
Piecemeal for each, until it settles on him
That wreath of incommunicable grief
Which is all mystery or nothing.

1937

Bagpipe Music

Louis MacNeice

It's no go the merrygoround, it's no go the rickshaw,
All we want is a limousine and a ticket for the peepshow.
Their knickers are made of crêpe-de-chine, their shoes are
    made of python,
Their halls are lined with tiger rugs and their walls with
    heads of bison.

John MacDonald found a corpse, put it under the sofa,
Waited till it came to life and hit it with a poker,
Sold its eyes for souvenirs, sold its blood for whisky,
Kept its bones for dumb-bells to use when he was fifty.

It's no go the Yogi-Man, it's no go Blavatsky,
All we want is a bank balance and a bit of skirt in a taxi.

Annie MacDougall went to milk, caught her foot in the
    heather,
Woke to hear a dance record playing of Old Vienna.
It's no go your maidenheads, it's no go your culture,
All we want is a Dunlop tyre and the devil mend the
    puncture.

The Laird o' Phelps spent Hogmanay declaring he was
    sober,
Counted his feet to prove the fact and found he had one
    foot over.
Mrs Carmichael had her fifth, looked at the job with
    repulsion,
Said to the midwife 'Take it away; I'm through with over-
    production'.

It's no go the gossip column, it's no go the Ceilidh,
All we want is a mother's help and a sugar-stick for the
    baby.

Willie Murray cut his thumb, couldn't count the damage,
Took the hide of an Ayrshire cow and used it for a bandage.
His brother caught three hundred cran when the seas were
    lavish,
Threw the bleeders back in the sea and went upon the
    parish.

It's no go the Herring Board, it's no go the Bible,
All we want is a packet of fags when our hands are idle.

It's no go the picture palace, it's no go the stadium,
It's no go the country cot with a pot of pink geraniums,
It's no go the Government grants, it's no go the elections,
Sit on your arse for fifty years and hang your hat on a
    pension.

It's no go my honey love, it's no go my poppet;
Work your hands from day to day, the winds will blow the
    profit.
The glass is falling hour by hour, the glass will fall for ever,
But if you break the bloody glass you won't hold up the
    weather.

Helena Petrovna Blavatsky (1831–1891) was an occultist and founder of the
Theosophical Society. The Herring Industry Board was tasked with overseeing
UK herring fisheries.

1937

Missing Dates

WILLIAM EMPSON

Slowly the poison the whole blood stream fills.
It is not the effort nor the failure tires.
The waste remains, the waste remains and kills.

It is not your system or clear sight that mills
Down small to the consequence a life requires;
Slowly the poison the whole blood stream fills.

They bled an old dog dry yet the exchange rills
Of young dog blood gave but a month's desires;
The waste remains, the waste remains and kills.

It is the Chinese tombs and the slag hills
Using the soil, and not the soil retires.
Slowly the poison the whole blood stream fills.

Not to have fire is to be a skin that shrills.
The complete fire is death. From partial fires
The waste remains, the waste remains and kills.

It is the poems you have lost, the ills
From missing dates, at which the heart expires.
Slowly the poison the whole blood stream fills.
The waste remains, the waste remains and kills.

1937

The Purse-Seine

—◦—

ROBINSON JEFFERS

Our sardine fishermen work at night in the dark of the
 moon; daylight or moonlight
They could not tell where to spread the net, unable to see the
 phosphorescence of the shoals of fish.
They work northward from Monterey, coasting Santa Cruz; off
 New Year's Point or off Pigeon Point
The look-out man will see some lakes of milk-color light on
 the sea's night-purple; he points, and the helmsman
Turns the dark prow, the motorboat circles the gleaming shoal
 and drifts out her seine-net. They close the circle
And purse the bottom of the net, then with great labor haul it
 in.

                                        I cannot tell you
How beautiful the scene is, and a little terrible, then, when the
 crowded fish
Know they are caught, and wildly beat from one wall to the
 other of their closing destiny the phosphorescent
Water to a pool of flame, each beautiful slender body sheeted
 with flame, like a live rocket
A comet's tail wake of clear yellow flame; while outside the
 narrowing
Floats and cordage of the net great sea-lions come up to watch,
 sighing in the dark; the vast walls of night
Stand erect to the stars.

                        Lately I was looking from a night mountain-top
On a wide city, the colored splendor, galaxies of light: how
 could I help but recall the seine-net
Gathering the luminous fish? I cannot tell you how beautiful
 the city appeared, and a little terrible.
I thought, We have geared the machines and locked all together
 into interdependence; we have built the great cities; now

There is no escape. We have gathered vast populations incapable
    of free survival, insulated
From the strong earth, each person in himself helpless, on all
    dependent. The circle is closed, and the net
Is being hauled in. They hardly feel the cords drawing, yet they
    shine already. The inevitable mass-disasters
Will not come in our time nor in our children's, but we and
    our children
Must watch the net draw narrower, government take all powers
    – or revolution, and the new government
Take more than all, add to kept bodies kept souls – or anarchy,
    the mass-disasters.

                        These things are Progress;
Do you marvel our verse is troubled or frowning, while it
    keeps its reason? Or it lets go, lets the mood flow
In the manner of the recent young men into mere hysteria,
    splintered gleams, crackled laughter. But they are quite
    wrong.
There is no reason for amazement: surely one always knew that
    cultures decay, and life's end is death.

1938

Port Bou

STEPHEN SPENDER

As a child holds a pet
Arms clutching but with hands that do not join
And the coiled animal looks through the gap
To outer freedom animal air,
So the earth-and-rock arms of this small harbour
Embrace but do not encircle the sea
Which, through a gap, vibrates into the ocean,
Where dolphins swim and liners throb.
In the bright winter sunlight I sit on the parapet
Of a bridge; my circling arms rest on a newspaper
And my mind is empty as the glittering stone
While I search for an image
(The one written above) and the words (written above)
To set down the childish headlands of Port Bou.
A lorry halts beside me with creaking brakes
And I look up at warm downwards-looking faces
Of militia men staring at my (French) newspaper.
'How do they write of our struggle over the frontier?'
I hold out the paper, but they cannot read it,
They want speech and to offer cigarettes.
In their waving flag-like faces the war finds peace. The
    famished mouths
Of rusted carbines lean against their knees,
Like leaning, rust-coloured, fragile reeds.
Wrapped in cloth – old granny in a shawl –
The stuttering machine-gun rests.
They shout – salute back as the truck jerks forward
Over the vigorous hill, beyond the headland.
An old man passes, his mouth dribbling,
From three rusted teeth, he shoots out: 'pom-pom-pom'.
The children run after; and, more slowly, the women;
Clutching their skirts, trail over the horizon.

Now Port Bou is empty, for the firing practice.
I am left alone on the parapet at the exact centre
Above the river trickling through the gulley, like that old
    man's saliva.
The exact centre, solitary as the bull's eye in a target.
Nothing moves against the background of stage-scenery
    houses
Save the skirring mongrels. The firing now begins
Across the harbour mouth, from headland to headland,
White flecks of foam whipped by lead from the sea.
An echo spreads its cat-o'-nine tails
Thrashing the flanks of neighbour hills.
My circling arms rest on the newspaper,
My mind is paper on which dust and words sift,
I assure myself the shooting is only for practice
But I am the coward of cowards. The machine-gun stitches
My intestines with a needle, back and forth;
The solitary, spasmodic, white puffs from the carbines
Draw fear in white threads back and forth through my body.

A man travelling on a British passport experienced no difficulty in crossing the
French-Spanish border in 1938. But the entire Pyrenees border, from Irún in the
west to Port Bou in the east, was soon to become highly sensitive after the Nazi
Wehrmacht occupied France in 1940. It was in Port Bou that Walter Benjamin
committed suicide in September 1940.

1938

In the Theatre
(*A true incident*)

———————◆◇◆———————

DANNIE ABSE

'Only a local anaesthetic was given because of the blood pressure problem. The patient, thus, was fully awake throughout the operation. But in those days – in 1938, in Cardiff, when I was Lambert Rogers' dresser – they could not locate a brain tumour with precision. Too much normal brain tissue was destroyed as the surgeon searched for it, before he felt the resistance of it . . . all somewhat hit and miss. One operation I shall never forget . . .'
Dr Wilfred Abse

Sister saying – 'Soon you'll be back in the ward,'
sister thinking – 'Only two more on the list,'
the patient saying – 'Thank you, I feel fine';
small voices, small lies, nothing untoward,
though, soon, he would blink again and again
because of the fingers of Lambert Rogers,
rash as a blind man's, inside his soft brain.

If items of horror can make a man laugh
then laugh at this: one hour later, the growth
still undiscovered, ticking its own wild time;
more brain mashed because of the probe's braille path;
Lambert Rogers desperate, fingering still;
his dresser thinking, 'Christ! Two more on the list,
a cisternal puncture and a neural cyst.'

Then, suddenly, the cracked record in the brain,
a ventriloquist voice that cried, 'You sod,
leave my soul alone, leave my soul alone,' –
the patient's dummy lips moving to that refrain,
the patient's eyes too wide. And, shocked,
Lambert Rogers drawing out the probe
with nurses, students, sister, petrified.

'Leave my soul alone, leave my soul alone,'
that voice so arctic and that cry so odd
had nowhere else to go – till the antique
gramophone wound down and the words began
to blur and slow, '. . . leave . . . my . . . soul . . .
  alone . . .'
to cease at last when something other died.
And silence matched the silence under snow.

Lambert Rogers (1897–1961) was one of the most eminent surgeons of his time.
Dr Wilfred Abse (1914–2005) was the brother of poet Dannie Abse, who was
himself a chest physician till his retirement.

1938

Lapis Lazuli

W. B. YEATS

For Harry Clifton

I have heard that hysterical women say
They are sick of the palette and fiddle-bow,
Of poets that are always gay,
For everybody knows or else should know
That if nothing drastic is done
Aeroplane and Zeppelin will come out,
Pitch like King Billy bomb-balls in
Until the town lie beaten flat.

All perform their tragic play,
There struts Hamlet, there is Lear,
That's Ophelia, that Cordelia;
Yet they, should the last scene be there,
The great stage curtain about to drop,
If worthy their prominent part in the play,
Do not break up their lines to weep.
They know that Hamlet and Lear are gay;
Gaiety transfiguring all that dread.
All men have aimed at, found and lost;
Black out; Heaven blazing into the head:
Tragedy wrought to its uttermost.
Though Hamlet rambles and Lear rages,
And all the drop-scenes drop at once
Upon a hundred thousand stages,
It cannot grow by an inch or an ounce.

On their own feet they came, or on shipboard,
Camel-back, horse-back, ass-back, mule-back,
Old civilisations put to the sword.
Then they and their wisdom went to rack:
No handiwork of Callimachus,

Who handled marble as if it were bronze,
Made draperies that seemed to rise
When sea-wind swept the corner, stands;
His long lamp-chimney shaped like the stem
Of a slender palm, stood but a day;
All things fall and are built again,
And those that build them again are gay.

Two Chinamen, behind them a third,
Are carved in lapis lazuli,
Over them flies a long-legged bird,
A symbol of longevity;
The third, doubtless a serving-man,
Carries a musical instrument.

Every discoloration of the stone,
Every accidental crack or dent,
Seems a water-course or an avalanche,
Or lofty slope where it still snows
Though doubtless plum or cherry-branch
Sweetens the little half-way house
Those Chinamen climb towards, and I
Delight to imagine them seated there;
There, on the mountain and the sky,
On all the tragic scene they stare.
One asks for mournful melodies;
Accomplished fingers begin to play.
Their eyes mid many wrinkles, their eyes,
Their ancient, glittering eyes, are gay.

In 1935 Yeats was given a lapis lazuli carving by Harry Clifton, the last squire of Lytham Hall, Lancashire. Zeppelins, named from their designer, were airships, used in the First World War for bombing but otherwise for civilian purposes. By the time of Yeats's poem, the Hindenburg disaster of 1937 had signalled that their useful life was over. King Billy was William III of Orange, who became King of England at the Glorious Revolution of 1688, when James II was deposed. In Ireland he subdued Catholic forces loyal to James. Callimachus was a Greek sculptor of the fifth century B.C.

1938

The Glen of Silence

‹◇›

HUGH MacDIARMID

πέφρικα τὰν ὠλεσίοικον
θεόν οὐ θεοῖζ ὁμοίαν
Aeschylus, *The Seven Against Thebes*

By this cold shuddering fit of fear
My heart divines a presence here,
Goddess or ghost yclept;
Wrecker of homes . . .

G. M. Cookson's translation, *vide*
Four Plays of Aeschylus, p. 142

Where have I 'heard' a silence before
Like this that only a lone bird's cries
And the sound of a brawling burn today
Serve in this desolate glen but to emphasize?

Every doctor knows it – the stillness of foetal death,
The indescribable silence over the abdomen then!
A silence literally 'heard' because of the way
It stands out in the auscultation of the abdomen.

Here is an identical silence picked out
By a bickering burn and a lone bird's wheeple
– The foetal death in this great 'cleared' glen
Where the *fear-tholladh nan tighean* has done its foul work
– The tragedy of an unevolved people!

The Gaelic phrase '*fear-tholladh nan tighean*' means 'the destroyer of homes'.

1938

Penal Law

<o>

AUSTIN CLARKE

Burn Ovid with the rest. Lovers will find
A hedge-school for themselves and learn by heart
All that the clergy banish from the mind,
When hands are joined and head bows in the dark.

Presumably Ovid's *Amores* and *Ars Amatoria* are meant in the first line.

1938

The Pacifist

Hilaire Belloc

Pale Ebenezer thought it wrong to fight,
But Roaring Bill (who killed him) thought it right.

1938

Snow in Europe

<o>

DAVID GASCOYNE

Out of their slumber Europeans spun
Dense dreams: appeasement, miracle, glimpsed flash
Of a new golden era; but could not restrain
The vertical white weight that fell last night
And made their continent a blank.

Hush, says the sameness of the snow,
The Ural and the Jura now rejoin
The furthest Arctic's desolation. All is one;
Sheer monotone: plain, mountain; country, town:
Contours and boundaries no longer show.

The warring flags hang colourless a while;
Now midnight's icy zero feigns a truce
Between the signs and seasons, and fades out
All shots and cries. But when the great thaw comes,
How red shall be the melting snow, how loud the drums!

Christmas, 1938

1939

In Memory of W. B. Yeats
(d. Jan. 1939)

◦

W. H. AUDEN

I

He disappeared in the dead of winter:
The brooks were frozen, the airports almost deserted,
And snow disfigured the public statues;
The mercury sank in the mouth of the dying day.
What instruments we have agree
The day of his death was a dark cold day.

Far from his illness
The wolves ran on through the evergreen forests,
The peasant river was untempted by the fashionable quays;
By mourning tongues
The death of the poet was kept from his poems.

But for him it was his last afternoon as himself,
An afternoon of nurses and rumours;
The provinces of his body revolted,
The squares of his mind were empty,
Silence invaded the suburbs,
The current of his feeling failed; he became his admirers.

Now he is scattered among a hundred cities
And wholly given over to unfamiliar affections,
To find his happiness in another kind of wood
And be punished under a foreign code of conscience.
The words of a dead man
Are modified in the guts of the living.

But in the importance and noise of to-morrow
When the brokers are roaring like beasts on the floor of
    the Bourse,

And the poor have the sufferings to which they are fairly
   accustomed,
And each in the cell of himself is almost convinced of his
   freedom,
A few thousand will think of this day
As one thinks of a day when one did something slightly
   unusual.
What instruments we have agree
The day of his death was a dark cold day.

II

You were silly like us; your gift survived it all:
The parish of rich women, physical decay,
Yourself. Mad Ireland hurt you into poetry.
Now Ireland has her madness and her weather still,
For poetry makes nothing happen: it survives
In the valley of its making where executives
Would never want to tamper, flows on south
From ranches of isolation and the busy griefs,
Raw towns that we believe and die in; it survives,
A way of happening, a mouth.

III

Earth, receive an honoured guest:
William Yeats is laid to rest.
Let the Irish vessel lie
Emptied of its poetry.

In the nightmare of the dark
All the dogs of Europe bark,
And the living nations wait,
Each sequestered in its hate;

Intellectual disgrace
Stares from every human face,
And the seas of pity lie
Locked and frozen in each eye.

Follow, poet, follow right
To the bottom of the night,
With your unconstraining voice
Still persuade us to rejoice;

With the farming of a verse
Make a vineyard of the curse,
Sing of human unsuccess
In a rapture of distress;

In the deserts of the heart
Let the healing fountain start,
In the prison of his days
Teach the free man how to praise.

1939

The Last Words of My English Grandmother

WILLIAM CARLOS WILLIAMS

There were some dirty plates
and a glass of milk
beside her on a small table
near the rank, disheveled bed –

Wrinkled and nearly blind
she lay and snored
rousing with anger in her tones
to cry for food,

Gimme something to eat –
They're starving me –
I'm all right I won't go
to the hospital. No, no, no

Give me something to eat
Let me take you
to the hospital, I said
and after you are well

you can do as you please.
She smiled, Yes
you do what you please first
then I can do what I please –

Oh, oh, oh! she cried
as the ambulance men lifted
her to the stretcher –
Is this what you call

making me comfortable?
By now her mind was clear –
Oh you think you're smart
you young people,

she said, but I'll tell you
you don't know anything.
Then we started.
On the way

we passed a long row
of elms. She looked at them
awhile out of
the ambulance window and said,

What are all those
fuzzy-looking things out there?
Trees? Well, I'm tired
of them and rolled her head away.

1939

Five Bells

‹o›

KENNETH SLESSOR

Time that is moved by little fidget wheels
Is not my Time, the flood that does not flow.
Between the double and the single bell
Of a ship's hour, between a round of bells
From the dark warship riding there below,
I have lived many lives, and this one life
Of Joe, long dead, who lives between five bells.

Deep and dissolving verticals of light
Ferry the falls of moonshine down. Five bells
Coldly rung out in a machine's voice. Night and water
Pour to one rip of darkness, the Harbour floats
In air, the Cross hangs upside-down in water.

Why do I think of you, dead man, why thieve
These profitless lodgings from the flukes of thought
Anchored in Time? You have gone from earth,
Gone even from the meaning of a name;
Yet something's there, yet something forms its lips
And hits and cries against the ports of space,
Beating their sides to make its fury heard.

Are you shouting at me, dead man, squeezing your face
In agonies of speech on speechless panes?
Cry louder, beat the windows, bawl your name!

But I hear nothing, nothing . . . only bells,
Five bells, the bumpkin calculus of Time.
Your echoes die, your voice is dowsed by Life,
There's not a mouth can fly the pygmy strait –
Nothing except the memory of some bones
Long shoved away, and sucked away, in mud;

And unimportant things you might have done,
Or once I thought you did; but you forgot,
And all have now forgotten — looks and words
And slops of beer; your coat with buttons off,
Your gaunt chin and pricked eye, and raging tales
Of Irish kings and English perfidy,
And dirtier perfidy of publicans
Groaning to God from Darlinghurst.

Five bells.

Then I saw the road, I heard the thunder
Tumble, and felt the talons of the rain
The night we came to Moorebank in slab-dark,
So dark you bore no body, had no face,
But a sheer voice that rattled out of air
(As now you'd cry if I could break the glass),
A voice that spoke beside me in the bush,
Loud for a breath or bitten off by wind,
Of Milton, melons, and the Rights of Man,
And blowing flutes, and how Tahitian girls
Are brown and angry-tongued, and Sydney girls
Are white and angry-tongued, or so you'd found.
But all I heard was words that didn't join
So Milton became melons, melons girls,
And fifty mouths, it seemed, were out that night,
And in each tree an Ear was bending down,
Or something had just run, gone behind grass,
When, blank and bone-white, like a maniac's thought,
The naphtha-flash of lightning slit the sky,
Knifing the dark with deathly photographs.
There's not so many with so poor a purse
Or fierce a need, must fare by night like that,
Five miles in darkness on a country track,
But when you do, that's what you think.

Five bells.

In Melbourne, your appetite had gone,
Your angers too; they had been leeched away
By the soft archery of summer rains
And the sponge-paws of wetness, the slow damp
That stuck the leaves of living, snailed the mind,
And showed your bones, that had been sharp with rage,
The sodden ecstasies of rectitude.
I thought of what you'd written in faint ink,
Your journal with the sawn-off lock, that stayed behind
With other things you left, all without use,
All without meaning now, except a sign
That someone had been living who now was dead:
'At Labassa. Room 6 × 8
On top of the tower; because of this, very dark
And cold in winter. Everything has been stowed
Into this room – 500 books all shapes
And colours, dealt across the floor
And over sills and on the laps of chairs;
Guns, photoes of many differant things
And differant curioes that I obtained . . .'

In Sydney, by the spent aquarium-flare
Of penny gaslight on pink wallpaper,
We argued about blowing up the world,
But you were living backward, so each night
You crept a moment closer to the breast,
And they were living, all of them, those frames
And shapes of flesh that had perplexed your youth,
And most your father, the old man gone blind,
With fingers always round a fiddle's neck,
That graveyard mason whose fair monuments
And tablets cut with dreams of piety
Rest on the bosoms of a thousand men
Stacked bone by bone, in quiet astonishment
At cargoes they had never thought to bear,
These funeral-cakes of sweet and sculptured stone.

Where have you gone? The tide is over you,
The turn of midnight water's over you,
As Time is over you, and mystery,
And memory, the flood that does not flow.
You have no suburb, like those easier dead
In private berths of dissolution laid –
The tide goes over, the waves ride over you
And let their shadows down like shining hair,
But they are Water; and the sea-pinks bend
Like lilies in your teeth, but they are Weed;
And you are only part of an Idea.
I felt the wet push its black thumb-balls in,
The night you died, I felt your eardrums crack,
And the short agony, the longer dream,
The Nothing that was neither long nor short;
But I was bound, and could not go that way,
But I was blind, and could not feel your hand.
If I could find an answer, could only find
Your meaning, or could say why you were here
Who now are gone, what purpose gave you breath
Or seized it back, might I not hear your voice?

I looked out of my window in the dark
At waves with diamond quills and combs of light
That arched their mackerel-backs and smacked the sand
In the moon's drench, that straight enormous glaze,
And ships far off asleep, and Harbour-buoys
Tossing their fireballs wearily each to each,
And tried to hear your voice, but all I heard
Was a boat's whistle, and the scraping squeal
Of seabirds' voices far away, and bells,
Five bells. Five bells coldly ringing out.

Five bells.

The poem was written to commemorate the death by drowning of Slessor's friend Joe Lynch in Sydney harbour in 1927. An account was left of the death by Philip Lindsay in *I'd Live the Same Life Over*. 'Loaded with bottles, he had been off to some North Shore party with Frank when, tiring of the slow progress of the ferry – or perhaps of life itself – he had sprung up, saying that he'd swim there quicker, and, fully dressed, dived overboard. A deckhand had leaped in after him, and lifebelts had been thrown. They saw Joe, Frank said, wave cheerfully and strike out for Milsons Point; then he had vanished in the moon light. Perhaps a shark got him, or a mermaid – as some said – or the load of bottles in his greasy old raincoat tugged him to the fishes: no one can tell, for the body was never found.'

1939

Walking on the Cliff

<><>

ANDREW YOUNG

But for a sleepy gull that yawned
  And spread its wings and dropping disappeared
This evening would have dawned
  To the eternity my flesh has feared.

For too intent on a blackcap
  Perched like a miser on the yellow furze
High over Birling Gap,
  That sang 'Gold is a blessing not a curse,'

How near I was to stepping over
  The brink where the gull dropped to soar beneath,
While now safe as a lover
  I walk the cliff-edge arm in arm with Death.

1939

The Thieves

ROBERT GRAVES

Lovers in the act dispense
With such meum-tuum sense
As might warningly reveal
What they must not pick or steal,
And their nostrum is to say:
'I and you are both away.'

After, when they disentwine
You from me and yours from mine,
Neither can be certain who
Was that I whose mine was you.
To the act again they go
More completely not to know.

Theft is theft and raid is raid
Though reciprocally made.
Lovers, the conclusion is
Doubled sighs and jealousies
In a single heart that grieves
For lost honour among thieves.

1939

Meeting Point

Louis MacNeice

Time was away and somewhere else,
There were two glasses and two chairs
And two people with the one pulse
(Somebody stopped the moving stairs):
Time was away and somewhere else.

And they were neither up nor down;
The stream's music did not stop
Flowing through heather, limpid brown,
Although they sat in a coffee shop
And they were neither up nor down.

The bell was silent in the air
Holding its inverted poise –
Between the clang and clang a flower,
A brazen calyx of no noise:
The bell was silent in the air.

The camels crossed the miles of sand
That stretched around the cups and plates;
The desert was their own, they planned
To portion out the stars and dates:
The camels crossed the miles of sand.

Time was away and somewhere else.
The waiter did not come, the clock
Forgot them and the radio waltz
Came out like water from a rock:
Time was away and somewhere else.

Her fingers flicked away the ash
That bloomed again in tropic trees:
Not caring if the markets crash
When they had forests such as these,
Her fingers flicked away the ash.

God or whatever means the Good
Be praised that time can stop like this,
That what the heart has understood
Can verify in the body's peace
God or whatever means the Good.

Time was away and she was here
And life no longer what it was,
The bell was silent in the air
And all the room one glow because
Time was away and she was here.

April, 1939

1939

'Say this city has ten million souls'

◄◇►

W. H. AUDEN

Say this city has ten million souls,
Some are living in mansions, some are living in holes:
Yet there's no place for us, my dear, yet there's no place for us.

Once we had a country and we thought it fair,
Look in the atlas and you'll find it there:
We cannot go there now, my dear, we cannot go there now.

In the village churchyard there grows an old yew.
Every spring it blossoms anew:
Old passports can't do that, my dear, old passports can't do
    that.

The consul banged the table and said:
'If you've got no passport you're officially dead':
But we are still alive, my dear, but we are still alive.

Went to a committee; they offered me a chair;
Asked me politely to return next year:
But where shall we go to-day, my dear, but where shall we go
    to-day?

Came to a public meeting; the speaker got up and said:
'If we let them in, they will steal our daily bread':
He was talking of you and me, my dear, he was talking of you
    and me.

Thought I heard the thunder rumbling in the sky;
It was Hitler over Europe, saying: 'They must die';
We were in his mind, my dear, we were in his mind.

Saw a poodle in a jacket fastened with a pin.
Saw a door opened and a cat let in:
But they weren't German Jews, my dear, but they weren't
    German Jews.

Went down to the harbour and stood upon the quay,
Saw the fish swimming as if they were free:
Only ten feet away, my dear, only ten feet away.

Walked through a wood, saw the birds in the trees;
They had no politicians and sang at their ease:
They weren't the human race, my dear, they weren't the
   human race.

Dreamed I saw a building with a thousand floors,
A thousand windows and a thousand doors;
Not one of them was ours, my dear, not one of them was
   ours.

Stood on a great plain in the falling snow;
Ten thousand soldiers marched to and fro:
Looking for you and me, my dear, looking for you and me.

March 1939

IV

1940–1945

War

WHEN HITLER invaded Poland in September 1939, Great Britain and France honoured their obligations by declaring war on Germany. They then did nothing. The spirit of appeasement was deeply ingrained and, while Neville Chamberlain remained Prime Minister, not a bomb was dropped on German territory. The French were equally concerned not to provoke their aggressive neighbours, who were therefore allowed to lay Poland waste without distraction.

The Phoney – or Bore – War, as this period was known, was, for the general population, a time of increasing anxiety. John Betjeman gently satirised the conflicting emotions of non-combatants who rightly suspected that they would soon find themselves in the firing line, while for those called to arms there was the listlessness of life in camp, evoked by Alun Lewis in 'All day it has rained . . .', and the mind-numbing inanities of Basic Training, brilliantly captured in Henry Reed's 'Lessons of the War'. While language was reduced by drill sergeants to the lowest common denominator ('Whatever you do, don't call the bleeders sheep'), the poets themselves were wary of high-flown patriotic gestures. The headlines might demand 'Where are the war poets?' but no one was going to fall into the same trap as Rupert Brooke in 1914. As T. S. Eliot put it with authoritative asperity, what was required was 'Not the expression of collective emotion / Imperfectly reflected in the daily papers.'

The one person prepared to pull out the rhetorical stops was not a poet at all, but the man who replaced Chamberlain. When Germany finally turned on France in May 1940, there was little resistance. As the demoralised French army was swept aside, and British troops retreated to the beaches of Dunkirk, the country turned to Winston Churchill, who warned 'I have nothing to offer but blood, toil, tears and sweat', while insisting, 'we shall never surrender'. As Britain stood alone against the might of Hitler's war machine, which was gearing up to invade, Churchill depended on the English language as the last bulwark against barbarism, with speech after speech designed to lift morale and shame defeatists. Immortalising the young pilots who saw off the Luftwaffe in the Battle of Britain – 'Never in the field of human conflict was so much owed by so many to so few' – he called on his beleaguered countrymen to stand firm against the devastation that Hitler's bombers proceeded to unleash: 'Let us . . . brace ourselves to our duties, and so bear ourselves that, if the British Empire and its commonwealth lasts for a thousand years, men will say, "This was their finest hour".' The German bombing campaign, beginning by targeting docks and factories, soon became an open attempt to batter the population into submission. H. D.'s 'The Walls Do Not Fall' viewed the conflict as an archetypal drama, setting her experience of London during the Blitz alongside the historical examples of cities that had resisted the onslaught of their enemies. Another poet in London during the bombing was Eliot, widely seen since the death of Yeats as the foremost poet of the English language. He carried on his work at Faber and Faber, still publishing books despite the paper shortage, and played his part in the war effort as a night-time fire watcher during the Blitz. His own creative efforts were focused on completing the meditative masterpieces ultimately gathered as *Four Quartets*. It would be crude simplification to say that they represented a celebration of what the war was being fought for, but, as 'East Coker' demonstrates, Eliot is concerned with the timeless continuities of English life, and the pursuit of a spiritual path completely antithetical to Nazism.

There were no Allied ground troops in mainland Europe, but other theatres of war were busy – North Africa, where the brilliant General Rommel swept from victory to victory; the Far East, where disaster threatened; and the Atlantic, across which the convoys ran the gauntlet of the U-boats to keep supplies of food and military equipment coming in from America. The war changed dramatically on 22 June 1941, when Hitler unleashed Operation Barbarossa on Russia, catching his co-signatory to the Nazi-Soviet non-aggression pact completely by surprise. The largest army ever amassed in European history (almost 3.6 million soldiers) rolled east, routing Stalin's

ill-prepared forces and ultimately reaching the outskirts of Moscow. Six months
later, the Japanese inflicted a similar shock with their pre-emptive air strike
on the American naval base Pearl Harbour. The British (fighting with their
colonial peoples) now had two mighty allies in the global conflagration. In
the short term, though, they benefitted little. A Japanese army fought its way
down the Malay peninsula and, after a manoeuvre of great military daring,
forced the fall of supposedly impregnable Singapore in February 1942, with
the ignominious surrender of 60,000 British, Australian and Indian troops.

A sense of the dispirited mood of the times is caught in Roy
Fuller's 'Spring 1942', and it wasn't until October of that year that a
much-needed victory was recorded. After a steady retreat across North
Africa, British forces made a stand under their newly appointed general,
Bernard Montgomery, outside El Alamein. With an advantage of numbers
and firepower (the epic battle of Stalingrad was draining the German
war machine), Montgomery broke through the Axis lines to achieve the
first land victory of the war. Churchill authorised the ringing of the
church bells which had been silenced since the hostilities broke out. A
young tank officer, Keith Douglas, served in the North Africa campaign,
and wrote an excellent memoir about his experiences, *Alamein to Zem
Zem*. In tank warfare you only saw your enemy when he surrendered
or when, as in 'Vergissmeinnicht', you came upon his rotting corpse.
Douglas was killed himself in Normandy a year later, leaving arguably
the best war poems of any Englishman in the conflict.

The entry of the Russians and Americans into the war had trans-
formed the conflict, and from the great turning point of Stalingrad the
outcome could not be in doubt. In the Pacific theatre, the epic struggle
against the Japanese took a heavy toll in casualties. Randall Jarrell saw
the pilots' war from close quarters, while Robinson Jeffers achieved an
extraordinary overview of the whole Pacific theatre in his astonishing
poem, 'The Eye'. In Europe, the western Allies at last mounted their
long-awaited invasion in June 1944, and the weeks after the Normandy
landings on D Day saw ferocious fighting. Louis Simpson's 'Carentan O
Carentan' is a counterpart to Henry Reed's poem in its eye for natural
beauty and its consciousness of lovers, and with its *faux-naïf* trimeter it
captures the terrible arrival of death in a place that might be idyllic. From
Normandy to Berlin, a ten-month ordeal of slaughter still stretched ahead,

but the European war finally ended on 8 May 1945, with Hitler dead in the bunker below his Chancellery and the thousand-year Reich in ruins.

In addition to bitter fighting, the advancing Allied armies had the horrific job of liberating the concentration camps. The Russians entered Auschwitz in January. A similar shock awaited British forces when they liberated Bergen-Belsen in April. Phillip Whitfield, a Captain in the Medical Corps, was confronted by 10,000 unburied corpses there, while of the 38,500 survivors as many as 28,000 died soon afterwards. Churchill called the Nazis' Final Solution, in which six million Jews and others were systematically murdered on an industrial scale, 'the greatest and most horrible crime ever committed in the whole history of the world'. A different kind of horror exploded above the cities of Hiroshima and Nagasaki in August 1945. In addition to destroying two cities, and swiftly ending Japan's stubborn resistance, the atomic bombs put mankind on notice of imminent extinction, under the threat of which all subsequent generations have lived. The Nazi genocide, and the shadow of the mushroom cloud, have transformed our understanding of what might be meant by human civilisation.

The Second World War was a war of fearful statistics, with the Soviet Union alone totalling military and civilian losses of between twenty and twenty-five million. Just as the annihilation of the six million, and the destruction of Hiroshima and Nagasaki, defy faith in the meaning of poetry, so too the sheer scale of death, suffering and loss in six short years is not easily amenable to words. But the poets nonetheless found ways of bearing witness to the enduring qualities of the human spirit. Alan Ross on an Arctic convoy picks up fortunate survivors from the icy waters. John Magee captures the exhilarating freedom of the dangerous skies in his immensely popular poem 'High Flight'. E. J. Scovell gives voice to one of the thousands displaced by the war's progress across Europe. Dorothy Parker writes an uncharacteristically tender poem absolving the young men sent far away of the inevitable infidelities of wartime. Claude McKay has no hesitation in reminding the United States of its own hypocrisies and imperfections. With peace at last restored, Dylan Thomas produces his compelling celebration of a magical Welsh childhood in 'Fern Hill'. And, many years later, Jeffrey Harrison's 'Sketch' points to a more promising future in which the wounds of war might even heal into friendship.

1940

Lessons of the War

HENRY REED

To Alan Michell
Vixi duellis nuper idoneus
Et militavi non sine gloria

I. NAMING OF PARTS

To-day we have naming of parts. Yesterday,
We had daily cleaning. And to-morrow morning,
We shall have what to do after firing. But to-day,
To-day we have naming of parts. Japonica
Glistens like coral in all of the neighbouring gardens,
    And to-day we have naming of parts.

This is the lower sling swivel. And this
Is the upper sling swivel, whose use you will see,
When you are given your slings. And this is the piling
    swivel,
Which in your case you have not got. The branches
Hold in the gardens their silent, eloquent gestures,
    Which in our case we have not got.

This is the safety-catch, which is always released
With an easy flick of the thumb. And please do not let
    me
See anyone using his finger. You can do it quite easy
If you have any strength in your thumb. The blossoms
Are fragile and motionless, never letting anyone see
    Any of them using their finger.

And this you can see is the bolt. The purpose of this
Is to open the breech, as you see. We can slide it
Rapidly backwards and forwards: we call this
Easing the spring. And rapidly backwards and forwards
The early bees are assaulting and fumbling the flowers:
   They call it easing the Spring.

They call it easing the Spring: it is perfectly easy
If you have any strength in your thumb: like the bolt,
And the breech, and the cocking-piece, and the point of
   balance,
Which in our case we have not got; and the almond-
   blossom
Silent in all of the gardens and the bees going backwards
   and forwards,
   For to-day we have naming of parts.

II. JUDGING DISTANCES

Not only how far away, but the way that you say it
Is very important. Perhaps you may never get
The knack of judging a distance, but at least you know
How to report on a landscape: the central sector,
The right of arc and that, which we had last Tuesday,
   And at least you know

That maps are of time, not place, so far as the army
Happens to be concerned – the reason being,
Is one which need not delay us. Again, you know
There are three kinds of tree, three only, the fir and the
   poplar,
And those which have bushy tops to; and lastly
   That things only seem to be things.

A barn is not called a barn, to put it more plainly,
Or a field in the distance, where sheep may be safely
   grazing.
You must never be over-sure. You must say, when reporting:
At five o'clock in the central sector is a dozen

Of what appear to be animals; whatever you do,
  Don't call the bleeders *sheep*.

I am sure that's quite clear; and suppose, for the sake of
    example,
The one at the end, asleep, endeavours to tell us
What he sees over there to the west, and how far away,
After first having come to attention. There to the west,
On the fields of summer the sun and the shadows bestow
  Vestments of purple and gold.

The still white dwellings are like a mirage in the heat,
And under the swaying elms a man and a woman
Lie gently together. Which is, perhaps, only to say
That there is a row of houses to the left of arc,
And that under some poplars a pair of what appear to be
    humans
  Appear to be loving.

Well that, for an answer, is what we might rightly call
Moderately satisfactory only, the reason being,
Is that two things have been omitted, and those are
    important.
The human beings, now: in what direction are they,
And how far away, would you say? And do not forget
  There may be dead ground in between.

There may be dead ground in between; and I may not
    have got
The knack of judging a distance; I will only venture
A guess that perhaps between me and the apparent lovers,
(Who, incidentally, appear by now to have finished,)
At seven o'clock from the houses, is roughly a distance
  Of about one year and a half.

The epigraph, from Horace (*Odes* III, 26), translates: 'Lately I have lived in the midst of battles, creditably enough, and have soldiered, not without glory.' In the Latin, Reed has substituted the word '*duellis*' (battles) for '*puellis*' (girls).

1940

'All day it has rained . . .'

ALUN LEWIS

All day it has rained, and we on the edge of the moors
Have sprawled in our bell-tents, moody and dull as boors,
Groundsheets and blankets spread on the muddy ground
And from the first grey wakening we have found
No refuge from the skirmishing fine rain
And the wind that made the canvas heave and flap
And the taut wet guy-ropes ravel out and snap.
All day the rain has glided, wave and mist and dream,
Drenching the gorse and heather, a gossamer stream
Too light to stir the acorns that suddenly
Snatched from their cups by the wild south-westerly
Pattered against the tent and our upturned dreaming faces.
And we stretched out, unbuttoning our braces,
Smoking a Woodbine, darning dirty socks,
Reading the Sunday papers – I saw a fox
And mentioned it in the note I scribbled home; –
And we talked of girls, and dropping bombs on Rome,
And thought of the quiet dead and the loud celebrities
Exhorting us to slaughter, and the herded refugees;
– Yet thought softly, morosely of them, and as indifferently
As of ourselves or those whom we
For years have loved, and will again
Tomorrow maybe love; but now it is the rain
Possesses us entirely, the twilight and the rain.
And I can remember nothing dearer or more to my heart
Than the child I watched in the woods on Saturday
Shaking down burning chestnuts for the schoolyard's merry
    play,

Or the shaggy patient dog who followed me
By Sheet and Steep and up the wooded scree
To the Shoulder o' Mutton where Edward Thomas
    brooded long
On death and beauty – till a bullet stopped his song.

A stone in memory of Edward Thomas was placed on Shoulder of Mutton hill, near his home in Hampshire, in 1937.

1940

In Westminster Abbey

JOHN BETJEMAN

Let me take this other glove off
  As the *vox humana* swells,
And the beauteous fields of Eden
  Bask beneath the Abbey bells.
Here, where England's statesmen lie,
Listen to a lady's cry.

Gracious Lord, oh bomb the Germans.
  Spare their women for Thy Sake,
And if that is not too easy
  We will pardon Thy Mistake.
But, gracious Lord, whate'er shall be,
Don't let anyone bomb me.

Keep our Empire undismembered
  Guide our Forces by Thy Hand,
Gallant blacks from far Jamaica,
  Honduras and Togoland;
Protect them Lord in all their fights,
And, even more, protect the whites.

Think of what our Nation stands for,
  Books from Boots' and country lanes,
Free speech, free passes, class distinction,
  Democracy and proper drains.
Lord, put beneath Thy special care
One-eighty-nine Cadogan Square.

Although dear Lord I am a sinner,
  I have done no major crime;
Now I'll come to Evening Service
  Whensoever I have the time.

So, Lord, reserve for me a crown,
And do not let my shares go down.

I will labour for Thy Kingdom,
    Help our lads to win the war,
Send white feathers to the cowards
    Join the Women's Army Corps,
Then wash the Steps around Thy Throne
In the Eternal Safety Zone.

Now I feel a little better,
    What a treat to hear Thy Word,
Where the bones of leading statesmen
    Have so often been interr'd.
And now, dear Lord, I cannot wait
Because I have a luncheon date.

1940

The Entertainment of War

◄◊►

ROY FISHER

I saw the garden where my aunt had died
And her two children and a woman from next door;
It was like a burst pod filled with clay.

A mile away in the night I had heard the bombs
Sing and then burst themselves between cramped houses
With bright soft flashes and sounds like banging doors;

The last of them crushed the four bodies into the ground,
Scattered the shelter, and blasted my uncle's corpse
Over the housetop and into the street beyond.

Now the garden lay stripped and stale; the iron shelter
Spread out its separate petals around a smooth clay saucer,
Small, and so tidy it seemed nobody had ever been there.

When I saw it, the house was blown clean by blast and care:
Relations had already torn out the new fireplaces;
My cousin's pencils lasted me several years.

And in his office notepad that was given me
I found solemn drawings in crayon of blondes without
    dresses.
In his lifetime I had not known him well.

Those were the things I noticed at ten years of age:
Those, and the four hearses outside our house,
The chocolate cakes, and my classmates' half-shocked envy.

But my grandfather went home from the mortuary
And for five years tried to share the noises in his skull,
Then he walked out and lay under a furze-bush to die.

When my father came back from identifying the daughter
He asked us to remind him of her mouth.
We tried. He said 'I think it was the one'.

These were marginal people I had met only rarely
And the end of the whole household meant that no grief was
    seen;
Never have people seemed so absent from their own deaths.

This bloody episode of four whom I could understand better
    dead
Gave me something I needed to keep a long story moving;
I had no pain of it; can find no scar even now.

But had my belief in the fiction not been thus buoyed up
I might, in the sigh and strike of the next night's bombs
Have realized a little what they meant, and for the first time
    been afraid.

1940

Native-born
◄◦►

EVE LANGLEY

In a white gully among fungus red
  Where serpent logs lay hissing at the air,
I found a kangaroo. Tall, dewy, dead,
  So like a woman, she lay silent there.
Her ivory hands, black-nailed, crossed on her breast,
  Her skin of sun and moon hues, fallen cold.
Her brown eyes lay like rivers come to rest
  And death had made her black mouth harsh and old.
Beside her in the ashes I sat deep
  And mourned for her, but had no native song
To flatter death, while down the ploughlands steep
  Dark young Camelli whistled loud and long,
'Love, liberty, and Italy are all.'
  Broad golden was his breast against the sun.
I saw his wattle whip rise high and fall
  Across the slim mare's flanks, and one by one
She drew the furrows after her as he
  Flapped like a gull behind her, climbing high,
Chanting his oaths and lashing soundingly,
  While from the mare came once a blowing sigh.
The dew upon the kangaroo's white side
  Had melted. Time was whirling high around,
Like the thin wommera, and from heaven wide
  He, the bull-roarer, made continuous sound.
Incarnate lay my country by my hand:
  Her long hot days, bushfires, and speaking rains,
Her mornings of opal and the copper band
  Of smoke around the sunlight on the plains.

Globed in fire-bodies the meat-ants ran
  To taste her flesh and linked us as we lay,
For ever Australian, listening to a man
  From careless Italy, swearing at our day.
When, golden-lipped, the eagle-hawks came down
  Hissing and whistling to eat of lovely her,
And the blowflies with their shields of purple brown
  Plied hatching to and fro across her fur,
I burnt her with the logs, and stood all day
  Among the ashes, pressing home the flame
Till woman, logs, and dreams were scorched away,
  And native with night, that land from whence they
  came.

1940

East Coker

T. S. Eliot

I

In my beginning is my end. In succession
Houses rise and fall, crumble, are extended,
Are removed, destroyed, restored, or in their place
Is an open field, or a factory, or a by-pass.
Old stone to new building, old timber to new fires,
Old fires to ashes, and ashes to the earth
Which is already flesh, fur and faeces,
Bone of man and beast, cornstalk and leaf.
Houses rise and die: there is a time for building
And a time for living and for generation
And a time for the wind to break the loosened pane
And to shake the wainscot where the field-mouse trots
And to shake the tattered arras woven with a silent motto.

In my beginning is my end. Now the light falls
Across the open field, leaving the deep lane
Shuttered with branches, dark in the afternoon,
Where you lean against a bank while a van passes,
And the deep lane insists on the direction
Into the village, in the electric heat
Hypnotised. In a warm haze the sultry light
Is absorbed, not refracted, by grey stone.
The dahlias sleep in the empty silence.
Wait for the early owl.

                    In that open field
If you do not come too close, if you do not come too
    close,
On a summer midnight, you can hear the music
Of the weak pipe and the little drum
And see them dancing around the bonfire

The association of man and woman
In daunsinge, signifying matrimonie –
A dignified and commodious sacrament.
Two and two, necessarye coniunction,
Holding eche other by the hand or the arm
Whiche betokeneth concorde. Round and round the fire
Leaping through the flames, or joined in circles,
Rustically solemn or in rustic laughter
Lifting heavy feet in clumsy shoes,
Earth feet, loam feet, lifted in country mirth
Mirth of those long since under earth
Nourishing the corn. Keeping time,
Keeping the rhythm in their dancing
As in their living in the living seasons
The time of the seasons and the constellations
The time of milking and the time of harvest
The time of the coupling of man and woman
And that of beasts. Feet rising and falling.
Eating and drinking. Dung and death.

  Dawn points, and another day
Prepares for heat and silence. Out at sea the dawn wind
Wrinkles and slides. I am here
Or there, or elsewhere. In my beginning.

II

What is the late November doing
With the disturbance of the spring
And creatures of the summer heat,
And snowdrops writhing under feet
And hollyhocks that aim too high
Red into grey and tumble down
Late roses filled with early snow?
Thunder rolled by the rolling stars
Simulates triumphal cars
Deployed in constellated wars
Scorpion fights against the Sun
Until the Sun and Moon go down

Comets weep and Leonids fly
Hunt the heavens and the plains
Whirled in a vortex that shall bring
The world to that destructive fire
Which burns before the ice-cap reigns.

That was a way of putting it – not very satisfactory:
A periphrastic study in a worn-out poetical fashion,
Leaving one still with the intolerable wrestle
With words and meanings. The poetry does not matter.
It was not (to start again) what one had expected.
What was to be the value of the long looked forward to,
Long hoped for calm, the autumnal serenity
And the wisdom of age? Had they deceived us,
Or deceived themselves, the quiet-voiced elders,
Bequeathing us merely a receipt for deceit?
The serenity only a deliberate hebetude,
The wisdom only the knowledge of dead secrets
Useless in the darkness into which they peered
Or from which they turned their eyes. There is, it seems to
    us,
At best, only a limited value
In the knowledge derived from experience.
The knowledge imposes a pattern, and falsifies,
For the pattern is new in every moment
And every moment is a new and shocking
Valuation of all we have been. We are only undeceived
Of that which, deceiving, could no longer harm.
In the middle, not only in the middle of the way
But all the way, in a dark wood, in a bramble,
On the edge of a grimpen, where is no secure foothold,
And menaced by monsters, fancy lights,
Risking enchantment. Do not let me hear
Of the wisdom of old men, but rather of their folly,
Their fear of fear and frenzy, their fear of possession,
Of belonging to another, or to others, or to God.
The only wisdom we can hope to acquire
Is the wisdom of humility: humility is endless.

The houses are all gone under the sea.

The dancers are all gone under the hill.

III

O dark dark dark. They all go into the dark,
The vacant interstellar spaces, the vacant into the vacant,
The captains, merchant bankers, eminent men of letters.
The generous patrons of art, the statesmen and the rulers,
Distinguished civil servants, chairman of many committees,
Industrial lords and petty contractors, all go into the dark,
And dark the Sun and Moon, and the Almanach de Gotha
And the Stock Exchange Gazette, the Directory of Directors,
And cold the sense and lost the motive of action.
And we all go with them, into the silent funeral,
Nobody's funeral, for there is no one to bury.
I said to my soul, be still, and let the dark come upon you
Which shall be the darkness of God. As, in a theatre,
The lights are extinguished, for the scene to be changed
With a hollow rumble of wings, with a movement of
    darkness on darkness,
And we know that the hills and the trees, the distant
    panorama
And the bold imposing façade are all being rolled away –
Or as, when an underground train, in the tube, stops too
    long between stations
And the conversation rises and slowly fades into silence
And you see behind every face the mental emptiness deepen
Leaving only the growing terror of nothing to think about;
Or when, under ether, the mind is conscious but conscious
    of nothing –
I said to my soul, be still, and wait without hope
For hope would be hope for the wrong thing; wait without
    love
For love would be love of the wrong thing; there is yet faith
But the faith and the love and the hope are all in the
    waiting.
Wait without thought, for you are not ready for thought:

So the darkness shall be the light, and the stillness the
    dancing.
Whisper of running streams, and winter lightning.
The wild thyme unseen and the wild strawberry,
The laughter in the garden, echoed ecstasy
Not lost, but requiring, pointing to the agony
Of death and birth.
                              You say I am repeating
Something I have said before. I shall say it again.
Shall I say it again? In order to arrive there,
To arrive where you are, to get from where you are not,
    You must go by a way wherein there is no ecstasy.
In order to arrive at what you do not know
    You must go by a way which is the way of ignorance.
In order to possess what you do not possess
    You must go by the way of dispossession.
In order to arrive at what you are not
    You must go through the way in which you are not.
And what you do not know is the only thing you know
And what you own is what you do not own
And where you are is where you are not.

                              IV

The wounded surgeon plies the steel
That questions the distempered part;
Beneath the bleeding hands we feel
The sharp compassion of the healer's art
Resolving the enigma of the fever chart.

Our only health is the disease
If we obey the dying nurse
Whose constant care is not to please
But to remind of our, and Adam's curse,
And that, to be restored, our sickness must grow worse.

The whole earth is our hospital
Endowed by the ruined millionaire,
Wherein, if we do well, we shall
Die of the absolute paternal care
That will not leave us, but prevents us everywhere.

The chill ascends from feet to knees,
The fever sings in mental wires.
If to be warmed, then I must freeze
And quake in frigid purgatorial fires
Of which the flame is roses, and the smoke is briars.

The dripping blood our only drink,
The bloody flesh our only food:
In spite of which we like to think
That we are sound, substantial flesh and blood –
Again, in spite of that, we call this Friday good.

V

So here I am, in the middle way, having had twenty years –
Twenty years largely wasted, the years of *l'entre deux guerres* –
Trying to learn to use words, and every attempt
Is a wholly new start, and a different kind of failure
Because one has only learnt to get the better of words
For the thing one no longer has to say, or the way in which
One is no longer disposed to say it. And so each venture
Is a new beginning, a raid on the inarticulate
With shabby equipment always deteriorating
In the general mess of imprecision of feeling,
Undisciplined squads of emotion. And what there is to
    conquer
By strength and submission, has already been discovered
Once or twice, or several times, by men whom one cannot
    hope
To emulate – but there is no competition –
There is only the fight to recover what has been lost
And found and lost again and again: and now, under
    conditions
That seem unpropitious. But perhaps neither gain nor loss.

For us, there is only the trying. The rest is not our business.
Home is where one starts from. As we grow older
The world becomes stranger, the pattern more complicated
Of dead and living. Not the intense moment
Isolated, with no before and after,
But a lifetime burning in every moment
And not the lifetime of one man only
But of old stones that cannot be deciphered.
There is a time for the evening under starlight,
A time for the evening under lamplight
(The evening with the photograph album).
Love is most nearly itself
When here and now cease to matter.
Old men ought to be explorers
Here and there does not matter
We must be still and still moving
Into another intensity
For a further union, a deeper communion
Through the dark cold and the empty desolation,
The wave cry, the wind cry, the vast waters
Of the petrel and the porpoise. In my end is my beginning.

Eliot visited East Coker in Somerset, from which his own English ancestors had left for the colonies in America in 1669, in 1937. He was later buried there, in the cemetery at St Michael's church. The sources of the poem, poetic and theological, are complex, but its central lamentation of mortality, and its hope for redemption, are expressed with a lambent lucidity.

1941

We Must Have a Speech from a Minister

NOËL COWARD

We must have a speech from a minister,
It's what we've been trained to expect.
We're faced with defeat and despair and disaster,
We couldn't be losing our Colonies faster,
We know that we haven't the guns to defend
The 'Mermaid' at Rye, or the pier at Southend;
You have no idea how we've grown to depend
In hours of crisis
On whacking great slices
Of verbal evasion and dissimulation,
A nice Governmental appeal to the Nation
We'd listen to gladly with awe and respect,
We know that the moment is sinister
And what we've been earnestly trained to expect,
When such moments we reach,
Is a lovely long speech,
(Not a comment or chat
About this, about that)
But a really long speech,
An extremely long speech,
An ambiguous speech from a minister.

We must have a speech from a minister,
We don't mind a bit who it is
As long as we get that drab lack of conviction,
That dismal, self-conscious, inadequate diction.
We find Mr Churchill a trifle uncouth;
His ill-repressed passion for telling the truth.
His 'Eye for an Eye' and his 'Tooth for a Tooth'
Is violent, too snappy,
We'd be far more happy

With some old Appeaser's inert peroration,
We'd give ourselves up to complete resignation,
Refusing to worry or get in a frizz.
We know that the moment is sinister,
We've already said we don't mind who it is,
We'd fight on the beach
For a really long speech,
(Not a breezy address,
Or a postscript on Hess)
But a lovely long speech,
A supremely long speech,
An embarrassing speech from a minister.

Hess was Rudolf Hess (1894–1987), Hitler's deputy, who flew to Scotland on 10 May 1941, apparently under the impression that he could negotiate peace between Germany and Britain. He remained a prisoner for the rest of his life.

1941

High Flight
<o>
JOHN MAGEE

Oh! I have slipped the surly bonds of Earth
And danced the skies on laughter-silvered wings;
Sunward I've climbed, and joined the tumbling mirth
Of sun-split clouds – and done a hundred things
You have not dreamed of – wheeled and soared and swung
High in the sunlit silence. Hov'ring there,
I've chased the shouting wind along, and flung
My eager craft through footless halls of air . . .
Up, up the long, delirious burning blue
I've topped the wind-swept heights with easy grace,
Where never lark, or even eagle flew –
And, while with silent, lifting mind I've trod
The high untrespassed sanctity of space,
Put out my hand and touched the face of God.

1941

from R.A.F.

———◦———

H.D.

I

He said, I'm just out of hospital,
but I'm still flying.

I answered, *of course*,
angry, prescient, knowing

what fire lay behind his wide stare,
what fury of desire

impelled him,
pretending not to notice

his stammer
and that now, in his agony to express himself

his speech failed
altogether,

and his eyes seemed to gather
in their white-heat,

all the fires of the wind,
fire of sleet,

snow like white-fire pellets,
congealed radium, planets

like snow-flakes:
and I thought,

the sun
is only a round platform

for his feet
to rest upon.

1941

Escape

—◦—

W. R. RODGERS

The roads of Europe are running away from the war,
Running fast over the mined bridges and past the men
Waiting there, with watch, ready to maim and arrest them,
And strong overhead the long snorings of the planes' tracks
Are stretching like rafters from end to end of their power.
Turn back, you who want to escape or want to forget
The ruin of all your regards. You will be more free
At the thoughtless centre of slaughter than you would be
Standing chained to the telephone-end while the world
  cracks.

1941

House and Land

—◇—

ALLEN CURNOW

Wasn't this the site, asked the historian,
Of the original homestead?
Couldn't tell you, said the cowman;
I just live here, he said,
Working for old Miss Wilson
Since the old man's been dead.

Moping under the bluegums
The dog trailed his chain
From the privy as far as the fowlhouse
And back to the privy again,
Feeling the stagnant afternoon
Quicken with the smell of rain.

There sat old Miss Wilson,
With her pictures on the wall,
The baronet uncle, mother's side,
And the one she called The Hall;
Taking tea from a silver pot
For fear the house might fall.

People in the *colonies*, she said,
Can't quite understand . . .
Why, from Waiau to the mountains
It was all father's land.

She's all of eighty said the cowman,
Down at the milking-shed.
I'm leaving here next winter.
Too bloody quiet, he said.

The spirit of exile, wrote the historian,
Is strong in the people still.
He reminds me rather, said Miss Wilson,
Of Harriet's youngest, Will.

The cowman, home from the shed, went drinking
With the rabbiter home from the hill.

The sensitive nor'west afternoon
Collapsed, and the rain came;
The dog crept into his barrel
Looking lost and lame.
But you can't attribute to either
Awareness of what great gloom
Stands in a land of settlers
With never a soul at home.

1941

What are Years?

⟨o⟩

MARIANNE MOORE

What is our innocence,
what is our guilt? All are
    naked, none is safe. And whence
is courage: the unanswered question,
the resolute doubt, –
dumbly calling, deafly listening – that
in misfortune, even death,
        encourages others
        and in its defeat, stirs

    the soul to be strong? He
sees deep and is glad, who
    accedes to mortality
and in his imprisonment rises
upon himself as
the sea in a chasm, struggling to be
free and unable to be,
        in its surrendering
        finds its continuing.

    So he who strongly feels,
behaves. The very bird,
    grown taller as he sings, steels
his form straight up. Though he is captive,
his mighty singing
says, satisfaction is a lowly
thing, how pure a thing is joy.
        This is mortality,
        this is eternity.

1941

To an Anti-Semite

CARL RAKOSI

So you fought for the Jews
in the last war
and have become a patriot again!

Why you thick-skulled liar
as impossible to offend
as to trust with an order,

you were never within
three thousand miles
of the front.

You fought the war
in Camp McKinley,
cleaning stables

and stealing out
into the moonlight
with the kitchen maids.

And now I find you
trying to drive the Jews
and Communists out of America!

1942

Spring 1942

◄○►

ROY FULLER

Once as we were sitting by
The failing sun, the thickening air,
The chaplain came against the sky
And quietly took a vacant chair.

And under the tobacco smoke:
'Freedom,' he said, and 'Good' and 'Duty.'
We stared as though a savage spoke.
The scene took on a singular beauty.

And we made no reply to that
Obscure, remote communication,
But only stared at where the flat
Meadow dissolved in vegetation.

And thought: O sick, insatiable
And constant lust; O death, our future;
O revolution in the whole
Of human use of man and nature!

1942

Survivors

ALAN ROSS

With the ship burning in their eyes
The white faces float like refuse
In the darkness – the water screwing
Oily circles where the hot steel lies.

They clutch with fingers frozen into claws
The lifebelts thrown from a destroyer,
And see, between the future's doors,
The gasping entrance of the sea.

Taken on board as many as lived, who
Had a mind left for living and the ocean,
They open eyes running with surf,
Heavy with the grey ghosts of explosion.

The meaning is not yet clear,
Where daybreak died in the smile –
And the mouth remained stiff
And grinning, stupid for a while.

But soon they joke, easy and warm,
As men will who have died once
Yet somehow were able to find their way –
Muttering about their food and pay.

Later, sleepless at night, the brain spinning
With cracked images, they won't forget
The confusion and the oily dead,
Nor yet the casual knack of living.

Ross joined the Royal Navy in 1941, and served for two years in the Arctic
convoys, aboard destroyers escorting supply ships to the Soviet Union. In
December 1942 he came close to death aboard HMS *Onslow*, in the Battle of
the Barents Sea.

1942

from The Walls Do Not Fall
——◄◇►——
H. D.

I

An incident here and there,
and rails gone (for guns)
from your (and my) old town square:

mist and mist-grey, no colour,
still the Luxor bee, chick and hare
pursue unalterable purpose

in green, rose-red, lapis;
they continue to prophesy
from the stone papyrus:

there, as here, ruin opens
the tomb, the temple; enter,
there as here, there are no doors:

the shrine lies open to the sky,
the rain falls, here, there
sand drifts; eternity endures:

ruin everywhere, yet as the fallen roof
leaves the sealed room
open to the air,

so, through our desolation,
thoughts stir, inspiration stalks us
through gloom:

unaware, Spirit announces the Presence;
shivering overtakes us,
as of old, Samuel:

trembling at a known street-corner,
we know not nor are known;
the Pythian pronounces – we pass on

to another cellar, to another sliced wall
where poor utensils show
like rare objects in a museum;

Pompeii has nothing to teach us,
we know crack of volcanic fissure,
slow flow of terrible lava,

pressure on heart, lungs, the brain
about to burst its brittle case
(what the skull can endure!):

over us, Apocryphal fire,
under us, the earth sway, dip of a floor,
slope of a pavement

where men roll, drunk
with a new bewilderment,
sorcery, bedevilment:

the bone-frame was made for
no such shock knit within terror,
yet the skeleton stood up to it:

the flesh? it was melted away,
the heart burnt out, dead ember,
tendons, muscles shattered, outer husk
    dismembered,

yet the frame held:
we passed the flame: we wonder
what saved us? what for?

1942

Death Valley

SORLEY MACLEAN

Some Nazi or other has said that the Fuehrer had restored to German manhood the 'right and joy of dying in battle'.

Sitting dead in 'Death Valley'
below the Ruweisat Ridge
a boy with his forelock down about his cheek
and his face slate-grey;

I thought of the right and the joy
that he got from his Fuehrer,
of falling in the field of slaughter
to rise no more;

of the pomp and the fame
that he had, not alone,
though he was the most piteous to see
in a valley gone to seed

with flies about grey corpses
on a dun sand
dirty yellow and full of the rubbish
and fragments of battle.

Was the boy of the band
who abused the Jews
and Communists, or of the greater
band of those

led, from the beginning of generations,
unwillingly to the trial
and mad delirium of every war
for the sake of rulers?

Whatever his desire or mishap,
his innocence or malignity,
he showed no pleasure in his death
below the Ruweisat Ridge.

1942

Beach Burial

◄◇►

KENNETH SLESSOR

Softly and humbly to the Gulf of Arabs
The convoys of dead sailors come;
At night they sway and wander in the waters far under,
But morning rolls them in the foam.

Between the sob and clubbing of the gunfire
Someone, it seems, has time for this,
To pluck them from the shallows and bury them in
    burrows
And tread the sand upon their nakedness;

And each cross, the driven stake of tidewood,
Bears the last signature of men,
Written with such perplexity, with such bewildered pity,
The words choke as they begin —

'*Unknown seaman*' — the ghostly pencil
Wavers and fades, the purple drips,
The breath of the wet season has washed their inscriptions
As blue as drowned men's lips,

Dead seamen, gone in search of the same landfall,
Whether as enemies they fought,
Or fought with us, or neither; the sand joins them
    together,
Enlisted on the other front.

El Alamein.

Slessor too was at El Alamein, and some of his vivid war despatches were collected later in *Bread and Wine* (1970).

1943

Cairo Jag

‹◦›

KEITH DOUGLAS

Shall I get drunk or cut myself a piece of cake,
a pasty Syrian with a few words of English
or the Turk who says she is a princess – she dances
apparently by levitation? Or Marcelle, Parisienne
always preoccupied with her dull dead lover:
she has all the photographs and his letters
tied in a bundle and stamped *Décedé* in mauve ink.
All this takes place in a stink of jasmin.

But there are the streets dedicated to sleep
stenches and the sour smells, the sour cries
do not disturb their application to slumber
all day, scattered on the pavement like rags
afflicted with fatalism and hashish. The women
offering their children brown-paper breasts
dry and twisted, elongated like the skull,
Holbein's signature. But this stained white town
is something in accordance with mundane conventions –
Marcelle drops her Gallic airs and tragedy
suddenly shrieks in Arabic about the fare
with the cabman, links herself so
with the somnambulists and legless beggars:
it is all one, all as you have heard.

But by a day's travelling you reach a new world
the vegetation is of iron
dead tanks, gun barrels split like celery
the metal brambles have no flowers or berries
and there are all sorts of manure, you can imagine
the dead themselves, their boots, clothes and possessions
clinging to the ground, a man with no head
has a packet of chocolate and a souvenir of Tripoli.

1943

Vergissmeinnicht

◄◊►

KEITH DOUGLAS

Three weeks gone and the combatants gone
returning over the nightmare ground
we found the place again, and found
the soldier sprawling in the sun.

The frowning barrel of his gun
overshadowing. As we came on
that day, he hit my tank with one
like the entry of a demon.

Look. Here in the gunpit spoil
the dishonoured picture of his girl
who has put: *Steffi. Vergissmeinnicht*
in a copybook gothic script.

We see him almost with content,
abased, and seeming to have paid
and mocked at by his own equipment
that's hard and good when he's decayed.

But she would weep to see today
how on his skin the swart flies move;
the dust upon the paper eye
and the burst stomach like a cave.

For here the lover and killer are mingled
who had one body and one heart.
And death who had the soldier singled
has done the lover mortal hurt.

The German word *Vergissmeinnicht* means 'forget me not' (both the flower and
the admonition).

1943

Sportsmen

KEITH DOUGLAS

'I think I am becoming a God.'

The noble horse with courage in his eye,
clean in the bone, looks up at a shellburst:
away fly the images of the shires
but he puts the pipe back in his mouth.

Peter was unfortunately killed by an 88;
it took his leg off; he died in the ambulance.
When I saw him crawling, he said:
It's most unfair, they've shot my foot off.

How then can I live among this gentle
obsolescent breed of heroes, and not weep?
Unicorns, almost. For they are fading into two legends
in which their stupidity and chivalry are celebrated;
the fool and the hero will be immortals.

These plains were a cricket pitch
and in the hills the tremendous drop fences
brought down some of the runners, who
under these stones and earth lounge still
in famous attitudes of unconcern. Listen
against the bullet cries the simple horn.

1943

Rattler Morgan

————◅◦►————

CHARLES CAUSLEY

Now his eyes are bright farthings
   And he spindles
In seas deeper than death.
   His lips are no longer wet with wine
But gleam with green salt
   And the Gulf Stream is his breath.

Now he is fumbled by ancient tides
   Among decks flagged with seaweed
But no flags sees he there.
   His fingers are washed to stone
And to phosphor
   And there are starfish in his hair.

(HMS *Cabbala*)

1943

Tapu

A. R. D. Fairburn

To stave off disaster, or bring the devil to heel,
  or to fight against fear, some carry a ring or a locket,
but I, who have nothing to lose by the turn of the wheel,
  and nothing to gain, I carry the world in my pocket.

For all I have gained, and have lost, is locked up in this
    thing,
this cup of cracked bone from the skull of a fellow long
    dead,
with a hank of thin yellowish hair fastened in with a ring.
  For a symbol of death and desire these tokens are wed.

The one I picked out of a cave in a windy cliff-face
where the old Maoris slept, with a curse on the stranger
    who moved,
in despite of tapu, but a splinter of bone from that place.
  The other I cut from the head of the woman I loved.

1944

Prodigy

<o>

CHARLES SIMIC

I grew up bent over
a chessboard.

I loved the word *endgame*.

All my cousins looked worried.

It was a small house
near a Roman graveyard.
Planes and tanks
shook its windowpanes.

A retired professor of astronomy
taught me how to play.

That must have been in 1944.

In the set we were using,
the paint had almost chipped off
the black pieces.

The white King was missing
and had to be substituted for.

I'm told but do not believe
that that summer I witnessed
men hung from telephone poles.

I remember my mother
blindfolding me a lot.

She had a way of tucking my head
suddenly under her overcoat.

In chess, too, the professor told me,
the masters play blindfolded,
the great ones on several boards
at the same time.

1944

A Refugee

E. J. SCOVELL

My heart had learnt the habit of earthly life
In an accustomed place.
My voice had learnt the habit of maternal
Sharpness and gentleness.

My thighs had learnt the speech of love. The house
And market tasks that show
So small a flower, rooting in hands and feet
Had matted my flesh through.

My husband died in the mercy of Russian snow.
My child died in the train,
In three days in the weeping cattle truck
From Breslau to Berlin.

I was not taught the song of extremity,
The dancing of duress.
All that I know of infinite is the intensity
Of finite tenderness.

All that I have of goodness is through love –
Their love my only worth.
My rigid arms set in the shape of their love
Have no more use on earth.

Breslau is today's Wroclaw (in Poland). In September 1944 it was transformed
by the German Wehrmacht into a fortress, and women, children and the elderly
were evacuated.

1944

War Song

DOROTHY PARKER

Soldier, in a curious land
  All across a swaying sea,
Take her smile and lift her hand –
  Have no guilt of me.

Soldier, when were soldiers true?
  If she's kind and sweet and gay,
Use the wish I send to you –
  Lie not lone till day!

Only, for the nights that were,
  Soldier, and the dawns that came,
When in sleep you turn to her
  Call her by my name.

1944

1944

Fife Tune

<o>

JOHN MANIFOLD

For Sixth Platoon, 308th ITC

One morning in spring
We marched from Devizes
All shapes and all sizes
Like beads on a string,
But yet with a swing
We trod the bluemetal
And full of high fettle
We started to sing.

She ran down the stair
A twelve-year-old darling
And laughing and calling
She tossed her bright hair;
Then silent to stare
At the men flowing past her –
There were all she could master
Adoring her there.

It's seldom I'll see
A sweeter or prettier;
I doubt we'll forget her
In two years or three,
And lucky he'll be
She takes for a lover
While we are far over
The treacherous sea.

1944

Carentan O Carentan

LOUIS SIMPSON

Trees in the old days used to stand
And shape a shady lane
Where lovers wandered hand in hand
Who came from Carentan.

This was the shining green canal
Where we came two by two
Walking at combat-interval.
Such trees we never knew.

The day was early June, the ground
Was soft and bright with dew.
Far away the guns did sound,
But here the sky was blue.

The sky was blue, but there a smoke
Hung still above the sea
Where the ships together spoke
To towns we could not see.

Could you have seen us through a glass
You would have said a walk
Of farmers out to turn the grass,
Each with his own hay-fork.

The watchers in their leopard suits
Waited till it was time,
And aimed between the belt and boot
And let the barrel climb.

I must lie down at once, there is
A hammer at my knee.
And call it death or cowardice,
Don't count again on me.

Everything's all right, Mother,
Everyone gets the same
At one time or another.
It's all in the game.

I never strolled, nor ever shall,
Down such a leafy lane.
I never drank in a canal,
Nor ever shall again.

There is a whistling in the leaves
And it is not the wind,
The twigs are falling from the knives
That cut men to the ground.

Tell me, Master-Sergeant,
The way to turn and shoot.
But the Sergeant's silent
That taught me how to do it.

O Captain, show us quickly
Our place upon the map.
But the Captain's sickly
And taking a long nap.

Lieutenant, what's my duty,
My place in the platoon?
He too's a sleeping beauty,
Charmed by that strange tune.

Carentan O Carentan
Before we met with you
We never yet had lost a man
Or known what death could do.

Carentan is a port in Normandy. The Battle of Carentan was fought between 10 and 15 June 1944 by forces of the US 101st Airborne Division, who took the town from defending German forces. Capture of Carentan was crucial if the Allied forces that had been landed on Utah and Omaha Beaches on D-Day (6 June) were to be united.

1944

The Mind is an Enchanting Thing

MARIANNE MOORE

is an enchanted thing
    like the glaze on a
katydid-wing
        subdivided by sun
        till the nettings are legion.
Like Gieseking playing Scarlatti;

like the apteryx-awl
    as a beak, or the
kiwi's rain-shawl
        of haired feathers, the mind
        feeling its way as though blind,
walks along with its eyes on the ground.

It has memory's ear
    that can hear without
having to hear.
        Like the gyroscope's fall,
        truly unequivocal
because trued by regnant certainty,

it is a power of
    strong enchantment. It
is like the dove-
        neck animated by
        sun; it is memory's eye;
it's conscientious inconsistency.

It tears off the veil; tears
    the temptation, the
mist the heart wears,
        from its eyes – if the heart

has a face; it takes apart
dejection. It's fire in the dove-neck's

iridescence; in the
   inconsistencies
of Scarlatti.
    Unconfusion submits
    its confusion to proof; it's
not a Herod's oath that cannot change.

The French-born German pianist Walter Gieseking (1895–1956) had a formidable repertoire which included the eighteenth-century Italian composer Domenico Scarlatti, though Gieseking's fame rested chiefly on his interpretations of Bach and Beethoven and also of modern composers such as Hindemith and Schoenberg, Debussy and Ravel. He did not go into exile but remained in Germany under the Nazis, and on a famous 1944 recording of Beethoven's Emperor Concerto (which Marianne Moore could not have been familiar with) anti-aircraft fire was audible in the background. Herod's oath is given to Salome (Matthew 14:7), offering her 'whatsoever she would ask', and is not broken even when she asks for the head of John the Baptist.

1944

The Eye

◄◦►

ROBINSON JEFFERS

The Atlantic is a stormy moat; and the Mediterranean,
The blue pool in the old garden,
More than five thousand years has drunk sacrifice
Of ships and blood, and shines in the sun; but here the
    Pacific –
Our ships, planes, wars are perfectly irrelevant.
Neither our present blood-feud with the brave dwarfs
Nor any future world-quarrel of westering
And eastering man, the bloody migrations, greed of power,
    clash of faiths –
Is a speck of dust on the great scale-pan.
Here from this mountain shore, headland beyond stormy
    headland plunging like dolphins through the blue
    sea-smoke
Into pale sea – look west at the hill of water: it is half the
    planet: this dome, this half-globe, this bulging
Eyeball of water, arched over to Asia,
Australia and white Antarctica: those are the eyelids that
    never close; this is the staring unsleeping
Eye of the earth; and what it watches is not our wars.

1945

Look within

CLAUDE MCKAY

Lord, let me not be silent while we fight
   In Europe Germans, Asia Japanese
For setting up a Fascist way of might
   While fifteen million Negroes on their knees
Pray for salvation from the Fascist yoke
   Of these United States. Remove the beam
(Nearly two thousand years since Jesus spoke)
   From your own eyes before the mote you deem
It proper from your neighbor's to extract!
   We bathe our lies in vapors of sweet myrrh,
And close our eyes not to perceive the fact!
   But Jesus said: You whited sepulchre,
Pretending to be uncorrupt of sin,
While worm-infested, rotten through within!

McKay is thinking first of Christ's words, 'Why beholdest thou the mote that is in thy brother's eye, but considerest not the beam that is in thine own eye?' (Matthew 7:3) and then, in the closing lines of the sonnet, of other words of Christ's, 'Ye are like unto whited sepulchres, which indeed appear beautiful outward, but are within full of dead men's bones, and of all uncleanness.' (Matthew 23:27).

1945

A Pilot from the Carrier

◄◦►

RANDALL JARRELL

Strapped at the center of the blazing wheel,
His flesh ice-white against the shattered mask,
He tears at the easy clasp, his sobbing breaths
Misting the fresh blood lightening to flame,
Darkening to smoke; trapped there in pain
And fire and breathlessness, he struggles free
Into the sunlight of the upper sky —
And falls, a quiet bundle in the sky,
The miles to warmth, to air, to waking:
To the great flowering of his life, the hemisphere
That holds his dangling years. In its long slow sway
The world steadies and is almost still . . .
He is alone; and hangs in knowledge
Slight, separate, estranged: a lonely eye
Reading a child's first scrawl, the carrier's wake —
The travelling milk-like circle of a miss
Beside the plant-like genius of the smoke
That shades, on the little deck, the little blaze
Toy-like as the glitter of the wing-guns,
Shining as the fragile sun-marked plane
That grows to him, rubbed silver tipped with flame.

1945

The Death of the Ball Turret Gunner

RANDALL JARRELL

From my mother's sleep I fell into the State,
And I hunched in its belly till my wet fur froze.
Six miles from earth, loosed from its dream of life,
I woke to black flak and the nightmare fighters.
When I died they washed me out of the turret with a
  hose.

Jarrell explained that, in the first of these poems, he used the word 'genius' in the sense of 'djinn' or 'geni'. For the second, he provided this note: 'A ball turret was a plexiglass sphere set into the belly of a B-17 or B-24, and inhabited by two .50 caliber machine-guns and one man, a short small man. When this gunner tracked with his machine-guns a fighter attacking his bomber from below, he revolved with the turret; hunched upside-down in his little sphere, he looked like the foetus in the womb. The fighters which attacked him were armed with cannon firing explosive shells. The hose was a steam hose.'

1945

Day of Liberation, Bergen-Belsen, May 1945

PHILLIP WHITFIELD

We build our own prison walls
but that day the doors fell open,
it was holiday time
in the death camp.

Lift him with courtesy,
this silent survivor.
Battle-dress doctors,
we took him from the truck
and put him to bed.

The moving skeleton
had crippled hands,
his skinny palms held secrets:
when I undid the joints I found
five wheat grains huddled there.
In the faces of other people
I witness my distress.

I close my eyes:
ten thousand wasted people
still piled in the flesh-pits.
Death of one is the death of all.
It is not the dead I pity.

The Nazi concentration camp at Bergen-Belsen, in Lower Saxony, was in fact
liberated, Whitfield's title notwithstanding, on 15 April 1945 (by the British 11th
Armoured Division). The many who had died there included Anne Frank. Whit-
field's phrase 'Death of one is the death of all' may echo the Talmudic 'He who
saves a single life saves the world entire'.

1945

Sketch

JEFFREY HARRISON

For Donald Richie

August 1945. The bombs
had fallen, the war was coming to an end.
By a deserted canal outside Shanghai,
a young American merchant marine ensign
sat sketching a pagoda. A rhythmic clanking,
rising behind the cicadas' shimmering scrim,
broke through to consciousness too late: he looked up
and saw a platoon of Japanese soldiers
marching toward him along the canal path.
Fear bolted through him, but he made himself
keep sketching as the soldiers filed past
behind him, his heart fisting when he saw,
out of the corner of his eye, the rear officer
veer toward him as the troops continued on.
He heard the crunch of boots against loose stones
halting at his back. The pencil stopped.
The sketchbook on his knee seemed far away,
as if seen through the wrong end of a telescope.
Then the page went blank and he saw nothing
except an image of the officer's raised sword
scything down on him, and of his head
splashing into the canal's stagnant water.
The officer barked something in Japanese,
a phrase that bored itself into the brain
of the young American, who took it to be
the formal pronouncement of his execution.
But the sword never fell, and the American
told me his story forty-three years later
while we were having lunch at the Press Club
on the top floor of a Tokyo high rise

with a view of the Imperial Palace.
Emperor Hirohito was dying,
and hundreds of people were standing in the rain
before the palace gates, waiting in line
to sign their last respects into a book.
From that height, their umbrellas seemed to form
the scales of a long, sinuous dragon.
'Which, after all, is an imperial symbol,'
said my host. But his story wasn't finished.
Not long after the war, he'd come to Japan
and found he loved the place. He never left.
Years later, after he'd learned Japanese,
the utterance from that day emerged intact,
like a dormant insect larva that had lodged
in his skull and was now coming back to life
as something wholly different: not a sentence
of death, but the phrase *Nakanaka yoi*,
meaning, in reference to the sketch, 'Not bad at all.'

In 1945, atomic bombs were dropped on Hiroshima (6 August) and Nagasaki (9 August), hastening the surrender of Japan to the Allied forces (15 August). Emperor Hirohito (1901–1989) was the 124th emperor of Japan according to the traditional order, reigning from 1926 until his death in 1989. It was under Hirohito's rule that the Japanese joined forces with the Italian Fascists and the Nazis. The dedicatee of Harrison's poem, Donald Richie (born 1924), is the American author of numerous books on Japanese culture.

1945

August, 1945

◄◊►

HOWARD NEMEROV

Feeble Caligula! to say
You wished mankind one only neck.
The dying guards might dance that day
At Auschwitz and at Maidanek,
Seeing their bloody seed begin to swell
Where the two cities fell.

That was our deed, without us done.
Great murder in the earth was set
That day to grow, and for us won
A present freedom to regret
Necessity, that once had made us, blind,
The saviors of mankind.

The pluming shadow of that plant,
A tragic actor now grown tall
To toppling, sounds the haughty cant
And birdlike flutes of sorrow, all
That power cracked at the root and manifest
In the burnt Phoenix' nest.

The words of Caligula (Roman Emperor from AD 37 to 41) were communicated to us by Suetonius, in *The Twelve Caesars*. (Caligula reportedly spoke of the Roman people, not of all mankind.) Maidanek was a Nazi concentration camp on the outskirts of Lublin, Poland.

1945

The Castle

◁◦▷

EDWIN MUIR

All through that summer at ease we lay,
And daily from the turret wall
We watched the mowers in the hay
And the enemy half a mile away.
They seemed no threat to us at all.

For what, we thought, had we to fear
With our arms and provender, load on load,
Our towering battlements, tier on tier,
And friendly allies drawing near
On every leafy summer road.

Our gates were strong, our walls were thick,
So smooth and high, no man could win
A foothold there, no clever trick
Could take us, have us dead or quick.
Only a bird could have got in.

What could they offer us for bait?
Our captain was brave and we were true . . .
There was a little private gate,
A little wicked wicket gate.
The wizened warder let them through.

Oh then our maze of tunnelled stone
Grew thin and treacherous as air.
The cause was lost without a groan,
The famous citadel overthrown,
And all its secret galleries bare.

How can this shameful tale be told?
I will maintain until my death
We could do nothing, being sold;
Our only enemy was gold,
And we had no arms to fight it with.

1945

Fern Hill

◄○►

DYLAN THOMAS

Now as I was young and easy under the apple boughs
About the lilting house and happy as the grass was green,
 The night above the dingle starry,
  Time let me hail and climb
 Golden in the heydays of his eyes,
And honoured among wagons I was prince of the apple
 towns
And once below a time I lordly had the trees and leaves
  Trail with daisies and barley
 Down the rivers of the windfall light.

And as I was green and carefree, famous among the barns
About the happy yard and singing as the farm was home,
 In the sun that is young once only.
  Time let me play and be
 Golden in the mercy of his means,
And green and golden I was huntsman and herdsman, the
 calves
Sang to my horn, the foxes on the hills barked clear and
 cold,
  And the sabbath rang slowly
 In the pebbles of the holy streams.

All the sun long it was running, it was lovely, the hay
Fields high as the house, the tunes from the chimneys, it
 was air
 And playing, lovely and watery
  And fire green as grass.
 And nightly under the simple stars
As I rode to sleep the owls were bearing the farm away,
All the moon long I heard, blessed among stables, the
 nightjars

Flying with the ricks, and the horses
  Flashing into the dark.

And then to awake, and the farm, like a wanderer white
With the dew, come back, the cock on his shoulder: it was all
  Shining, it was Adam and maiden,
    The sky gathered again
  And the sun grew round that very day.
So it must have been after the birth of the simple light
In the first, spinning place, the spellbound horses walking
  warm
    Out of the whinnying green stable
      On to the fields of praise.

And honoured among foxes and pheasants by the gay house
Under the new made clouds and happy as the heart was long,
  In the sun born over and over,
    I ran my heedless ways,
  My wishes raced through the house high hay
And nothing I cared, at my sky blue trades, that time allows
In all his tuneful turning so few and such morning songs
  Before the children green and golden
    Follow him out of grace,

Nothing I cared, in the lamb white days, that time would take
  me
Up to the swallow thronged loft by the shadow of my hand,
  In the moon that is always rising,
    Nor that riding to sleep
  I should hear him fly with the high fields
And wake to the farm forever fled from the childless land.
Oh as I was young and easy in the mercy of his means,
    Time held me green and dying
  Though I sang in my chains like the sea.

V

1946–1968
Peace and Cold War

A FTER THE greatest conflict in the world's history, an estimated sixty
million people had lost their lives, more than half of them civilians.
Cities had been reduced to rubble, factories flattened, infrastructures
destroyed. If the First World War had enforced the conclusion that civili-
sation was 'botched', the Second World War taught the grimmer lesson
that in reality there was no such thing as civilisation. In 'The Shield of
Achilles' Auden denounced the brutality to which mankind has been
enslaved from time immemorial, in terms informed by recent history.
Thetis, the mother of Achilles, looks into her son's shield in the hope
of finding images of peace, order and prosperity, but instead finds
totalitarian oppression at an individual level, the abject abdication of
basic human values: kindness, tolerance, love. The Indian poet Nissim
Ezekiel developed a similar theme of disillusion in 'The Double Horror'
– for all the possibilities of good within the world, human complicity
in the negative seems certain to condemn humanity to a bleak future.
If Australian poet Judith Wright employed military imagery to establish
the threat to her lovers in 'The Company of Lovers', the message was
not least that the menace Auden had expressed immediately before the
war, in '"Say this city has ten million souls"', had not been mitigated
by the blood-letting.

Elizabeth Bishop, who spent much of her life travelling, reminds us
of the exhilaration implicit in cartography, but around the world maps
were being re-drawn to reflect new realities of power. While half the
countries of Europe fell under Stalin's empire of satellite states, behind

what Churchill dubbed the 'Iron Curtain', across the globe Britain's tired imperial pretensions were succumbing to the unstoppable pressure for independence. India was the first to go, released by the Labour government which replaced Churchill's war coalition in the election landslide of 1945. However, the divide between the Hindu majority and the Muslim minority meant that the sub-continent had to be divided, creating the new nation of Pakistan. Partition, as it was known, appeared to be a political necessity, but its human cost was high. Although a ruinous civil war was avoided, the bloodshed that followed British withdrawal was appalling, with thousands losing their lives in sectarian massacres.

By the end of the Forties, poets (like everyone else) were beginning to sense the uneasiness of the new peace and project imaginary versions of the war which really would end all war. Kingsley Amis recasts murderous geo-political rivalries as an Agatha Christie-style country house murder story, while Edwin Muir's 'The Horses' is a bleakly moving post-nuclear holocaust pastoral. The conflict with which the new decade opened did not lead to apocalypse, but as the first 'hot' war between the West and Communism, Korea was a sour foretaste of the possibilities of mutual destruction, especially when China offered military support to her Stalinist southern neighbour, North Korea. R. A. K. Mason's sonnet of scathing reproof to veteran American General Douglas MacArthur sounds a note of moral fury that would be heard many times over through the Cold War.

To seek for a thread running through the poetry of the Fifties is to be confronted by many different and often incompatible narratives. That fact in itself is eloquent of the changed nature of life in the second half of the twentieth century, when the old certainties were felt to have lost their purchase and validity. For Gwendolyn Brooks, the American experience was expressed in a gently observant poem about the vast disparities in wealth – and life-expectancy – between the well-off whites and the slum-dwelling blacks. For Adrienne Rich, the same endless class divide is viewed through the other end of the telescope, recording an uncle ruminating on cultural benefits of wealth and the dangerous threat from the discontented have-nots. The Fifties saw the rise of the Beats in America, led by the novelists Jack Kerouac and William Burroughs and poet Allen Ginsberg, who shot to fame with outspoken and outlandish counter-culture poems which he read to enraptured young audiences. Poems like 'America' and 'Howl' scandalised the nation with their rejection of unquestioned certainties concerning patriotism, religion, sexual orientation and drug use. Like his Russian counterpart, Yevgeny Yevtushenko, Ginsberg extended the poet's remit, travelling the world as an unofficial ambassador for peace and goodwill. Ginsberg found a home for his poetry with City Lights, San Francisco, run by fellow poet Lawrence Ferlinghetti, who was a similarly radical sensibility, writing copiously about the manifest injustices that have plagued humanity down the ages. In the poem here, he holds up the terrifying realism of the great Spanish painter Goya as a mirror to contemporary America.

These were American identities not envisioned in the polished, poised poetry of Richard Wilbur, or the open-to-all *parlando* of Elizabeth Bishop's 'At the Fishhouses', or indeed the newly candid but formally and socially astute poetry of Lowell, Snodgrass, Sexton and Berryman. Confession, a complex idea with a lineage from St Augustine through Rousseau to Salvador Dalí's *Secret Life*, was identified by critics as the main impulse behind a new sensibility of self in American writing. W. D. Snodgrass wrote with arresting honesty about the aftermath of a messy divorce, focusing particularly on the effect on his young daughter in *Heart's Needle*, a book which influenced Anne Sexton among others. Robert Lowell also broke through with his dazzling *Life Studies*, which ranged through the seamier side of his patrician family history and introduced a new, colloquial voice which could discuss any subject, however personal. Frank O'Hara too, though he pursued a distinctive aesthetic programme, implicitly places a high valuation on the self as he builds up – in 'The Day Lady Died' – a picture of an ordinary day in New York impacted by the announcement of the death of the great black singer, Billie Holiday.

The explosion of 'confessional' poetry centred upon the self came out of the US. Elsewhere, poets had other emphases to place. R. D. FitzGerald's return to the early days of Australia, when it was not much more than a penal colony, follows the thread of history back to a doctor forbear whose job it was to attend the brutal floggings meted out to prisoners in the local jail. The poem is one that raises questions rather than answering them, and the self who concludes 'I've my own faults to face' makes the statement without any taint of exhibitionism or ostentation. FitzGerald's countrywoman Judith Wright conceives an imitation of Christ for a 'new' continent in 'The Lost Man', and confronts questions of cultural and racial guilt and atonement in 'At Cooloolah'. Another Australian, David Campbell, playfully telescopes the abyss between royalty and an ordinary commoner happy to offer his bedroom to the Queen *in* dream *extremis*, while the old wives in Shaw Neilson's poem take a grim consolation in the face of a young woman's beauty, noting that while 'her love was finery . . . her shroud was plain'.

The poetic shroud Dylan Thomas prepared for his schoolmaster father was anything but plain, and his fine poem, 'Do not go gentle into that good night', manages to celebrate fiercely even as hope ebbs away inevitably on the deathbed. Does the injunction to 'rage' already implicitly part company with Christian thinking? Many of course could not sustain belief, not only because of the challenge the century's history posed to it, but also because so much evidence now pointed in directions that took the individual away from faith. Philip Larkin might be described as the laureate of lost faith, and in 'Church Going' rehearsed the strong pull of the traditional forms and observances, even as he embarrassed himself by sending them up. Mocking the mock-solemnities of the church service gives way to a gracious acceptance of organised religion's role and the role of lovingly sustained buildings: 'A serious house on serious earth it is' is the insight of a man who has taken the very substantial trouble to understand what seriousness is. An equally rich understanding of final seriousness, though textured and expressed in very different ways, informs Jon Silkin's lament for a dead one-year-old son, and Michael Hamburger's disquisition on Adolf Eichmann.

As the Sixties dawned, the world remained a dangerous place. The Chinese put down a revolt against their illegal rule by the Tibetans; in South Africa the apartheid regime also resorted to violence when its pass laws provoked civil unrest; and the United States was about to embark on its gravest military engagement since 1945, Vietnam. In the 1960 Presidential election, John F. Kennedy beat Richard Nixon to the White House. Despite his charisma, and the promise of a 'New Frontier' at home, Kennedy's brutally shortened term in office coincided with an escalation of the Cold War. Fidel Castro's successful revolution in Cuba gave his sponsor, the Soviet Union, a potential launchpad into a suddenly vulnerable America. With the botched attempt to reverse the revolution, which ended catastrophically at the Bay of Pigs, the two sides were left in an uneasy stand-off, and the possibility of the imminent destruction of the entire world in a nuclear war became a commonplace topic. 'All autumn, the chafe and jar / of nuclear war,' as Robert Lowell puts it in 'Fall 1961', adding the despairing thought: 'A father's no shield / for his child.' Richard Wilbur wrote the great poem of nuclear dread in 'Advice to a Prophet' in that same year, before the Cuban missile crisis peaked, and was resolved, in 1962. Paul Muldoon captures the knife-edge nature of the crisis in a vignette from his Irish boyhood, 'Cuba'.

The following year, the world was again united in horror when Kennedy was shot dead as his motorcade proceeded through Dallas. His had been a mercurial rise to global pre-eminence, but his legacy, which included the Vietnam war, has been subject to extensive revisionist reappraisal. New Zealander C. K. Stead voiced his reservations succinctly, while Robert Lowell captured something of the new, bleaker mood with a powerful poem, 'For the Union Dead', which contrasts legendary courage and sacrifice from the Civil War period with the greedy, compromised, self-serving cynicism of the present day. His friend and poetic rival John Berryman similarly sifted history for its contemporary meanings in his idiosyncratic, authoritative sequence of Dream Songs.

Across the Atlantic in England, Ted Hughes had married Sylvia Plath in the union that was to become an obsession to generations of scholars and feminists. Hughes was still a student at Cambridge when he met the visiting American graduate who became the most famous woman poet of the second half of the century, and, because of the tragic outcome of her relationship with Hughes, a feminist icon. Hughes had achieved his first popularity with poems that imaginatively entered the violent world of natural predators such as the hawk, jaguar, or fox. Immensely talented, Plath was also intensely ambitious, and fell on Hughes as a kindred creative spirit. She started publishing poems, but it was not until the relationship with Hughes disintegrated that the full force of her talent was released. In a spectacular spate of dark creativity, especially in October 1962, she wrote the poems that made her famous, later collected in Ariel (1965). She committed suicide in 1963. Years later – near the end of his own life, and after a lifetime's silence – Hughes published a series of autobiographical poems about the relationship. 'Epiphany', with its unusual story of being offered a fox cub on a London street, suggests the highly-charged world Hughes inhabited.

Basil Bunting, friend and disciple of Ezra Pound, and a minor name until his re-emergence in the Sixties, returned home after a lifetime's travel and excavated his masterpiece, *Briggflatts*, from the history and legends of Eric Bloodaxe. The opening pastoral section, set in the secluded countryside of West Yorkshire and Cumbria, is one of the high achievements of post-war English poetry, and seems scarcely to belong to the same social universe as that to which a British Prime Minister, noting the return (in 1957) of prosperity after years of tightened belts, had addressed the words, 'You've never had it so good'. Of course material well-being and the security of a well-paid job could not be guaranteed to produce happiness. But the truth was that Sixties Britain was no longer the country either of Basil Bunting or of Harold Macmillan. If it belonged to anyone, it belonged to The Beatles. The equivalent of the new pop music in poetry was the quirky, irreverent Merseysound of Roger McGough, Brian Patten and Adrian Henri, capturing the mood of everyday life in everyday (cummings-influenced) language.

Around the world, the younger generation were beginning to realise that this new world, a world that might put the old mistakes behind it, was theirs to make. Louis Simpson's telling words – 'grave by grave we civilize the ground' – epitomised the new view taken by 'the West' of itself. Leaders everywhere were perceived as middle-aged men in suits with no understanding of the aspirations of the hippy alternative to 'straight' society. As the war escalated in Vietnam, a tide of protest flooded across the Western world. Race riots were triggered in America by the assassination of the charismatic civil rights leader, Dr Martin Luther King, while in France student protests brought anarchy to the streets of Paris. When they were joined by the workers, the ageing President Charles de Gaulle, and indeed the French Republic, appeared to be tottering. And protest was not confined to 'the West'. There were stirrings behind the Iron Curtain: under a new, popular and liberal leader, Alexander Dubcek, Czechoslavakia had been basking in a period of reform, the Prague Spring, enjoying freedoms not experienced in a generation. The affront to Soviet authority brought Russian tanks into Prague, crushing the experiment in which the Czechs had hoped to prove it was possible to have 'communism with a human face'.

The late Sixties can be seen with hindsight to have had a singularly troubled relationship with the spiritual life, obsessively seeking salvation by material means, on the streets or in the stores. The quasi-cultic following that has been drawn to the figure of Thomas Merton in the decades since his death in Bangkok in 1968 makes an illuminating study. Equally illuminating is a profoundly thoughtful poem by Australian poet A. D. Hope, in which he looks back beyond the world's immediate troubles to reflect on an engraving of a body – that of a pregnant woman dragged from the river. The engraving possesses the historical significance of being the first representation of the unborn foetus in the womb. The significance of the poem is great as well, for the cogent passion with which it urges us, in the midst of our 'intellectual quest', to think of the 'questions . . . which we fail to ask'. The loose-at-all-ends post-war decades had need of the reminder.

1946

The Hawthorn Hedge

Judith Wright

How long ago she planted the hawthorn hedge –
she forgets how long ago –
that barrier thorn across the hungry ridge;
thorn and snow.

It is twice as tall as the rider on the tall mare
who draws his reins to peer
in through the bee-hung blossom. Let him stare.
No one is here:

Only the mad old girl from the hut on the hill,
unkempt as an old tree.
She will hide away if you wave your hand or call;
she will not see.

Year-long, wind turns her grindstone heart and whets
a thornbranch like a knife,
shouting in winter 'Death'; and when the white bud sets,
more loudly, 'Life'.

She has forgotten when she planted the hawthorn hedge,
that thorn, that green, that snow;
birdsong and sun dazzled across the ridge –
it was long ago.

Her hands were strong in the earth, her glance on the sky,
her song was sweet on the wind.
The hawthorn hedge took root, grew wild and high
to hide behind.

1946

The Company of Lovers

—◄◦►—

JUDITH WRIGHT

We meet and part now over all the world.
We, the lost company,
take hands together in the night, forget
the night in our brief happiness, silently.
We who sought many things, throw all away
for this one thing, one only,
remembering that in the narrow grave
we shall be lonely.

Death marshals up his armies round us now.
Their footsteps crowd too near.
Lock your warm hand above the chilling heart
and for a time I live without my fear.
Grope in the night to find me and embrace,
for the dark preludes of the drums begin,
and round us, round the company of lovers,
Death draws his cordons in.

1946

A Peasant

R. S. THOMAS

Iago Prytherch his name, though, be it allowed,
Just an ordinary man of the bald Welsh hills,
Who pens a few sheep in a gap of cloud.
Docking mangels, chipping the green skin
From the yellow bones with a half-witted grin
Of satisfaction, or churning the crude earth
To a stiff sea of clods that glint in the wind –
So are his days spent, his spittled mirth
Rarer than the sun that cracks the cheeks
Of the gaunt sky perhaps once in a week.
And then at night see him fixed in his chair
Motionless, except when he leans to gob in the fire.
There is something frightening in the vacancy of his mind.
His clothes, sour with years of sweat
And animal contact, shock the refined,
But affected, sense with their stark naturalness.
Yet this is your prototype, who, season by season
Against siege of rain and the wind's attrition,
Preserves his stock, an impregnable fortress
Not to be stormed even in death's confusion.
Remember him, then, for he, too, is a winner of wars,
Enduring like a tree under the curious stars.

1946

The Map

——◄◊►——

ELIZABETH BISHOP

Land lies in water; it is shadowed green.
Shadows, or are they shallows, at its edges
showing the line of long sea-weeded ledges
where weeds hang to the simple blue from green.
Or does the land lean down to lift the sea from under,
drawing it unperturbed around itself?
Along the fine tan sandy shelf
is the land tugging at the sea from under?

The shadow of Newfoundland lies flat and still.
Labrador's yellow, where the moony Eskimo
has oiled it. We can stroke these lovely bays,
under a glass as if they were expected to blossom,
or as if to provide a clean cage for invisible fish.
The names of seashore towns run out to sea,
the names of cities cross the neighboring mountains
– the printer here experiencing the same excitement
as when emotion too far exceeds its cause.
These peninsulas take the water between thumb and finger
like women feeling for the smoothness of yard-goods.

Mapped waters are more quiet than the land is,
lending the land their waves' own conformation:
and Norway's hare runs south in agitation,
profiles investigate the sea, where land is.
Are they assigned, or can the countries pick their colors?
– What suits the character or the native waters best.
Topography displays no favorites; North's as near as West.
More delicate than the historians' are the map-makers'
    colors.

1946

Mr Gradgrind's Country

SYLVIA TOWNSEND WARNER

There was a dining-room, there was a drawing-room,
There was a billiard-room, there was a morning-room,
There were bedrooms for guests and bedrooms for sons
    and daughters,
In attic and basement there were ample servants' quarters,
There was a modern bathroom, a strong-room, and a
    conservatory.
In the days of England's glory.

There were Turkish carpets, there were Axminster carpets,
There were oil paintings of Vesuvius and family portraits,
There were mirrors, ottomans, wash-hand-stands and
    tantaluses,
There were port, sherry, claret, liqueur, and champagne
    glasses,
There was a solid brass gong, a grand piano, antlers,
    decanters, and a gentlemen's lavatory,
In the days of England's glory.

There was marqueterie and there was mahogany,
There was a cast of the Dying Gladiator in his agony,
There was the 'Encyclopaedia Britannica' in a revolving
    bookcase,
There were finger-bowls, asparagus-tongs, and islets of real
    lace:
They stood in their own grounds and were called
    Chatsworth, Elgin, or Tobermory,
In the days of England's glory.

But now these substantial gentlemen's establishments
Are like a perspective of disused elephants,
And the current Rajahs of industry flash past their wide
    frontages

343

Far, far away to the latest things in labour-saving cottages,
Where with Russell lupins, jade ash-trays, some Sealyham
    terriers, and a migratory
Cook they continue the story.

This biting account of the taste and mores of the affluent middle classes at the
height of English power – written (as the 'elephants' and 'Rajahs' hint) as the
approaching independence of India signalled that that power was definitively
at an end, even if the new captains of industry still had money – takes its title
from Mr Thomas Gradgrind in Dickens' novel *Hard Times* (1854), a character
conceived as a damning critique of the limits of utilitarian, materialist-minded
philistinism. The 'Dying Gladiator', or Dying Gaul, is one of the most celebrated
sculptures to have survived from the ancient world. The Roman copy of a lost
Greek original is in the Capitoline Museum in Rome; copies of it are in other
museums, and its popularity was so great in the nineteenth century that plaster
copies were mass-produced.

344

1947

The View of the Castle

WELDON KEES

The castle is mortgaged now, my dear,
The mortgage is overdue:
The moat, the tower, the beautiful yards,
The silverware and the frightening guards;
Although it's still on the postal cards,
The castle is mortgaged now, my dear;
They whisper its days are few.

The castle's been cracking for years, my dear,
And has not been properly cleaned;
The rooms are draughty and bring on colds,
The pantries are covered with unpleasant moulds,
It's thought rather queer the foundation holds
After so many years, my dear;
And it's best not to speak of the beams.

The princesses were whores, my dear,
The princesses were whores;
The queen looks on with unconcern,
The king tries hard to seem strong and stern,
Yet neither of them was much startled to learn
That the princesses were whores, my dear,
And the prince was covered with sores.

This is the castle then, my dear,
With its justly famous view.
There are other historic sights in store –
Battlegrounds, parks we might explore,
The hundreds of monuments to war;
Now that you've seen the castle, my dear,
We'll see them before we're through.

1947

Epic

◇

PATRICK KAVANAGH

I have lived in important places, times
When great events were decided, who owned
That half a rood of rock, a no-man's land
Surrounded by our pitchfork-armed claims.
I heard the Duffys shouting 'Damn your soul'
And old McCabe stripped to the waist, seen
Step the plot defying blue cast-steel –
'Here is the march along these iron stones'.
That was the year of the Munich bother. Which
Was more important? I inclined
To lose my faith in Ballyrush and Gortin
Till Homer's ghost came whispering to my mind.
He said: I made the Iliad from such
A local row. Gods make their own importance.

Kavanagh's wryly understated phrase 'the Munich bother' refers to the agreement
of September 1938, by which Britain and France agreed to Germany's absorption
of the Sudetenland, then part of Czechoslovakia. British Prime Minister Neville
Chamberlain returned home speaking of 'peace in our time', but the Czechs
had been betrayed, and the Anglo-French policy of appeasement was profoundly
controversial. The outbreak of war a year later showed it to have been misguided,
as Kavanagh knew.

1947

Partition

<◇>

W. H. AUDEN

Unbiased at least he was when he arrived on his mission,
Having never set eyes on this land he was called to partition
Between two peoples fanatically at odds,
With their different diets and incompatible gods.
'Time,' they had briefed him in London, 'is short. It's too late
For mutual reconciliation or rational debate:
The only solution now lies in separation.
The Viceroy thinks, as you will see from his letter,
That the less you are seen in his company the better,
So we've arranged to provide you with other accommodation.
We can give you four judges, two Moslem and two Hindu,
To consult with, but the final decision must rest with you.'

Shut up in a lonely mansion, with police night and day
Patrolling the gardens to keep assassins away,
He got down to work, to the task of settling the fate
Of millions. The maps at his disposal were out of date
And the Census Returns almost certainly incorrect,
But there was no time to check them, no time to inspect
Contested areas. The weather was frightfully hot,
And a bout of dysentery kept him constantly on the trot,
But in seven weeks it was done, the frontiers decided,
A continent for better or worse divided.

The next day he sailed for England, where he quickly forgot
The case, as a good lawyer must. Return he would not,
Afraid, as he told his Club, that he might get shot.

Louis Mountbatten, Earl Mountbatten of Burma (1900–79), was appointed by
Britain's post-war Labour government to oversee Indian independence, as the
last Viceroy of the sub-continent under British rule. More than twelve million
people were displaced in the process of partition into India and Pakistan, and
the accompanying violence between the Hindu and Muslim communities is
estimated to have cost up to a million lives.

1948

Child on Top of a Greenhouse

Theodore Roethke

The wind billowing out the seat of my britches,
My feet crackling splinters of glass and dried putty,
The half-grown chrysanthemums staring up like accusers,
Up through the streaked glass, flashing with sunlight,
A few white clouds all rushing eastward,
A line of elms plunging and tossing like horses,
And everyone, everyone pointing up and shouting!

Speaking to the BBC in 1953 of the greenhouse that was central to a number of the poems in his collection *The Lost Son and Other Poems* (1948), Roethke described it as 'both heaven and hell', saying: 'It was a universe, several worlds, which, even as a child, one worried about.'

1948

The Last War

<small>◄○►</small>

KINGSLEY AMIS

The first country to die was normal in the evening,
Ate a good but plain dinner, chatted with some friends
Over a glass, and went to bed soon after ten;
And in the morning was found disfigured and dead.
  That was a lucky one.

At breakfast the others heard about it, and kept
Their eyes on their plates. Who was guilty? No one knew,
But by lunch-time three more would never eat again.
The rest appealed for frankness, quietly cocked their guns,
  Declared 'This can't go on'.

They were right. Only the strongest turned up for tea:
The old ones with the big estates hadn't survived
The slobbering blindfold violence of the afternoon.
One killer or many? Was it a gang, or all-against-all?
  Somebody must have known.

But each of them sat there watching the others, until
Night came and found them anxious to get it over.
Then the lights went out. A few might have lived, even
    then;
Innocent, they thought (at first) it still mattered what
  You had or hadn't done.

They were wrong. One had been lenient with his servants;
Another ran an island brothel, but rarely left it;
The third owned a museum, the fourth a remarkable gun;
The name of a fifth was quite unknown, but in the end
  What was the difference? None.

Homicide, pacifist, crusader, tyrant, adventurer, boor
Staggered about moaning, shooting into the dark.
Next day, to tidy up as usual, the sun came in
When they and their ammunition were all finished,
   And found himself alone.

Upset, he looked them over, to separate, if he could,
The assassins from the victims, but every face
Had taken on the flat anonymity of pain;
And soon they'll all smell alike, he thought, and felt sick,
   And went to bed at noon.

1949

Let it go

WILLIAM EMPSON

It is this deep blankness is the real thing strange.
　The more things happen to you the more you can't
　　Tell or remember even what they were.

The contradictions cover such a range.
　The talk would talk and go so far aslant.
　　You don't want madhouse and the whole thing
　　there.

1950

Sonnet to MacArthur's Eyes

R. A. K. MASON

*General MacArthur looked down on the bodies of four young
Korean soldiers. 'That's a good sight for my old eyes,' he said.
Newspaper report*

I have known old eyes that had seen many more
aspects of warfare than this man has seen –
eyes that had looked on Gallipoli or the keen
edge of battle with the Boer or in even older war
had known Balaclava and the Mutiny's evil score:
such eyes as I've known them old have always been
eager to see spring flowers and the youth who mean
mankind's spring after war's winter. Never before

Have I known of anyone whose old eyes rejoice
to see young men lying dead in their own land,
never have I known one who of his own choice
follows up the machines of death to take his stand
over the slain and in a quavering voice
declaim his joy at youth dead beneath his hand

September, 1950

US General Douglas MacArthur played a key role in the Pacific theatre in the
Second World War, especially in the Philippines. Following the North Korean
invasion of South Korea in June 1950, he commanded the United Nations forces
fighting with the South Koreans, until he was relieved of his command in April
1951. In the poem, Mason recalls conversations with old men who were veterans
of the Gallipoli campaign (in the First World War), of the Boer War (1899–1902),
of the Battle of Balaclava (1854, during the Crimean War) and of the Indian
Mutiny of 1857.

1950

Beverly Hills, Chicago

GWENDOLYN BROOKS

'and the people live till they have white hair'
– E. M. Price

The dry brown coughing beneath their feet,
(Only a while, for the handyman is on his way)
These people walk their golden gardens.
We say ourselves fortunate to be driving by today.

That we may look at them, in their gardens where
The summer ripeness rots. But not raggedly.
Even the leaves fall down in lovelier patterns here.
And the refuse, the refuse is a neat brilliancy.

When they flow sweetly into their houses
With softness and slowness touched by that everlasting
    gold,
We know what they go to. To tea. But that does not
    mean
They will throw some little black dots into some water
    and add sugar and the juice of the cheapest lemons
    that are sold,
While downstairs that woman's vague phonograph
    bleats, 'Knock me a kiss.'
And the living all to be made again in the sweatingest
    physical manner
Tomorrow . . . Not that anybody is saying that these
    people have no trouble.
Merely that it is trouble with a gold-flecked beautiful
    banner.

Nobody is saying that these people do not ultimately
    cease to be. And
Sometimes their passings are even more painful than
    ours.
It is just that so often they live till their hair is white.
They make excellent corpses, among the expensive
    flowers . . .

Nobody is furious. Nobody hates these people.
At least, nobody driving by in this car.
It is only natural, however, that it should occur to us
How much more fortunate they are than we are.

It is only natural that we should look and look
At their wood and brick and stone
And think, while a breath of pine blows,
How different these are from our own.

We do not want them to have less.
But it is only natural that we should think we have
    not enough.
We drive on, we drive on.
When we speak to each other our voices are a little
    gruff.

1951

The Uncle Speaks in the Drawing Room

ADRIENNE RICH

I have seen the mob of late
Standing sullen in the square,
Gazing with a sullen stare
At window, balcony, and gate.
Some have talked in bitter tones,
Some have held and fingered stones.

These are follies that subside.
Let us consider, none the less,
Certain frailties of glass
Which, it cannot be denied,
Lead in times like these to fear
For crystal vase and chandelier.

Not that missiles will be cast;
None as yet dare lift an arm.
But the scene recalls a storm
When our grandsire stood aghast
To see his antique ruby bowl
Shivered in a thunder-roll.

Let us only bear in mind
How these treasures handed down
From a calmer age passed on
Are in the keeping of our kind.
We stand between the dead glass-blowers
And murmurings of missile-throwers.

1951

'Do not go gentle into that good night'

◀◉▶

DYLAN THOMAS

Do not go gentle into that good night,
Old age should burn and rave at close of day;
Rage, rage against the dying of the light.

Though wise men at their end know dark is right,
Because their words had forked no lightning they
Do not go gentle into that good night.

Good men, the last wave by, crying how bright
Their frail deeds might have danced in a green bay,
Rage, rage against the dying of the light.

Wild men who caught and sang the sun in flight,
And learn, too late, they grieved it on its way,
Do not go gentle into that good night.

Grave men, near death, who see with blinding sight
Blind eyes could blaze like meteors and be gay,
Rage, rage against the dying of the light.

And you, my father, there on the sad height,
Curse, bless, me now with your fierce tears, I pray.
Do not go gentle into that good night.
Rage, rage against the dying of the light.

1951

Sarajevo

LAWRENCE DURRELL

Bosnia. November. And the mountain roads
Earthbound but matching perfectly these long
And passionate self-communings counter-march,
Balanced on scarps of trap, ramble or blunder
Over traverses of cloud: and here they move,
Mule-teams like insects harnessed by a bell
Upon the leaf-edge of a winter sky,

And down at last into this lap of stone
Between four cataracts of rock: a town
Peopled by sleepy eagles, whispering only
Of the sunburnt herdsman's hopeless ploy:
A sterile earth quickened by shards of rock
Where nothing grows, not even in his sleep,

Where minarets have twisted up like sugar
And a river, curdled with blond ice, drives on
Tinkling among the mule-teams and the mountaineers,
Under the bridges and the wooden trellises
Which tame the air and promise us a peace
Harmless with nightingales. None are singing now.

No history much? Perhaps. Only this ominous
Dark beauty flowering under veils,
Trapped in the spectrum of a dying style:
A village like an instinct left to rust,
Composed around the echo of a pistol-shot.

The 'pistol-shot' recalls the assassination in Sarajevo of Austrian Archduke Franz
Ferdinand on 28 June 1914, the event that triggered the First World War.

1952

The Shield of Achilles

W. H. AUDEN

She looked over his shoulder
    For vines and olive trees,
Marble well-governed cities
    And ships upon untamed seas,
But there on the shining metal
    His hands had put instead
An artificial wilderness
    And a sky like lead.

A plain without a feature, bare and brown,
   No blade of grass, no sign of neighbourhood,
Nothing to eat and nowhere to sit down,
   Yet, congregated on its blankness, stood
   An unintelligible multitude,
A million eyes, a million boots in line,
Without expression, waiting for a sign.

Out of the air a voice without a face
   Proved by statistics that some cause was just
In tones as dry and level as the place:
   No one was cheered and nothing was discussed;
   Column by column in a cloud of dust
They marched away enduring a belief
Whose logic brought them, somewhere else, to grief.

She looked over his shoulder
    For ritual pieties,
White flower-garlanded heifers,
    Libation and sacrifice,
But there on the shining metal
    Where the altar should have been,
She saw by his flickering forge-light
    Quite another scene.

Barbed wire enclosed an arbitrary spot
  Where bored officials lounged (one cracked a joke)
And sentries sweated for the day was hot:
  A crowd of ordinary decent folk
  Watched from without and neither moved nor spoke
As three pale figures were led forth and bound
To three posts driven upright in the ground.

The mass and majesty of this world, all
  That carries weight and always weighs the same
Lay in the hands of others; they were small
  And could not hope for help and no help came:
  What their foes liked to do was done, their shame
Was all the worst could wish; they lost their pride
And died as men before their bodies died.

    She looked over his shoulder
      For athletes at their games,
    Men and women in a dance
      Moving their sweet limbs
    Quick, quick, to music,
      But there on the shining shield
    His hands had set no dancing-floor
      But a weed-choked field.

A ragged urchin, aimless and alone,
  Loitered about that vacancy, a bird
Flew up to safety from his well-aimed stone:
  That girls are raped, that two boys knife a third,
  Were axioms to him, who'd never heard
Of any world where promises were kept,
Or one could weep because another wept.

The thin-lipped armourer,
  Helphaestos hobbled away,
Thetis of the shining breasts
  Cried out in dismay
At what the god had wrought
  To please her son, the strong
Iron-hearted man-slaying Achilles
  Who would not live long.

Hephaestos was commissioned to make new armour for Achilles, by Achilles'
mother Thetis, in the eighteenth book of Homer's *Iliad*.

1952

The Double Horror

◄○►

NISSIM EZEKIEL

I am corrupted by the world, continually
Reduced to something less than human by the crowd,
Newspapers, cinemas, radio features, speeches
Demanding peace by men with grim warlike faces,
Posters selling health and happiness in bottles,
Large returns for small investments, in football pools
Or self-control, six easy lessons for a pound,
Holidays in Rome for writing praise of toothpastes,
The jungle growth of what so obviously intends
To suck life from life, leaving you and me corrupted.

Those who say Comrade are merely slaves and those
Who will not be my brothers share the acrid shame
Of being unwanted, unloved, incompetent
As leaders, disloyal servants, always alone.
Unpolitical I still embrace the sterile
Whore of private politics, sign a manifesto,
Call a meeting, work on committees; I agree
Something must be done but secretly rejoice
When fifty thousand Chinese have been killed,
I who, as a child, wept to see a rat destroyed.

Corrupted by the world I must infect the world
With my corruption. This double horror holds me
Like a nightmare from which I cannot wake, denounced
Only by myself, to others harmless, hero,
Sage, poet, conversationalist, connoisseur
Of coffee, guide to modern Indian Art
Or Greek antiquities. Only being what I am
Hurts, and hurts the world although it does not know.
Between the world and me there is a frightful
Equipoise, as infected I corrupt the world.

The 'fifty thousand Chinese' referred to as 'killed' were casualties in the civil war
between Communists and Nationalists, which had resumed in China after the
end of the Second World War. It ended with the proclamation of the People's
Republic by Mao Zedong in October 1949. Chiang Kai-Shek's remaining
Nationalist forces retreated to Taiwan.

1953

The Lost Man

⟨◦⟩

JUDITH WRIGHT

To reach the pool you must go through the rain-forest –
through the bewildering midsummer of darkness
lit with ancient fern,
laced with poison and thorn.
You must go by the way he went – the way of the
    bleeding
hands and feet, the blood on the stones like flowers,
under the hooded flowers
that fall on the stones like blood.
To reach the pool you must go by the black valley,
among the crowding columns made of silence,
under the hanging clouds
of leaves and voiceless birds.
To go by the way he went to the voice of the water,
where the priest stinging-tree waits with his whips and
    fevers,
under the hooded flowers
that fall from the trees like blood,
you must forget the song of the gold bird dancing
over tossed light; you must remember nothing
except the drag of darkness
that draws your weakness under.
To go by the way he went, you must find beneath you
that last and faceless pool, and fall. And falling
find between breath and death
the sun by which you live.

1954

from Rites

◄◦►

EDWARD KAMAU BRATHWAITE

If uh wasn't there to see fuh meself,
I would'a never believe it,
I would'a never believe it.

But I say it once an' I say it agen:
when things goin' good, you cahn touch
we; but leh murder start an' you cahn fine a man to hole
   up de side.

Like when Laker come on.
Goin' remember what happenin' then
for the rest o' me life.

This Laker a quiet tall heavy-face fellow
who before he start to do anything ser'ous
is hitch up he pants round he belly.

He bowlin' off-breaks.
Int makin' no fuss
jus' toss up de firs'

one an' *bap!*
Clyde play forward firm
an' de ball hit he pad

an' fly up over de wicket.
Boy, *dis* is cricket!
Laker shift weight

an' toss up de secon';
it pitchin' off-stump an' comin'back sharp
wid de men in de leg trap shinin' like shark.

Clyde stretchin' right out like a man in de dark
an' he kill it.
'N . . . O . . . O . . . O', from de schoolboys, 'hit it, hit it'.

Boy, dis is *cricket*.
Then Laker come down wid he third
one. He wrap up de ball in de palm

o' he han' like a package
AN' MAKE CLYDE WALCOTT LOOK FOOLISH.
Mister man, could'a hear

all de flies that was buzzin' out there
round de bread carts; could'a hear
if de empire fart.

An' then blue murder start:
'Kill one o'dem, Clyde', some wise-
wun was shoutin', 'knock he skull off;

doan let them tangle you up in no leg trap;
use de feet dat God give you!'
Ev'ry blabber mout' talkin',

ev'ry man jack givin' advice;
but we so frighten now at what happenin' there
we could piss we pants if we doan have a care.

'*Swing de bat, man*', one feller was shoutin';
an' Clyde swing de bat but de bat miss
de ball an' de ball hit he pad

an' he pad went biff
like you beatin' bed
an' de empire han' stick

in de air
like Francis who dead
an' de bess o' we batsmen out.

The crowd so surprise you int hearin'a shout.
Ev'ry mout' loss.
But I say it once an' I say it agen:

when things goin' good, you cahn touch
we; but leh murder start
an' ol man, you cahn fine a man to hole up de
   side . . .

West Indian Clyde Walcott was one of the great batsmen of the twentieth century with a Test average of 56.68. He was knighted for services to cricket in 1994. Jim Laker was one of England's finest spinners, famous for his record nineteen wickets in a Test match against Australia in 1956.

1954

Church Going

PHILIP LARKIN

Once I am sure there's nothing going on
I step inside, letting the door thud shut.
Another church: matting, seats, and stone,
And little books; sprawlings of flowers, cut
For Sunday, brownish now; some brass and stuff
Up at the holy end; the small neat organ;
And a tense, musty, unignorable silence,
Brewed God knows how long. Hatless, I take off
My cycle-clips in awkward reverence,

Move forward, run my hand around the font.
From where I stand, the roof looks almost new –
Cleaned, or restored? Someone would know: I don't.
Mounting the lectern, I peruse a few
Hectoring large-scale verses, and pronounce
'Here endeth' much more loudly than I'd meant.
The echoes snigger briefly. Back at the door
I sign the book, donate an Irish sixpence,
Reflect the place was not worth stopping for.

Yet stop I did: in fact I often do,
And always end much at a loss like this,
Wondering what to look for; wondering, too,
When churches fall completely out of use
What we shall turn them into, if we shall keep
A few cathedrals chronically on show,
Their parchment, plate and pyx in locked cases,
And let the rest rent-free to rain and sheep.
Shall we avoid them as unlucky places?

Or, after dark, will dubious women come
To make their children touch a particular stone;
Pick simples for a cancer; or on some
Advised night see walking a dead one?
Power of some sort or other will go on
In games, in riddles, seemingly at random;
But superstition, like belief, must die,
And what remains when disbelief has gone?
Grass, weedy pavement, brambles, buttress, sky,

A shape less recognisable each week,
A purpose more obscure. I wonder who
Will be the last, the very last, to seek
This place for what it was; one of the crew
That tap and jot and know what rood-lofts were?
Some ruin-bibber, randy for antique,
Or Christmas-addict, counting on a whiff
Of gown-and-bands and organ-pipes and myrrh?
Or will he be my representative,

Bored, uninformed, knowing the ghostly silt
Dispersed, yet tending to this cross of ground
Through suburb scrub because it held unspilt
So long and equably what since is found
Only in separation – marriage, and birth,
And death, and thoughts of these – for which was built
This special shell? For, though I've no idea
What this accoutred frowsty barn is worth,
It pleases me to stand in silence here;

A serious house on serious earth it is,
In whose blent air all our compulsions meet,
Are recognised, and robed as destinies.
And that much never can be obsolete,
Since someone will forever be surprising
A hunger in himself to be more serious,
And gravitating with it to this ground,
Which, he once heard, was proper to grow wise in,
If only that so many dead lie round.

1954

The Wound

◄○►

Thom Gunn

The huge wound in my head began to heal
About the beginning of the seventh week.
Its valleys darkened, its villages became still:
For joy I did not move and dared not speak,
Not doctors would cure it, but time, its patient skill.

And constantly my mind returned to Troy.
After I sailed the seas I fought in turn
On both sides, sharing even Helen's joy
Of place, and growing up — to see Troy burn —
As Neoptolemus, that stubborn boy.

I lay and rested as prescription said.
Maneuvered with the Greeks, or sallied out
Each day with Hector. Finally my bed
Became Achilles' tent, to which the lout
Thersites came reporting numbers dead.

I was myself: subject to no man's breath:
My own commander was my enemy.
And while my belt hung up, sword in the sheath,
Thersites shambled in and breathlessly
Cackled about my friend Patroclus' death.

I called for armor, rose, and did not reel.
But, when I thought, rage at his noble pain
Flew to my head, and turning I could feel
My wound break open wide. Over again
I had to let those storm-lit valleys heal.

The names of Trojan Hector and Greek Achilles, and of the beautiful Helen
whose abduction led to the Trojan War, are of course familiar from Homer's *Iliad*.
Neoptolemus is Achilles' son, and Patroclus Achilles' friend.

1954

Death of a Son
(who died in a mental hospital aged one)

JON SILKIN

Something has ceased to come along with me.
Something like a person: something very like one.
And there was no nobility in it
Or anything like that.

Something was there like a one year
Old house, dumb as stone. While the near buildings
Sang like birds and laughed
Understanding the pact

They were to have with silence. But he
Neither sang nor laughed. He did not bless silence
Like bread, with words.
He did not forsake silence.

But rather, like a house in mourning
Kept the eye turned in to watch the silence while
The other houses like birds
Sang around him.

And the breathing silence neither
Moved nor was still.

I have seen stones: I have seen brick
But this house was made up of neither bricks nor stone
But a house of flesh and blood
With flesh of stone

And bricks for blood. A house
Of stones and blood in breathing silence with the other
Birds singing crazy on its chimneys.
But this was silence,

This was something else, this was
Hearing and speaking though he was a house drawn
    Into silence, this was
        Something religious in his silence,

  Something shining in his quiet,
This was different this was altogether something else:
    Though he never spoke, this
        Was something to do with death.

  And then slowly the eye stopped looking
Inward. The silence rose and became still.
The look turned to the outer place and stopped,
    With the birds still shrilling around him.
      And as if he could speak

He turned over on his side with his one year
Red as a wound
He turned over as if he could be sorry for this
And out of his eyes two great tears rolled, like stones, and
  he died.

1955

At Cooloolah

JUDITH WRIGHT

The blue crane fishing in Cooloolah's twilight
has fished there longer than our centuries.
He is the certain heir of lake and evening,
and he will wear their colour till he dies;

but I'm a stranger, come of a conquering people.
I cannot share his calm, who watch his lake,
being unloved by all my eyes delight in
and made uneasy, for an old murder's sake.

Those dark-skinned people who once named Cooloolah
knew that no land is lost or won by wars,
for earth is spirit; the invader's feet will tangle
in nets there and his blood be thinned by fears.

Riding at noon and ninety years ago,
my grandfather was beckoned by a ghost –
a black accoutred warrior armed for fighting,
who sank into bare plain, as now into time past.

White shores of sand, plumed reed and paperbark,
clear heavenly levels frequented by crane and swan –
I know that we are justified only by love,
but oppressed by arrogant guilt, have room for none.

And walking on clean sand among the prints
of bird and animal, I am challenged by a driftwood spear
thrust from the water; and, like my grandfather,
must quiet a heart accused by its own fear.

The date of the grandfather's vision – 'ninety years ago' – suggests that he was at
Cooloolah, in Queensland, for the gold rush of 1867.

1955

Frankie and Johnny in 1955
—◦—
KIT WRIGHT

Many of the men wore damned great flannel trousers
With double-breasted blazers. Double-breasted women wore
 blouses

With pleated skirts or shiny black haunch-hugging dresses
On the night and the morning of the twin unpleasantnesses –

His shooting, her hanging – while I myself wore shorts,
Snakebelt and aertex, suitable for summer sports,

When Albert Pierrepoint hanged Ruth Ellis high
In Holloway Prison and I was too young to cry –

She, to die. Poor Ruth, I say:
She whipped out a .38, blew her lover away.

Now, Ruth was the last woman hanged on British earth
And David Blakely was of moneyed birth –

Public school, army, obsessed with racing cars,
Which he talked about all the time in clubs and bars –

Was a total shit, some say, which I think untrue –
I think he was as much of a shit as me or you –

Some say he was charming and friendly – alas for charm –
The grave leaves never a trace – well, he did her harm,

But not as much harm as she did him that day
She whipped out a damned great gun and she blew him away.

Well, Ruth was the Little Club night-club manageress
And had been through, seen through, much distress

Long before the killing. She'd a war-time child
By a GI who ditched her, divorce suit filed

From a mad alcoholic dentist who smashed her about:
Then: semi-pro loving in clubs. No doubt

Of the matter at all, time worked her so
Little Ruth was as hard as nails and as soft as snow

And the hurt she felt, and the love, and the hate
She fired point-blank from a damned great .38.

Oh, the reason little Ruth was standing in the dock
Was she loved him in the morning and she loved him round
the clock

But people were stealing him. Ruth said, 'Well,
Can't see my loving man here, I'll see him in hell' –

And she wanted to die, did die, which she needn't have done
But she said in court, with that Smith and Wesson gun

She'd a fancy to kill him – wed him with a big black
trousseau?
Yes, she wanted to die. But he didn't wish to do so

And I count it a shame that by South End Green
She wasted her lover with a damned great hand-machine.

She'd a powder compact that played *La Vie En Rose*,
She was taking French lessons, she'd a special film-actress
pose

For photos, she was slender, she'd a small white face like an
ox-eyed
Daisy and hair of pure peroxide

(That probably hanged her – at the trial a smart
Juror noted down: 'She's a TYPICAL WEST END TART')

And Blakely was a handsome and a likeable youth –
Spoilt ponce, too, violent bastard to Ruth,

Some say. Who's to judge? Oh, the judge could judge that day
He slipped on his little black cap and he slid her away.

Not much to say. She loved him but she hadn't got him.
Waited by the pub and when he came out she shot him

With a mixed spray of bullets to his head, his lungs, his
    heart:
It was theatre, my lovely, performance art,

But you didn't want to do it, they didn't want to do it to
    you
And they snipped your pretty white throat pretty nearly in
    two

Because, entirely, it was 1955:
Oh, I wish you were here, I wish you were alive

And I wish above all things unmade, junked down the spout,
That damned great side-arm that took your loving man out.

Your lifetime later, I think how nothing is freed
By time from its shadow, opacity of need,

The instant when it happens, *in situ*, on spec –
How nothing but detail breaks anyone's heart or
    neck –

Of how, little Ruth, in the first year of rock-and-roll,
You could tip young David down into the hole

Or how they could hang you on a Holloway hanging tree,
Poor little Ruth Ellis, two months before ITV.

'Frankie and Johnny' is a traditional American song, and story, of unclear origins, in which Frankie finds that her man Johnny is having an affair with another woman and shoots him dead. There have been numerous treatments in various media, including films with Elvis Presley (1966) and with Al Pacino and Michelle Pfeiffer (1991). Kit Wright's poem transfers the outline of the story to the case of Ruth Ellis (1926–55), the last woman to be executed in the UK, who was hanged for the murder of her lover, David Blakely. Albert Pierrepoint (1905–92) was for many years the UK's official hangman, the third in his family to hold the position, and in that office executed several hundred people (many of them Nazi war criminals).

1955

The Horses

—◄◦►—

EDWIN MUIR

Barely a twelvemonth after
The seven days war that put the world to sleep,
Late in the evening the strange horses came.
By then we had made our covenant with silence,
But in the first few days it was so still
We listened to our breathing and were afraid.
On the second day
The radios failed; we turned the knobs; no answer.
On the third day a warship passed us, heading north,
Dead bodies piled on the deck. On the sixth day
A plane plunged over us into the sea. Thereafter
Nothing. The radios dumb;
And still they stand in corners of our kitchens,
And stand, perhaps, turned on, in a million rooms
All over the world. But now if they should speak,
If on a sudden they should speak again,
If on the stroke of noon a voice should speak,
We would not listen, we would not let it bring
That old bad world that swallowed its children quick
At one great gulp. We would not have it again.
Sometimes we think of the nations lying asleep,
Curled blindly in impenetrable sorrow,
And then the thought confounds us with its strangeness.

The tractors lie about our fields; at evening
They look like dank sea-monsters couched and waiting.
We leave them where they are and let them rust:
'They'll moulder away and be like other loam.'
We make our oxen drag our rusty ploughs,
Long laid aside. We have gone back
Far past our fathers' land.
                           And then, that evening

Late in the summer the strange horses came.
We heard a distant tapping on the road,
A deepening drumming; it stopped, went on again
And at the corner changed to hollow thunder.
We saw the heads
Like a wild wave charging and were afraid.
We had sold our horses in our fathers' time
To buy new tractors. Now they were strange to us
As fabulous steeds set on an ancient shield
Or illustrations in a book of knights.
We did not dare go near them. Yet they waited,
Stubborn and shy, as if they had been sent
By an old command to find our whereabouts
And that long-lost archaic companionship.
In the first moment we had never a thought
That they were creatures to be owned and used.
Among them were some half-a-dozen colts
Dropped in some wilderness of the broken world,
Yet new as if they had come from their own Eden.
Since then they have pulled our ploughs and borne our
    loads,
But that free servitude still can pierce our hearts.
Our life is changed; their coming our beginning.

1956

America

ALLEN GINSBERG

America I've given you all and now I'm nothing.
America two dollars and twentyseven cents January 17, 1956.
I can't stand my own mind.
America when will we end the human war?
Go fuck yourself with your atom bomb.
I don't feel good don't bother me.
I won't write my poem till I'm in my right mind.
America when will you be angelic?
When will you take off your clothes?
When will you look at yourself through the grave?
When will you be worthy of your million Trotskyites?
America why are your libraries full of tears?
America when will you send your eggs to India?
I'm sick of your insane demands.
When can I go into the supermarket and buy what I need with
    my good looks?
America after all it is you and I who are perfect not the next
    world.
Your machinery is too much for me.
You made me want to be a saint.
There must be some other way to settle this argument.
Burroughs is in Tangiers I don't think he'll come back it's sinister.
Are you being sinister or is this some form of practical joke?
I'm trying to come to the point.
I refuse to give up my obsession.
America stop pushing I know what I'm doing.
America the plum blossoms are falling.
I haven't read the newspapers for months, everyday somebody
    goes on trial for murder.
America I feel sentimental about the Wobblies.
America I used to be a communist when I was a kid I'm not
    sorry.

I smoke marijuana every chance I get.

I sit in my house for days on end and stare at the roses in the
closet.

When I go to Chinatown I get drunk and never get laid.

My mind is made up there's going to be trouble.

You should have seen me reading Marx.

My psychoanalyst thinks I'm perfectly right.

I won't say the Lord's Prayer.

I have mystical visions and cosmic vibrations.

America I still haven't told you what you did to Uncle Max after
he came over from Russia.

I'm addressing you.

Are you going to let your emotional life be run by *Time*
Magazine?

I'm obsessed by *Time Magazine*.

I read it every week.

Its cover stares at me every time I slink past the corner
candystore.

I read it in the basement of the Berkeley Public Library.

It's always telling me about responsibility. Businessmen are serious.
Movie producers are serious. Everybody's serious but me.

It occurs to me that I am America.

I am talking to myself again.

Asia is rising against me.

I haven't got a chinaman's chance.

I'd better consider my national resources.

My national resources consist of two joints of marijuana millions
of genitals an unpublishable private literature that jetplanes
1400 miles an hour and twentyfive-thousand mental
institutions.

I say nothing about my prisons nor the millions of
underprivileged who live in my flowerpots under the light of
five hundred suns.

I have abolished the whorehouses of France, Tangiers is the next
to go.

My ambition is to be President despite the fact that I'm a
Catholic.

America how can I write a holy litany in your silly mood?

I will continue like Henry Ford my strophes are as individual as
his automobiles more so they're all different sexes.

America I will sell you strophes $2500 apiece $500 down on
your old strophe

America free Tom Mooney

America save the Spanish Loyalists

America Sacco & Vanzetti must not die

America I am the Scottsboro boys.

America when I was seven momma took me to Communist Cell
meetings they sold us garbanzos a handful per ticket a ticket
costs a nickel and the speeches were free everybody was
angelic and sentimental about the workers it was all so sincere
you have no idea what a good thing the party was in 1835
Scott Nearing was a grand old man a real mensch Mother
Bloor the Silk-strikers' Ewig-Weibliche made me cry I once
saw the Yiddish orator Israel Amter plain. Everybody must
have been a spy.

America you don't really want to go to war.

America it's them bad Russians.

Them Russians them Russians and them Chinamen. And them
Russians.

The Russia wants to eat us alive. The Russia's power mad. She
wants to take our cars from out our garages.

Her wants to grab Chicago. Her needs a Red *Reader's Digest*. Her
wants our auto plants in Siberia. Him big bureaucracy running
our fillingstations.

That no good. Ugh. Him make Indians learn read. Him need big
black niggers. Hah. Her make us all work sixteen hours a day.
Help.

America this is quite serious.

America this is the impression I get from looking in the
television set.

America is this correct?

I'd better get right down to the job.

It's true I don't want to join the Army or turn lathes in precision
parts factories, I'm nearsighted and psychopathic anyway.

America I'm putting my queer shoulder to the wheel.

Berkeley, January 17, 1956

William S. Burroughs, subsequently the author of *Naked Lunch*, spent time in Morocco because homosexual partners and drugs were readily available there. By "the Wobblies" Ginsberg means the Industrial Workers of the World, an international union. Tom Mooney (1882–1942) was a political activist and labour leader, who was, controversially, convicted of an anarchist bombing in 1916. He was pardoned in 1939 after twenty-two years in prison. Similarly, Sacco and Vanzetti polarised American opinion when tried for murder (they were executed), and the nine black defendants in a gang rape case at Scottsboro, Alabama, found themselves at the centre of one of the stormiest legal controversies in US history. Radical activist Scott Nearing (1883–1983) and Ella Reeve "Mother" Bloor (1862–1951) were campaigners for socialist and pacifist causes. The silk strikers protested in 1913 in Paterson, New Jersey, shutting down all three hundred mills in the city. Ginsberg's association with this women-led strike of "das Ewig-Weibliche", the eternal female principle which, according to Goethe's *Faust*, forever draws us onward, is presumably meant as a reflection on the energy and power of women. Israel Amter (1881–1954) was a founder member of the US Communist Party. Ginsberg's extraordinary litany profiles an alternative, anti-establishment view of America.

1956

Sinalóa

◀◦▶

EARLE BIRNEY

Si, señor, is halligators here, your guidebook say it,
si, jaguar in the montañas, maybe helephants, quién sabe?
You like, those palm trees in the sunset? Certamente very
  nice,
it happen each night in the guía tourista.
But who the hell eat jaguar, halligator, you heat them?
Mira my fren, wat this town need is muy big breakwater –
  I like take hax to them jeezly palmas.

So you want buy machete? Por favor, I give you
sousand machetes you give me one grand bulldozer, hey?
Wat this country is lack, señor, is real good goosin,
is need pinehapple shove hup her bottom
(sure, sure, is bella all those water-ayacints)
is need drains for sugarcane in them pitorescos swamps –
  and shoot all them anarquista egrets.

Hokay, you like bugambilla, ow you say, flower-hung cliffs?
Is how old, the Fort? Is Colhuan, muy viejo, before Moses,
  no?
Is for you, señor, take em away, send us helevator for w'eat.
It like me to see all them fine boxcar stuff full rice,
sugar, flax, all rollin down to those palmstudded ports
were Cortez and all that crap (you heat history?) –
  and bugger the pink flamingos.

Amigo, we make you present all them two-weel hoxcart,
you send em Québec, were my brudder was learn to be
    padre —
we take ditchdiggers, tractors, Massey-Arris yes?
Sinalóa want ten sousand mile irrigation canals,
absolutamente. Is fun all that organ-cactus fence?
Is for the birds, señor; is more better barbwire, verdad? —
    and chingar those cute little burros.

Sin argumento, my fren, is a beautiful music,
all them birds. Pero, wy you no like to hear combos,
refrigerator trucks? Is wonderful on straight new ighway
jampack with melons, peppers, bananas, tomatoes, si, si . . .
Chirrimoyas? Mangos? You like! Is for Indros, solamente,
is bruise, no can ship, is no bueno, believe me, señor —
    and defecar on those goddam guidebook.

Sinalóa is a state in northwestern Mexico. Massey Harris was for many years the leading US maker of tractors (the company merged to become Massey Ferguson in the Fifties).

1956

At the Fishhouses

ELIZABETH BISHOP

Although it is a cold evening,
down by one of the fishhouses
an old man sits netting,
his net, in the gloaming almost invisible,
a dark purple-brown,
and his shuttle worn and polished.
The air smells so strong of codfish
it makes one's nose run and one's eyes water.
The five fishhouses have steeply peaked roofs
and narrow, cleated gangplanks slant up
to storerooms in the gables
for the wheelbarrows to be pushed up and down on.
All is silver: the heavy surface of the sea,
swelling slowly as if considering spilling over,
is opaque, but the silver of the benches,
the lobster pots, and masts, scattered
among the wild jagged rocks,
is of an apparent translucence
like the small old buildings with an emerald moss
growing on their shoreward walls.
The big fish tubs are completely lined
with layers of beautiful herring scales
and the wheelbarrows are similarly plastered
with creamy iridescent coats of mail,
with small iridescent flies crawling on them.
Up on the little slope behind the houses,
set in the sparse bright sprinkle of grass,
is an ancient wooden capstan,
cracked, with two long bleached handles
and some melancholy stains, like dried blood,
where the ironwork has rusted.
The old man accepts a Lucky Strike.

He was a friend of my grandfather.
We talk of the decline in the population
and of codfish and herring
while he waits for a herring boat to come in.
There are sequins on his vest and on his thumb.
He has scraped the scales, the principal beauty,
from unnumbered fish with that black old knife,
the blade of which is almost worn away.

Down at the water's edge, at the place
where they haul up the boats, up the long ramp
descending into the water, thin silver
tree trunks are laid horizontally
across the gray stones, down and down
at intervals of four or five feet.

Cold dark deep and absolutely clear,
element bearable to no mortal,
to fish and to seals . . . One seal particularly
I have seen here evening after evening.
He was curious about me. He was interested in music;
like me a believer in total immersion,
so I used to sing him Baptist hymns.
I also sang 'A Mighty Fortress Is Our God.'
He stood up in the water and regarded me
steadily, moving his head a little.
Then he would disappear, then suddenly emerge
almost in the same spot, with a sort of shrug
as if it were against his better judgment.
Cold dark deep and absolutely clear,
the clear gray icy water . . . Back, behind us,
the dignified tall firs begin.
Bluish, associating with their shadows,
a million Christmas trees stand
waiting for Christmas. The water seems suspended
above the rounded gray and blue-gray stones.
I have seen it over and over, the same sea, the same,
slightly, indifferently swinging above the stones,
icily free above the stones,

above the stones and then the world.
If you should dip your hand in,
your wrist would ache immediately,
your bones would begin to ache and your hand would
   burn
as if the water were a transmutation of fire
that feeds on stones and burns with a dark gray flame.
If you tasted it, it would first taste bitter,
then briny, then surely burn your tongue.
It is like what we imagine knowledge to be:
dark, salt, clear, moving, utterly free,
drawn from the cold hard mouth
of the world, derived from the rocky breasts
forever, flowing and drawn, and since
our knowledge is historical, flowing, and flown.

1956

A Baroque Wall-Fountain in the Villa Sciarra

RICHARD WILBUR

For Dore and Adja

Under the bronze crown
Too big for the head of the stone cherub whose feet
   A serpent has begun to eat,
Sweet water brims a cockle and braids down

     Past spattered mosses, breaks
On the tipped edge of a second shell, and fills
   The massive third below. It spills
In threads then from the scalloped rim, and makes

     A scrim or summery tent
For a faun-ménage and their familiar goose.
   Happy in all that ragged, loose
Collapse of water, its effortless descent

     And flatteries of spray,
The stocky god upholds the shell with ease,
   Watching, about his shaggy knees,
The goatish innocence of his babes at play;

     His fauness all the while
Leans forward, slightly, into a clambering mesh
   Of water-lights, her sparkling flesh
In a saecular ecstasy, her blinded smile

     Bent on the sand floor
Of the trefoil pool, where ripple-shadows come
   And go in swift reticulum,
More addling to the eye than wine, and more

Interminable to thought
Than pleasure's calculus. Yet since this all
    Is pleasure, flash, and waterfall,
Must it not be too simple? Are we not

    More intricately expressed
In the plain fountains that Maderna set
    Before St Peter's – the main jet
Struggling aloft until it seems at rest

    In the act of rising, until
The very wish of water is reversed,
    That heaviness borne up to burst
In a clear, high, cavorting head, to fill

    With blaze, and then in gauze
Delays, in a gnatlike shimmering, in a fine
    Illumined version of itself, decline,
And patter on the stones its own applause?

    If that is what men are
Or should be, if those water-saints display
    The pattern of our areté,
What of these showered fauns in their bizarre,

    Spangled, and plunging house?
They are at rest in fulness of desire
    For what is given, they do not tire
Of the smart of the sun, the pleasant water-douse

    And riddled pool below,
Reproving our disgust and our ennui
    With humble insatiety.
Francis, perhaps, who lay in sister snow

    Before the wealthy gate
Freezing and praising, might have seen in this
    No trifle, but a shade of bliss –
That land of tolerable flowers, that state

As near and far as grass
Where eyes become the sunlight, and the hand
Is worthy of water: the dreamt land
Toward which all hungers leap, all pleasures pass.

The Villa Sciarra is in Rome, as is St Peter's, the frontal extension of which was designed by Carlo Maderna (1556–1629), who added the fountains in the piazza. Randall Jarrell described this as 'one of the most marvellously beautiful, one of the most nearly perfect poems any American has written', and Australian poet Alan Wearne reported in his obituary of John Forbes (see p. 708) that Forbes, at first glance surely less likely than Jarrell to recognise the strength of Wilbur, particularly admired this poem.

1957

Not Waving but Drowning

‹o›

STEVIE SMITH

Nobody heard him, the dead man,
But still he lay moaning:
I was much further out than you thought
And not waving but drowning.

Poor chap, he always loved larking
And now he's dead
It must have been too cold for him his heart gave way,
They said.

Oh, no no no, it was too cold always
(Still the dead one lay moaning)
I was much too far out all my life
And not waving but drowning.

1957

I Remember

————◄◊►————

STEVIE SMITH

It was my bridal night I remember,
An old man of seventy-three
I lay with my young bride in my arms,
A girl with t.b.
It was wartime, and overhead
The Germans were making a particularly heavy raid on
  Hampstead.
What rendered the confusion worse, perversely
Our bombers had chosen that moment to set out for
  Germany.
Harry, do they ever collide?
I do not think it has ever happened,
Oh my bride, my bride.

1957

Waikato Railstop

◄◦►

KENDRICK SMITHYMAN

Two suicides, not in the one season
   exactly, as we count what is materially
a season: principally I remember for
this railstop a so ordinary quality,
   so neutral, it may be
     distinguished for,

by, what was unusual there, as though
   intensely they shot peepholes through February's
smoke and haze revealing, instantaneous and
all-summing, purest motives, marrying perdition
   with action. Do not, please,
     misrepresent

the hamlet as an enthusiasm
   for the mortuary-minded in a death-centred
democracy. That certain young women should find
themselves unseasonably with child is to be
   understood and even
     an interest

to those on outlying farms. There was also
   an engineer who built an aircraft in his backyard,
which he could not fly; ambition was not licensed
to go soaring. Such an ascent measures most days'
   custom of being flat.
     You may set off

one day from another if you wish or
   if you can, skirting their outlook in the sandy
pinebelts while the Highway on the slight ridge above
consigns traffic elsewhere and a rake of coal-cars
   retreating south does not
     hurry, clacking

into the crossing and out, nor disturbs
   mynahs and bulbuls from their squabbling. Let orchard
and vineyard tally freights of purpose. You do well
or wither and rot where, to entertain your summer
   listening, the child's play
     musketry of

gorsepods fusillades at no target big
   enough to miss. Admiring does not get you far.
Wattleseeds crushed underfoot stink as from a knoll
you track further across the swamp ravelling out
   and winding mazily
     acres of peat

smoke their signals but no one, slouching hot,
   cares to separate smoke hulk from thundery cumulus.
Noon massed above blackens cloudland and a cuckold
below, seething skein by skein impartially.
   Outside the billiard room
     a truck backfires.

1958

In Goya's greatest scenes we seem to see
◄◦►
LAWRENCE FERLINGHETTI

In Goya's greatest scenes we seem to see
                the people of the world
    exactly at the moment when
      they first attained the title of
              'suffering humanity'
     They writhe upon the page
         in a veritable rage
            of adversity
     Heaped up
       groaning with babies and bayonets
           under cement skies
   in an abstract landscape of blasted trees
    bent statues bats wings and beaks
       slippery gibbets
     cadavers and carnivorous cocks
  and all the final hollering monsters
   of the
           'imagination of disaster'
  they are so bloody real
         it is as if they really still existed

And they do

Only the landscape is changed

They still are ranged along the roads
    plagued by legionaires
         false windmills and demented roosters

They are the same people
>> only further from home
> on freeways fifty lanes wide
> on a concrete continent
>> spaced with bland billboards
>> illustrating imbecile illusions of happiness

The scene shows fewer tumbrils
>> but more maimed citizens
>>> in painted cars
> and they have strange license plates
and engines
>> that devour America

Goya is the great Spanish artist Francisco José de Goya y Lucientes (1746–1828). Ferlinghetti chiefly has in mind the *Desastres de la Guerra* (Disasters of War), the series of prints Goya began in 1810, recording the horrors of the Napoleonic wars as experienced on the Iberian peninsula. They were not published till 1863.

1958

The Whitsun Weddings

‹o›

PHILIP LARKIN

That Whitsun, I was late getting away:
  Not till about
One-twenty on the sunlit Saturday
Did my three-quarters-empty train pull out,
All windows down, all cushions hot, all sense
Of being in a hurry gone. We ran
Behind the backs of houses, crossed a street
Of blinding windscreens, smelt the fish-dock; thence
The river's level drifting breadth began,
Where sky and Lincolnshire and water meet.

All afternoon, through the tall heat that slept
  For miles inland,
A slow and stopping curve southwards we kept.
Wide farms went by, short-shadowed cattle, and
Canals with floatings of industrial froth;
A hothouse flashed uniquely: hedges dipped
And rose: and now and then a smell of grass
Displaced the reek of buttoned carriage-cloth
Until the next town, new and nondescript,
Approached with acres of dismantled cars.

At first, I didn't notice what a noise
  The weddings made
Each station that we stopped at: sun destroys
The interest of what's happening in the shade,
And down the long cool platforms whoops and skirls
I took for porters larking with the mails,
And went on reading. Once we started, though,
We passed them, grinning and pomaded, girls
In parodies of fashion, heels and veils,
All posed irresolutely, watching us go,

As if out on the end of an event
  Waving goodbye
To something that survived it. Struck, I leant
More promptly out next time, more curiously,
And saw it all again in different terms:
The fathers with broad belts under their suits
And seamy foreheads; mothers loud and fat;
An uncle shouting smut; and then the perms,
The nylon gloves and jewellery-substitutes,
The lemons, mauves, and olive-ochres that

Marked off the girls unreally from the rest.
  Yes, from cafés
And banquet-halls up yards, and bunting-dressed
Coach-party annexes, the wedding-days
Were coming to an end. All down the line
Fresh couples climbed aboard: the rest stood round;
The last confetti and advice were thrown,
And, as we moved, each face seemed to define
Just what it saw departing: children frowned
At something dull; fathers had never known

Success so huge and wholly farcical;
  The women shared
The secret like a happy funeral;
While girls, gripping their handbags tighter, stared
At a religious wounding. Free at last,
And loaded with the sum of all they saw,
We hurried towards London, shuffling gouts of steam.
Now fields were building-plots, and poplars cast
Long shadows over major roads, and for
Some fifty minutes, that in time would seem

Just long enough to settle hats and say
  I nearly died,
A dozen marriages got under way.
They watched the landscape, sitting side by side
– An Odeon went past, a cooling tower,
And someone running up to bowl – and none
Thought of the others they would never meet

Or how their lives would all contain this hour.
I thought of London spread out in the sun,
Its postal districts packed like squares of wheat:

There we were aimed. And as we raced across
    Bright knots of rail
Past standing Pullmans, walls of blackened moss
Came close, and it was nearly done, this frail
Travelling coincidence; and what it held
Stood ready to be loosed with all the power
That being changed can give. We slowed again,
And as the tightened brakes took hold, there swelled
A sense of falling, like an arrow-shower
Sent out of sight, somewhere becoming rain.

An Odeon was a cinema, in a national chain.

1959

The Wind at Your Door

◀◦▶

R. D. FitzGerald

To Mary Gilmore

My ancestor was called on to go out –
a medical man, and one such must by law
wait in attendance on the pampered knout
and lend his countenance to what he saw,
lest the pet, patting with too bared a claw,
be judged a clumsy pussy. Bitter and hard,
see, as I see him, in that jailhouse yard.

Or see my thought of him: though time may keep
elsewhere tradition or a portrait still,
I would not feel under his cloak of sleep
if beard there or smooth chin, just to fulfil
some canon of precision. Good or ill
his blood's my own; and scratching in his grave
could find me more than I might wish to have.

Let him then be much of the middle style
of height and colouring; let his hair be dark
and his eyes green; and for that slit, the smile
that seemed inhuman, have it cruel and stark,
but grant it could be too the ironic mark
of all caught in the system – who the most,
the doctor or the flesh twined round that post?

There was a high wind blowing on that day;
for one who would not watch, but looked aside,
said that when twice he turned it blew his way
splashes of blood and strips of human hide
shaken out from the lashes that were plied
by one right-handed, one left-handed tough,
sweating at this paid task, and skilled enough.

That wind blows to your door down all these years.
Have you not known it when some breath you drew
tasted of blood? Your comfort is in arrears
of just thanks to a savagery tamed in you
only as subtler fears may serve in lieu
of thong and noose – old savagery which has built
your world and laws out of the lives it spilt.

For what was jailyard widens and takes in
my country. Fifty paces of stamped earth
stretch; and grey walls retreat and grow so thin
that towns show through and clearings – new raw birth
which burst from handcuffs – and free hands go forth
to win tomorrow's harvest from a vast
ploughland – the fifty paces of that past.

But see it through a window barred across,
from cells this side, facing the outer gate
which shuts on freedom, opens on its loss
in a flat wall. Look left now through the grate
at buildings like more walls, roofed with grey slate
or hollowed in the thickness of laid stone
each side the court where the crowd stands this noon.

One there with the officials, thick of build,
not stout, say burly (so this obstinate man
ghosts in the eyes) is he whom enemies killed
(as I was taught) because the monopolist clan
found him a grit in their smooth-turning plan,
too loyally active on behalf of Bligh.
So he got lost; and history passed him by.

But now he buttons his long coat against
the biting gusts, or as a gesture of mind,
habitual; as if to keep him fenced
from stabs of slander sticking him from behind,
sped by the schemers never far to find
in faction, where approval from one source
damns in another clubroom as of course.

This man had Hunter's confidence, King's praise;
and settlers on the starving Hawkesbury banks
recalled through twilight drifting across their days
the doctor's fee of little more than thanks
so often; and how sent by their squeezed ranks
he put their case in London. I find I lack
the hateful paint to daub him wholly black.

Perhaps my life replies to his too much
through veiling generations dropped between.
My weakness here, resentments there, may touch
old motives and explain them, till I lean
to the forgiveness I must hope may clean
my own shortcomings; since no man can live
in his own sight if it will not forgive.

Certainly I must own him whether or not
it be my will. I was made understand
this much when once, marking a freehold lot,
my papers suddenly told me it was land
granted to Martin Mason. I felt his hand
heavily on my shoulder, and knew what coil
binds life to life through bodies, and soul to soil.

There, over to one corner, a bony group
of prisoners waits; and each shall be in turn
tied by his own arms in a human loop
about the post, with his back bared to learn
the price of seeking freedom. So they earn
three hundred rippling stripes apiece, as set
by the law's mathematics against the debt.

These are the Irish batch of Castle Hill,
rebels and mutineers, my countrymen
twice over: first, because of those to till
my birthplace first, hack roads, raise roofs; and then
because their older land time and again
enrolls me through my forebears; and I claim
as origin that threshold whence we came.

One sufferer had my surname, and thereto
'Maurice', which added up to history once;
an ignorant dolt, no doubt, for all that crew
was tenantry. The breed of clod and dunce
makes patriots and true men: could I announce
that Maurice as my kin I say aloud
I'd take his irons as heraldry, and be proud.

Maurice is at the post. Its music lulls,
one hundred lashes done. If backbone shows
then play the tune on buttocks! But feel his pulse;
that's what a doctor's for; and if it goes
lamely, then dose it with these purging blows –
which have not made him moan; though, writhing there,
'Let my neck be,' he says, 'and flog me fair.'

One hundred lashes more, then rest the flail.
What says the doctor now? 'This dog won't yelp;
he'll tire you out before you'll see him fail;
here's strength to spare; go on!' Ay, pound to pulp;
yet when you've done he'll walk without your help,
and knock down guards who'd carry him being bid,
and sing no song of where the pikes are hid.

It would be well if I could find, removed
through generations back – who knows how far? –
more than a surname's thickness as a proved
bridge with that man's foundations. I need some star
of courage from his firmament, a bar
against surrenders: faith. All trials are less
than rain-blacked wind tells of that old distress.

Yet I can live with Mason. What is told
and what my heart knows of his heart, can sort
much truth from falsehood, much there that I hold
good clearly or good clouded by report;
and for things bad, ill grows where ills resort:
they were bad times. None know what in his place
they might have done. I've my own faults to face.

The dedicatee, Dame Mary Gilmore, attempted to found a socialist 'New Australia' in Paraguay in the 1890s, but lived most of her life as a journalist and poet in Australia, and at her death was given a state funeral. FitzGerald's reference to William Bligh (1754–1817), who had sailed with Cook, is not to the time of the unforgotten mutiny (1789) but to his later years (1805–8) as Governor of New South Wales, when he was again deposed in the course of a rebellion.

1959

To the Western World

Louis Simpson

A siren sang, and Europe turned away
From the high castle and the shepherd's crook.
Three caravels went sailing to Cathay
On the strange ocean, and the captains shook
Their banners out across the Mexique Bay.

And in our early days we did the same.
Remembering our fathers in their wreck
We crossed the sea from Palos where they came
And saw, enormous to the little deck,
A shore in silence waiting for a name.

The treasures of Cathay were never found.
In this America, this wilderness
Where the axe echoes with a lonely sound,
The generations labor to possess
And grave by grave we civilize the ground.

The three caravels seeking the treasures of China (and the Indies) were those of
Christopher Columbus, who set sail in 1492, on the voyage that would discover
'America', from Palos de la Frontera.

1959

Eisenhower's Visit to Franco, 1959

―◇―

JAMES WRIGHT

'. . . we die of cold, and not of darkness.'
– Unamuno

The American hero must triumph over
The forces of darkness.
He has flown through the very light of heaven
And come down in the slow dusk
Of Spain.

Franco stands in a shining circle of police.
His arms open in welcome.
He promises all dark things
Will be hunted down.

State police yawn in the prisons.
Antonio Machado follows the moon
Down a road of white dust,
To a cave of silent children
Under the Pyrenees.
Wine darkens in stone jars in villages.
Wine sleeps in the mouths of old men, it is a dark red
    color.

Smiles glitter in Madrid.
Eisenhower has touched hands with Franco, embracing
In a glare of photographers.
Clean new bombers from America muffle their engines
And glide down now.

Their wings shine in the searchlights
Of bare fields,
In Spain.

General Dwight David 'Ike' Eisenhower (1890–1969), who had supreme command of the Allied forces in Europe at D-Day and until the end of the Second World War, subsequently served as President of the US from 1953 till 1961. Though relations with Spanish dictator General Francisco Franco were controversial, Eisenhower signed a bilateral defence agreement in his first year in office, putting concerns of Cold War strategy first, and in 1959 paid a state visit to Franco which many saw as conferring legitimacy on the dictator's regime.

1959

The Day Lady Died

FRANK O'HARA

It is 12:20 in New York a Friday
three days after Bastille day, yes
it is 1959 and I go get a shoeshine
because I will get off the 4:19 in Easthampton
at 7:15 and then go straight to dinner
and I don't know the people who will feed me

I walk up the muggy street beginning to sun
and have a hamburger and a malted and buy
an ugly NEW WORLD WRITING to see what the poets
in Ghana are doing these days
                                    I go on to the bank
and Miss Stillwagon (first name Linda I once heard)
doesn't even look up my balance for once in her life
and in the GOLDEN GRIFFIN I get a little Verlaine
for Patsy with drawings by Bonnard although I do
think of Hesiod, trans. Richmond Lattimore or
Brendan Behan's new play or *Le Balcon* or *Les Nègres*
of Genet, but I don't, I stick with Verlaine
after practically going to sleep with quandariness

and for Mike I just stroll into the PARK LANE
Liquor Store and ask for a bottle of Strega and
then I go back where I came from to 6th Avenue
and the tobacconist in the Ziegfeld Theatre and
casually ask for a carton of Gauloises and a carton
of Picayunes, and a NEW YORK POST with her face on it

and I am sweating a lot by now and thinking of
leaning on the john door in the 5 SPOT
while she whispered a song along the keyboard
to Mal Waldron and everyone and I stopped breathing

Jazz singer Billie Holiday died at the age of forty-four on 17 July 1959. In the closing lines, O'Hara remembers her in performance at a club, accompanied by jazz pianist Malcolm Earl Waldron (1925–2002).

1959

from Heart's Needle

W. D. SNODGRASS

IV

No one can tell you why
the season will not wait;
   the night I told you I
must leave, you wept a fearful rate
      to stay up late.

Now that it's turning Fall,
we go to take our walk
   among municipal
flowers, to steal one off its stalk,
      to try and talk.

We huff like windy giants
scattering with our breath
   gray-headed dandelions;
Spring is the cold wind's aftermath.
      The poet saith.

But the asters, too, are gray,
ghost-gray. Last night's cold
   is sending on their way
petunias and dwarf marigold,
      hunched sick and old.

Like nerves caught in a graph,
the morning-glory vines
   frost has erased by half
still scrawl across their rigid twines.
      Like broken lines

of verses I can't make.
In its unravelling loom
we find a flower to take,
with some late buds that might still bloom,
back to your room.

Night comes and the stiff dew.
I'm told a friend's child cried
because a cricket, who
had minstrelled every night outside
her window, died.

The first of Snodgrass's four marriages ended in divorce in 1953. The poems of the title sequence in *Heart's Needle* are addressed to his daughter from that marriage.

1959

Skunk Hour

◄◦►

ROBERT LOWELL

For Elizabeth Bishop

Nautilus Island's hermit
heiress still lives through winter in her Spartan cottage;
her sheep still graze above the sea.
Her son's a bishop. Her farmer
is first selectman in our village,
she's in her dotage.

Thirsting for
the hierarchic privacy
of Queen Victoria's century,
she buys up all
the eyesores facing her shore,
and lets them fall.

The season's ill —
we've lost our summer millionaire,
who seemed to leap from an L. L. Bean
catalogue. His nine-knot yawl
was auctioned off to lobstermen.
A red fox stain covers Blue Hill.

And now our fairy
decorator brightens his shop for fall,
his fishnet's filled with orange cork,
orange, his cobbler's bench and awl,
there is no money in his work,
he'd rather marry.

One dark night,
my Tudor Ford climbed the hill's skull,
I watched for love-cars. Lights turned down,
they lay together, hull to hull,
where the graveyard shelves on the town . . .
My mind's not right.

A car radio bleats,
'Love, O careless Love . . .' I hear
my ill-spirit sob in each blood cell,
as if my hand were at its throat . . .
I myself am hell,
nobody's here –

only skunks, that search
in the moonlight for a bite to eat.
They march on their soles up Main Street:
white stripes, moonstruck eyes' red fire
under the chalk-dry and spar spire
of the Trinitarian Church.

I stand on top
of our back steps and breathe the rich air –
a mother skunk with her column of kittens swills the
     garbage pail.
She jabs her wedge head in a cup
of sour cream, drops her ostrich tail,
and will not scare.

L. L. Bean is an American mail-order company, still happily in business.

1960

The Woman at the Washington Zoo

RANDALL JARRELL

The saris go by me from the embassies.

Cloth from the moon. Cloth from another planet.
They look back at the leopard like the leopard.

And I . . .
        this print of mine, that has kept its color
Alive through so many cleanings; this dull null
Navy I wear to work, and wear from work, and so
To my bed, so to my grave, with no
Complaints, no comment: neither from my chief,
The Deputy Chief Assistant, nor his chief –
Only I complain . . . this serviceable
Body that no sunlight dyes, no hand suffuses
But, dome-shadowed, withering among columns,
Wavy beneath fountains – small, far-off, shining
In the eyes of animals, these beings trapped
As I am trapped but not, themselves, the trap,
Aging, but without knowledge of their age,
Kept safe here, knowing not of death, for death –
Oh, bars of my own body, open, open!

The world goes by my cage and never sees me.
And there come not to me, as come to these,
The wild beasts, sparrows pecking the llamas' grain,
Pigeons settling on the bears' bread, buzzards
Tearing the meat the flies have clouded . . .
                                        Vulture,
When you come for the white rat that the foxes left,

Take off the red helmet of your head, the black
Wings that have shadowed me, and step to me as man:
The wild brother at whose feet the white wolves fawn,
To whose hand of power the great lioness
Stalks, purring . . .
                    You know what I was,
You see what I am: change me, change me!

1960

from The Avenue Bearing the Initial of Christ into the New World

GALWAY KINNELL

II

The fishmarket closed, the fishes gone into flesh.
The smelts draped on each other, fat with roe,
The marble cod hacked into chunks on the counter,
Butterfishes mouths still open, still trying to eat,
Porgies with receding jaws hinged apart
In a grimace of dejection, as if like cows
They had died under the sledgehammer, perches
In grass-green armor, spotted squeteagues
In the melting ice meek-faced and croaking no more,
Mud-eating mullets buried in crushed ice,
Tilefishes with scales like bits of chickenfat,
Spanish mackerels with buttercups on the flanks,
Pot-bellied pikes, two-tone flounders
After the long contortion of pushing both eyes
To the brown side that they might look up,
Lying brown side down, like a mass laying-on of hands,
Or the oath-taking of an army.
The only things alive are the carp
That drift in the black tank in the rear,
Kept living for the usual reason, that they have not died,
And perhaps because the last meal was garbage and they might
    begin smelling
On dying, before the customer got halfway home.
They nudge each other, to be netted,
The sweet flesh to be lifted thrashing into the air,
To be slugged, and then to keep on living
While they are opened on the counter.
Fishes do not die exactly, it is more

That they go out of themselves, the visible part
Remains the same, there is little pallor,
Only the cataracted eyes that have not shut ever
Must look through the mist which crazed Homer.

These are the vegetables of the deep,
The Sheol-flowers of darkness, swimmers
Of denser darknesses where the sun's rays bend for the last
    time
And in the sky there burns this shifty jellyfish
That degenerates and flashes and re-forms.

Fishes are nailed to the wood,
The big Jew stands like Christ, nailing them to the wood,
He scrapes the knife up the grain, the scales fly,
He unnails them, reverses them, nails them again,
Scrapes and the scales fly. He lops off the heads,
Shakes out the guts as if they did not belong in the first place,
And they are flesh for the first time in their lives.

> Dear Frau—:
>   Your husband, —, died in the Camp Hospital on
> —. May I express my sincere sympathy on your bereave-
> ment. — was admitted to the Hospital on — with severe
> symptoms of exhaustion, complaining of difficulties in
> breathing and pains in the chest. Despite competent
> medication and devoted medical attention, it proved
> impossible, unfortunately, to keep the patient alive. The
> deceased voiced no final requests.
>   Camp Commandant, —

On 5th Street Bunko Certified Embalmer Catholic
Leans in his doorway drawing on a Natural Bloom Cigar.
He looks up the street. Even the Puerto Ricans are Jews
And the Chinese Laundry closes on Saturday.

1960

Epiphany

TED HUGHES

London. The grimy lilac softness
Of an April evening. Me
Walking over Chalk Farm Bridge
On my way to the tube station.
A new father – slightly light-headed
With the lack of sleep and the novelty.
Next, this young fellow coming towards me.

I glanced at him for the first time as I passed him
Because I noticed (I couldn't believe it)
What I'd been ignoring.

Not the bulge of a small animal
Buttoned into the top of his jacket
The way colliers used to wear their whippets –
But its actual face. Eyes reaching out
Trying to catch my eyes – so familiar!
The huge ears, the pinched, urchin expression –
The wild confronting stare, pushed through fear,
Between the jacket lapels.
                              'It's a fox-cub!'
I heard my own surprise as I stopped.
He stopped. 'Where did you get it? What
Are you going to do with it?'
                              A fox-cub
On the hump of Chalk Farm Bridge!

'You can have him for a pound.' 'But
Where did you find it? What will you do with it?'
'Oh, somebody'll buy him. Cheap enough
At a pound.' And a grin.
                              What I was thinking
Was – what would you think? How would we fit it

Into our crate of space? With the baby?
What would you make of its old smell
And its mannerless energy?
And as it grew up and began to enjoy itself
What would we do with an unpredictable,
Powerful, bounding fox?
The long-mouthed, flashing temperament?
That necessary nightly twenty miles
And that vast hunger for everything beyond us?
How would we cope with its cosmic derangements
Whenever we moved?
The little fox peered past me at other folks,
At this one and at that one, then at me.
Good luck was all it needed.
Already past the kittenish
But the eyes still small,
Round, orphaned-looking, woebegone
As if with weeping. Bereft
Of the blue milk, the toys of feather and fur,
The den life's happy dark. And the huge whisper
Of the constellations
Out of which Mother had always returned.
My thoughts felt like big, ignorant hounds
Circling and sniffing around him.

                      Then I walked on
As if out of my own life.
I let that fox-cub go. I tossed it back
Into the future
Of a fox-cub in London and I hurried
Straight on and dived as if escaping
Into the Underground. If I had paid,
If I had paid that pound and turned back
To you, with that armful of fox –

If I had grasped that whatever comes with a fox
Is what tests a marriage and proves it a marriage –
I would not have failed the test. Would you have failed it?
But I failed. Our marriage had failed.

1960

Pike

Pike, three inches long, perfect
Pike in all parts, green tigering the gold.
Killers from the egg: the malevolent aged grin.
They dance on the surface among the flies.

Or move, stunned by their own grandeur,
Over a bed of emerald, silhouette
Of submarine delicacy and horror.
A hundred feet long in their world.

In ponds, under the heat-struck lily pads –
Gloom of their stillness:
Logged on last year's black leaves, watching upwards.
Or hung in an amber cavern of weeds

The jaws' hooked clamp and fangs
Not to be changed at this date;
A life subdued to its instrument;
The gills kneading quietly, and the pectorals.

Three we kept behind glass,
Jungled in weed: three inches, four,
And four and a half: fed fry to them –
Suddenly there were two. Finally one

With a sag belly and the grin it was born with.
And indeed they spare nobody.
Two, six pounds each, over two feet long,
High and dry and dead in the willow-herb –

One jammed past its gills down the other's gullet:
The outside eye stared: as a vice locks –
The same iron in this eye
Though its film shrank in death.

A pond I fished, fifty yards across,
Whose lilies and muscular tench
Had outlasted every visible stone
Of the monastery that planted them –

Stilled legendary depth:
It was as deep as England. It held
Pike too immense to stir, so immense and old
That past nightfall I dared not cast

But silently cast and fished
With the hair frozen on my head
For what might move, for what eye might move.
The still splashes on the dark pond,

Owls hushing the floating woods
Frail on my ear against the dream
Darkness beneath night's darkness had freed,
That rose slowly towards me, watching.

1960

From Tibet

‹o›

DOM MORAES

I

For me my dark words are
Quickened by your bright hair,
But I have come too far
To a strange country where
Tree-fingers point towards
Darkness, and I lack words.

The yaks like clumps of wool
Stump through red poison-flowers,
So red, so beautiful,
A dream rises and towers
Beyond me, till I stand,
Your hand warm in my hand.

But I must ride with Das,
A small man quick with hope
Toward the invaded slope,
Cloud-fastened, ice-ribbed, where
A few hawks shriek and stare.

I shall keep warm above
The valleys hazed and far
For these days I find love
In poem, wind and star,
Wiser than I am wise,
You have lent me your eyes.

II

Today the rare pale sun
Appears, and the mules snort,

Das writes his press report –
We have seen no Chinese.
No fighting has begun.
The hawks sleep in the trees.

I have seen enough
Of this valley and this death.
I would not waste my breath
Mourning, but be a hawk
Who would take wing far off
Before the approaching dark.

Like cinders the red flowers
Brush fire across my sleeve.
I shall remount and leave
Taking no backward look,
And then collect these hours
In a travel book.

My book will tell the truth
But it will not be true,
Till I return to you,
My truth, my miracle.
While I keep my old faith
In you, I shall write well.

My page will be of stone
Where the bright water scrawls
The truth of Time, which falls
From times when, you not there,
I would recall, alone,
The colour of your hair.

After the Dalai Lama fled to India in 1959, following the Chinese occupation of Tibet, Dom Moraes was among the first to interview him. He spent several months working as a journalist in Tibet.

1960

Our Sharpeville

INGRID DE KOK

I was playing hopscotch on the slate
when the miners roared past in lorries,
their arms raised, signals at a crossing,
their chanting foreign and familiar,
like the call and answer of road gangs
across the veld, building hot arteries
from the heart of the Transvaal mine.

I ran to the gate to watch them pass.
And it seemed like a great caravan
moving across the desert to an oasis
I remembered from my Sunday-school book:
olive trees, a deep jade pool,
men resting in clusters after a long journey,
the danger of the mission still around them,
and night falling, its silver stars just like the ones
you got for remembering your Bible texts.

Then my grandmother called from behind the front door,
her voice a stiff broom over the steps:
'Come inside; they do things to little girls.'

For it was noon, and there was no jade pool.
Instead, a pool of blood that already had a living name
and grew like a shadow as the day lengthened.

The dead, buried in voices that reached even my gate,
the chanting men on the ambushed trucks,
these were not heroes in my town,
but maulers of children,
doing things that had to remain nameless.
And our Sharpeville was this fearful thing
that might tempt us across the well-swept streets.

If I had turned I would have seen
brocade curtains drawn tightly across sheer net ones,
known there were eyes behind both,
heard the dogs pacing the locked yard next door.
But, walking backwards, all I felt was shame,
at being a girl, at having been found at the gate,
at having heard my grandmother lie
and at the fear her lie might be true.
Walking backwards, called back,
I returned to the closed rooms, home.

On 21 March 1960, in Sharpeville, near Johannesburg, a confrontation of about twenty thousand black protesters with police turned violent. The police fired into the crowd, killing sixty-nine protesters. Ingrid de Kok, a white South African, was a nine-year-old at the time, growing up in the mining town of Stilfontein.

1961

In a Cold Season

MICHAEL HAMBURGER

I

Words cannot reach him in his prison of words
Whose words killed men because those men were words
Women and children who to him were numbers
And still are numbers though reiterated
Launched into air to circle out of hearing
And drop unseen, their metal shells not broken.
Words cannot reach him though I spend more words
On words reporting words reiterated
When in his cage of words he answered words
That told how with his words he murdered men
Women and children who were words and numbers
And he remembered or could not remember
The words and numbers they reiterated
To trap in words the man who killed with words.
Words cannot reach the children, women, men
Who were not words or numbers till they died
Because ice-packed in terror shrunk minds clung
To numbers words that did not sob or whimper
As children do when packed in trucks to die
That did not die two deaths as mothers do
Who see their children packed in trucks to die.

II

Yet, Muse of the IN-trays, OUT-trays,
Shall he be left uncelebrated
For lack of resonant numbers calculated
To denote your hero, and our abstract age?
Rather in the appropriate vocabulary

Let a memorandum now be drawn up –
Carbon copies to all whom it may concern –
A monument in kind, a testimonial
To be filed for further reference
And to circulate as required.
Adolf Eichmann, civil servant (retired):
A mild man, meticulous in his ways,
As distinctly averse to violence
As to all other irregularities
Perpetrated in his presence,
Rudeness of speech or deportment,
Infringements of etiquette
Or downright incompetence, the gravest offence;
With a head for figures, a stable family life,
No abnormalities.

Never lost his temper on duty
Even with subordinates, even with elements earmarked
For liquidation;
Never once guilty of exceeding his authority
But careful always to confine his ambitions
Within the limits laid down for personnel of his grade.
Never, of course, a maker of policy,
But in its implementation at office level,
Down to the detailed directive, completely reliable;
Never, perhaps, indispensable,
Yet difficult to replace
Once he had mastered the formalities
Of his particular department
And familiarized himself with his responsibilities
As a specialist in the organization
Of the transport and disposal of human material –
In short, an exemplary career.

III

Words words his words – and half his truth perhaps
If blinking, numb in moonlight and astray
A man can map the landmarks trace the shapes

That may be mountains icebergs or his tears
And he whose only zeal was to convert
Real women children men to words and numbers
Added to be subtracted leaving nothing
But aggregates and multiples of nothing
Can know what made him adept in not knowing
Feel what it was he could not would not feel –
And caged in words between their death his death
No place no time for memory to unfreeze
The single face that would belie his words
The single cry that proved his numbers wrong.

Probing his words with their words my words fail.
Cold cold with words I cannot break the shell
And almost dare not lest his whole truth be
To have no core but unreality.

IV

I heard no cry, nor saw her dying face,
Have never known the place, the day,
Whether by bullet, gas or deprivation
They finished her off who was old and ill enough
To die before long in her own good time;
Only that when they came to march her out of her
    human world,
Creaking leather couch, mementoes, widow's urn,
They made her write a postcard to her son in England.
'Am going on a journey'; and that all those years
She had refused to travel even to save her life.
Too little I know of her life, her death,
Forget my last visit to her at the age of nine,
The goodbye like any other that was the last,
Only recall that she, mother of five, grandmother,
Freely could share with a child all her little realm;
Recall her lapdog who trembled and snapped up cheese –
Did they kill her lapdog also, or drive him away? –
And the bigger dog before that, a French bulldog, stuffed
To keep her company still after his early death.

Three goldfishes I recall, one with a hump on his back
That lived for years though daily she brushed her fishes
Under the kitchen tap to keep them healthy and clean;
And how she conspired with us children,
Bribed us with sweets if we promised not to tell
Our father that she, who was diabetic,
Kept a pillbox of sweets in her handbag
To eat like a child in secret –
When neither could guess that sweets would not cause her
    death.
A wireless set with earphones was part of the magic
She commanded and freely dispensed,
Being childlike herself and guileless and wise . . .

Too little I know of her wisdom, her life,
Only that, guileless, she died deprived
Of her lapdog even, stuffed bulldog and pillbox of sweets.

V

And yet and yet I would not have him die
Caged in his words their words – one deadly word
Setting the seal on unreality
Adding one number to the millions dead
Subtracting nothing from death dividing nothing
Silencing him who murdered words with words
Not one shell broken, not one word made flesh.
Nor in my hatred would imprison him
Who never free in fear and hatred served
Another's hatred which again was fear
So little life in him he dared not pity
Or if he pitied dared not act on pity;
But show him pity now for pity's sake
And for their sake who died for lack of pity;
Break from the husk at last one naked grain
That still may grow where the massed carrion lay
Bones piled on bones their only mourners bones
The inconceivable aggregate of the dead
Beyond all power to mourn or to avenge;

See man in him spare woman child in him
Though in the end he neither saw nor spared –
Peel off the husk for once and heed the grain,
Plant it though he sowed nothing poisoned growth;
Dare break one word and words may yet be whole.

Adolf Eichmann (1906–62) was one of the principal architects and organisers of the Nazi genocide. After the Second World War he escaped to Argentina, where he was abducted on 11 May 1960 by Mossad agents and smuggled to Israel. His trial in Jerusalem, which began on 11 April 1961, was closely followed throughout the world. Eichmann appealed against the death sentence handed down in December, but it was upheld the following May by the Israeli Supreme Court, and he was hanged on 31 May 1962. Hannah Arendt, the German Jewish political philosopher, who had lived in the US since 1941, reported on the trial for *The New Yorker*, and subsequently published *Eichmann in Jerusalem* in 1963, coining the phrase 'the banality of evil' to describe Eichmann's conduct.

1961

My Grandmother

ELIZABETH JENNINGS

She kept an antique shop – or it kept her.
Among Apostle spoons and Bristol glass,
The faded silks, the heavy furniture,
She watched her own reflection in the brass
Salvers and silver bowls, as if to prove
Polish was all, there was no need of love.

And I remember how I once refused
To go out with her, since I was afraid.
It was perhaps a wish not to be used
Like antique objects. Though she never said
That she was hurt, I still could feel the guilt
Of that refusal, guessing how she felt.

Later, too frail to keep a shop, she put
All her best things in one long narrow room.
The place smelt old, of things too long kept shut,
The smell of absences where shadows come
That can't be polished. There was nothing then
To give her own reflection back again.

And when she died I felt no grief at all,
Only the guilt of what I once refused.
I walked into her room among the tall
Sideboards and cupboards – things she never used
But needed; and no finger-marks were there,
Only the new dust falling through the air.

1961

The Taxis

LOUIS MACNEICE

In the first taxi he was alone tra-la,
No extras on the clock. He tipped ninepence
But the cabby, while he thanked him, looked askance
As though to suggest someone had bummed a ride.

In the second taxi he was alone tra-la
But the clock showed sixpence extra; he tipped according
And the cabby from out his muffler said: 'Make sure
You have left nothing behind tra-la between you.'

In the third taxi he was alone tra-la
But the tip-up seats were down and there was an extra
Charge of one-and-sixpence and an odd
Scent that reminded him of a trip to Cannes.

As for the fourth taxi, he was alone
Tra-la when he hailed it but the cabby looked
Through him and said: 'I can't tra-la well take
So many people, not to speak of the dog.'

1961

Advice to a Prophet

◁◦▷

RICHARD WILBUR

When you come, as you soon must, to the streets of our
 city
Mad-eyed from stating the obvious,
Not proclaiming our fall but begging us
In God's name to have self-pity,

Spare us all word of the weapons, their force and range,
The long numbers that rocket the mind;
Our slow, unreckoning hearts will be left behind,
Unable to fear what is too strange.

Nor shall you scare us with talk of the death of the race.
How should we dream of this place without us? –
The sun mere fire, the leaves untroubled about us,
A stone look on the stone's face?

Speak of the world's own change. Though we cannot
 conceive
Of an undreamt thing, we know to our cost
How the dreamt cloud crumbles, the vines are blackened by
 frost,
How the view alters. We could believe,

If you told us so, that the white-tailed deer will slip
Into perfect shade, grown perfectly shy,
The lark avoid the reaches of our eye,
The jack-pine lose its knuckled grip

On the cold ledge, and every torrent burn
As Xanthus once, its gliding trout
Stunned in a twinkling. What should we be without
The dolphin's arc, the dove's return,

432

These things in which we have seen ourselves and spoken?
Ask us, prophet, how we shall call
Our natures forth when that live tongue is all
Dispelled, that glass obscured or broken

In which we have said the rose of our love and the clean
Horse of our courage, in which beheld
The singing locust of the soul unshelled,
And all we mean or wish to mean.

Ask us, ask us whether with the worldless rose
Our hearts shall fail us; come demanding
Whether there shall be lofty or long standing
When the bronze annals of the oak-tree close.

In book XXI of Homer's *Iliad*, Hephaestus is commanded by his mother to 'burn
the trees on Xanthus' banks, and set the very river on fire'.

1961

Fall 1961

◄○►

ROBERT LOWELL

Back and forth, back and forth
goes the tock, tock, tock
of the orange, bland, ambassadorial
face of the moon
on the grandfather clock.

All autumn, the chafe and jar
of nuclear war;
we have talked our extinction to death.
I swim like a minnow
behind my studio window.

Our end drifts nearer,
the moon lifts,
radiant with terror.
The state
is a diver under a glass bell.

A father's no shield
for his child.
We are like a lot of wild
spiders crying together,
but without tears.

Nature holds up a mirror.
One swallow makes a summer.
It's easy to tick
off the minutes,
but the clockhands stick.

Back and forth!
Back and forth, back and forth –
my one point of rest
is the orange and black
oriole's swinging nest!

1962

Cuba

◄◊►

PAUL MULDOON

My eldest sister arrived home that morning
In her white muslin evening dress.
'Who the hell do you think you are,
Running out to dances in next to nothing?
As though we hadn't enough bother
With the world at war, if not at an end.'
My father was pounding the breakfast-table.

'Those Yankees were touch and go as it was –
If you'd heard Patton in Armagh –
But this Kennedy's nearly an Irishman
So he's not much better than ourselves.
And him with only to say the word.
If you've got anything on your mind
Maybe you should make your peace with God.'

I could hear May from beyond the curtain.
'Bless me, Father, for I have sinned.
I told a lie once, I was disobedient once.
And, Father, a boy touched me once.'
'Tell me, child. Was this touch immodest?
Did he touch your breast, for example?'
'He brushed against me, Father. Very gently.'

In October 1962 the world came closer to nuclear war than at any other time
when the US confronted the USSR over its missile installations in Cuba.

1962

Apocalypse

D.J. ENRIGHT

'After the New Apocalypse, very few members were still in possession of their instruments. Hardly a musician could call a decent suit his own. Yet, by the early summer of 1945, strains of sweet music floated on the air again. While the town still reeked of smoke, charred buildings and the stench of corpses, the Philharmonic Orchestra bestowed the everlasting and imperishable joy which music never fails to give.'

From *The Muses on the Banks of the Spree*,
a Berlin tourist brochure

It soothes the savage doubts.
One Bach outweighs ten Belsens. If 200,000 people
Were remaindered at Hiroshima, the sales of So-and-So's
New novel reached a higher figure in as short a time.
So, imperishable paintings reappeared:
Texts were reprinted:
Public buildings reconstructed:
Human beings reproduced.

After the Newer Apocalypse, very few members
Were still in possession of their instruments
(Very few were still in possession of their members),
And their suits were chiefly indecent.
Yet, while the town still reeked of smoke etc.,
The Philharmonic Trio bestowed, etc.

A civilization vindicated,
A race with three legs still to stand on!
True, the violin was shortly silenced by leukaemia,
And the pianoforte crumbled softly into dust.
But the flute was left. And one is enough.
All, in a sense, goes on. All is in order.

And the ten-tongued mammoth larks,
The forty-foot crickets and the elephantine frogs
Decided that the little chap was harmless,
At least he made no noise, on the banks of whatever river
    it used to be.

One day, a reed-warbler stepped on him by accident.
However, all, in a sense, goes on. Still the everlasting and
    imperishable joy
Which music never fails to give is being given.

1962

Blowin' in the Wind

BOB DYLAN

How many roads must a man walk down
Before you call him a man?
How many seas must a white dove sail
Before she sleeps in the sand?
Yes, 'n' how many times must the cannon balls fly
Before they're forever banned?
The answer, my friend, is blowin' in the wind,
The answer is blowin' in the wind.

Yes, 'n' how many years can a mountain exist
Before it's washed to the sea?
Yes, 'n' how many years can some people exist
Before they're allowed to be free?
Yes, 'n' how many times can a man turn his head,
And pretend that he just doesn't see?
The answer, my friend, is blowin' in the wind,
The answer is blowin' in the wind.

Yes, 'n' how many times must a man look up
Before he can see the sky?
Yes, 'n' how many ears must one man have
Before he can hear people cry?
Yes, 'n' how many deaths will it take till he knows
That too many people have died?
The answer, my friend, is blowin' in the wind,
The answer is blowin' in the wind.

1962

You were wearing

KENNETH KOCH

You were wearing your Edgar Allan Poe printed
   cotton blouse.
In each divided up square of the blouse was a
   picture of Edgar Allan Poe.
Your hair was blonde and you were cute. You asked
   me, 'Do most boys think that most girls are bad?'
I smelled the mould of your seaside resort hotel
   bedroom on your hair held in place by a John
   Greenleaf Whittier clip.
'No,' I said, 'it's girls who think that boys are bad.'
   Then we read *Snowbound* together
And ran around in an attic, so that a little of the
   blue enamel was scraped off my George
   Washington, Father of His Country, shoes.

Mother was walking in the living room, her Strauss
   Waltzes comb in her hair.
We waited for a time and then joined her, only to
   be served tea in cups painted with pictures of
   Herman Melville
As well as with illustrations from his book *Moby Dick*
   and from his novella *Benito Cereno*.
Father came in wearing his Dick Tracy necktie:
   'How about a drink, everyone?'
I said, 'Let's go outside a while.' Then we went onto
   the porch and sat on the Abraham Lincoln swing.

You sat on the eyes, mouth, and beard part, and I sat
on the knees.
In the yard across the street we saw a snowman
holding a garbage can lid smashed into a likeness
of the mad English king, George the Third.

In this withering critique of commodification, Koch names writers (Poe, Whittier, Melville), presidents (Washington, Lincoln), a king (George III), a comic strip detective (Dick Tracy), and a composer (Strauss).

1962

Mothers and Daughters

DAVID CAMPBELL

The cruel girls we loved
Are over forty,
Their subtle daughters
Have stolen their beauty;

And with a blue stare
Of cool surprise,
They mock their anxious mothers
With their mothers' eyes.

1962

All My Pretty Ones
◆◇◆

ANNE SEXTON

> *All my pretty ones?*
> *Did you say all? O hell-kite! All?*
> *What! all my pretty chickens and their dam*
> *At one fell swoop? . . .*
> *I cannot but remember such things were,*
> *That were most precious to me.*
>
> *Macbeth*

Father, this year's jinx rides us apart
where you followed our mother to her cold slumber,
a second shock boiling its stone to your heart,
leaving me here to shuffle and disencumber
you from the residence you could not afford:
a gold key, your half of a woollen mill,
twenty suits from Dunne's, an English Ford,
the love and legal verbiage of another will,
boxes of pictures of people I do not know.
I touch their cardboard faces. They must go.

But the eyes, as thick as wood in this album,
hold me. I stop here, where a small boy
waits in a ruffled dress for someone to come . . .
for this soldier who holds his bugle like a toy
or for this velvet lady who cannot smile.
Is this your father's father, this commodore
in a mailman suit? My father, time meanwhile
has made it unimportant who you are looking for.
I'll never know what these faces are all about.
I lock them into their book and throw them out.

This is the yellow scrapbook that you began
the year I was born; as crackling now and wrinkly

as tobacco leaves: clippings where Hoover outran
the Democrats, wiggling his dry finger at me
and Prohibition; news where the *Hindenburg* went
down and recent years where you went flush
on war. This year, solvent but sick, you meant
to marry that pretty widow in a one-month rush.
But before you had that second chance, I cried
on your fat shoulder. Three days later you died.

These are the snapshots of marriage, stopped in places.
Side by side at the rail toward Nassau now;
here, with the winner's cup at the speedboat races,
here, in tails at the Cotillion, you take a bow,
here, by our kennel of dogs with their pink eyes,
running like show-bred pigs in their chain-link pen;
here, at the horseshow where my sister wins a prize;
and here, standing like a duke among groups of men.
Now I fold you down, my drunkard, my navigator,
my first lost keeper, to love or look at later.

I hold a five-year diary that my mother kept
for three years, telling all she does not say
of your alcoholic tendency. You overslept,
she writes. My God, father, each Christmas Day
with your blood, will I drink down your glass
of wine? The diary of your hurly-burly years
goes to my shelf to wait for my age to pass.
Only in this hoarded span will love persevere.
Whether you are pretty or not, I outlive you,
bend down my strange face to yours and forgive you.

Sexton's title is from *Macbeth* IV, ii, 216. Herbert Hoover was (Republican) President of the US from 1929 to 1933. The LZ 129 *Hindenburg*, a German passenger airship, went up in flames as it was docking at Lakehurst, New Jersey, on 6 May 1937.

1962

The Bee Meeting

◄◇►

SYLVIA PLATH

Who are these people at the bridge to meet me? They are
    the villagers –
The rector, the midwife, the sexton, the agent for bees.
In my sleeveless summery dress I have no protection,
And they are all gloved and covered, why did nobody tell me?
They are smiling and taking out veils tacked to ancient hats.

I am nude as a chicken neck, does nobody love me?
Yes, here is the secretary of bees with her white shop smock,
Buttoning the cuffs at my wrists and the slit from my neck to
    my knees.
Now I am milkweed silk, the bees will not notice.
They will not smell my fear, my fear, my fear.

Which is the rector now, is it that man in black?
Which is the midwife, is that her blue coat?
Everybody is nodding a square black head, they are knights in
    visors,
Breastplates of cheesecloth knotted under the armpits.
Their smiles and their voices are changing. I am led through a
    beanfield.

Strips of tinfoil winking like people,
Feather dusters fanning their hands in a sea of bean flowers,
Creamy bean flowers with black eyes and leaves like bored
    hearts.
Is it blood clots the tendrils are dragging up that string?
No, no, it is scarlet flowers that will one day be edible.

Now they are giving me a fashionable white straw Italian hat
And a black veil that molds to my face, they are making me
    one of them.
They are leading me to the shorn grove, the circle of hives.

Is it the hawthorn that smells so sick?
The barren body of hawthorn, etherizing its children.

Is it some operation that is taking place?
It is the surgeon my neighbors are waiting for,
This apparition in a green helmet,
Shining gloves and white suit.
Is it the butcher, the grocer, the postman, someone I know?

I cannot run, I am rooted, and the gorse hurts me
With its yellow purses, its spiky armory.
I could not run without having to run forever.
The white hive is snug as a virgin,
Sealing off her brood cells, her honey, and quietly humming.

Smoke rolls and scarves in the grove.
The mind of the hive thinks this is the end of everything.
Here they come, the outriders, on their hysterical elastics.
If I stand very still, they will think I am cow-parsley,
A gullible head untouched by their animosity,

Not even nodding, a personage in a hedgerow.
The villagers open the chambers, they are hunting the queen.
Is she hiding, is she eating honey? She is very clever.
She is old, old, old, she must live another year, and she knows
    it.
While in their fingerjoint cells the new virgins

Dream of a duel they will win inevitably,
A curtain of wax dividing them from the bride flight,
The upflight of the murderess into a heaven that loves her.
The villagers are moving the virgins, there will be no killing.
The old queen does not show herself, is she so ungrateful?

I am exhausted, I am exhausted —
Pillar of white in a blackout of knives.
I am the magician's girl who does not flinch.
The villagers are untying their disguises, they are shaking
    hands.
Whose is that long white box in the grove, what have they
    accomplished, why am I cold.

1962

Lady Lazarus

◀◦▶

SYLVIA PLATH

I have done it again.
One year in every ten
I manage it –

A sort of walking miracle, my skin
Bright as a Nazi lampshade,
My right foot

A paperweight,
My face a featureless, fine
Jew linen.

Peel off the napkin
O my enemy.
Do I terrify? –

The nose, the eye pits, the full set of teeth?
The sour breath
Will vanish in a day.

Soon, soon the flesh
The grave cave ate will be
At home on me

And I a smiling woman.
I am only thirty.
And like the cat I have nine times to die.

This is Number Three.
What a trash
To annihilate each decade.

What a million filaments.
The peanut-crunching crowd
Shoves in to see

Them unwrap me hand and foot –
The big strip tease.
Gentlemen, ladies

These are my hands
My knees.
I may be skin and bone,

Nevertheless, I am the same, identical woman.
The first time it happened I was ten.
It was an accident.

The second time I meant
To last it out and not come back at all.
I rocked shut

As a seashell.
They had to call and call
And pick the worms off me like sticky pearls.

Dying
Is an art, like everything else.
I do it exceptionally well.

I do it so it feels like hell.
I do it so it feels real.
I guess you could say I've a call.

It's easy enough to do it in a cell.
It's easy enough to do it and stay put.
It's the theatrical

Comeback in broad day
To the same place, the same face, the same brute
Amused shout:

'A miracle!'
That knocks me out.
There is a charge

For the eyeing of my scars, there is a charge
For the hearing of my heart –
It really goes.

And there is a charge, a very large charge
For a word or a touch
Or a bit of blood

Or a piece of my hair or my clothes.
So, so, Herr Doktor.
So, Herr Enemy.

I am your opus,
I am your valuable,
The pure gold baby

That melts to a shriek.
I turn and burn.
Do not think I underestimate your great concern.

Ash, ash —
You poke and stir.
Flesh, bone, there is nothing there —

A cake of soap,
A wedding ring,
A gold filling.

Herr God, Herr Lucifer
Beware
Beware.

Out of the ash
I rise with my red hair
And I eat men like air.

For the raising of Lazarus, see John 11: 1–44. The image of the Nazi lampshade originates in reports that Ilse Koch, sadistic wife of the commandant of Buchenwald concentration camp, had had a lampshade made for her out of human skin. At the time of her trial for war crimes in 1947 this piece of evidence could not be found.

1963

Prize-Giving

GWEN HARWOOD

Professor Eisenbart, asked to attend
a girls' school speech night as an honoured guest
and give the prizes out, rudely declined;
but from indifference agreed, when pressed
with dry scholastic jokes, to change his mind,
to grace their humble platform, and to lend

distinction (of a kind not specified)
to the occasion. Academic dress
became him, as he knew. When he appeared
the girls whirred with an insect nervousness,
the Head in humbler black flapped round and steered
her guest, superb in silk and fur, with pride

to the best seat beneath half-hearted blooms
tortured to form the school's elaborate crest.
Eisenbart scowled with violent distaste,
then recomposed his features to their best
advantage: deep in thought, with one hand placed
like Rodin's Thinker. So he watched the room's

mosaic of young heads. Blonde, black, mouse-brown
they bent for their Headmistress' opening prayer.
But underneath a light (no accident
of seating, he felt sure), with titian hair
one girl sat grinning at him, her hand bent
under her chin in mockery of his own.

Speeches were made and prizes given. He shook
indifferently a host of virgin hands.
'Music!' The girl with titian hair stood up,
hitched at a stocking, winked at nearby friends,
and stood before him to receive a cup
of silver chased with curious harps. He took

her hand, and felt its voltage fling his hold
from his calm age and power; suffered her strange
eyes, against reason dark, to take his stare
with her to the piano, there to change
her casual schoolgirl's for a master's air.
He forged his rose-hot dream as Mozart told

the fullness of all passion or despair
summoned by arrogant hands. The music ended,
Eisenbart teased his gown while others clapped,
and peered into a trophy which suspended
his image upside down: a sage fool trapped
by music in a copper net of hair.

The Thinker (*Le Penseur*) is a celebrated piece by the French sculptor Auguste
Rodin (1840–1917).

1963

The Australian Dream

————◦————

DAVID CAMPBELL

The doorbell buzzed. It was past three o'clock.
The steeple-of-Saint-Andrew's weathercock
Cried silently to darkness, and my head
Was bronze with claret as I rolled from bed
To ricochet from furniture. Light! Light
Blinded the stairs, the hatstand sprang upright,
I fumbled with the lock, and on the porch
Stood the Royal Family with a wavering torch.

'We hope,' the Queen said, 'we do not intrude.
The pubs were full, most of our subjects rude.
We came before our time. It seems the Queen's
Command brings only, "Tell the dead marines!"
We've come to you.' I must admit I'd half
Expected just this visit. With a laugh
That put them at their ease, I bowed my head.
'Your Majesty is most welcome here,' I said.
'My home is yours. There is a little bed
Downstairs, a boiler-room, might suit the Duke.'

He thanked me gravely for it and he took
Himself off with a wave. 'Then the Queen Mother?
She'd best bed down with you. There is no other
But my wide bed. I'll curl up in a chair.'
The Queen looked thoughtful. She brushed out her hair
And folded up *The Garter* on a pouf.
'Distress was the first commoner, and as proof
That queens bow to the times,' she said, 'we three
Shall share the double bed. Please follow me.'

I waited for the ladies to undress –
A sense of fitness, even in distress,
Is always with me. They had tucked away
Their state robes in the lowboy; gold crowns lay
Upon the bedside tables; ropes of pearls
Lassoed the plastic lampshade; their soft curls
Were spread out on the pillows and they smiled.
'Hop in,' said the Queen Mother. In I piled
Between them to lie like a stick of wood.
I couldn't find a thing to say. My blood
Beat, but like rollers at the ebb of tide.
'I hope your Majesties sleep well,' I lied.
A hand touched mine and the Queen said, 'I am
Most grateful to you, Jock. Please call me Ma'am.'

1963

Dallas, 1963

◄○►

C.K. STEAD

Caesar, you were everybody's baby
But not mine.
I thought the broken warhorse that doddered before
Alone made you shine.
But when your head leaked blood on the lap of the world
Like those your mistakes murdered,
I thought it was the golden apple
And the holy wine.

American President John F. Kennedy was assassinated in Dallas, Texas, on 22 November 1963.

1964

For the Union Dead

———————◦———————

ROBERT LOWELL

'Relinquunt Omnia Servare Rem Publicam.'

The old South Boston Aquarium stands
in a Sahara of snow now. Its broken windows are boarded.
The bronze weathervane cod has lost half its scales.
The airy tanks are dry.

Once my nose crawled like a snail on the glass;
my hand tingled
to burst the bubbles
drifting from the noses of the cowed, compliant fish.

My hand draws back. I often sigh still
for the dark downward and vegetating kingdom
of the fish and reptile. One morning last March,
I pressed against the new barbed and galvanized

fence on the Boston Common. Behind their cage,
yellow dinosaur steamshovels were grunting
as they cropped up tons of mush and grass
to gouge their underworld garage.

Parking spaces luxuriate like civic
sandpiles in the heart of Boston.
A girdle of orange, Puritan-pumpkin colored girders
braces the tingling Statehouse,

shaking over the excavations, as it faces Colonel Shaw
and his bell-cheeked Negro infantry
on St Gaudens' shaking Civil War relief,
propped by a plank splint against the garage's earthquake.

Two months after marching through Boston,
half the regiment was dead;
at the dedication,
William James could almost hear the bronze Negroes breathe.

Their monument sticks like a fishbone
in the city's throat.
Its Colonel is as lean
as a compass-needle.

He has an angry wrenlike vigilance,
a greyhound's gentle tautness;
he seems to wince at pleasure,
and suffocate for privacy.

He is out of bounds now. He rejoices in man's lovely,
peculiar power to choose life and die –
when he leads his black soldiers to death,
he cannot bend his back.

On a thousand small town New England greens,
the old white churches hold their air
of sparse, sincere rebellion; frayed flags
quilt the graveyards of the Grand Army of the Republic.

The stone statues of the abstract Union Soldier
grow slimmer and younger each year –
wasp-wasted, they doze over muskets
and muse through their sideburns . . .

Shaw's father wanted no monument
except the ditch,
where his son's body was thrown
and lost with his 'niggers.'

The ditch is nearer.
There are no statues for the last war here;
on Boylston Street, a commercial photograph
shows Hiroshima boiling

over a Mosler Safe, the 'Rock of Ages'
that survived the blast. Space is nearer.
When I crouch to my television set,
the drained faces of Negro school-children rise like balloons.

Colonel Shaw
is riding on his bubble,
he waits
for the blessèd break.

The Aquarium is gone. Everywhere,
giant finned cars nose forward like fish;
a savage servility
slides by on grease.

The Latin epigraph, which translates as 'they gave up everything to serve the republic', is the inscription on the Shaw memorial described in the sixth quatrain of the poem. Colonel Robert Gould Shaw commanded the all-black 54th Regiment in the American Civil War. The memorial, erected in 1897, was a collaboration between architect Stanford White (1853–1906) and sculptor Augustus Saint Gaudens (1848–1907). William James (1842–1910), psychologist, philosopher, and brother of novelist Henry James, himself had two younger brothers who fought in the Civil War.

1964

Anxiety

◄○►

FRANK O'HARA

I'm having a real day of it.
                    There was
something I had to do. But what?
There are no alternatives, just
the one something.
               I have a drink,
it doesn't help – far from it!
                  I
feel worse. I can't remember how
I felt, so perhaps I feel better.
No. Just a little darker.
             If I could
get really dark, richly dark, like
being drunk, that's the best that's
open as a field. Not the best,

but the best except for the impossible
pure light, to be as if above a vast
prairie, rushing and pausing over
the tiny golden heads in deep grass.

But still now, familiar laughter low
from a dark face, affection human and often even –

motivational? the warm walking night
                          wandering
amusement of darkness, lips,
                and
the light, always in wind. Perhaps
that's it: to clean something. A window?

1964

Dream Song 41

◄○►

JOHN BERRYMAN

If we sang in the wood (and Death is a German expert)
while snows flies, chill, after so frequent knew
so many all of nothing,
for lead & fire, it's not we would assert
particulars, but animal; cats mew,
horses scream, man sing.

Or: men psalm. Man palms his ears and moans.
Death is a German expert. Scrambling, sitting,
spattering, we hurry.
I try to. Odd & trivial, atones
somehow for *my* escape a bullet splitting
my trod-on instep, fiery.

The cantor bubbled, rattled. The Temple burned.
Lurch with me! phantoms of Varshava. Slop!
When I used to be,
who haunted, stumbling, sewers, my sacked shop,
roofs, a dis-world *ai!* Death was a German
home-country.

'Death is a German expert' translates the words 'Der Tod ist ein Meister aus
Deutschland', from the 'Todesfuge' ('Fugue of Death') by Paul Celan (1920–
70). The modulation to 'a German home-country' at the close recalls Heinrich
Heine's 'I once had a German homeland. It was a dream.' (Both poets were
Jewish.) Varshava is Warsaw.

1965

from Briggflatts

BASIL BUNTING

Brag, sweet tenor bull,
descant on Rawthey's madrigal,
each pebble its part
for the fells' late spring.
Dance tiptoe, bull,
black against may.
Ridiculous and lovely
chase hurdling shadows
morning into noon.
May on the bull's hide
and through the dale
furrows fill with may,
paving the slowworm's way.

A mason times his mallet
to a lark's twitter,
listening while the marble rests,
lays his rule
at a letter's edge,
fingertips checking,
till the stone spells a name
naming none,
a man abolished.
Painful lark, labouring to rise!
The solemn mallet says:
In the grave's slot
he lies. We rot.

Decay thrusts the blade,
wheat stands in excrement
trembling. Rawthey trembles.
Tongue stumbles, ears err
for fear of spring.

Rub the stone with sand,
wet sandstone rending
roughness away. Fingers
ache on the rubbing stone.
The mason says: Rocks
happen by chance.
No one here bolts the door,
love is so sore.

Stone smooth as skin,
cold as the dead they load
on a low lorry by night.
The moon sits on the fell
but it will rain.
Under sacks on the stone
two children lie,
hear the horse stale,
the mason whistle,
harness mutter to shaft,
felloe to axle squeak,
rut thud the rim,
crushed grit.

Stocking to stocking, jersey to jersey,
head to a hard arm,
they kiss under the rain,
bruised by their marble bed.
In Garsdale, dawn;
at Hawes, tea from the can.
Rain stops, sacks
steam in the sun, they sit up.
Copper-wire moustache,
sea-reflecting eyes
and Baltic plainsong speech
declare: By such rocks
men killed Bloodaxe.

Fierce blood throbs in his tongue,
lean words.
Skulls cropped for steel caps

huddle round Stainmore.
Their becks ring on limestone,
whisper to peat.
The clogged cart pushes the horse downhill.
In such soft air
they trudge and sing,
laying the tune frankly on the air.
All sounds fall still,
fellside bleat,
hide-and-seek peewit.

Her pulse their pace,
palm countering palm,
till a trench is filled,
stone white as cheese
jeers at the dale.
Knotty wood, hard to rive,
smoulders to ash;
smell of October apples.
The road again,
at a trot.
Wetter, warmed, they watch
the mason meditate
on name and date.

Rain rinses the road,
the bull streams and laments.
Sour rye porridge from the hob
with cream and black tea,
meat, crust and crumb.
Her parents in bed
the children dry their clothes.
He has untied the tape
of her striped flannel drawers
before the range. Naked
on the pricked rag mat
his fingers comb
thatch of his manhood's home.

Gentle generous voices weave
over bare night
words to confirm and delight
till bird dawn.
Rainwater from the butt
she fetches and flannel
to wash him inch by inch,
kissing the pebbles.
Shining slowworm part of the marvel.
The mason stirs:
Words!
Pens are too light.
Take a chisel to write.

Every birth a crime,
every sentence life.
Wiped of mould and mites
would the ball run true?
No hope of going back.
Hounds falter and stray,
shame deflects the pen.
Love murdered neither bleeds nor stifles
but jogs the draftsman's elbow.
What can he, changed, tell
her, changed, perhaps dead?
Delight dwindles. Blame
stays the same.

Brief words are hard to find,
shapes to carve and discard:
Bloodaxe, king of York,
king of Dublin, king of Orkney.
Take no notice of tears;
letter the stone to stand
over love laid aside lest
insufferable happiness impede
flight to Stainmore,
to trace
lark, mallet,

becks, flocks
and axe knocks.

Dung will not soil the slowworm's
mosaic. Breathless lark
drops to nest in sodden trash;
Rawthey truculent, dingy.
Drudge at the mallet, the may is down,
fog on fells. Guilty of spring
and spring's ending
amputated years ache after
the bull is beef, love a convenience.
It is easier to die than to remember.
Name and date
split in soft slate
a few months obliterate.

A photograph that can be viewed on the website of Durham University's Basil Bunting Poetry Centre shows Bunting in 1980 beside the Rawthey, a river in Cumbria, in front of a gate on which are painted the words, 'Beware bull'. Bloodaxe was the Viking leader Eric Bloodaxe, killed at Stainmore in 954.

1965

Old Woman

Iain Crichton Smith

And she, being old, fed from a mashed plate
as an old mare might droop across a fence
to the dull pastures of its ignorance.
Her husband held her upright while he prayed

to God who is all-forgiving to send down
some angel somewhere who might land perhaps
in his foreign wings among the gradual crops.
She munched, half dead, blindly searching the spoon.

Outside, the grass was raging. There I sat
imprisoned in my pity and my shame
that men and women having suffered time
should sit in such a place, in such a state

and wished to be away, yes, to be far away
with athletes, heroes, Greek or Roman men
who pushed their bitter spears into a vein
and would not spend an hour with such decay.

'Pray God,' he said, 'we ask you, God,' he said.
The bowed back was quiet. I saw the teeth
tighten their grip around a delicate death.
And nothing moved within the knotted head

but only a few poor veins as one might see
vague wishless seaweed floating on a tide
of all the salty waters where had died
too many waves to mark two more or three.

1965

Questions of Travel
◄○►

ELIZABETH BISHOP

There are too many waterfalls here; the crowded streams
hurry too rapidly down to the sea,
and the pressure of so many clouds on the mountaintops
makes them spill over the sides in soft slow-motion,
turning to waterfalls under our very eyes.
— For if those streaks, those mile-long, shiny, tearstains,
aren't waterfalls yet,
in a quick age or so, as ages go here,
they probably will be.
But if the streams and clouds keep travelling, travelling,
the mountains look like the hulls of capsized ships,
slime-hung and barnacled.

Think of the long trip home.
Should we have stayed at home and thought of here?
Where should we be today?
Is it right to be watching strangers in a play
in this strangest of theatres?
What childishness is it that while there's a breath of life
in our bodies, we are determined to rush
to see the sun the other way around?
The tiniest green hummingbird in the world?
To stare at some inexplicable old stonework,
inexplicable and impenetrable,
at any view,
instantly seen and always, always delightful?
Oh, must we dream our dreams
and have them, too?
And have we room
for one more folded sunset, still quite warm?

But surely it would have been a pity
not to have seen the trees along this road,
really exaggerated in their beauty,
not to have seen them gesturing
like noble pantomimists, robed in pink.
– Not to have had to stop for gas and heard
the sad, two-noted, wooden tune
of disparate wooden clogs
carelessly clacking over
a grease-stained filling-station floor.
(In another country the clogs would all be tested.
Each pair there would have identical pitch.)
– A pity not to have heard
the other, less primitive music of the fat brown bird
who sings above the broken gasoline pump
in a bamboo church of Jesuit baroque:
three towers, five silver crosses.
– Yes, a pity not to have pondered,
blurr'dly and inconclusively,
on what connection can exist for centuries
between the crudest wooden footwear
and, careful and finicky,
the whittled fantasies of wooden cages.
– Never to have studied history in
the weak calligraphy of songbirds' cages.
– And never to have had to listen to rain
so much like politicians' speeches:
two hours of unrelenting oratory
and then a sudden golden silence
in which the traveller takes a notebook, writes:

'Is it lack of imagination that makes us come
to imagined places, not just stay at home?
Or could Pascal have been not entirely right
about just sitting quietly in one's room?

Continent, city, country, society:
the choice is never wide and never free.
And here, or there . . . No. Should we have stayed at home,
wherever that may be?'

Blaise Pascal (1623–62) observed that all humanity's misfortunes came from not being able to sit quietly in one's room.

1966

A Walk in Würzburg

◀◇▶

WILLIAM PLOMER

Passing a dull red college block
Of the bygone, full-fed, Kaiser time,
When the tribal mercury welled up
Ready to burst, is to wonder if inside
That institute some intent and hairy head,
Bored by the strut of the show-off turkey-cock,
Through steel-rimmed ovals used at that time perhaps
To peer with love, pure love, of finding out;

Is to wonder who now may be tunnelling there
For an unknown vein, or perhaps with the sifting hand
Of an archaeologist-in-reverse
Dredging towards a treasure the future hides.
Bombs broke the wigged Baroque only yards away,
But his thoughtful back would be that of a sage
Averted from fractured dreams, unhealable wounds,
Revenges, ruined walls, undruggable nerves.

By chance to see an inconspicuous plaque
On that otherwise unadorned wall, is to learn
That here, right here, a miracle struck
Which altered us all – as Gutenberg did,
Daguerre, or Freud; is to feel what the pious feel,
Quite carried away to find they face
Unawares a place of sublime prestige,
Where a saint flared out of the chrysalid stage.

Not to have known about this! That here,
That nowhere else in the wasteful, wilful,
Death-wishing world, here Röntgen focused his ray
And the eye first saw right through the skin,
So that now without knives we see what is wrong
Or is going to be wrong. We still need a ray
To coax the delicate wings from the commonplace husk
And detect why the horde we are destroys itself.

Plomer refers to Johannes Gutenberg (c. 1398–1468), who invented printing from movable type; Louis Daguerre (1787–1851), inventor of the photographic process (the daguerreotype) that bears his name; Sigmund Freud (1856–1939), the father of psychoanalysis; and Wilhelm Röntgen (1845–1923), the German physicist who in 1895 detected what subsequently became known as X-rays, work which brought him the first Nobel Prize in Physics, in 1901. He conducted this research while at the University of Würzburg, a city in Franconia (in southeastern Germany) which, as Plomer notes in passing, was heavily bombed during the Second World War.

1966

At Rest from the Grim Place

◄◦►

ARTHUR NORTJE

The sergeant laughs with strong teeth,
his jackboots nestle under the springbok horns.
Those bayonets are silent,
the spear of the nation gone to the ground.
Warriors prowl in the stars of their dungeons.
I've seen the nebulae of a man's eyes
squirm with pain, he sang his life
through cosmic volleys. They call it
genital therapy, the blond bosses.

Why is there no more news?
Bluetits scuffle in the eaves of England,
an easy summer shimmers on the water.
Fields of peace, I lie here
in the music of your gaze
so beautiful we seem no strangers.

Curling smoke, a white butt is
brother to my lips and fingers.
You watch the ash on grass blades gently crumble.
Your hands are small as roses,
they cancel memory.

Once going down to the sea through the mountains
my limbs felt freedom in the glide of air:
over the bridge at the window I found
speech an impossible cry.
Under the fatal shadows spun down the chasm
my heart squirmed in the throat of snaking water.
I have since forgotten what they call that place.

1966

Mortality

◄◦►

JOHN BETJEMAN

The first-class brains of a senior civil servant
   Shiver and shatter and fall
As the steering column of his comfortable Humber
   Batters in the bony wall.
All those delicate little re-adjustments
   'On the one hand, if we proceed
With the *ad hoc* policy hitherto adapted
   To individual need . . .
On the other hand, too rigid an arrangement
   Might, of itself, perforce . . .
I would like to submit for the Minister's concurrence
   The following alternative course,
Subject to revision and reconsideration
   In the light our experience gains . . .'
And this had to happen at the corner where the by-pass
   Comes into Egham out of Staines.
That very near miss for an All Souls' Fellowship
   The recent compensation of a 'K' –
The first-class brains of a senior civil servant
   Are sweetbread on the road today.

A 'K' is a knighthood.

1967

A Miltonic Sonnet for Mr Johnson on His Refusal of Peter Hurd's Official Portrait

———— ‹○› ————

RICHARD WILBUR

Heir to the office of a man not dead
Who drew our Declaration up, who planned
Range and Rotunda with his drawing-hand
And harbored Palestrina in his head,
Who would have wept to see small nations dread
The imposition of our cattle-brand,
With public truth at home mistold or banned,
And in whose term no army's blood was shed,

Rightly you say the picture is too large
Which Peter Hurd by your appointment drew,
And justly call that Capitol too bright
Which signifies our people in your charge;
Wait, Sir, and see how time will render you,
Who talk of vision but are weak of sight.

6 January 1967

Lyndon B. Johnson (1908–73) succeeded Kennedy as president and was elected in his own right in 1964. His massive escalation of American military involvement in Vietnam was controversial and unpopular, and, to Wilbur's mind, very much at odds with the thinking of Thomas Jefferson (1743–1826), principal author of the American Declaration of Independence and third President of the US, who is described though not named in Wilbur's opening lines. American artist Peter Hurd (1904–84) was commissioned to paint Johnson's official portrait, but the President disliked it intensely.

1967

Waking Early Sunday Morning

ROBERT LOWELL

O to break loose, like the chinook
salmon jumping and falling back,
nosing up to the impossible
stone and bone-crushing waterfall –
raw-jawed, weak-fleshed there, stopped by ten
steps of the roaring ladder, and then
to clear the top on the last try,
alive enough to spawn and die.

Stop, back off. The salmon breaks
water, and now my body wakes
to feel the unpolluted joy
and criminal leisure of a boy –
no rainbow smashing a dry fly
in the white run is free as I,
here squatting like a dragon on
time's hoard before the day's begun!

Vermin run for their unstopped holes;
in some dark nook a fieldmouse rolls
a marble, hours on end, then stops;
the termite in the woodwork sleeps –
listen, the creatures of the night
obsessive, casual, sure of foot,
go on grinding, while the sun's
daily remorseful blackout dawns.

Fierce, fireless mind, running downhill.
Look up and see the harbor fill:
business as usual in eclipse
goes down to the sea in ships –
wake of refuse, dacron rope,
bound for Bermuda or Good Hope,
all bright before the morning watch
the wine-dark hulls of yawl and ketch.

I watch a glass of water wet
with a fine fuzz of icy sweat,
silvery colors touched with sky,
serene in their neutrality –
yet if I shift, or change my mood,
I see some object made of wood,
background behind it of brown grain,
to darken it, but not to stain.

O that the spirit could remain
tinged but untarnished by its strain!
Better dressed and stacking birch,
or lost with the Faithful at Church –
anywhere, but somewhere else!
And now the new electric bells,
clearly chiming, 'Faith of our fathers,'
and now the congregation gathers.

O Bible chopped and crucified
in hymns we hear but do not read,
none of the milder subtleties
of grace or art will sweeten these
stiff quatrains shovelled out four-square –
they sing of peace, and preach despair;
yet they gave darkness some control,
and left a loophole for the soul.

No, put old clothes on, and explore
the corners of the woodshed for
its dregs and dreck: tools with no handle,
ten candle-ends not worth a candle,

old lumber banished from the Temple,
damned by Paul's precept and example,
cast from the kingdom, banned in Israel,
the wordless sign, the tinkling cymbal.

When will we see Him face to face?
Each day, He shines through darker glass –
In this small town where everything
is known, I see His vanishing
emblems, His white spire and flag-
pole sticking out above the fog,
like old white china doorknobs, sad,
slight, useless things to calm the mad.

Hammering military splendor,
top-heavy Goliath in full armor –
little redemption in the mass
liquidations of their brass,
elephant and phalanx moving
with the times and still improving,
when that kingdom hit the crash:
a million foreskins stacked like trash . . .

Sing softer! But what if a new
diminuendo brings no true
tenderness, only restlessness,
excess, the hunger for success,
sanity of self-deception
fixed and kicked by reckless caution,
while we listen to the bells—
anywhere, but somewhere else!

O to break loose. All life's grandeur
is something with a girl in summer . . .
elated as the President
girdled by his establishment
this Sunday morning, free to chaff
his own thoughts with his bear-cuffed staff,
swimming nude, unbuttoned, sick
of his ghost-written rhetoric!

No weekends for the gods now. Wars
flicker, earth licks its open sores,
fresh breakage, fresh promotions, chance
assassinations, no advance.
Only man thinning out his kind
sounds through the Sabbath noon, the blind
swipe of the pruner and his knife
busy about the tree of life . . .

Pity the planet, all joy gone
from this sweet volcanic cone;
peace to our children when they fall
in small war on the heels of small
war – until the end of time
to police the earth, a ghost
orbiting forever lost
in our monotonous sublime.

The words 'face to face' and 'darker glass' echo St. Paul (1 Corinthians 13:12).
The president glimpsed in the poem was Johnson. Lowell had refused Johnson's
invitation to attend the White House Festival of Arts in 1965, and in 1967 joined
the famous protest march on the Pentagon (described by Norman Mailer in his
novel *The Armies of the Night*).

1967

Sonnet 71

<o>

JOHN BERRYMAN

Our Sunday morning when dawn-priests were applying
Wafer and wine to the human wound, we laid
Ourselves to cure ourselves down: I'm afraid
Our vestments wanted, but Francis' friends were crying
In the nave of pines, sun-satisfied, and flying
Subtle as angels about the barricade
Boughs made over us, deep in a bed half made
Needle-soft, half the sea of our simultaneous dying.

'Death is the mother of beauty.' Awry no leaf
Shivering with delight, we die to be well . . .
Careless with sleepy love, so long unloving.
What if our convalescence must be brief
As we are, the matin meet the passing bell?. . .
About our pines our sister, wind, is moving.

'Francis' friends' are birds, the 'friends' of St Francis of Assisi. 'Death is the mother
of beauty' is quoted from Wallace Stevens' 'Sunday Morning' (see p. 113).

1967

Let Me Die a Youngman's Death

━━━━━━◁◇▷━━━━━━

ROGER McGOUGH

Let me die a youngman's death
not a clean & inbetween
the sheets holywater death
not a famous-last-words
peaceful out of breath death

When I'm 73
& in constant good tumour
may I be mown down at dawn
by a bright red sports car
on my way home
from an allnight party

Or when I'm 91
with silver hair
& sitting in a barber's chair
may rival gangsters
with hamfisted tommyguns burst in
& give me a short back & insides

Or when I'm 104
& banned from the Cavern
may my mistress
catching me in bed with her daughter
& fearing her son
cut me up into little pieces
& throw away every piece but one

Let me die a youngman's death
not a free from sin tiptoe in
candle wax & waning death
not a curtains drawn by angels borne
'what a nice way to go' death

The Cavern was a Liverpool club where the Beatles played in the early days of
their career. It is still in business.

1967

For the Anniversary of My Death

W. S. MERWIN

Every year without knowing it I have passed the day
When the last fires will wave to me
And the silence will set out
Tireless traveller
Like the beam of a lightless star

Then I will no longer
Find myself in life as in a strange garment
Surprised at the earth
And the love of one woman
And the shamelessness of men
As today writing after three days of rain
Hearing the wren sing and the falling cease
And bowing not knowing to what

1967

'It out-Herods Herod. Pray you, avoid it.'

ANTHONY HECHT

Tonight my children hunch
Toward their Western, and are glad
As, with a Sunday punch,
The Good casts out the Bad.

And in their fairy tales
The warty giant and witch
Get sealed in doorless jails
And the match-girl strikes it rich.

I've made myself a drink.
The giant and witch are set
To bust out of the clink
When my children have gone to bed.

All frequencies are loud
With signals of despair;
In flash and morse they crowd
The rondure of the air.

For the wicked have grown strong,
Their numbers mock at death,
Their cow brings forth its young,
Their bull engendereth.

Their very fund of strength,
Satan, bestrides the globe;
He stalks its breadth and length
And finds out even Job.

Yet by quite other laws
My children make their case;
Half God, half Santa Claus,
But with my voice and face,

A hero comes to save
The poorman, beggarman, thief,
And make the world behave
And put an end to grief.

And that their sleep be sound
I say this childermas
Who could not, at one time,
Have saved them from the gas.

Hecht's title is taken from Hamlet's advice to the visiting players in Act III, scene ii of Shakespeare's *Hamlet*. The advice means that they should not cut crazy capers in the way that the character of Herod, in the mediaeval mystery plays, had licence to, but Hecht has in mind that the Nazi genocide far outdid the thousands of innocents slaughtered by the Biblical Herod (Matthew 2:16).

1968

On an Engraving by Casserius

A. D. HOPE

For Dr John Z. Bowers

Set on this bubble of dead stone and sand,
Lapped by its frail balloon of lifeless air,
Alone in the inanimate void, they stand,
These clots of thinking molecules who stare
Into the night of nescience and death,
And, whirled about with their terrestrial ball,
Ask of all being its motion and its frame:
This of all human images takes my breath;
Of all the joys in being a man at all,
This folds my spirit in its quickening flame.

Turning the leaves of this majestic book
My thoughts are with those great cosmographers,
Surgeon adventurers who undertook
To probe and chart time's other universe.
This one engraving holds me with its theme:
More than all maps made in that century
Which set true bearings for each cape and star,
De Quiros' vision or Newton's cosmic dream,
This reaches towards the central mystery
Of whence our being draws and what we are.

It came from that great school in Padua:
Casserio and Spiegel made this page.
Vesalius, who designed the *Fabrica*,
There strove, but burned his book at last in rage;
Fallopius by its discipline laid bare
The elements of this Humanity
Without which none knows that which treats the soul;

Fabricius talked with Galileo there:
Did those rare spirits in their colloquy
Divine in their two skills the single goal?

'One force that moves the atom and the star;'
Says Galileo, 'one basic law beneath
All change!' 'Would light from Achernar
Reveal how embryon forms within its sheath?'
Fabricius asks, and smiles. Talk such as this,
Ranging the bounds of our whole universe,
Could William Harvey once have heard? And once
Hearing, strike out that strange hypothesis,
Which in *De Motu Cordis* twice recurs,
Coupling the heart's impulsion with the sun's?

Did Thomas Browne at Padua, too, in youth
Hear of their talk of universal law
And form that notion of particular truth
Framed to correct a science they foresaw,
That darker science of which he used to speak
In later years and called the Crooked Way
Of Providence? Did *he* foresee perhaps
An age in which all sense of the unique,
And singular dissolves, like ours today,
In diagrams, statistics, tables, maps?

Not here! The graver's tool in this design
Aims still to give not general truth alone,
Blue-print of science or data's formal line:
Here in its singularity he has shown
The image of an individual soul;
Bodied in this one woman, he makes us see
The shadow of his anatomical laws.
An artist's vision animates the whole,
Shines through the scientist's detailed scrutiny
And links the person and the abstract cause.

Such were the charts of those who pressed beyond
Vesalius their master, year by year
Tracing each bone, each muscle, every frond
Of nerve until the whole design lay bare.
Thinking of this dissection, I descry
The tiers of faces, their teacher in his place,
The talk at the cadaver carried in:
'A woman – with child'; I hear the master's dry
Voice as he lifts a scalpel from its case:
'With each new step in science, we begin.'

Who was she? Though they never knew her name,
Dragged from the river, found in some alley at dawn,
This corpse none cared, or dared perhaps, to claim,
The dead child in her belly still unborn,
Might have passed, momentary as a shooting star,
Quenched like the misery of her personal life,
Had not the foremost surgeon of Italy,
Giulio Casserio of Padua,
Bought her for science, questioned her with his knife,
And drawn her for his great *Anatomy*;

Where still in the abundance of her grace,
She stands among the monuments of time
And, with a feminine delicacy displays
His elegant dissection: the sublime
Shaft of her body opens like a flower
Whose petals, folded back expose the womb,
Cord and placenta and the sleeping child,
Like instruments of music in a room
Left when her grieving Orpheus left his tower
Forever, for the desert and the wild.

Naked she waits against a tideless shore,
A sibylline stance, a noble human frame
Such as those old anatomists loved to draw.
She turns her head as though in trouble or shame,
Yet with a dancer's gesture holds the fruit
Plucked, though not tasted, of the Fatal Tree.
Something of the first Eve is in this pose
And something of the second in the mute
Offering of her child in death to be
Love's victim and her flesh its mystic rose.

No figure with wings of fire and back-swept hair
Swoops with his: Blessed among Women!; no sword
Of the spirit cleaves or quickens her; yet there
She too was overshadowed by the Word,
Was chosen, and by her humble gift of death
The lowly and the poor in heart give tongue,
Wisdom puts down the mighty from their seat;
The vile rejoice and rising, hear beneath
Scalpel and forceps, tortured into song,
Her body utter their magnificat.

Four hundred years since first that cry rang out:
Four hundred years, the patient, probing knife
Cut towards its answer – yet we stand in doubt:
Living, we cannot tell the source of life.
Old science, old certainties that lit our way
Shrink to poor guesses, dwindle to a myth.
Today's truths teach us how we were beguiled;
Tomorrow's how blind our vision of today.
The universals we thought to conjure with
Pass: there remain the mother and the child.

Loadstone, loadstar, alike to each new age,
There at the crux of time they stand and scan,
Past every scrutiny of prophet or sage,
Still unguessed prospects in this venture of Man.
To generations which we leave behind,
They taught a difficult, selfless skill: to show
The mask beyond the mask beyond the mask;
To ours another vista, where the mind
No longer asks for answers, but to know:
What questions are there which we fail to ask?

Who knows, but to the age to come they speak
Words that our own is still unapt to hear:
'These are the limits of all you sought and seek;
More our yet unborn nature cannot bear.
Learn now that all man's intellectual quest
Was but the stirrings of a foetal sleep;
The birth you cannot haste and cannot stay
Nears its appointed time; turn now and rest
Till that new nature ripens, till the deep
Dawns with that unimaginable day.'

Julius Casserius (Giulio Cesare Casseri, 1552–1616) succeeded 'the father of embryology', Hieronymus Fabricius (1533–1619), as professor of anatomy at the University of Padua in Italy. At that time, the 'great school in Padua' led the world in modern anatomical research. The earlier generation had been led by two others referred to by Hope: Gabriel Fallopius (1523–1562), and Flemish-born Andreas Vesalius (1514–64), creator of the *De humani corporis fabrica*, a compendium of anatomical illustrations, one of the most influential of all books in this area of medical science. Casserius followed Vesalius' example in producing (with Adriaan van de Spiegel, 1578–1625) a book of anatomical pictures, among them one which depicted for the first time ever the unborn foetus in the mother's womb. It was this landmark illustration that provided Hope with the subject for this poem. Others mentioned in the poem who studied at Padua are William Harvey (1578–1657), the English physician who identified the circulation of the blood, and the English writer Sir Thomas Browne (1605–82). Hope makes further mention of others whose visions affected the course of human thought and life: Newton and Galileo are familiar, but less well known to non-Australians is Captain Pedro Fernandez de Quiros (c. 1563–1615), the Portuguese-born Spanish navigator who explored the Pacific in search of Terra Australis. Hope's poem is dedicated to Dr John Zimmerman Bowers (1913–93), an influential American medical historian.

1968

May 1968

◄◊►

SHARON OLDS

When the Dean said we could not cross campus
until the students gave up the buildings,
we lay down, in the street,
we said the cops will enter this gate
over us. Lying back on the cobbles,
I saw the buildings of New York City
from dirt level, they soared up
and stopped, chopped off – above them, the sky,
the night air over the island.
The mounted police moved, near us,
while we sang, and then I began to count,
12, 13, 14, 15,
I counted again, 15, 16, one
month since the day on that deserted beach,
17, 18, my mouth fell open,
my hair on the street,
if my period did not come tonight
I was pregnant. I could see the sole of a cop's
shoe, the gelding's belly, its genitals –
if they took me to Women's Detention and did
the exam on me, the speculum,
the fingers – I gazed into the horse's tail
like a comet-train. All week, I had
thought about getting arrested, half-longed
to give myself away. On the tar –
one brain in my head, another,
in the making, near the base of my tail –
I looked at the steel arc of the horse's
shoe, the curve of its belly, the cop's
nightstick, the buildings streaming up
away from the earth. I knew I should get up
and leave, but I lay there looking at the space

above us, until it turned deep blue and then
ashy, colorless, *Give me this one
night*, I thought, *and I'll give this child
the rest of my life*, the horses' heads,
this time, drooping, dipping, until
they slept in a circle around my body and my daughter.

1968 was the pre-eminent year of protest in many parts of the world, notably
France, Germany, the UK and the US.

1968

Elegy

◄○►

DEREK WALCOTT

Our hammock swung between Americas,
we miss you, Liberty. Che's
bullet-riddled body falls,
and those who cried, the Republic must first die
to be reborn, are dead,
the freeborn citizen's ballot in the head.
Still, everybody wants to go to bed
with Miss America. And, if there's no bread,
let them eat cherry pie.

But the old choice of running, howling, wounded
wolf-deep in her woods,
while the white papers snow on
genocide is gone;
no face can hide
its public, private pain,
wincing, already statued.

Some splintered arrowhead lodged in her brain
sets the black singer howling in his bear trap,
shines young eyes with the brightness of the mad,
tires the old with her residual sadness;
and yearly lilacs in her dooryards bloom,
and the cherry orchard's surf
blinds Washington and whispers
to the assassin in his furnished room
of an ideal America, whose flickering screens
show, in slow herds, the ghosts of the Cheyennes
scuffling across the staked and wired plains
with whispering, rag-bound feet,

while the farm couple framed in their Gothic door
like Calvin's saints, waspish, pragmatic, poor,
gripping the devil's pitchfork
stare rigidly towards the immortal wheat.

6 June 1968

Ernesto 'Che' Guevara, the Argentine-born Cuban revolutionary, was executed
in Bolivia in 1967. Walcott's poem bears the date on which Robert Kennedy,
younger brother of assassinated President John F. Kennedy and himself a US
Senator and presidential candidate in 1968, was assassinated. The closing lines
glance at Grant Wood's celebrated painting of 1930, *American Gothic*.

1968

Ballad of the Bread Man
◀◦▶

CHARLES CAUSLEY

Mary stood in the kitchen
  Baking a loaf of bread.
An angel flew in through the window.
  'We've a job for you,' he said.

'God in his big gold heaven,
  Sitting in his big blue chair,
Wanted a mother for his little son.
  Suddenly saw you there.'

Mary shook and trembled,
  'It isn't true what you say.'
'Don't say that,' said the angel.
  'The baby's on its way.'

Joseph was in the workshop
  Planing a piece of wood.
'The old man's past it,' the neighbours said.
  'That girl's been up to no good.'

'And who was that elegant fellow,'
  They said, 'in the shiny gear?'
The things they said about Gabriel
  Were hardly fit to hear.

Mary never answered,
  Mary never replied.
She kept the information,
  Like the baby, safe inside.

It was election winter.
  They went to vote in town.
When Mary found her time had come
  The hotels let her down.

The baby was born in an annexe
  Next to the local pub.
At midnight, a delegation
  Turned up from the Farmers' Club.

They talked about an explosion
  That made a hole in the sky,
Said they'd been sent to the Lamb & Flag
  To see God come down from on high.

A few days later a bishop
  And a five-star general were seen
With the head of an African country
  In a bullet-proof limousine.

'We've come,' they said, 'with tokens
  For the little boy to choose.'
Told the tale about war and peace
  In the television news.

After them came the soldiers
  With rifle and bomb and gun,
Looking for enemies of the state.
  The family had packed and gone.

When they got back to the village
  The neighbours said, to a man,
'That boy will never be one of us,
  Though he does what he blessed well can.'

He went round to all the people
  A paper crown on his head.
Here is some bread from my father.
  Take, eat, he said.

Nobody seemed very hungry.
  Nobody seemed to care.
Nobody saw the god in himself
  Quietly standing there.

He finished up in the papers.
   He came to a very bad end.
He was charged with bringing the living to life.
   No man was that prisoner's friend.

There's only one kind of punishment
   To fit that kind of a crime.
They rigged a trial and shot him dead.
   They were only just in time.

They lifted the young man by the leg,
   They lifted him by the arm,
They locked him in a cathedral
   In case he came to harm.

They stored him safe as water
   Under seven rocks.
One Sunday morning he burst out
   Like a jack-in-the-box.

Through the town he went walking.
   He showed them the holes in his head.
Now do you want any loaves? he cried.
   'Not today,' they said.

1968

Siena in Sixty-eight

<o>

CHARLES TOMLINSON

The town band, swaying dreamily on its feet,
    Under the portraits of Gramsci and Ho,
Play 'Selections from *Norma*', and the moon,
    Casta diva, mounts up to show
How high the sky is over harvested Tuscany,
    Over this communist conviviality within the wall
Of a fortress that defends nothing at all.

History turns to statues, to fancy dress
    And the stylishness of Guevara in his bonnet. Here,
Red-bloused, forgetful sales girls
    For the revolution, flirt with the males
At a bookstore under an awning of red:
    Lenin, Che, Debray and Mao –
The unbought titles, pristinely serried.

'Realism and sobriety' one might write of the art show:
    In *No to Repression*, a procession of women
With raised fists, shouts No, No, No.
    And between *American Bombers* and *Black Boy Cleaning
    Shoes*,
Somebody, unteachably out of step,
    Has gouged intently into paint
The stigmata of St Francis in *Miracle of the Saint*.

Consciences drowse this summer night
    Warmed by the after-glow. Fragrance of cooking
Weighs on the sense already fed by it,
    The wild boar turning and turning on its spit;
And the air too greasily replete to lift the red flag,
    The morning headlines grow fainter in the dusk:
'Where is Dubcek?' 'Tanks on the streets of Prague.'

Che Guevara makes another appearance here, as does Ho Chi Minh (1890–
1969), Communist leader of North Vietnam, and Communist theorist Antonio
Gramsci (1891–1937). These names, with those of Lenin and Mao, were on the
lips of student protesters all over Europe in 1968. (Régis Debray, born 1940, who
has since played a significant part in French public life, was then celebrated by
students for his culture criticism and for having fought with Che in Bolivia.)
Tomlinson's poem notes the mixed feelings Italy brought to the 1968 agendas,
but ends with the Soviet invasion of Czechoslovakia on 20 August of that year,
and the downfall of reformist Czech prime minister Alexander Dubcek.

1968

August, 1968

W. H. AUDEN

The Ogre does what ogres can,
Deeds quite impossible for Man,
But one prize is beyond his reach,
The Ogre cannot master Speech:
About a subjugated plain,
Among its desperate and slain,
The Ogre stalks with hands on hips,
While drivel gushes from his lips.

Auden's ogre may owe something to Goya's colossus in his painting of that title, dating from between 1808 and 1812.

1968

Dream Song 105

<o>

JOHN BERRYMAN

As a kid I believed in democracy: I
'saw no alternative' – teaching at The Big Place I ah
put it in practice:
we'd time for one long novel: to a vote –
Gone with the Wind they voted: I crunched 'No'
and we sat down with *War & Peace*.

As a man I believed in democracy (nobody
ever learns *anything*): only one lazy day
my assistant, called James Dow,
& I were chatting, in a failure of meeting of minds,
and I said curious 'What are your real politics?'
'Oh, I'm a monarchist.'

Finishing his dissertation, in Political Science.
I resign. The universal contempt for Mr Nixon,
whom never I liked but who
alert & gutsy served us years under a dope,
since dynasty K swarmed in. Let's have a King
maybe, before a few mindless votes.

1968

Dream Song 343

<o>

John Berryman

Another directory form to be corrected.
Henry did one years & years agone for *Who's Who*,
wasn't that enough?
Why does the rehearsal of the public events of his life
always strike him as a list of failures, pal?
Where is childhood,

from which he recovered, & where are the moments of
　　love?
his three-day drunk at the fête of St Tropez?
his inn-garden in Kyoto?
his moments with Sonya? the pool-apron in Utah whereon
　　he lay
the famous daughter? of the famous mother? O
there were more than enough whereof

to whet an entry, rather than this silliness
of jobs, awards, books. He took a hard look
at the programme of the years
and struck his hardened palms across his ears
& 'Basta!' cried: I should　　have been a noted crook
or cat in a loud slum yes.

1968

Crossing the Border

Norman MacCaig

I sit with my back to the engine, watching
the landscape pouring away out of my eyes.
I think I know where I'm going and have
some choice in the matter.

I think, too, that this was a country
of bog-trotters, moss-troopers,
fired ricks and roof-trees in the black night – glinting
on tossed horns and red blades.
I think of lives
bubbling into the harsh grass.

What difference now?
I sit with my back to the future, watching
time pouring away into the past. I sit, being helplessly
lugged backwards
through the Debatable Lands of history, listening
to the execrations, the scattered cries, the
falling of roof-trees
in the lamentable dark.

1968

One Cigarette

<o>

EDWIN MORGAN

No smoke without you, my fire.
After you left,
your cigarette glowed on in my ashtray
and sent up a long thread of such quiet grey
I smiled to wonder who would believe its signal
of so much love. One cigarette
in the non-smoker's tray.
As the last spire
trembles up, a sudden draught
blows it winding into my face.
Is it smell, is it taste?
You are here again, and I am drunk on your tobacco
    lips.
Out with the light.
Let the smoke lie back in the dark.
Till I hear the very ash
sigh down among the flowers of brass
I'll breathe, and long past midnight, your last kiss.

1968

Death of Thomas Merton

◄◇►

HARRY CLIFTON

Losing altitude, you can see below you the flames
Of the Tet Offensive, giving the lie to your visions
Of Eastern mystics, like uncensored newsreel
In which the slaves of history are spreading the blame –
And so your mind records it, a sin of omission
In a mystic journal. Meanwhile the wheels
Descend for Bangkok, with one of the Catholic great,
In late October, Nineteen Sixty Eight.

A clean declaration. One a.m. and you're through
The bulletproof glass of security, like a conscience
Filtered through judgement, leaving behind
Temptations you were dead to, years ago –
Hippies frisked for heroin, women and incense
For the American soldiers. Only the life of the mind
You hide on your person – all the rest you can shed
Like a stale narcotic. Shortly, you'll be dead.

So wake before daylight, breakfast alone,
Remembering what you came for. Below you a river
Seeps out of Buddhist heartlands, not in meditation
But in commerce, irrigating zones
Of military fleshpots, where the barges deliver
Rice and Thai girls, and a drifting vegetation
Drags at the chains of destroyers, moored in Bangkok –
And you wait to be chauffeured, at nine o'clock,

To the other side of the city . . .

                            Spiritual masters
Shrunken to skin and bone, await you in silence
On a neutral ground of Buddhas, golden and hollow,
Smiling from inner space, beyond disaster
To an old complacency. Starving for non-violence

In saffron robes, their shavenheaded followers
Beg on the streets. From an airconditioned car
You can see them in passing, as cut off as you are –

Cut off from each other, disconnected by history
In Paris and Calcutta, linked alone by the airspace
Of a temporal pilgrimage. Diplomatic immunity,
This is your saving grace – to restore mystery
To a common weal, and resurrect from disgrace
The nonpolitical, kneeling in the unity
Of a moment's prayer, with the Dalai Lama and
    wife –
For the flash-photographers of *Time* and *Life*.

Judas has other betrayals. At your last supper
In a Hungarian restaurant, among friends in Bangkok,
It's left to the Chinese waiter to overprice you –
So unworldly. You can switch from corruption
Suddenly into wisdom, through an electric shock
Turning your hair white, resolving your crisis
Into anticlimax. But it leaves you dead,
With a powerline shortcircuited through your head . . .

A small embarrassment, for the United States –
Your motherhouse at Gethsemani awaits
Its anti-hero. A gaggle of monks are released
To New Haven for the day, to identify and separate
Among the Vietnam dead, the maimed in crates
From an Air Force plane, this body of a priest
And holy fool – from beyond the international
Dateline, and the jungle war with the irrational.

Thomas Merton (1915–1968) was born in France to a New Zealand father and American mother, and took US citizenship in 1949. Monk, writer, social activist, he led a life of spiritual quest which has served as an inspiration to many. He died away from his 'motherhouse at Gethsemani' (an abbey in Kentucky), in the course of a visit to Asia which had included a meeting with the Dalai Lama and took him on to Bangkok, where an accident resulted in his electrocution. The aftermath of the Tet Offensive, launched by the North Vietnamese against the South earlier that year, was still raging.

1969–1988
From the Moon to Berlin

B Y THE 1960s, the mass medium of television had become the communicative common currency of developed societies, and was increasingly well understood – so much so, that Canadian culture critic Marshall McLuhan's general insight that 'the medium is the message' could be re-stated by John Updike, in a poem about Apollo 11's landing on the moon, in tones of high tedium. 'Man, am I sick / of the moon. / We've turned it into one big / television screen.' Conceding that seeing Neil Armstrong on the surface of the moon 'was worth sitting up for', Updike concluded that the media had 'swamped the message'. Auden – fusing two words ('apparatchik' and 'sputnik') from the vocabulary of America's space race rivals, the Soviet Russians – designated the three US astronauts 'apparatniks', and in comparing their exploit with that of Homer's heroes he agreed with Updike, observing that at least Hector's deeds were not covered by television. For William Plomer, the whole lunar adventure boiled down to the one word 'claptrap'.

'The West' was wearying of its own superfluity. The world of political stand-off and the world of consumer materialism were alike prompting recoil and rejection. The very medium that had brought the 'Ed Sullivan Show', or 'The Black and White Minstrel Show', into households the length and breadth of the US or the UK, had also shown endless re-runs of Kennedy's assassination, the riots in Paris and London, and the Soviet tanks in Prague. The surplus of post-War energy that had fuelled the conspicuous consumption of the Fifties imploded into the anti-Establishment politics of youth culture across 'the West' in the Sixties and onward into the Seventies. It was bliss, of course, to be alive in the dawn of flower power. And even if the culture of the 68-ers was itself predicated on consumption, their simple and outspoken plea for life and peace resonated throughout the world, across all the divides of cultures and generations. In the more thoughtful poetry of the years that followed, that resonance appeared in fundamental notes of openness, doubt and self-scrutiny.

The openness is overwhelmingly apparent when the conservative Australian James McAuley lets down his guard and writes of his parents, when New Zealander James Baxter talks with God or with his dead father, or, in the late Seventies, when Peter Porter, anguished after the suicide of his first wife, imagines her at his study door at night, asking if he has work to do – or will he come to bed? The great upheaval in emotional honesty that had been accomplished by Lowell, Plath, Sexton and Berryman issued in reams of ungifted magazine verse in the Sixties and Seventies, but also had the important effect of midwifing the candour and tenderness of other major poets.

A keynote of poetry in the late Sixties and through the Seventies was its doubt. John Berryman's thoughts about a public account of life that excludes 'moments with Sonya', Peter Redgrove's dalliance with dark undersides of existence in his imagined curiosity shop, and Douglas Stewart's enterprising portrayal of the Reverend Henry White as 'the most innocent of mankind', all imply considered thought about the nature of the good life, and doubts about the value of partial accounts. Arun Kolatkar's 'The Priest', from his landmark collection *Jejuri*, amiably substitutes humour, doubt, and the evidence of the senses, for any system of belief that the priest may stand for. And the certainty shortly before death of Baxter and Berryman, who wrote with passion of God after leading self-indulgent lives, reads like a defiant, self-deceiving denial of doubt.

The self-scrutiny apparent throughout the work of a Heaney, a Mahon or a Porter is strongest when both the personal and the national, cultural identity are examined, and in the mid-Seventies these three poets coincidentally published defining poems that stand among the finest achievements of recent decades. Seamus Heaney's

'Punishment' steps outside the confines of its own troubled time in Ireland to meditate on a terrible example of tribal retribution, and returns from that meditation to confront the poet's own difficult, ambiguous position on sectarian violence. Derek Mahon's magisterial contemplation of a shed in the grounds of a burnt-out, abandoned hotel places Ireland's ghosts, and the presence of the past in the present, within dizzyingly extended perspectives, both in time and in place, so that we understand the Irish condition to be the human condition. And Peter Porter's 'On First Looking into Chapman's Hesiod' – rich in aphorism, sharp in its understanding of ancient and modern, 'Old' World and 'New' – seamlessly joins the needs of the questing individual (the poet from Brisbane had made his life in London) with a searching analysis of Australian national identity. Les Murray recognised the 'high importance as a cultural document' of Porter's poem, and, while entering caveats, agreed that 'our culture is still in its Boeotian phase'. The detail of the bi-plane crop-dusting lucerne, in David Malouf's Horatian poem of 1970, showed another major Australian writer reaching the same conclusion.

In a period when US supremacy was felt globally to bring problems as well as benefits, when Britain, having divested itself of an empire and embarked on closer but fraught relations with the rest of Europe, seemed unsure of its future, and when 'new' nations such as Australia realised they had hit their stride, inquiry into national identity was all-important. Larkin's 'Going, Going' was not only an environmentalist jeremiad, it was also a lament for the decline of Britain. For the United States, scrutiny of national identity turned upon the workings of democracy, and the war in Vietnam. Even before the Watergate affair, John Berryman could refer in passing to the 'universal contempt for Mr Nixon' apparently without any fear of being controversial. Howard Nemerov, like Kipling reviewing the First World War, knew that the elders never fail to find causes for the young to die in; he was also scathing about the egotistical self-delusion of poets penning lines against the Vietnam war. (His two well-taken squibs appear here, as it happens, beside Douglas Stewart's vision of 'the most harmless, the most innocent of mankind', which can be read in this context as the most diffident of peace poems.) Later, when Hollywood was turning out its movies, and the American nation, and individual Vietnam veterans, were coming to terms with defeat in a traumatic war, Yusef Komunyakaa visited the Vietnam Veterans Memorial and discovered that its black stone played tricks.

The Seventies and Eighties proved to be the heyday of the proxy wars. The terror of brinkmanship kept the fingers of the USA and the USSR off their buttons. The acronym MAD (Mutually Assured Destruction) said it all. But in 'the place where death is planned', in Vikram Seth's phrase, business continued as usual. Every year brought its new deployments of missiles, its new peace movement groupings and demonstrations, its wars of words, its arms limitation talks. And in places remote from Moscow or Washington, the Cold War was hot: James Fenton writing of Cambodia, Carolyn Forché of El Salvador, and Landeg White of a raid into Zambia, were first-hand observers of events that everyone followed on a daily basis. Perhaps it was an era half in love with easeful death. The shadow cast by the Second World War persisted long and dark, and poems by Geoffrey Hill, Derek Mahon, Andrew Motion and Jorie Graham almost suggest a reluctance to come out from under that shadow. (Even Hugo Williams's childhood memories retain 'before the war' as their semi-mythic starting-point.) Tony Harrison's magisterial poem 'The Mother of the Muses' takes the nature of memory, and its involvement in the intractable history of the twentieth century, as its subject, and the result is a meditation of triumphantly tragic compass. The evils of the Troubles brought expressions of grief and anger from Irish poets, Durcan, Heaney, Longley and Carson among them. And the long process of coming to terms with the British Empire produced in Derek Walcott a poet who could not only turn his back on the old imagined centre and write of the true centre that is wherever life is fully lived, but could also take the Conradian tools of imperial critique and, in 'Koenig of the River', craft a new 'Ozymandias', a constructed world in which it has become meaningless to claim that 'victory was in sight'.

If it is true that consumption followed privation after 1945, and that the upheaval of the Sixties was as much a revolt against hardened materialism as against the continuation of war by other, colder means, what was the inner story of the Seventies and Eighties, when even a chess series between grand masters could become a proxy war? One answer must be that many of the stories that preoccupied the media of the day apparently offered paltry purchase to poets' imaginations. From the Chinese cultural revolution, the fall of Allende in Chile, or the Watergate affair, to the women protesters encamped at Greenham Common, the stories that made headlines for weeks, even months or years, were reflected only rarely, and rarely well, in thoughtful, effective poetry. And the notorious fashions and pop music of the Seventies, the sports icons and sporting occasions (even the terrorist attack on the 1972 Munich Olympics), the movies from *Jaws* to the Indiana Jones and *Star Wars* series, all existed in a universe that poetry was largely content to ignore. As the fate of the world was decided (it seemed) at Reykjavik or Camp David, the calm, quiet realm of the spirit drew lyrical meditations from Welsh poets R. S. Thomas and Gillian Clarke, from New Zealanders Allen Curnow and James Baxter, from Canadians Phyllis Webb, Roo Borson and Robert Bringhurst; it drew poems of love from W. S. Graham, Seamus Heaney and Michael Ondaatje, poems of compassion and loss from Don Coles, Douglas Dunn and Sharon Olds. The greatness of the still centre of humanity, and the reasons why it will abide beyond all headlines, are made luminous in their work.

The inner story was that humanity understood that its greatest resource was its humanity, and learned to be comfortable with an oppositional relationship to the headline world of power politics. When Richard Wilbur cast the knife-edge balance of nuclear politics in the form of a fable, he was not misjudging his tone, he was choosing a register that caught precisely the widely-shared sense of knowing (alas) what was what. When C. K. Williams observed his president 'completely unafraid' in his 'absurd protective booties' at the site of the Three Mile Island accident (at a nuclear power plant in Pennsylvania), his laconic comment was, 'the fool'. As the Cold War moved into a fifth decade, Vincent O'Sullivan's Pilate, having 'killed a god', was a man who had 'dabbled in chaos' and voted 'as you do'. Two striking poems about city dumps written a decade apart – Robert Gray's 'Flames and Dangling Wire' in the late Seventies, and Elizabeth Spires's 'The Woman on the Dump' in the late Eighties – shared visions of infernal fires, but salvaged from their hellish despond a hope that grew from the sheer vitality of the human spirit: in the survival of radio sounds from a concert hall, still travelling 'around the arc of the universe', Gray's apocalyptic poem placed what faith it could (even a delusory faith) in artistic creation, while for Spires, telling of the woman's pointless labours, it was the sheer indefatigability of her effort, 'saving everything / that can be saved', that was valuable – her sheer determination to find 'The *the*'. Ahead, uncannily prefigured in Charles Boyle's visionary poem 'The Chess Player', lay the transformation that bore the name of Berlin.

1969

Seven New Ways of Looking at the Moon

——◦——

JOHN UPDIKE

July 21, 1969

I

Man, am I sick
    of the moon.
We've turned it into one big
    television screen,
one more littered campsite,
one more high school yearbook
    signed, 'Lots of luck,
        Richard Nixon.'

II

Still, seeing Armstrong's strong leg
float down in creepy silhouette
    that first stark second
    was worth sitting up for.
Then it got too real, and seemed
    a George Pal Puppettoon
    called 'Men on the Moon,'
mocked up on a Ping-Pong table.

III

Never again will I think of Houston
as full of rich men in cowboy hats:
    it is full
of numbers that like to talk
    and cajole.
They say, 'Neil, start gathering rocks now'
and, 'Buzz, about time to get back into
    your module.'

IV

And how about little Luna
    snooping around
like a rusty private eye
    casing the motel
where we'd set up the tryst?

V

There was a backyard something
    that happened after
they put up the flag and laid out
the solar tinfoil and dug some holes.
    I had been there before,
playing marbles under a line of wash,
skinning my knees on the lack of grass.

VI

Since St Paul filed his bulletins
standing headlines have been claiming
    SECOND COMING.
Now the type was broken up and used:
    MOON SEDUCING,
one 'c' turned sideways as a 'u'.
Since no one came, we went.

VII

Well, I don't know. The media
have swamped the message, but anyway
      God bless the men.
      I loved the way they ran,
like bear-foot ghosts let out of school to say
that Death is probably O.K.
if all it means is being in the sky.
      Which answers why.

Updike's poem is dated to the day on which Neil Armstrong, then Buzz Aldrin,
American astronauts from the Apollo 11 mission, became the first humans to
walk on the moon.

1969

Moon Landing

<o>

W. H. AUDEN

It's natural the Boys should whoop it up for
so huge a phallic triumph, an adventure
   it would not have occurred to women
   to think worth while, made possible only

because we like huddling in gangs and knowing
the exact time: yes, our sex may in fairness
   hurrah the deed, although the motives
   that primed it were somewhat less than *menschlich*.

A grand gesture. But what does it period?
What does it osse? We were always adroiter
   with objects than lives, and more facile
   at courage than kindness: from the moment

the first flint was flaked this landing was merely
a matter of time. But our selves, like Adam's,
   still don't fit us exactly, modern
   only in this – our lack of decorum.

Homer's heroes were certainly no braver
than our Trio, but more fortunate: Hector
   was excused the insult of having
   his valor covered by television.

Worth *going* to see? I can well believe it.
Worth *going*? Mneh! I once rode through a desert
   and was not charmed: give me a watered
   lively garden, remote from blatherers

about the New, the von Brauns and their ilk, where
on August mornings I can count the morning
   glories, where to die has a meaning,
   and no engine can shift my perspective.

Unsmudged, thank God, my Moon still queens the
    Heavens
as She ebbs and fulls, a Presence to glop at,
    Her Old Man, made of grit not protein,
    still visits my Austrian several

with His old detachment, and the old warnings
still have power to scare me: Hybris comes to
    an ugly finish, Irreverence
    is a greater oaf than Superstition.

Our apparatniks will continue making
the usual squalid mess called History:
    all we can pray for is that artists,
    chefs and saints may still appear to blithe it.

The 'Trio' was Armstrong and Aldrin (see note to previous poem) and the third astronaut on the Apollo 11 mission, Michael Collins. Auden's reference to 'von Brauns' means Wernher von Braun (1912–77), the German rocket engineer who developed the V-2 military rockets during the Second World War and later, in the US (he became a US citizen in 1955), played a key role in the American space programme.

1969

To the Moon and Back

◁◇▷

WILLIAM PLOMER

countdown	takeoff
moonprints	rockbox
splashdown	claptrap

1969

Because

James McAuley

My father and my mother never quarrelled.
They were united in a kind of love
As daily as the *Sydney Morning Herald*,
Rather than like the eagle or the dove.

I never saw them casually touch,
Or show a moment's joy in one another.
Why should this matter to me now so much?
I think it bore more hardly on my mother,

Who had more generous feelings to express.
My father had dammed up his Irish blood
Against all drinking praying fecklessness,
And stiffened into stone and creaking wood.

His lips would make a switching sound, as though
Spontaneous impulse must be kept at bay.
That it was mainly weakness I see now,
But then my feelings curled back in dismay.

Small things can pit the memory like a cyst:
Having seen other fathers greet their sons,
I put my childish face up to be kissed
After an absence. The rebuff still stuns

My blood. The poor man's curt embarrassment
At such a delicate proffer of affection
Cut like a saw. But home the lesson went:
My tenderness thenceforth escaped detection.

My mother sang *Because*, and *Annie Laurie*,
White Wings, and other songs; her voice was sweet.
I never gave enough, and I am sorry;
But we were all closed in the same defeat.

People do what they can; they were good people,
They cared for us and loved us. Once they stood
Tall in my childhood as the school, the steeple.
How can I judge without ingratitude?

Judgment is simply trying to reject
A part of what we are because it hurts.
The living cannot call the dead collect:
They won't accept the charge, and it reverts.

It's my own judgment day that I draw near,
Descending in the past, without a clue,
Down to that central deadness: the despair
Older than any hope I ever knew.

1969

Tabletalk

◄◦►

JAMES McAULEY

In tabletalk my father used to tell
Of the escaped nun kidnapped by a priest;
Or innocent girls in the confessional,
Closeted in the dark with some gross beast.

By contrast, Anglican restraint was good:
It kept religion in its proper place. –
What all this talk was for, I understood
Only long after; but it left a trace.

In an unguarded moment once, I drew
Deserved rebuke for letting on I had
A plan of reading the whole Bible through:
He thought this a quick way of going mad.

On relatives my parents were agreed:
Too much association doesn't do,
And doubly so with the bog-Irish breed –
They're likely to want something out of you.

On friendship too the doctrine was as cold:
They're only making use of you you'll find;
Prudence consists in learning to withhold
The natural impulse of the sharing mind.

What is the wisdom that a child needs most?
Ours was distrust, a coating behind the eye
We took in daily with the mutton roast,
The corned-beef salad, and the shepherd's pie.

1970

Reading Horace outside Sydney, 1970

DAVID MALOUF

The distance is deceptive: Sydney glitters invisible
in its holocaust of air, just thirty miles away, in Rome
two thousand years from here, a goosequill scrapes, two crack
    divisions
are hurled against a furclad, barbarous northern people pushing

south into history; small throats are cut at committee tables,
a marriage dies in bed; bald officials like old pennies
worn smooth by time and trade were once my copper-keen
    schoolfellows,
who studied Cicero and shook their heads over the fall

of virtue in high places; now on pills twelve storeys high
in air, they shake their heads and fall and pause and walk again.
Somewhere across a border shabby barefoot warriors
stumble into grass, an empire mourns, in small wars seeking

safe boundaries against death. Over the traffic, over the harbour,
    lions
roar, schoolboys scramble out of nightmares, mineral stocks
fall with a noiseless crash, the sigh of millions; cicadas
are heard, shrill under stones, in the long suspension of our
    breath.

Out here wheat breathes and surges, poplars flare. On the
    highway lorries
throb towards city squares. High in the blue a Cessna biplane
crop-dusting lucerne turns to catch the sun. The brilliant granule
climbs on out of sight. Its shadow dances in my palm.

Cicero (106–43 BC) was a philosopher statesman, arguably the greatest of
Rome's political thinkers. The generation that divided his life from that of the
poet Horace (65–8 BC) saw the immense conflicts that ushered in the change
from republic to empire.

1970

Incident
<o>
FRANCIS WEBB

If ONLY to create a simpler ruffian with no gun . . .
I give you our dayroom at twelve: dinner overdue:
Flyscreens bowdlerising the garrulous sun:
Discreet odours of stew:
Honest plastic chairs: senile patter of doctor telly:
Our dreams of tart tea and innocuous blasé bread.
And into this shop of shades, like a blade in the belly,
Someone comes with the news. 'McMurtrie's dead'.

Why, there were tablets in felicitous reticules
To lower like sheets daily comas upon the void.
Cheap tobacco fumes wavered like seaweed about our hulls.
Our limpets laboured like God.
And upon these lacquers and languors, this stygian vision,
Comes a smear, a sneer, a spinnaker working like a head.
Bulging and billowing in travail, this imposition
Of the thug Time of the timeless. McMurtrie's dead.

Might have seen him asail in some ward or other;
Might have borrowed a smoke (pay you back tomorrow);
But now, with poor petty Charon in all sorts of bother
To moor him – laughter nor sorrow –
He comes like a clipper with stunsails in white rigmarole.
Oceans and latitudes wrestle in his rigging; unsaid
Any word or oath of clearance or parole;
Only that frail occult murmur, 'McMurtrie's dead'.

McMurtrie once bruised his shins or pondered a flower:
O colossal revelation and prophecy,
O silver yards and hands all ashake with power!
Two thousand light-years into sky
He peered once, pulled at the breast, or kissed a woman.
Strange spasms of speculation whisper and are fed
By his swelling tackle – he knows all, he is superhuman
And can trump the last tricks of space. McMurtrie's dead.

For a time and half a time, unfathomable minute,
Greaved with silence and laughter he stood and strode,
With doodling bootmarks claimed for his own a planet.
Concupiscence? Rectitude?
One puny sense is eternal – he had five.
Things that he fingered (crucifix, ashtray, bed)
Are gulls in his shroudings. Transfigured and alive
Without taunt of terror or stillness. McMurtrie's dead.

1970

from Jerusalem Sonnets

JAMES K. BAXTER

1

The small grey cloudy louse that nests in my beard
Is not, as some have called it, 'a pearl of God' –

No, it is a fiery tormentor
Waking me at two a.m.

Or thereabouts, when the lights are still on
In the houses in the pa, to go across thick grass

Wet with rain, feet cold, to kneel
For an hour or two in front of the red flickering

Tabernacle light – what He sees inside
My meandering mind I can only guess –

A madman, a nobody, a raconteur
Whom He can joke with – 'Lord,' I ask Him,

'Do You or don't You expect me to put up with lice?'
His silent laugh still shakes the hills at dawn.

5

Man, my outdoor lavatory
Has taken me three days to build –

A trench cut deep into the clay,
Then four posts, some rusty fencing wire

And a great fort of bracken
Intertwined – a noble structure

Like the gardens of Babylon, made to hide

My defecation from the eyes of the nuns –

And this morning I found a fat green frog
Squatting in the trench – I lifted him out

Against his will and set him free,
But I am trapped in the ditch of ownership

Wondering if the next gale at night
Will flatten the whole ziggurat and leave me to shit naked.

18

Yesterday I planted garlic,
Today, sunflowers – 'the non-essentials first'

Is a good motto – but these I planted in honour of
The Archangel Michael and my earthly friend,

Illingworth, Michael also, who gave me the seeds –
And they will turn their wild pure golden discs

Outside my bedroom, following Te Ra
Who carries fire for us in His terrible wings

(Heresy, man!) – and if He wanted only
For me to live and die in this old cottage,

It would be enough, for the angels who keep
The very stars in place resemble most

These green brides of the sun, hopelessly in love with
Their Master and Maker, drunkards of the sky.

36

Brother Ass, Brother Ass, you are full of fancies,
You want this and that – a woman, a thistle,

A poem, a coffeebreak, a white bed, no crabs;
And now you complain of the weight of the Rider

Who will set you free to gallop in the light of the sun!
Ah well, kick Him off then, and see how you go

Lame-footed in the brambles; your disconsolate bray
Is ugly in my ears – long ago, long ago,

The battle was fought and the issue decided
As to who would be King – go on, little donkey

Saddled and bridled by the Master of the world,
Be glad you can distinguish not an inch of the track,

That the stones are sharp, that your hide can itch,
That His true weight is heavy on your back.

37

Colin, you can tell my words are crippled now;
The bright coat of art He has taken away from me

And like the snail I crushed at the church door
My song is my stupidity;

The words of a homely man I cannot speak,
Home and bed He has taken away from me;

Like an old horse turned to grass I lift my head
Biting at the blossoms of the thorn tree;

Prayer of priest or nun I cannot use,
The songs of His house He has taken away from me;

As blind men meet and touch each other's faces
So He is kind to my infirmity;

As the cross is lifted and the day goes dark
Rule over myself He has taken away from me.

A pa is a Maori village, and Te Ra is the Maori sun god. 'Brother Ass' was the expression used by St Francis of Assisi for his body. Michael Illingworth (1932–88) moved to New Zealand from England in 1951, and worked as a photographer and artist. The unrhymed, irregular sonnets Baxter wrote in his isolation at the Jerusalem settlement were addressed to his friend Colin Durning, to whom he sometimes spoke directly and by name (as in sonnet 37).

1970

'I leave this at your ear'

W. S. GRAHAM

For Nessie Dunsmuir

I leave this at your ear for when you wake,
A creature in its abstract cage asleep.
Your dreams blindfold you by the light they make.

The owl called from the naked-woman tree
As I came down by the Kyle farm to hear
Your house silent by the speaking sea.

I have come late but I have come before
Later with slaked steps from stone to stone
To hope to find you listening for the door.

I stand in the ticking room. My dear, I take
A moth kiss from your breath. The shore gulls cry.
I leave this at your ear for when you wake.

Nessie Dunsmuir (1909–99) was Graham's wife.

1971

Spoon

CHARLES SIMIC

An old spoon
Bent, gouged,
Polished to an evil
Glitter.

It has bitten
Into my life –
This kennel-bone
Sucked thin.

Now, it is a living
Thing: ready
To scratch a name
On a prison wall –

Ready to be passed on
To the little one
Just barely
Beginning to walk.

1971

A Leopard Lives in a Muu Tree

JONATHAN KARIARA

A leopard lives in a Muu tree
Watching my home
My lambs are born speckled
My wives tie their skirts tight
And turn away –
Fearing mottled offspring.
They bathe when the moon is high
Soft and fecund
Splash cold mountain stream water on their nipples
Drop their skin skirts and call obscenities.
I'm besieged
I shall have to cut down the Muu tree
I'm besieged
I walk about stiff
Stroking my loins.
A leopard lives outside my homestead
Watching my women
I have called him elder, the one-from-the-same-womb
He peers at me with slit eyes
His head held high
My sword has rusted in the scabbard.
My wives purse their lips
When owls call for mating
I'm besieged
They fetch cold mountain water
They crush the sugar cane
But refuse to touch my beer horn.
My fences are broken
My medicine bags torn

The hair on my loins is singed
The upright post at the gate has fallen
My women are frisky
The leopard arches over my homestead
Eats my lambs
Resuscitating himself.

1971

Vultures

◄◦►

CHINUA ACHEBE

In the grayness
and drizzle of one despondent
dawn unstirred by harbingers
of sunbreak a vulture
perching high on broken
bone of a dead tree
nestled close to his
mate his smooth
bashed-in head, a pebble
on a stem rooted in
a dump of gross
feathers, inclined affectionately
to hers. Yesterday they picked
the eyes of a swollen
corpse in a waterlogged
trench and ate the
things in its bowel. Full
gorged they chose their roost
keeping the hollowed remnant
in easy range of cold
telescopic eyes . . .
    Strange
indeed how love in other
ways so particular
will pick a corner
in that charnel house
tidy it and coil up there, perhaps
even fall asleep – her face
turned to the wall!
. . . Thus the Commandant at Belsen
Camp going home for
the day with fumes of

human roast clinging
rebelliously to his hairy
nostrils will stop
at the wayside sweetshop
and pick up a chocolate
for his tender offspring
waiting at home for Daddy's
return . . .
    Praise bounteous
providence if you will
that grants even an ogre
its glowworm
tenderness encapsulated
in icy caverns of a cruel
heart or else despair
for in the very germ
of that kindred love is
lodged the perpetuity
of evil.

1972

The Curiosity-Shop

PETER REDGROVE

It was a Borgia-pot, he told me,
A baby had been distilled alive into the pottery,
He recommended the cream, it would make a mess of
anybody's face;
My grief moved down my cheeks in a slow mass like
ointment.

Or there was this undine-vase, if you shook it
The spirit made a silvery tinkling inside;
Flat on the table, it slid so that it pointed always towards the
sea.
A useful compass, he said.
I could never unseal this jar, tears would never stop flowing
towards the sea.

Impatiently he offered me the final item, a ghoul-sack,
I was to feed it with rats daily unless I had a great enemy
Could be persuaded to put his head inside;
That's the one! I said,
That's the sackcloth suit sewn for the likes of me
With my one love's grief, and my appetite for curiosity.

Undine was a water nymph in central European legend, and has appeared in
many media, from Friedrich de la Motte Fouqué's novella of 1811 to the 1958
ballet by Hans Werner Henze (choreographed by Frederick Ashton for Margot
Fonteyn), from John William Waterhouse's 1872 painting to Seamus Heaney's
poem of 1969.

1972

Going, Going

⊸◦⊷

Philip Larkin

I thought it would last my time –
The sense that, beyond the town,
There would always be fields and farms,
Where the village louts could climb
Such trees as were not cut down;
I knew there'd be false alarms

In the papers about old streets
And split-level shopping, but some
Have always been left so far;
And when the old part retreats
As the bleak high-risers come
We can always escape in the car.

Things are tougher than we are, just
As earth will always respond
However we mess it about;
Chuck filth in the sea, if you must:
The tides will be clean beyond.
– But what do I feel now? Doubt?

Or age, simply? The crowd
Is young in the M1 café;
Their kids are screaming for more –
More houses, more parking allowed,
More caravan sites, more pay.
On the Business Page, a score

Of spectacled grins approve
Some takeover bid that entails
Five per cent profit (and ten
Per cent more in the estuaries): move
Your works to the unspoilt dales
(Grey area grants)! And when

You try to get near the sea
In summer . . .

              It seems, just now,
To be happening so very fast;
Despite all the land left free
For the first time I feel somehow
That it isn't going to last,

That before I snuff it, the whole
Boiling will be bricked in
Except for the tourist parts –
First slum of Europe: a role
It won't be so hard to win,
With a cast of crooks and tarts.

And that will be England gone,
The shadows, the meadows, the lanes,
The guildhalls, the carved choirs.
There'll be books; it will linger on
In galleries; but all that remains
For us will be concrete and tyres.

Most things are never meant.
This won't be, most likely: but greeds
And garbage are too thick-strewn
To be swept up now, or invent
Excuses that make them all needs.
I just think it will happen, soon.

1972

Natural History

❮o❯

ROBERT PENN WARREN

In the rain the naked old father is dancing, he will get wet.
The rain is sparse, but he cannot dodge all the drops.

He is singing a song, but the language is strange to me.

The mother is counting her money like mad, in the sunshine.
Like shuttles her fingers fly, and the sum is clearly
    astronomical.
Her breath is sweet as bruised violets, and her smile sways like
    daffodils reflected in a brook.

The song of the father tells how at last he understands.
That is why the language is strange to me.

That is why clocks all over the continent have stopped.

The money the naked old mother counts is her golden
    memories of love.
That is why I see nothing in her maniacally busy fingers.

That is why all flights have been canceled out of Kennedy.

As much as I hate to, I must summon the police.
For their own good, as well as that of society, they must be
    put under surveillance.

They must learn to stay in their graves. That is what graves
    are for.

1972

Certainty Before Lunch

◆

JOHN BERRYMAN

NINETY percent of the mass of the Universe
(90%!) may be gone in collapsars,
pulseless, lightless, forever, if they exist.
My friends the probability man & I

& his wife the lawyer are taking a country walk
in the flowerless April snow in exactly two hours
and maybe won't be back. Finite & unbounded
the massive spirals absolutely fly

distinctly apart, by math *and* observation,
current math, this morning's telescopes
& inference. My wife is six months gone
so won't be coming. That mass must be somewhere!

or not? just barely possibly *may not*
BE anywhere? My Lord, I'm glad we don't
on x or y depend for Your being there.
I know You are there. The sweat is, I am here.

When Berryman wrote this poem, the word 'collapsars' was used to refer to what shortly became known by the now familiar term 'black holes'.

1972

from Autumn Testament

JAMES K. BAXTER

11

At times when I walk beside the budding figtree
Or on the round stones by the river,

I meet the face of my dead father
With one or two white bristles on his chin

The safety razor missed. When he was younger
He'd hold the cut-throat with the ivory handle

And bring it with one deft stroke down his jowl,
Leaving the smooth blue skin. 'Old man,' I say,

'Long loved by me, still loved by many,
Is there a chance your son will ever join you

'In the kingdom of the summer stars?' He leaves me
Without a word, but like a touch behind him,

Greener the bulge of fruit among the figleaves,
Hotter the bright eye of the noonday sun.

22

To pray for an easy heart is no prayer at all
Because the heart itself is the creaking bridge

On which we cross these Himalayan gorges
From bluff to bluff. To sweat out the soul's blood

Midnight after midnight is the ministry of Jacob,
And Jacob will be healed. This body that shivers

In the foggy cold, tasting the sour fat,
Was made to hang like a sack on its thief's cross,

Counting it better than bread to say the words of Christ,
'*Eli! Eli!*' The Church will be shaken like a

Blanket in the wind, and we are the fleas that fall
To the ground for the dirt to cover. Brother thief,

You who are lodged in my ribcage, do not rail at
The only gate we have to paradise.

29

I think the Lord on his axe-chopped cross
Is laughing as usual at my poems,

My solemn metaphors, my ladder-climbing dreams,
For he himself is incurably domestic,

A family man who never lifted a sword,
An only son with a difficult mother,

If you understand my thought. He has saddled me again
With the cares of a household, and no doubt

Has kept me away from Otaki
Because I'd spout nonsense, and wear my poverty

As a coat of vanity. Down at the Mass
Today, as Francie told me to, I took Communion

For her (and Siân as well) cursing gently
The Joker who won't let me shuffle my own pack.

33

'Mother, your statue by the convent path
Has chips of plaster scattered round it

'Where rain or frost have stripped you of your mantle –'
'It doesn't matter.' 'As you know, in winter

'I often kneel there under the knife-edged moon
Praying for –' 'I hear those prayers.'

'Mother, your blue gown seems like stone,
Too rigid –' 'What they make of me

'Is never what I am.' 'Our Church looks to the young
Like a Medusa; they want to be –'

'Free, yes; Christ is the only Master.'
'They are taught to judge themselves.' 'Suffer it.'

'But sin –' 'I see no sin. My secret is
I hold the Child I was given to hold.'

On the cross, Jesus 'cried with a loud voice, saying, *Eli, Eli, lama sabachthani?* That
is to say, My God, my God, why hast thou forsaken me?' (Matthew 27: 46)

1973

B Flat

───────◆◇◆───────

DOUGLAS STEWART

Sing softly, Muse, the Reverend Henry White
Who floats through time as lightly as a feather
Yet left one solitary gleam of light
Because he was the Selborne naturalist's brother

And told him once how on warm summer eves
When moonlight filled all Fyfield to the brim
And yearning owls were hooting to their loves
On church and barn and oak-tree's leafy limb

He took a common half-a-crown pitch-pipe
Such as the masters used for harpsichords
And through the village trod with silent step
Measuring the notes of those melodious birds

And found that each one sang, or rather hooted,
Precisely in the measure of B flat.
And that is all that history has noted;
We know no more of Henry White than that.

So, softly, Muse, in harmony and conformity
Pipe up for him and all such gentle souls
Thus in the world's enormousness, enormity,
So interested in music and in owls;

For though we cannot claim his crumb of knowledge
Was worth much more than virtually nil
Nor hail him for vast enterprise or courage,
Yet in my mind I see him walking still

With eager ear beneath his clerical hat
Through Fyfield village sleeping dark and blind,
Oh surely as he piped his soft B flat
The most harmless, the most innocent of mankind.

The 'Selborne naturalist' was Gilbert White (1720–93), who remains well known
for *The Natural History and Antiquities of Selborne* (1789).

1973

On Getting Out of Vietnam

HOWARD NEMEROV

Theseus, if he did destroy the Minotaur
(It's hard to say, that may have been a myth),
Was careful not to close the labyrinth.
So After kept on looking like Before:
Back home in Athens still the elders sent
Their quota of kids to Knossos, confident
They would find something to die of, and for.

1973

On Being Asked for a Peace Poem

HOWARD NEMEROV

Here is Joe Blow the poet
Sitting before the console of the giant instrument
That mediates his spirit to the world.
He flexes his fingers nervously,
He ripples off a few scale passages
(Shall I compare thee to a summer's day?)
And resolutely readies himself to begin
His poem about the War in Vietnam.

This poem, he figures, is
A sacred obligation: all by himself,
Applying the immense leverage of art,
He is about to stop this senseless war.
So Homer stopped that dreadful thing at Troy
By giving the troops the Iliad to read instead;
So Wordsworth stopped the Revolution when
He felt that Robespierre had gone too far;
So Yevtushenko was invited in the *Times*
To keep the Arabs out of Israel
By smiting once again his mighty lyre.
Joe smiles. He sees the Nobel Prize
Already, and the reading of his poem
Before the General Assembly, followed by
His lecture to the Security Council
About the Creative Process; probably
Some bright producer would put it on TV.
Poetry might suddenly be the in thing.

Only trouble was, he didn't have
A good first line, though he thought that for so great
A theme it would be right to start with O,
Something he would not normally have done,

543

O

And follow on by making some demands
Of a strenuous sort upon the Muse
Polyhymnia of Sacred Song, that Lady
With the fierce gaze and implacable small smile.

Russian poet Yevgeny Yevtushenko (born 1933) was at the peak of his popularity and influence in the Sixties and Seventies, and had established a sharp international profile by criticising the Soviet authorities on numerous occasions. Nemerov's irony insists on reminding us that poets are powerless.

1974

In Memory of Those Murdered in the Dublin Massacre, May 1974

——◄o►——

PAUL DURCAN

In the grime-ridden sunlight in the downtown Wimpy bar
I think of all the crucial aeons – and of the labels
That freedom fighters stick onto the lost destinies of unborn
   children;
The early morning sunlight carries in the whole street from
   outside;
The whole wide street from outside through the plate-glass
   windows;
Wholly, sparklingly, surgingly, carried in from outside;
And the waitresses cannot help but be happy and gay
As they swipe at the tabletops with their dishcloths –
Such a moment as would provide the heroic freedom fighter
With his perfect meat.
And I think of those heroes – heroes? – heroes.

And as I stand up to walk out –
The aproned old woman who's been sweeping the floor
Has mop stuck in bucket, leaning on it;
And she's trembling all over, like a flower in the breeze.
She'd make a mighty fine explosion now, if you were to blow
   her up;
An explosion of petals, of aeons, and the waitresses too, flying
   breasts and limbs,
For a free Ireland.

The poem is a response to the Dublin and Monaghan car bombings of 17 May
1974.

1975

Punishment

◄○►

SEAMUS HEANEY

I can feel the tug
of the halter at the nape
of her neck, the wind
on her naked front.

It blows her nipples
to amber beads,
it shakes the frail rigging
of her ribs.

I can see her drowned
body in the bog,
the weighing stone,
the floating rods and boughs.

Under which at first
she was a barked sapling
that is dug up
oak-bone, brain-firkin:

her shaved head
like a stubble of black corn,
her blindfold a soiled bandage,
her noose a ring

to store
the memories of love.
Little adulteress,
before they punished you

you were flaxen-haired,
undernourished, and your
tar-black face was beautiful.
My poor scapegoat,

I almost love you
but would have cast, I know,
the stones of silence.
I am the artful voyeur

of your brain's exposed
and darkened combs,
your muscles' webbing
and all your numbered bones:

I who have stood dumb
when your betraying sisters,
cauled in tar,
wept by the railings,

who would connive
in civilized outrage
yet understand the exact
and tribal, intimate revenge.

1975

A Disused Shed in Co. Wexford

◄◦►

DEREK MAHON

'Let them not forget us, the weak
souls among the asphodels.'
Seferis, *Mythistorema*

For J. G. Farrell

Even now there are places where a thought might grow –
Peruvian mines, worked out and abandoned
To a slow clock of condensation,
An echo trapped for ever, and a flutter
Of wild flowers in the lift-shaft,
Indian compounds where the wind dances
And a door bangs with diminished confidence,
Lime crevices behind rippling rain-barrels,
Dog corners for bone burials;
And in a disused shed in Co. Wexford,

Deep in the grounds of a burnt-out hotel,
Among the bathtubs and the washbasins
A thousand mushrooms crowd to a keyhole.
This is the one star in their firmament
Or frames a star within a star.
What should they do there but desire?
So many days beyond the rhododendrons
With the world waltzing in its bowl of cloud,
They have learnt patience and silence
Listening to the rooks querulous in the high wood.

They have been waiting for us in a foetor
Of vegetable sweat since civil war days,
Since the gravel-crunching, interminable departure
Of the expropriated mycologist.
He never came back, and light since then

Is a keyhole rusting gently after rain.
Spiders have spun, flies dusted to mildew
And once a day, perhaps, they have heard something –
A trickle of masonry, a shout from the blue
Or a lorry changing gear at the end of the lane.

There have been deaths, the pale flesh flaking
Into the earth that nourished it;
And nightmares, born of these and the grim
Dominion of stale air and rank moisture.
Those nearest the door grow strong –
'Elbow room! Elbow room!'
The rest, dim in a twilight of crumbling
Utensils and broken pitchers, groaning
For their deliverance, have been so long
Expectant that there is left only the posture.

A half century, without visitors, in the dark –
Poor preparation for the cracking lock
And creak of hinges; magi, moonmen,
Powdery prisoners of the old regime,
Web-throated, stalked like triffids, racked by drought
And insomnia, only the ghost of a scream
At the flash-bulb firing-squad we wake them with
Shows there is life yet in their feverish forms.
Grown beyond nature now, soft food for worms,
They lift frail heads in gravity and good faith.

They are begging us, you see, in their wordless way,
To do something, to speak on their behalf
Or at least not to close the door again.
Lost people of Treblinka and Pompeii!
'Save us, save us,' they seem to say,
'Let the god not abandon us

Who have come so far in darkness and in pain.
We too had our lives to live.
You with your light meter and relaxed itinerary,
Let not our naive labours have been in vain!'

Though it helps to know that Treblinka was a Nazi extermination camp, and Pompeii was the city buried when Vesuvius erupted in AD 79, the key to unlocking this masterly poem is in fact in the epigraph. George Seferis (1900–71), one of the greatest Greek poets of the twentieth century, was awarded the Nobel Prize in 1963. Asphodels, in Greek mythology, are the flowers that grow in the underworld. Novelist J. G. Farrell (1935–79) is most celebrated for his trilogy on the decline of the British Empire, one of which, *Troubles* (1970), is set in a decaying hotel, the Majestic, in County Wexford in the years immediately after the First World War.

1975

On First Looking into Chapman's Hesiod

PETER PORTER

For 5p at a village fête I bought
Old Homer-Lucan who popped Keats's eyes,
Print smaller than the Book of Common Prayer
But Swinburne at the front, whose judgement is
Always immaculate. I'll never read a tenth
Of it in what life I have left to me
But I did look at *The Georgics*, as he calls
The Works and Days, and there I saw, not quite
The view from Darien but something strange
And balking – Australia, my own country
And its edgy managers – in the picture of
Euboeaen husbandry, terse family feuds
And the minds of gods tangential to the earth.

Like a Taree smallholder splitting logs
And philosophizing on his dangling billies,
The poet mixes hard agrarian instances
With sour sucks to his brother. Chapman, too,
That perpetual motion poetry machine,
Grinds up the classics like bone meal from
The abbatoirs. And the same blunt patriotism,
A long-winded, emphatic, kelpie yapping
About our land, our time, our fate, our strange
And singular way of moons and showers, lakes
Filling oddly – yes, Australians are Boeotians,
Hard as headlands, and, to be fair, with days
As robust as the Scythian wind on stone.

To teach your grandmother to suck eggs
Is a textbook possibility in New South Wales
Or outside Ascra. And such a genealogy too!
The Age of Iron is here, but oh the memories
Of Gold – pioneers preaching to the stringybarks,

Boring the land to death with verses and with
Mental Homes. 'Care-flying ease' and 'Gift-
devouring kings' become the Sonata of the Shotgun
And Europe's Entropy; for 'the axle-tree, the quern,
The hard, fate-fostered man' you choose among
The hand castrator, kerosene in honey tins
And mystic cattlemen: the Land of City States
Greets Australia in a farmer's gods.

Hesiod's father, caught in a miserable village,
Not helped by magic names like Helicon,
Sailed to improve his fortunes, and so did
All our fathers – in turn, their descendants
Lacked initiative, other than the doctors' daughters
Who tripped to England. Rough-nosed Hesiod
Was sure of his property to a slip-rail –
Had there been grants, he'd have farmed all
Summer and spent winter in Corinth
At the Creative Writing Class. Chapman, too,
Would vie with Steiner for the Pentecostal
Silver Tongue. Some of us feel at home nowhere,
Others in one generation fuse with the land.

I salute him then, the blunt old Greek whose way
Of life was as cunning as organic. His poet
Followers still make me feel déraciné
Within myself. One day they're on the campus,
The next in wide hats at a branding or
Sheep drenching, not actually performing
But looking the part and getting instances
For odes that bruise the blood. And history,
So interior a science it almost seems
Like true religion – who would have thought
Australia was the point of all that craft
Of politics in Europe? The apogee, it seems,
Is where your audience and its aspirations are.

'The colt, and mule, and horn-retorted steer' –
A good iambic line to paraphrase.
Long storms have blanched the million bones
Of the Aegean, and as many hurricanes
Will abrade the headstones of my native land:
Sparrows acclimatize but I still seek
The permanently upright city where
Speech is nature and plants conceive in pots,
Where one escapes from what one is and who
One was, where home is just a postmark
And country wisdom clings to calendars,
The opposite of a sunburned truth-teller's
World, haunted by precepts and the Pleiades.

Porter adapts his title from 'On First Looking into Chapman's Homer', a cele-
brated sonnet written in October 1816 by John Keats (1795–1821), and refers to
its final line in his phrase 'the view from Darien'. Chapman was dubbed 'Homer-
Lucan' by fellow poet Samuel Daniel for his strengths as a translator. Porter's
poem is a sustained cultural meditation on analogies between ancient Greece
and Australia, and in its turn prompted a penetrating essay by fellow-countryman
Les Murray, 'On Sitting Back and Thinking about Porter's Boeotia'. Steiner is the
extraordinary polymath and culture critic George Steiner.

1976

One Art

————◄◦►————

ELIZABETH BISHOP

The art of losing isn't hard to master;
so many things seem filled with the intent
to be lost that their loss is no disaster.

Lose something every day. Accept the fluster
of lost door keys, the hour badly spent.
The art of losing isn't hard to master.

Then practice losing farther, losing faster:
places, and names, and where it was you meant
to travel. None of these will bring disaster.

I lost my mother's watch. And look! my last, or
next-to-last, of three loved houses went.
The art of losing isn't hard to master.

I lost two cities, lovely ones. And, vaster,
some realms I owned, two rivers, a continent.
I miss them, but it wasn't a disaster.

– Even losing you (the joking voice, a gesture
I love) I shan't have lied. It's evident
the art of losing's not too hard to master
though it may look like (*Write* it!) like disaster.

1976

The Priest

ARUN KOLATKAR

An offering of heel and haunch
on the cold altar of the culvert wall
the priest waits.

Is the bus a little late?
The priest wonders.
Will there be a puran poli in his plate?

With a quick intake of testicles
at the touch of the rough cut, dew drenched stone
he turns his head in the sun

to look at the long road winding out of sight
with the evenlessness
of the fortune line on a dead man's palm.

The sun takes up the priest's head
and pats his cheek
familiarly like the village barber.

The bit of betel nut
turning over and over on his tongue
is a mantra.

It works.
The bus is no more just a thought in his head.
It's now a dot in the distance

and under his lazy lizard stare
it begins to grow
slowly like a wart upon his nose.

With a thud and a bump
the bus takes a pothole as it rattles past the priest
and paints his eyeballs blue.

The bus goes round in a circle.
Stops inside the bus station and stands
purring softly in front of the priest.

A catgrin on its face
and a live, ready to eat pilgrim
held between its teeth.

1976

The Abandoned British Cemetery at Balasore

JAYANTA MAHAPATRA

This is history.
I would not disturb it: the ruins of stone and marble,
the crumbling wall of brick, the coma of alienated decay.
How exactly should the archaic dead make me behave?

A hundred and fifty years ago
I might have lived. Now nothing offends my ways.
A quietness of bramble and grass holds me to a weed.
Will it matter if I know who the victims were, who
    survived?

And yet, awed by the forgotten dead,
I walk around them: thirty-nine graves, their legends
floating in a twilight of baleful littoral,
the flaking history my intrusion does not animate.

Awkward in the silence, a scrawny lizard
watches the drama with its shrewd, hooded gaze.
And a scorpion, its sting drooping,
two eerie arms spread upon the marble, over an alien name.

In the circle the epitaphs run: Florence R—, darling wife
of Captain R— R—, aged nineteen, of cholera . . .
Helen, beloved daughter of Mr & Mrs—, of cholera,
aged seventeen, in the year of our Lord, eighteen hundred . . .

Of what concern to me is a vanished Empire?
Or the conquest of my ancestors' timeless ennui?
It is the dying young who have the power to show
what the heart will hide, the grass shows no more.

Who watches now in the dark near the dead wall?
The tribe of grass in the cracks of my eyes?
It is the cholera still, death's sickly trickle,
that plagues the sleepy shacks beyond this hump of earth,

moving easily, swiftly, with quick power
through both past and present, the increasing young,
into the final bone, wearying all truth with ruin.
This is the iron

rusting in the vanquished country, the blood's unease,
the useless rain upon my familiar window;
the tired triumphant smile left behind by the dead
on a discarded anchor half-sunk in mud beside the graves:

out there on the earth's unwavering gravity
where it waits like a deity perhaps
for the elaborate ceremonial of a coming generation
to keep history awake, stifle the survivor's issuing cry.

1977

The Future

LES MURRAY

There is nothing about it. Much science fiction is set there
but is not about it. Prophecy is not about it.
It sways no yarrow stalks. And crystal is a mirror.
Even the man we nailed on a tree for a lookout
said little about it; he told us evil would come.
We see, by convention, a small living distance into it
but even that's a projection. And all our projections
fail to curve where it curves.
                              It is the black hole
out of which no radiation escapes to us.
The commonplace and magnificent roads of our lives
go on some way through cityscape and landscape
or steeply sloping, or scree, into that sheer fall
where everything will be that we have ever sent there,
compacted, spinning – except perhaps us, to see it.
It is said we see the start.
                              But, from here, there's a blindness.
The side-heaped chasm that will swallow all our present
blinds us to the normal sun that may be imagined
shining calmly away on the far side of it, for others
in their ordinary day. A day to which all our portraits,
ideals, revolutions, denim and deshabille
are quaintly heartrending. To see those people is impossible,
to greet them, mawkish. Nonetheless, I begin:
'When I was alive—'
                    and I am turned around
to find myself looking at a cheerful picnic party,
the women decently legless, in muslin and gloves,
the men in beards and weskits, with the long
cheroots and duck trousers of the better sort,
relaxing on a stone verandah. Ceylon, or Sydney.
And as I look, I know they are utterly gone,

each one on his day, with pillow, small bottles, mist,
with all the futures they dreamed or dealt in, going
down to that engulfment everything approaches;
with the man on the tree, they have vanished into the Future.

1977

from Crying in Early Infancy

‹o›

JOHN TRANTER

Today broke like a china plate,
rain and cloud, drifting smoke;
tonight fell like a suiciding athlete
or a bad joke.
I went to bed with a startling headache
and was distinctly no better when I woke,
I remained dumb in the company of those
who were happy only when I spoke.

Something new has moved uncomfortably close,
something not previously seen:
a talent for aiming the poisoned dart,
for detecting the touch of the unclean,
for discovering that, in the pure of heart,
there is something unforgivably obscene.

This is the forty-fourth poem in Tranter's sequence of irregular sonnets, *Crying in Early Infancy*.

1978

The List

◄◇►

U. A. FANTHORPE

Flawlessly typed, and spaced
At the proper intervals,
Serene and lordly, they pace
Along tomorrow's list
Like giftbearers on a frieze.

In tranquil order, arrayed
With the basic human equipment –
A name, a time, a number –
They advance on the future.

Not more harmonious who pace
Holding a hawk, a fish, a jar
(The customary offerings)
Along the Valley of the Kings.

Tomorrow these names will turn nasty,
Senile, pregnant, late,
Handicapped, handcuffed, unhandy,
Muddled, moribund, mute,

Be stained by living. But here,
Orderly, equal, right,
On the edge of tomorrow, they pause
Like giftbearers on a frieze

With the proper offering,
A time, a number, a name.
I am the artist, the typist;
I did my best for them.

1978

An Exequy

◄◦►

PETER PORTER

In wet May, in the months of change,
In a country you wouldn't visit, strange
Dreams pursue me in my sleep,
Black creatures of the upper deep –
Though you are five months dead, I see
You in guilt's iconography,
Dear Wife, lost beast, beleaguered child,
The stranded monster with the mild
Appearance, whom small waves tease,
(Andromeda upon her knees
In orthodox deliverance)
And you alone of pure substance,
The unformed form of life, the earth
Which Piero's brushes brought to birth
For all to greet as myth, a thing
Out of the box of imagining.

This introduction serves to sing
Your mortal death as Bishop King
Once hymned in tetrametric rhyme
His young wife, lost before her time;
Though he lived on for many years
His poem each day fed new tears
To that unreaching spot, her grave,
His lines a baroque architrave
The Sunday poor with bottled flowers
Would by-pass in their mourning hours,
Esteeming ragged natural life
('Most dearly loved, most gentle wife'),
Yet, looking back when at the gate
And seeing grief in formal state
Upon a sculpted angel group,
Were glad that men of god could stoop

To give the dead a public stance
And freeze them in their mortal dance.

The words and faces proper to
My misery are private – you
Would never share your heart with those
Whose only talent's to suppose,
Nor from your final childish bed
Raise a remote confessing head –
The channels of our lives are blocked,
The hand is stopped upon the clock,
No-one can say why hearts will break
And marriages are all opaque:
A map of loss, some posted cards,
The living house reduced to shards,
The abstract hell of memory,
The pointlessness of poetry –
These are the instances which tell
Of something which I know full well,
I owe a death to you – one day
The time will come for me to pay
When your slim shape from photographs
Stands at my door and gently asks
If I have any work to do
Or will I come to bed with you.
O *scala enigmatica*,
I'll climb up to that attic where
The curtain of your life was drawn
Some time between despair and dawn –
I'll never know with what halt steps
You mounted to this plain eclipse
But each stair now will station me
A black responsibility
And point me to that shut-down room,
'This be your due appointed tomb.'

I think of us in Italy:
Gin-and-chianti-fuelled, we
Move in a trance through Paradise,
Feeding at last our starving eyes,
Two people of the English blindness
Doing each masterpiece the kindness
Of discovering it – from Baldovinetti
To Venice's most obscure jetty.
A true unfortunate traveller, I
Depend upon your nurse's eye
To pick the altars where no Grinner
Puts us off our tourists' dinner
And in hotels to bandy words
With Genevan girls and talking birds,
To wear your feet out following me
To night's end and true amity,
And call my rational fear of flying
A paradigm of Holy Dying –
And, oh my love, I wish you were
Once more with me, at night somewhere
In narrow streets applauding wines,
The moon above the Apennines
As large as logic and the stars,
Most middle-aged of avatars,
As bright as when they shone for truth
Upon untried and avid youth.

The rooms and days we wandered through
Shrink in my mind to one – there you
Lie quite absorbed by peace – the calm
Which life could not provide is balm
In death. Unseen by me, you look
Past bed and stairs and half-read book
Eternally upon your home,
The end of pain, the left alone.

I have no friend, or intercessor,
No psychopomp or true confessor
But only you who know my heart
In every cramped and devious part –
Then take my hand and lead me out,
The sky is overcast by doubt,
The time has come, I listen for
Your words of comfort at the door,
O guide me through the shoals of fear –
'*Fürchte dich nicht, ich bin bei dir.*'

Porter's title signals the modelling of his poem on 'The Exequy', written in iambic tetrameter couplets by Henry King (1592–1669) in memory of his first wife, Anne, who died in 1624. Porter's first wife had committed suicide in 1974. Piero is Piero della Francesca (c. 1415–92), the Italian Renaissance artist, and Baldovinetti is a Florentine painter of the same period, Alessio Baldovinetti (c. 1425–99). The words '*Fürchte dich nicht, ich bin bei dir*', from Isaiah 41:10 ('Fear thou not; for I am with thee'), are the title of a motet by Bach, BWV 228. Of the passage beginning 'I owe a death to you', Craig Raine remarked: 'These are not fine lines. They are great poetry.'

1978

Bride and Groom Lie Hidden for Three Days

TED HUGHES

She gives him his eyes, she found them
Among some rubble, among some beetles

He gives her her skin
He just seemed to pull it down out of the air
                              and lay it over her
She weeps with fearfulness and astonishment

She has found his hands for him,
                    and fitted them freshly at the wrists
They are amazed at themselves,
                              they go feeling all over her

He has assembled her spine,
                    he cleaned each piece carefully
And sets them in perfect order
A superhuman puzzle but he is inspired
She leans back twisting this way and that,
                              using it and laughing incredulous

Now she has brought his feet, she is connecting them
So that his whole body lights up

And he has fashioned her new hips
With all fittings complete and with newly wound coils,
                              all shiningly oiled
He is polishing every part,
                    he himself can hardly believe it

They keep taking each other to the sun,
                              they find they can easily
To test each new thing at each new step
And now she smooths over him the plates of his skull
So that the joints are invisible

And now he connects her throat,
                    her breasts and the pit of her stomach
With a single wire

She gives him his teeth, tying their roots
                    to the centrepin of his body

He sets the little circlets on her fingertips
She stitches his body here and there
                    with steely purple silk
He oils the delicate cogs of her mouth
She inlays with deep-cuts scrolls the nape of his neck
He sinks into place the inside of her thighs

So, gasping with joy, with cries of wonderment
Like two gods of mud
Sprawling in the dirt, but with infinite care

They bring each other to perfection.

1978

Flames and Dangling Wire
◀◦▶

ROBERT GRAY

On a highway over the marshland.
Off to one side, the smoke of different fires in a row,
like fingers spread and dragged to smudge:
it is an always-burning dump.

Behind us, the city
driven like stakes into the earth.
A waterbird lifts above the swamp
as a turtle moves on the Galapagos shore.

We turn off down a gravel road,
approaching the dump. All the air wobbles
in some cheap mirror.
There is a fog over the hot sun.

Now the distant buildings are stencilled in the smoke.
And we come to a landscape of tin cans,
of cars like skulls,
that is rolling in its sand dune shapes.

Amongst these vast grey plastic sheets of heat,
shadowy figures
who seem engaged in identifying the dead –
they are the attendants, in overalls and goggles,

forking over rubbish on the dampened fires.
A sour smoke
is hauled out everywhere,
thin, like rope. And there are others moving – scavengers.

As in hell the devils
might pick about through our souls, for vestiges
of appetite
with which to stimulate themselves,

so these figures
seem to wander, disconsolate, with an eternity
in which to turn up
some peculiar sensation.

We get out and move about also.
The smell is huge,
blasting the mouth dry:
the tons of rotten newspaper, and great cuds of cloth . . .

And standing where I see the mirage of the city
I realize I am in the future.
This is how it shall be after men have gone.
It will be made of things that worked.

A labourer hoists an unidentifiable mulch
on his fork, throws it in the flame:
something flaps
like the rag held up in 'The Raft of the Medusa'.

We approach another, through the smoke,
and for a moment he seems that demon with the long
    barge pole.
– It is a man, wiping his eyes.
Someone who worked here would have to weep,

and so we speak. The rims beneath his eyes are wet
as an oyster, and red.
Knowing all that he does about us,
how can he avoid a hatred of men?

Going on, I notice an old radio, that spills
its dangling wire –
and I realize that somewhere the voices it received
are still travelling,

skidding away, riddled, around the arc of the universe;
and with them, the horse-laughs, and the Chopin
which was the sound of the curtains lifting,
one time, to a coast of light.

'The Raft of the Medusa' is a painting by Théodore Géricault (1791–1824).

1978

'Christmas Trees'

GEOFFREY HILL

Bonhoeffer in his skylit cell
bleached by the flares' candescent fall,
pacing out his own citadel,

restores the broken themes of praise,
encourages our borrowed days,
by logic of his sacrifice.

Against wild reasons of the state
his words are quiet but not too quiet.
We hear too late or not too late.

The German Lutheran pastor Dietrich Bonhoeffer was one of the key figures in the German resistance to Hitler, a founder of the Confessing Church, and was executed at Flossenbürg concentration camp on 9 April 1945, just a month before the end of the Second World War in Europe. From their appearance as they fell through the night sky, incendiary bombs were nicknamed 'Christmas trees' by the German civilian population.

1979

Koenig of the River

◄◦►

DEREK WALCOTT

Koenig knew now there was no one on the river.
Entering its brown mouth choking with lilies
and curtained with midges, Koenig poled the shallop
past the abandoned ferry and the ferry piles
coated with coal dust. Staying aboard, he saw, up
in a thick meadow, a sand-coloured mule,
untethered, with no harness, and no signs
of habitation round the ruined factory wheel
locked hard in rust, and through whose spokes the vines
of wild yam leaves leant from overweight;
the wild bananas in the yellowish sunlight
were dugged like aching cows with unmilked fruit.
This was the last of the productive mines.
Only the vegetation here looked right.
A crab of pain scuttled shooting up his foot
and fastened on his neck, at the brain's root.
He felt his reason curling back like parchment
in this fierce torpor. Well, he no longer taxed
and tired what was left of his memory;
he should thank heaven he had escaped the sea,
and anyway, he had demanded to be sent
here with the others – why get this river vexed
with his complaints? Koenig wanted to sing,
suddenly, if only to keep the river company –
this was a river, and Koenig, his name meant King.

They had all caught the missionary fever:
they were prepared to expiate the sins
of savages, to tame them as he would tame this river
subtly, as it flowed, accepting its bends;
he had seen how other missionaries met their ends –
swinging in the wind, like a dead clapper when

a bell is broken, if that sky was a bell –
for treating savages as if they were men,
and frightening them with talk of heaven and hell.
But I have forgotten our journey's origins,
mused Koenig, and our purpose. He knew it was noble,
based on some phrase, forgotten, from the Bible,
but he felt bodiless, like a man stumbling from
the pages of a novel, not a forest,
written a hundred years ago. He stroked his uniform,
clogged with the hooked burrs that had tried
to pull him, like the other drowning hands whom
his panic abandoned. The others had died,
like real men, by death. I, Koenig, am a ghost,
ghost-king of rivers. Well, even ghosts must rest.
If he knew he was lost he was not lost.
It was when you pretended that you were a fool.
He banked and leaned tiredly on the pole.
If I'm a character called Koenig, then I
shall dominate my future like a fiction
in which there is a real river and real sky,
so I'm not really tired, and should push on.

The lights between the leaves were beautiful,
and, as in that far life, now he was grateful
for any pool of light between the dull, usual
clouds of life: a sunspot haloed his tonsure;
silver and copper coins danced on the river;
his head felt warm – the light danced on his skull
like a benediction. Koenig closed his eyes,
and he felt blessed. It made direction sure.
He leant on the pole. He must push on some more.
He said his name. His voice sounded German,
then he said 'river,' but what was German
if he alone could hear it? *Ich spreche Deutsch*
sounded as genuine as his name in English,
Koenig in Deutsch, and, in English, King.
Did the river want to be called anything?
He asked the river. The river said nothing.

Around the bend the river poured its silver
like some remorseful mine, giving and giving
everything green and white: white sky, white
water, and the dull green like a drumbeat
of the slow-sliding forest, the green heat;
then, on some sandbar, a mirage ahead:
fabric of muslin sails, spiderweb rigging,
a schooner, foundered on black river mud,
was rising slowly up from the riverbed,
and a top-hatted native reading an inverted
newspaper.
      'Where's our Queen?' Koenig shouted.
'Where's our Kaiser?'
        The nigger disappeared.
Koenig felt that he himself was being read
like the newspaper or a hundred-year-old novel.
'The Queen dead! Kaiser dead!' the voices shouted.
And it flashed through him those trunks were not wood
but that the ghosts of slaughtered Indians stood
there in the mangroves, their eyes like fireflies
in the green dark, and that like hummingbirds
they sailed rather than ran between the trees.
The river carried him past his shouted words.
The schooner had gone down without a trace.
'There was a time when we ruled everything,'
Koenig sang to his corrugated white reflection.
'The German Eagle and the British Lion,
we ruled worlds wider than this river flows,
worlds with dyed elephants, with tasselled howdahs,
tigers that carried the striped shade when they rose
from their palm coverts; men shall not see these days
again; our flags sank with the sunset on the dhows
of Egypt; we ruled rivers as huge as the Nile,
the Ganges, and the Congo, we tamed, we ruled
you when our empires reached their blazing peak.'
This was a small creek somewhere in the world,
never mind where – victory was in sight.
Koenig laughed and spat in the brown creek.

The mosquitoes now were singing to the night
that rose up from the river, the fog uncurled
under the mangroves. Koenig clenched each fist
around his barge-pole sceptre, as a mist
rises from the river and the page goes white.

1979

The Visitor

CAROLYN FORCHÉ

In Spanish he whispers there is no time left.
It is the sound of scythes arcing in wheat,
the ache of some field song in Salvador.
The wind along the prison, cautious
as Francisco's hands on the inside, touching
the walls as he walks, it is his wife's breath
slipping into his cell each night while he
imagines his hand to be hers. It is a small country.

There is nothing one man will not do to another.

1979

Casualty

<o>

SEAMUS HEANEY

I

He would drink by himself
And raise a weathered thumb
Towards the high shelf,
Calling another rum
And blackcurrant, without
Having to raise his voice,
Or order a quick stout
By a lifting of the eyes
And a discreet dumb-show
Of pulling off the top;
At closing time would go
In waders and peaked cap
Into the showery dark,
A dole-kept breadwinner
But a natural for work.
I loved his whole manner,
Sure-footed but too sly,
His deadpan sidling tact,
His fisherman's quick eye
And turned observant back.

Incomprehensible
To him, my other life.
Sometimes, on his high stool,
Too busy with his knife
At a tobacco plug
And not meeting my eye,
In the pause after a slug
He mentioned poetry.
We would be on our own

And, always politic
And shy of condescension,
I would manage by some trick
To switch the talk to eels
Or lore of the horse and cart
Or the Provisionals.

But my tentative art
His turned back watches too:
He was blown to bits
Out drinking in a curfew
Others obeyed, three nights
After they shot dead
The thirteen men in Derry.
PARAS THIRTEEN, the walls said,
BOGSIDE NIL. That Wednesday
Everybody held
His breath and trembled.

II

It was a day of cold
Raw silence, wind-blown
Surplice and soutane:
Rained-on, flower-laden
Coffin after coffin
Seemed to float from the door
Of the packed cathedral
Like blossoms on slow water.
The common funeral
Unrolled its swaddling band,
Lapping, tightening
Till we were braced and bound
Like brothers in a ring.
But he would not be held
At home by his own crowd
Whatever threats were phoned,
Whatever black flags waved.

I see him as he turned
In that bombed offending place,
Remorse fused with terror
In his still knowable face,
His cornered outfaced stare
Blinding in the flash.

He had gone miles away
For he drank like a fish
Nightly, naturally
Swimming towards the lure
Of warm lit-up places,
The blurred mesh and murmur
Drifting among glasses
In the gregarious smoke.
How culpable was he
That last night when he broke
Our tribe's complicity?
'Now you're supposed to be
An educated man,'
I hear him say. 'Puzzle me
The right answer to that one.'

III

I missed his funeral,
Those quiet walkers
And sideways talkers
Shoaling out of his lane
To the respectable
Purring of the hearse . . .
They move in equal pace
With the habitual
Slow consolation
Of a dawdling engine,
The line lifted, hand
Over fist, cold sunshine
On the water, the land

Banked under fog: that morning
I was taken in his boat,
The screw purling, turning
Indolent fathoms white,
I tasted freedom with him.
To get out early, haul
Steadily off the bottom,
Dispraise the catch, and smile
As you find a rhythm
Working you, slow mile by mile,
Into your proper haunt
Somewhere, well out, beyond . . .

Dawn-sniffing revenant,
Plodder through midnight rain,
Question me again.

The thirteen marchers shot dead in Derry (or Londonderry) were killed on 30 January 1972 ('Bloody Sunday') by soldiers of the First Battalion Parachute Regiment.

1979

The Old Moscow Woman

—◇—

RALPH GUSTAFSON

The woman this morning sweeps the pavement
Of Kuibysheva Street,
Branches of spring tied to an old stick,
Brushing along last night's bits
Of paper, cigarette ends, dirt,
Keeping the city clean for this morning's
Traffic. By night it will have to be done
All over again. She looks happy.
What is this happiness? Grandchildren,
Soup on the stove, an hour's relief
From pain, Lenin sleeping nearby?
The street will always be dirty.
Mankind is imperfect.
Politics and bad manners
Leave his detritus
On the perfect peace. We
Do not understand one another.
The street will have to be swept again.
New York, Moscow, Montreal,
It is the same. Man is careless,
He drops the wrappings from his hands,
The torn paper, even the newspaper
With the news of the world
He leaves behind him to be picked up
By someone else. The wind is cold.
This is September. Soon the snow
Will cover the shivering gutter
And the plough will supersede the broom.
We all feel it. No matter the labour.

Snow and death come.
Do they not?
And yet this woman sweeps,
For a few kopeks,
Lentils for her soup,
And is happy.
What is this Moscow?
This humanity?

1979

Tar

◄◇►

C. K. WILLIAMS

The first morning of Three Mile Island: those first disquieting,
    uncertain, mystifying hours.
All morning a crew of workmen have been tearing the old
    decrepit roof off our building,
and all morning, trying to distract myself, I've been wandering
    out to watch them
as they hack away the leaden layers of asbestos paper and
    disassemble the disintegrating drains.
After half a night of listening to the news, wondering how to
    know a hundred miles downwind
if and when to make a run for it and where, then a coming
    bolt awake at seven
when the roofers we've been waiting for since winter sent their
    ladders shrieking up our wall,
we still know less than nothing: the utility company continues
    making little of the accident,
the slick federal spokesmen still have their evasions in some
    semblance of order.
Surely we suspect now we're being lied to, but in the meantime,
    there are the roofers,
setting winch-frames, sledging rounds of tar apart, and there I
    am, on the curb across, gawking.

I never realized what brutal work it is, how matter-of-factly and
    harrowingly dangerous.
The ladders flex and quiver, things skid from the edge, the
    materials are bulky and recalcitrant.
When the rusty, antique nails are levered out, their heads pull
    off; the underroofing crumbles.
Even the battered little furnace, roaring along as patient as a
    donkey, chokes and clogs,
a dense, malignant smoke shoots up, and someone has to fiddle
    with a cock, then hammer it,

583

before the gush and stench will deintensify, the dark, Dantean
broth wearily subside.
In its crucible, the stuff looks bland, like licorice, spill it, though,
on your boots or coveralls,
it sears, and everything is permeated with it, the furnace gunked
with burst and half-burst bubbles,
the men themselves so completely slashed and mucked they
seem almost from another realm, like trolls.
When they take their break, they leave their brooms standing at
attention in the asphalt pails,
work gloves clinging like Br'er Rabbit to the bitten shafts, and
they slouch along the precipitous lip,
the enormous sky behind them, the heavy noontime air alive
with shimmers and mirages.

Sometime in the afternoon I had to go inside: the advent of our
vigil was upon us.
However much we didn't want to, however little we would do
about it, we'd understood:
we were going to perish of all this, if not now, then soon, if not
soon, then someday.
Someday, some final generation, hysterically aswarm beneath an
atmosphere as unrelenting as rock,
would rue us all, anathematize our earthly comforts, curse our
surfeits and submissions.
I think I know, though I might rather not, why my roofers stay
so clear to me and why the rest,
the terror of that time, the reflexive disbelief and distancing, all
we should hold on to, dims so.
I remember the president in his absurd protective booties,
looking absolutely unafraid, the fool.
I remember a woman on the front page glaring across the misty
Susquehanna at those looming stacks.
But, more vividly, the men, silvered with glitter from the
shingles, clinging like starlings beneath the eaves.

Even the leftover carats of tar in the gutter, so black they
    seemed to suck the light out of the air.
By nightfall kids had come across them: every sidewalk on the
    block was scribbled with obscenities and hearts.

On 28 March 1979 a partial core meltdown occurred in the reactor at the Three
Mile Island nuclear power plant near Harrisburg, Pennsylvania. (The US Presi-
dent at the time was Jimmy Carter.)

1980

Why Brownlee Left

PAUL MULDOON

Why Brownlee left, and where he went,
Is a mystery even now.
For if a man should have been content
It was him; two acres of barley,
One of potatoes, four bullocks,
A milker, a slated farmhouse.
He was last seen going out to plough
On a March morning, bright and early.

By noon Brownlee was famous;
They had found all abandoned, with
The last rig unbroken, his pair of black
Horses, like man and wife,
Shifting their weight from foot to
Foot, and gazing into the future.

1980

Cumberland Station

DAVE SMITH

Gray brick, ash, hand-bent railings, steps so big
it takes hours to mount them, polished oak
pews holding the slim hafts of sun, and one
splash of the *Pittsburgh Post-Gazette*. The man
who left Cumberland gone, come back, no job
anywhere. I come here alone, shaken
the way I came years ago to ride down
mountains in Big Daddy's cab. He was
the first set cold in the black meadow.

Six rows of track gleam, thinned, rippling
like water on walls where famous engines steam, half
submerged in frothing crowds with something
to celebrate and plenty to eat. One engineer takes
children for a free ride, a frolic
like an earthquake. Ash cakes their hair.
I am one of those who walked uphill
through flowers of soot to zing
scared to death into the world.

Now whole families afoot cruise South Cumberland
for something to do, no jobs, no money for bars,
the old stories cracked like wallets.

This time there's no fun in coming back. The second
death. My roundhouse uncle coughed his youth
into a gutter. His son, the third, slid on the ice,
losing his need to drink himself
stupidly dead. In this vaulted hall
I think of all the dirt poured down
from shovels and trains and empty pockets.
I stare into the huge malignant headlamps
circling the gray walls and catch a stuttered

glimpse of faces stunned like deer on a track,
children getting drunk, shiny as Depression apples.

Churning through the inner space of this godforsaken
wayside, I feel the ground try to upchuck and I dig
my fingers in my temples to bury a child
diced on a cowcatcher, a woman smelling
alkaline from washing out the soot.
Where I stood in that hopeless, hateful room
will not leave me. The scarf of smoke I saw
over a man's shoulder runs through me
like the sored Potomac River.

Grandfather, you ask why I don't visit you
now you have escaped the ticket-seller's cage
to fumble hooks and clean the Shakespeare reels.
What could we catch? I've been sitting in the pews
thinking about us a long time, long enough to see
a man can't live in jobless, friendless Cumberland
anymore. The soot owns even the fish.

I keep promising I'll come back, we'll get out,
you and me, like brothers, and I mean it.
A while ago a man with the look of a demented
    cousin
shuffled across this skittery floor and snatched up
the *Post-Gazette* and stuffed it in his coat
and nobody gave a damn because nobody cares
who comes or goes here or even who steals
what nobody wants: old news, photographs
of dead diesels behind chipped glass
swimming into Cumberland Station.

I'm the man who stole it and I wish you were here
to beat the hell out of me for it because
what you said a long time ago welts my face
and won't go away. I admit
it isn't mine even if it's nobody else's.

Anyway, that's all I catch this trip — bad
news. I can't catch my nephew's life, my uncle's,
Big Daddy's, yours, or the ash-haired kids'
who fell down to sleep here after the war.

Outside new families pick their way along tracks
you and I have walked home on many nights.
Every face on the walls goes on smiling,
and, Grandfather, I wish I had the guts
to tell you this is a place I hope
I never have to go through again.

1981

Anne Frank Huis

◂◦▸

ANDREW MOTION

Even now, after twice her lifetime of grief
and anger in the very place, whoever comes
to climb these narrow stairs, discovers how
the bookcase slides aside, then walks through
shadow into sunlit rooms, can never help

but break her secrecy again. Just listening
is a kind of guilt: the Westerkirk repeats
itself outside, as if all time worked round
towards her fear, and made each stroke
die down on guarded streets. Imagine it –

three years of whispering and loneliness
and plotting, day by day, the Allied line
in Europe with a yellow chalk. What hope
she had for ordinary love and interest
survives her here, displayed above the bed

as pictures of her family; some actors;
fashions chosen by Princess Elizabeth.
And those who stoop to see them find
not only patience missing its reward,
but one enduring wish for chances

like my own: to leave as simply
as I do, and walk at ease
up dusty tree-lined avenues, or watch
a silent barge come clear of bridges
settling their reflections in the blue canal.

The house in which Anne Frank and her family lived, and then went into hiding (in secret rooms, the *Achterhuis*) in the hope of evading capture by German occupying forces, was at 263 Prinsengracht in Amsterdam. The *Achterhuis* was raided on 4 August 1944 and Anne and her family were deported to Germany. Only her father, Otto, survived the war (at Auschwitz). Anne herself died at Belsen in March 1945. Her diary, which became one of the most famous publications of the twentieth century, was published in Dutch as *Het Achterhuis* in 1947, and in English translation in 1952. The Westerkirk is a church close to her Amsterdam home, across the canal. Magazine clippings of Princess Elizabeth, today's Queen Elizabeth II, which she had stuck to the wall, can still be seen today in the house, which is maintained as a museum.

1981

Bad Run at King's Rest

—◄◦►—

DOUGLAS LIVINGSTONE

Clanking past the crest of a dune:
in the foreground, a group of urchins
straighten up, yelling. They scatter and run.

The big loggerhead turtle lay
swimming among human footprints, beached;
shell split by an errant propeller-blade.

Its flippers bloody where some lout's
hacking had ripped nails for medicines
or trophies. Both its eyes stabbed or pecked out.

It raised its beak to scream or pant,
the exhalations making no sound.
Dumping my bottles on the heaving sand,

I moved – lifelong stand-in for thought –
avoiding the still dangerous beak,
asking pardon, cut the leathery throat.

Rinse off queasily. Circle wide,
back, past that inert, spread-eagled mound.
Call dumbly on gulls, on incoming tides.

1981

from War Music

—◇—

CHRISTOPHER LOGUE

Cut to the strip between the rampart and the ditch.

   The air near Ajax was so thick with arrows, that,
As they came, their shanks tickered against each other.
And under them the Trojans swarmed so thick
Ajax outspread his arms, turned his spear flat,
And simply *pushed*. Yet they came clamouring back until
So many Trojans had a go at him
The iron chaps of Ajax' helmet slapped his cheeks
To soft red pulp, and his head reached back and forth
Like a clapper inside a bell made out of sword blades.
   Maybe, even with no breath left,

Big Ajax might have stood it yet; yet
Big and all as he was, Prince Hector meant to burn that
   ship,
And God was pleased to let him.

   Pulling the Trojans back a yard or two
He baited Ajax with his throat; and Ajax took.
As the spear lifted, Hector skipped in range;
As Ajax readied, Hector bared his throat again;
And, as Ajax lunged, Prince Hector jived on his heel
And snicked the haft clean through its neck
Pruning the eighteen-incher – Aie! – it was good to watch
Big Ajax and his spear blundering about for, O,
Two seconds went before he noticed it had gone.
   But when he noticed it he knew
God stood by Hector's elbow, not by his;
That God was pleased with Hector, not with Ajax;
And, sensibly enough, he fled.

   The ship was burned.

October.
The hungry province grows restive.
The Imperial army must visit the frontier.
Dawn.
The captains arrive behind standards;
A tiger's face carved on each lance-butt.
And equipment for a long campaign
Is issued to every soldier.
First light.
Men stand behind the level feathers of their breath.
A messenger runs from the pearl-fringed tent.
The captains form a ring. They read.
The eldest one points north. The others nod.
Likewise his heroes stood around Achilles, listening.
And the Myrmidons began to arm and tramp about the
    beach.
First sunlight off the sea like thousands of white birds.

Salt haze.

Imagine wolves: an hour ago the pack
Hustled a stag, then tore it into shreds.
Now they have gorged upon its haunch
They need a drink to wash their curry down.
So, sniffing out a pool, they loll their long,
Thin, sharp-pointed tongues in it; and as they lap
Piping shadows idle off their chops,
And infiltrate the water like rose smoke.

Likewise his Myrmidons,
Their five commanders, right,
Patroclus on his left,
And the onshore wind behind Achilles' voice:

'Excellent killers of men!
Today Patroclus leads; and by tonight,
You, behind him, will clear the Trojans from our ditch.
And who at twilight fails to bring
At least one Trojan head to deck the palings of our camp
Can sleep outside with Agamemnon's trash.'

The columns tightened.
The rim of each man's shield
Overlapped the face of his neighbour's shield
Like clinkered hulls – as shipwrights call them when they
    lay
Strake over strake, caulked against seas.
    As they moved off, the columns tightened more;
And from above it seemed five wide black straps
Studded with bolts were being drawn across the sand.

    Swarming up and off the beach
Patroclus swung the Myrmidons right at the ships.
    Keeping it on their right they streamed
Along the camp's main track; one side, the battered palisade;
On the other, ships.
    Things were so close you could not see your front;
And from the footplate of his wheels, Patroclus cried:
    'For Achilles!'
As the enemies closed.

    The Trojans lay across the ship
Most of them busy seeing that it burned.
Others slid underneath and were so occupied
Knocking away the chocks that kept it upright
They did not see Patroclus stoop.
But those above did.
    In less time than it takes to dip and light a match
Achilles' helmet loomed above their cheeks
With Myrmidons splayed out on either side
Like iron wings.
    Dropping the pitch
They reached for javelins, keelspikes, boat-hooks, Kai!
Anything to keep Achilles off –
Have he and Agamemnon patched things up?

    Patroclus aimed his spear where they were thickest.
That is to say,
Around Sarpedon's chariot commander, Akafact.
    But as Patroclus threw
The ship's mast flamed from stem to peak and fell

Lengthwise across the incident.
   Its fat waist clubbed the tiller deck
And the long pine hull flopped sideways.
   Those underneath got crunched,
And howling Greeks ran up
To pike the others as they slithered off.
   This fate was not for Akafact.
Because the mast's peak hit the sand no more than six
Feet from Patroclus' car, the horses shied
Spoiling his cast. Nothing was lost.
   As Akafact fell back, back arched,
God blew the javelin straight; and thus
Mid-air, the cold bronze apex sank
Between his teeth and tongue, parted his brain,
Pressed on, and stapled him against the upturned hull.
His dead jaw gaped. His soul
Crawled off his tongue and vanished into sunlight.

1982

Dead Soldiers

‹o›

JAMES FENTON

When His Excellency Prince Norodom Chantaraingsey
Invited me to lunch on the battlefield
I was glad of my white suit for the first time that day.
They lived well, the mad Norodoms, they had style.
The brandy and the soda arrived in crates.
Bricks of ice, tied around with raffia,
Dripped from the orderlies' handlebars.

And I remember the dazzling tablecloth
As the APCs fanned out along the road,
The dishes piled high with frogs' legs,
Pregnant turtles, their eggs boiled in the carapace,
Marsh irises in fish sauce
And inflorescence of a banana salad.

On every bottle, Napoleon Bonaparte
Pleaded for the authenticity of the spirit.
They called the empties Dead Soldiers
And rejoiced to see them pile up at our feet.

Each diner was attended by one of the other ranks
Whirling a table-napkin to keep off the flies.
It was like eating between rows of morris dancers –
Only they didn't kick.

On my left sat the prince;
On my right, his drunken aide.
The frogs' thighs leapt into the sad purple face
Like fish to the sound of a Chinese flute.
I wanted to talk to the prince. I wish now
I had collared his aide, who was Saloth Sar's brother.
We treated him as the club bore. He was always
Boasting of his connections, boasting with a head-shake.
Or by pronouncing of some doubtful phrase.

And well might he boast. Saloth Sar, for instance,
Was Pol Pot's real name. The APCs
Fired into the sugar palms but met no resistance.

In a diary, I refer to Pol Pot's brother as the Jockey Cap.
A few weeks later, I find him 'in good form
And very skeptical about Chantaraingsey.'
'But one eats well there,' I remark.
'So one should,' says the Jockey Cap:
'The tiger always eats well,
It eats the raw flesh of the deer,
And Chantaraingsey was born in the year of the tiger.
So, did they show you the things they do
With the young refugee girls?'

And he tells me how he will one day give me the gen.
He will tell me how the prince financed the casino
And how the casino brought Lon Nol to power.
He will tell me this.
He will tell me all these things.
All I must do is drink and listen.

In those days, I thought that when the game was up
The prince would be far, far away –
In a limestone faubourg, on the promenade at Nice,
Reduced in circumstances but well enough provided for.
In Paris, he would hardly require his private army.
The Jockey Cap might suffice for café warfare,
And matchboxes for APCs.

But we were always wrong in these predictions.
It was a family war. Whatever happened,
The principals were obliged to attend its issue.
A few were cajoled into leaving, a few were expelled,
And there were villains enough, but none of them
Slipped away with the swag.

For the prince was fighting Sihanouk, his nephew,
And the Jockey Cap was ranged against his brother
Of whom I remember nothing more
Than an obscure reputation for virtue.

I have been told that the prince is still fighting
Somewhere in the Cardamoms or the Elephant Mountains.
But I doubt that the Jockey Cap would have survived his
    good connections.
I think the lunches would have done for him –
Either the lunches or the dead soldiers.

Cambodia achieved independence from French rule in 1953, and became a constitutional monarchy under King Norodom Sihanouk, who abdicated two years later in order to become Prime Minister. His government was toppled in 1970 by a military coup led by Lon Nol (1913–85), who was sympathetic to the US, but this new administration was quickly threatened by the Communist Khmer Rouge. Fenton's poem is set in the early Seventies, during the heavy fighting – punctuated by massive US bombing raids aimed at breaking the Khmer Rouge – that finally brought the Khmer Rouge to power in 1975. The narrator of the poem is accompanying nationalist, anti-Communist forces, and is lunching with a member of the Cambodian royal family, Prince Norodom Chantaraingsey (c. 1924–c. 1976). APCs are armoured personnel carriers. After the Khmer Rouge took power, under Pol Pot (Saloth Sar, 1928–98), a reign of terror ensued that cost between one and three million Cambodians their lives.

1982

I Found South African Breweries Most Hospitable

KIT WRIGHT

Meat smell of blood in locked rooms I cannot smell it,
Screams of the brave in torture loges I never heard nor
  heard of
Apartheid I wouldn't know how to spell it,
None of these things am I paid to believe a word of
For I am a stranger to cant and contumely.
I am a professional cricketer.
My only consideration is my family.

I get my head down nothing to me or mine
Blood is geysering now from ear, from mouth, from eye,
How they take a fresh guard after breaking the spine,
I must play wherever I like or die
So spare me your news your views spare me your homily.
I am a professional cricketer.
My only consideration is my family.

Electrodes wired to their brains they should have had
  helmets,
Balls wired up they should have been wearing a box,
The danger was the game would turn into a stalemate,
Skin of their feet burnt off I like thick woollen socks
With buckskin boots that accommodate them roomily
For I am a professional cricketer.
My only consideration is my family.

They keep falling out of the window they must be clumsy
And unprofessional not that anyone told me,
Spare me your wittering spare me your whimsy,
Sixty thousand pounds is what they sold me
And I have no brain. I am an anomaly.
I am a professional cricketer.
My only consideration is my family.

The system of racial segregation known as 'apartheid' (separateness) was enforced in South Africa from 1948 to 1994. The International Cricket Conference suspended South Africa from international cricket competition in 1970, and blacklisted players on 'rebel tours' that visited South Africa despite the sanction. Wright's poem is voiced for one such player.

1982

from Very Indian Poems in Indian English
<small>◄◦►</small>

NISSIM EZEKIEL

1. THE PATRIOT

I am standing for peace and non-violence.
Why world is fighting fighting,
Why all people of world
Are not following Mahatma Gandhi,
I am simply not understanding.
Ancient Indian Wisdom is 100% correct.
I should say even 200% correct.
But Modern generation is neglecting –
Too much going for fashion and foreign thing.

Other day I'm reading in newspaper
(Every day I'm reading *Times* of India
To improve my English Language)
How one goonda fellow
Throw stone at Indirabehn.
Must be student unrest fellow, I am thinking.
Friends, Romans, Countrymen, I am saying (to
    myself)
Lend me the ears.
Everything is coming –
Regeneration, Remuneration, Contraception.
Be patiently, brothers and sisters.
You want one glass lassi?
Very good for digestion.
With little salt lovely drink,
Better than wine;
Not that I am ever tasting the wine.
I'm the total teetotaller, completely total.
But I say
Wine is for the drunkards only.

What you think of prospects of world peace?
Pakistan behaving like this,
China behaving like that,
It is making me very sad, I am telling you.
Really, most harassing me.
All men are brothers, no?
In India also
Gujaraties, Maharashtrians, Hindiwallahs
All brothers –
Though some are having funny habits.
Still, you tolerate me,
I tolerate you,
One day Ram Rajya is surely coming.

You are going?
But you will visit again
Any time, any day,
I am not believing in ceremony.
Always I am enjoying your company.

A goonda is a ruffian. Ram Rajya (Rama's Kingdom) is a utopian vision of a just
kingdom on earth.

1982

The Lovesleep
—◆◇◆—
GAVIN EWART

In an exciting world of love-bites, nipple-nipping,
unbuttoning and unzipping,
kisses that are
the highest kind of communication,
the lovers experience their timeless elation;

perhaps they reach those peaks where, like a bomb
    exploding,
the angels sing, encoding
ecstasies that
our language can never really deal with –
its nouns and its adjectives that no one can feel with;

but when the woman lies in the man's arms – soft,
    sleeping,
in perfect trust, and keeping
faith, you might say,
that is the truest peace and disarming –
no one can sleep in the arms of an enemy, however
    charming.

1982

A Reliable Service

ALLEN CURNOW

The world can end any time
it likes, say, 10.50 a.m.
of a bright winter Saturday,

that's when the *Bay Belle*
casts off, the diesels are picking
up step, the boatmaster leans

to the wheel, the white water
shoves Paihia jetty back.
Nobody aboard but the two of us.

Fifteen minutes to Russell
was once upon a time
before, say, 10.50 a.m.

The ketch slogging seaward
off Kororàreka Point,
the ensign arrested in

mid-flap, are printed and
pinned on a wall at the end
of the world. No lunch

over there either, the place
at the beach is closed. The *Bay
Belle* is painted bright

blue from stem to stern.
She lifts attentively. That
will be all, I suppose.

The setting of the poem is the Bay of Islands on the North Island of New
Zealand.

1982

Questions for the Old Woman
—◄◊►—

ROBERT BRINGHURST

From the hills of your breasts to the ruined wells
of your eyes is how many miles, old woman?
And how many days to the outwash fans
and gravelled channels of your thighs?

Old woman, what do we know but the swollen
thumb of the tongue against the cranium?
What do we know but the bloodshot
knuckles of the eyes,

the sting of the light in the tightening
fist, the ache of the darkness caked
in the hand? What do we know but the innocent
songs of the lungs in their cage never mating?

What do we know but the dry rasp
of a banjo pick against paper, the whisper
of blood against wood in the stunted trunk
of a tree, uprooted and running?

1982

The Water-Diviner

GILLIAN CLARKE

His fingers tell water like prayer.
He hears its voice in the silence
through fifty feet of rock
on an afternoon dumb with drought.

Under an old tin bath, a stone,
an upturned can, his copper pipe
glints with discovery. We dip our hose
deep into the dark, sucking its dryness,

till suddenly the water answers,
not the little sound we know,
but a thorough bass too deep
for the naked ear, shouts through the hose

a word we could not say, or spell, or remember,
something like 'dŵr . . . dŵr'.

The word 'dŵr' is Welsh and means water.

1982

from Landslides

‹○›

DON COLES

When a breath of early freshness
Blows over you, even now
When a breath of a kind of
Fullness re-opens the hiding place
Behind the leaves –

When he parted them
To find you hiding there,
Even now when your young father
Parts the leaves,
Always his face

Bending close towards
Thrilled laughter –
What kings, what legends!
Who is here now to find you
As you were,

Who is here to find you before
The roamings into womanhood,
To find you among the leaves?
Press my hand if you know.
Press it anyway.

Don Coles' thirteen-part sequence 'Landslides' records visits to his mother in a 'gericare centre'.

1983

History

---◦►---

JORIE GRAHAM

Into whose ear the deeds are spoken. The only
listener. So I believed
he would remember everything, the murmuring trees,
the sunshine's zealotry, its deep
unevenness. For history
is the opposite
of the eye
for whom, for instance, six million bodies in portions
of hundreds and
the flowerpots broken by a sudden wind stand as
equivalent. What more
is there
than fact? *I'll give ten thousand dollars to the man*
who proves the holocaust really
occurred said the exhausted solitude
in San Francisco
in 1980. Far in the woods
in a faded photograph
in 1942 the man with his own
genitalia in his mouth and hundreds of
slow holes
a pitchfork has opened
over his face
grows beautiful. The ferns and deepwood
lilies catch
the eye. Three men in ragged uniforms
with guns keep laughing
nervously. They share the day
with him. A bluebird
sings. The feathers of the shade touch every inch
of skin – the hand holding down the delicate gun,
the hands holding down the delicate

hips. And the sky
is visible between the men, between
the trees, a blue spirit
enveloping
anything. Late in the story, in northern Italy,
a man cuts down some trees for winter
fuel. We read this in the evening
news. Watching the fire burn late
one night, watching it change and change, a hand grenade,
lodged in the pulp the young tree
grew around, explodes, blinding the man, killing
his wife. Now who
will tell the children
fairytales? The ones where simple
crumbs over the forest
floor endure
to help us home?

Graham's rhetorical question 'who/will tell the children/fairytales?' indirectly
restates Theodor Adorno's dictum that to write poetry after Auschwitz is barbaric.

1983

Wounds

MICHAEL LONGLEY

Here are two pictures from my father's head –
I have kept them like secrets until now:
First, the Ulster Division at the Somme
Going over the top with 'Fuck the Pope!'
'No Surrender!': a boy about to die,
Screaming 'Give 'em one for the Shankill!'
'Wilder than Gurkhas' were my father's words
Of admiration and bewilderment.
Next comes the London-Scottish padre
Resettling kilts with his swagger-stick,
With a stylish backhand and a prayer.
Over a landscape of dead buttocks
My father followed him for fifty years.
At last, a belated casualty,
He said – lead traces flaring till they hurt –
'I am dying for King and Country, slowly.'
I touched his hand, his thin head I touched.

Now, with military honours of a kind,
With his badges, his medals like rainbows,
His spinning compass, I bury beside him
Three teenage soldiers, bellies full of
Bullets and Irish beer, their flies undone.
A packet of Woodbines I throw in,
A lucifer, the Sacred Heart of Jesus
Paralysed as heavy guns put out
The night-light in a nursery for ever;
Also a bus-conductor's uniform –
He collapsed beside his carpet-slippers
Without a murmur, shot through the head
By a shivering boy who wandered in
Before they could turn the television down

Or tidy away the supper dishes.
To the children, to a bewildered wife,
I think 'Sorry Missus' was what he said.

The 36th (Ulster) Division fought at the Battle of the Somme in northern France in 1916. Gurkha soldiers from Nepal have fought in the British Army since the early nineteenth century, and a Brigade of Gurkhas still exists. Woodbines were a brand of cigarette.

1983

Raid

LANDEG WHITE

The bombers strike, and shapes
in the photograph scatter, already dying:
the flames cling like water.
When the napalm
has eaten through their lives, only
bulldozers can assuage our horror:
the red trench swallows the charred corpses.

Bombers, and grass huts,
and people in charity clothing queueing
for flour. It keeps raining
and is called revenge
for the tourists ambushed, the baby
hacked in bed, the burning
mission with its women raped and bludgeoned.

None of the guilty are killed:
the avaricious, the psychopathic,
the leaders, power-gluttonous.
But guilt, like human
flesh, clings. We eat, drink,
vote and read, and cannot trace
the graves or name a single murdered child.

Landeg White writes: 'The raid was early 1979 by the Smith-Muzerewa regime
in Rhodesia-Zimbabwe on a ZAPU refugee camp just outside Lusaka. It was
very horrible, a napalm air raid, killing mostly women and children. One of the
buildings hit was a school and a friend described for me pages from *Romeo and
Juliet* fluttering around. There were similar raids but with ground troops on the
ZANU camp at Chimoio in Mozambique. But it was the Lusaka raid was closest
to my then home.'

1983

These Boys

JOHN WHITWORTH

These boys, fifteen, sixteen, seventeen, heeding
Not God nor social worker, being young the old therefore
Abjure. Her few pounds and her radio they care for

And steal, but do not care to leave her bleeding,
Nor break her flaky arms, nor black her eyes,
Nor crack with a brick her skull, though this is common.

Into her stair cupboard they scoop the little woman
Where, in her own damp and dark, at length she dies,
Of all deaths surely the most terrible.

What's to be done with such as these our children,
The untaught, the unfit, the unkind, the unnatural?
What right have we to pity or to pardon?

O bury them deep, deep in desolate places.
Stop eyes, ears, mouths with earth. My face is not these faces.
Each day somewhere the same, or worse disgraces.

1984

Visitors: Armthorpe, August 1984

IAN McMILLAN

Four of them, sitting in the kitchen
drinking tea, I imagine saucers.
I am probably wrong about the saucers.
A hot August day in the kitchen.

'The back door was unlocked
but they kicked it in.
Police said "Send the bastards out"
then the policeman jammed the door

into my face'. I imagine a kitchen,
I am probably wrong about the saucers.
I imagine heartbroken saucers
with patterns of flowers.

Armthorpe near Doncaster was one of the scenes of fiercest confrontations
between police and strikers during the miners' strike of 1984.

1984

The Roys

ARVIND KRISHNA MEHROTRA

We've rented a flat in Ghosh Buildings, Albert Road,
And the Roys live across the street. Mr Roy,
General Merchant, dresses in white
Drill trousers, long-sleeved cotton shirts,
And looks like a friendly barn-owl.
His sons are in school with me. Ganesh,
The eldest, has a gleaming forehead,
A shelled-egg complexion, a small
Equilateral mouth; he belongs to a mystical
Group of philatelists. Together with Shaporjee,
The tallow-white Parsi next door, and Roger Dutt,
The school's aromatic geography teacher, he goes up
In a hot-air balloon and, on the leeward
Side of a Stanley Gibbons catalogue, comes down
Near a turret in Helvetia or Magyar,
Stamp-sized snowflake-like countries
Whose names dissolve like jujubes on my tongue.
We play French cricket, seven-tiles, I-spy, and Injuns.
Our tomahawks are butter knives, our crow
Feathers are real, and riding out from behind
Plaza Talkies we ambush the cowboys of Civil Lines.
Ganesh doesn't join our games. The future,
He seems to say, is not a doodle on the back
Of an envelope but a scarp to be climbed
Alone. He attends a WUS meeting in Stockholm
And opens a restaurant in the heart of town.
I go there in early youth for Jamaican coffee,
In early middle age to use its toilet.
Without getting up from the cash desk he shakes my hand,
'How's the English Department?' he asks, 'How's
Rajamani? Is Mishra a professor now? Is it true? What are
Things coming to?' While I listen to him

My piss travels down the left trouser leg
Into my sock, and then my restless son drags me
Towards a shoe store and buys his first pair of
Naughty Boys. Seen from the road,
Mr Roy's shop is a P & O liner anchored in midstream.
Inside, it's an abandoned coal pit. A film
Of darkness wraps the merchandise; a section of the far
Wall conceals the mouth of a cave, leading
To an underground spring; the air, dry and silvery
At the entrance, is moist and sea-green, furry
To the touch; the display cases, embedded
In the floor, are stuffed with a galleon's treasure;
Finned toffees peer at customers through glass jars.
Every afternoon Mr Roy goes home for his
Siesta and Ramesh, his second son, still wearing
A crumpled school uniform, takes over the town's
Flagship. At 3 p.m. the roads melt, becoming
Impassable, and canvas-backed chicks
Protect shop-fronts against heatstroke.
For the next two hours the sun, stationed above
A traffic island, lays siege to the town, and the only
Movement is of leaves falling
So slowly that midway through their descent their colours
Change. The two waxen shop-assistants
Melt in their sticks, Ramesh sits beside
The cash box with an open sesame
Look in his eye, and I have the well
All to myself. Looking up its bejewelled
Shaft, I make out, in the small
Light coming in through the well-mouth,
Bottles of ketchup, flying cigarillos,
Death-feigning penknives, tooth powders, inexpensive
Dragon china dinner sets, sapphire-blue packets
Of detergent, wooden trays holding skeins
Of thread, jade-coloured boxes of hosiery, rolled-gold
Trinkets, mouth-watering dark tan shoe polish, creams
And hula hoops. Driven by two ceiling fans,
The freighter moves. Land drops from sight.

Though binoculars are trained on the earth's dip,
The eye is monopolized by afterimages of land:
I hold a negative against the light,
And now I'm received into the negative I'm holding.
At 5 p.m. the spell is broken. The sun
Calls it a day and goes down and Mr Roy comes
To clear away the jungle that has grown around his shop and I
Run out with a stolen packet of razor blades.
Where stealing's easy, hiding stolen goods is tough.
A pink stamp issued on Elizabeth's coronation
Cannot be traced to a cigarette tin buried among
Clothes, but what do I do with an album that has
The owner's name rubber stamped
All over it? I give lessons to five-year-old Suresh
In the pleasures of stealing.
For each first-day cover he brings, I press
My View-Master against his mongoloid eye
And let him look through it once. Then one day, while we're
Having lunch, I see a policeman framed in the door.
The food in my mouth hardens into a lump
Of plaster of Paris. Afterwards, I lose my voice
And so does everyone around me. Believe me when I say
There's nothing more sad than a tropical evening,
When auctioneers buy dead advocates' libraries
And there's all the time in the world and nowhere to go.
Anil, their cousin, takes out his autograph-book.
'Just in case,' he says, 'you become famous.'
He has said this to every boy in school.
'Do you think,' he asks me, 'I can get Peeks's
Grandfather's autograph?' Peeks's grandfather is a retired
Chief Justice and gets his pension in sterling.
Anil squints at a marble
In the hollow of his palm
But can't make out if it's an oblong. His sister, hairy
As a sloth bear, sits in the verandah, absorbed
In our game. Her mind, too, is half her age.
Through broken tiles in the roof
Sunbeams let themselves down and she screams

Before they strike her. She vanishes
Inside a blackbeetle and crawls on my skin;
I smell the bouquet of my spittled thumb
And it works like hartshorn. Charlie Hyde, nicknamed
Bony Arse, is the only other person
To so affect me. We go our different ways and sometimes
We cross Albert Road together or meet outside
A chemist's. Anil has a tabletop head and bulging
Irisless eyes. He nods; I nod. It's like watching
From a distance two men one doesn't know
Recognize each other. Anil sets himself up
As a dealer in office equipment
And then as a distributor for Number Ten cigarettes.
He fails at both jobs and is given shock therapy.

1984

A View of a View

◄○►

FUNSO AIYEJINA

For Ropo Sekoni

From the babylonic heights
of a Lagos high rise hotel
with balconies overlooking dawn
(a silver canvas on the Atlantic),
my eyes threaded the horizon
to a fisherman in the distance
silent and erect in his dug-out
as he prepares to cast his net
before the arrival of trawlers,
patient and stoic, like death
waiting for the appropriate tide
to come ashore with the ultimate gift
for the hotel's resident five-star guests
(chameleons with wardrobes for all occasions)
whose coded lives are made purer and safer
by the equivocation of every official probe.

1984

Stones

SHIRLEY KAUFMAN

When you live in Jerusalem you begin
to feel the weight of stones.
You begin to know the word
was made stone, not flesh.

They dwell among us. They crawl
up the hillsides and lie down
on each other to build a wall.
They don't care about prayers,
the small slips of paper
we feed them between the cracks.

They stamp at the earth
until the air runs out
and nothing can grow.

They stare at the sun without blinking
and when they've had enough,
make holes in the sky
so the rain will run down their faces.

They sprawl all over the town
with their pitted bodies. They want
to be water, but nobody
strikes them anymore.

Sometimes at night I hear them
licking the wind to drive it crazy.
There's a huge rock lying on my chest
and I can't get up.

1984

In Modern Dress

CRAIG RAINE

A pair of blackbirds
warring in the roses,
one or two poppies

losing their heads,
the trampled lawn
a battlefield of dolls.

Branch by pruned branch,
a child has climbed
the family tree

to queen it over us:
we groundlings search
the flowering cherry

till we find her face,
its pale prerogative
to rule our hearts.

Sir Walter Raleigh
trails his comforter
about the muddy garden,

a full-length Hilliard
in miniature hose
and padded pants.

How rakishly upturned
his fine moustache
of oxtail soup,

foreshadowing, perhaps,
some future time
of altered favour,

stuck in the high chair
like a pillory, features
pelted with food.

So many expeditions
to learn the history
of this little world:

I watch him grub
in the vegetable patch
and ponder the potato

in its natural state
for the very first time,
or found a settlement

of leaves and sticks,
cleverly protected
by a circle of stones.

But where on earth
did he manage to find
that cigarette end?

Rain and wind.
The day disintegrates.
I observe the lengthy

inquisition of a worm
then go indoors to face
a scattered armada

of picture hooks
on the dining room floor,
the remains of a ruff

on my glass of beer,
Sylvia Plath's *Ariel*
drowned in the bath.

Washing hair, I kneel
to supervise a second rinse
and act the courtier:

tiny seed pearls,
tingling into sight,
confer a kind of majesty.

And I am author
of this toga'd tribune
on my aproned lap,

who plays his part
to an audience of two,
repeating my words.

The imagery in this idyll of two young children, girl and boy, in a garden, draws systematically on the Elizabethan era, from explorers such as Raleigh (c. 1552–1618) and the plants introduced to Europe (potato, tobacco) through the visual arts – discovering the face of the girl in the flowering cherry tree is like discovering the face of Queen Elizabeth I amid the lace and brocade in a portrait miniature by Nicholas Hilliard (c. 1547–1619) – to the Shakespearean associations of Ariel (with *The Tempest*) and the toga'd tribunes who appear in the first scene of *Julius Caesar*.

1984

The Underground

SEAMUS HEANEY

There we were in the vaulted tunnel running,
You in your going-away coat speeding ahead
And me, me then like a fleet god gaining
Upon you before you turned to a reed

Or some new white flower japped with crimson
As the coat flapped wild and button after button
Sprang off and fell in a trail
Between the Underground and the Albert Hall.

Honeymooning, moonlighting, late for the Proms,
Our echoes die in that corridor and now
I come as Hansel came on the moonlit stones
Retracing the path back, lifting the buttons

To end up in a draughty lamplit station
After the trains have gone, the wet track
Bared and tensed as I am, all attention
For your step following and damned if I look back.

Heaney's imagery echoes the *Metamorphoses* of Ovid and the story of Hansel and
Gretel as recorded by the Brothers Grimm.

1984

'My loves are dying'

————◁◦▷————

PHYLLIS WEBB

My loves are dying. Or is it that my love
is dying, day by day, brief life, brief candle,

a flame, *flambeau*, torch, alive, singing
somewhere in the shadow: Here, this way, here.

Hear the atoms ambling, the genes a-tick
in grandfather's clock, in the old bones of beach.

Sun on the Sunday water in November.
Dead leaves on wet ground. The ferry leaves on time.

Time in your flight – O – a wristwatch strapped
to my heart, ticking erratically, winding down.

1984

The Cinnamon Peeler

MICHAEL ONDAATJE

If I were a cinnamon peeler
I would ride your bed
and leave the yellow bark dust
on your pillow.

Your breasts and shoulders would reek
you could never walk through markets
without the profession of my fingers
floating over you. The blind would
stumble certain of whom they approached
though you might bathe
under rain gutters, monsoon.

Here on the upper thigh
at this smooth pasture
neighbour to your hair
or the crease
that cuts your back. This ankle.
You will be known among strangers
as the cinnamon peeler's wife.

I could hardly glance at you
before marriage
never touch you
– your keen nosed mother, your rough brothers.
I buried my hands
in saffron, disguised them
over smoking tar,
helped the honey gatherers . . .

When we swam once
I touched you in water
and our bodies remained free,
you could hold me and be blind of smell.
You climbed the bank and said

          this is how you touch other women
the grass cutter's wife, the lime burner's daughter.
And you searched your arms
for the missing perfume

      and knew

      what good is it
to be the lime burner's daughter
left with no trace
as if not spoken to in the act of love
as if wounded without the pleasure of a scar.

You touched
your belly to my hands
in the dry air and said
I am the cinnamon
peeler's wife. Smell me.

1985

Tangerines

HUGO WILLIAMS

'Before the war' was once-upon-a-time
by 1947. I had to peer through cigarette smoke
to see my parents in black and white
lounging on zebra skins, while doormen stood by doors
in pale grey uniforms.

I wished I was alive before the war
when Tony and Mike rode their bicycles into the lake,
but after the war was where I had to stay,
upstairs in the nursery, with Nanny
and the rocking-horse. It sounded more fun
to dance all night and fly to France for breakfast.
But after the war I had to go to bed.

In my prisoner's pyjamas, I looked through
banisters into that polished, pre-war place
where my parents lived. If I leaned out
I could see the elephant's foot
tortured with shooting sticks
and a round mirror which filled from time to time
with hats and coats and shouts,
then emptied like a bath.

Every summer my parents got in the car
and drove back through the war to the South of France.
I longed to go with them, but I was stuck
in 1948 with Nanny Monkenbeck.

They sent me sword-shaped eucalyptus leaves
and purple, pre-war flowers, pressed
between the pages of my first letters. One year
a box of tangerines arrived for me from France.

I hid behind the sofa in my parents' bedroom,
eating my way south to join them.

1985

Empty Wardrobes
——◦——
DOUGLAS DUNN

I sat in a dress shop, trying to look
As dapper as a young ambassador
Or someone who'd impressed me in a book,
A literary rake or movie star.

Clothes are a way of exercising love.
False? A little. And did she like it? Yes.
Days, days, romantic as Rachmaninov,
A ploy of style, and now not comfortless.

She walked out from the changing-room in brown,
A pretty smock with its embroidered fruit;
Dress after dress, a lady-like red gown
In which she flounced, a smart career-girl's suit.

The dress she chose was green. She found it in
Our clothes-filled cabin trunk. The pot-pourri,
In muslin bags, was full of where and when.
I turn that scent like a memorial key.

But there's that day in Paris, that I regret,
When I said No, franc-less and husbandly.
She browsed through hangers in the Lafayette,
And that comes back tonight, to trouble me.

Now there is grief the couturier, and grief
The needlewoman mourning with her hands,
And grief the scattered finery of life,
The clothes she gave as keepsakes to her friends.

The Galeries Lafayette are a ten-storey department store on boulevard Hauss-mann in Paris, developed from a fashion store opened in a haberdasher's shop at 1 rue Lafayette, in 1893.

1985

'This is unclean . . .'

PETER READING

This is unclean: to eat turbots on Tuesdays,
tying the turban unclockwise at cockcrow,
cutting the beard in a south-facing mirror,
wearing the mitre whilst sipping the Bovril,
chawing the pig and the hen and the ox-tail,
kissing of crosses with peckers erected,
pinching of bottoms (except in a yashmak),
flapping of cocks at the star-spangled-banner,
snatching the claret-pot off of the vicar,
munching the wafer without genuflexion,
facing the East with the arse pointing backwards,
thinking of something a little bit risqué,
raising the cassock to show off the Y-fronts,
holding a Homburg without proper licence,
chewing the cud with another man's cattle,
groping the ladies – or gentry – o'Sundays,
leaving the tip on the old-plum-tree-shaker,
speaking in physics instead of the Claptrap,
failing to pay due obeisance to monkeys,
loving the platypus more than the True Duck,
death without Afterlife, smirking in Mecca,
laughing at funny hats, holding the tenet
how that the Word be but fucking baloney,
failing to laud the Accipiter which Our Lord saith is
Wisdom.

Started by *Australopithecus*, these are
time-honoured Creeds (and all unHoly doubters
shall be enlightened by Pious Devices:
mayhems of tinytots, low flying hardwares,
kneecappings, letterbombs, deaths of the firstborns,
total extinctions of infidel unclean wrong-godded others).

1985

The Mother of the Muses
(In memoriam Emmanuel Stratas,
born Crete 1903, died Toronto 1987)

———————◄◊►———————

TONY HARRISON

After I've lit the fire and looked outside
and found us snowbound and the roads all blocked,
anxious to prove my memory's not ossified
and the way into that storehouse still unlocked,
as it's easier to remember poetry,
I try to remember, but soon find it hard,
a speech from *Prometheus* a boy from Greece BC
scratched, to help him learn it, on a shard.

I remember the museum, and I could eke
his scratch marks out, and could complete
the . . . however many lines there were of Greek
and didn't think it then much of a feat.
But now, not that much later, when I find
the verses I once knew beyond recall
I resolve to bring all yesterday to mind,
our visit to your father, each fact, *all*.

Seeing the Home he's in 's made me obsessed
with remembering those verses I once knew
and setting myself this little memory test
I don't think, at the moment, I'll come through.
It's the Memory, Mother of the Muses, bit.
Prometheus, in words I do recall reciting
but can't quote now, and they're so apposite,
claiming he gave Mankind the gift of writing,

along with fire the Gods withheld from men
who'd lived like ants in caves deprived of light
they could well end up living in again
if we let what flesh first roasted on ignite

a Burning of the Books far more extreme
than any screeching Führer could inspire,
the dark side of the proud Promethean dream
our globe enveloped in his gift of fire.

He bequeathed to baker and to bombardier,
to help benighted men develop faster,
two forms of fire, the gentle one in here,
and what the *Luftwaffe* unleashed, *and* the Lancaster.
One beneficial and one baleful form,
the fire I lit a while since in the grate
that's keeping me, as I sit writing, warm
and what gutted Goethestrasse on this date,

beginning yesterday to be precise
and shown on film from forty years ago
in a Home for the Aged almost glazed with ice
and surrounded by obliterating snow.
We had the choice of watching on TV
Dresden destroyed, then watching its rebirth,
or, with the world outside too blizzardful to see,
live, the senile not long for this earth.

Piles of cracked ice tiles where ploughs try to push
the muddied new falls onto shattered slates,
the glittering shrapnel of grey frozen slush,
a blitz debris fresh snow obliterates
along with what was cleared the day before
bringing even the snowploughs to a halt.
And their lives are frozen solid and won't thaw
with no memory to fling its sparks of salt.

The outer world of blur reflects their inner,
these Rest Home denizens who don't quite know
whether they've just had breakfast, lunch, or dinner,
or stare, between three lunches, at the snow.
Long icicles from the low roof meet
the frozen drifts below and block their view
of flurry and blizzard in the snowed-up street
and of a sky that for a month has shown no blue.

Elsie's been her own optometrist,
measuring the daily way her sight declines
into a growing ball of flashing mist.
She trains her failing sight on outside signs:
the church's COME ALIVE IN '85!
the small hand on the *Export A* ad clock,
the flashing neon on the truck-stop dive
pulsing with strobe lights and jukebox rock,

the little red Scottie on the STOOP & SCOOP
but not the cute eye cast towards its rear,
the little rounded pile of heaped red poop
the owners are required to bend and clear.
To imagine herself so stooping is a feat
as hard as that of gymnasts she has seen
lissom in white leotards compete
in trampolining on the TV screen.

There's one with mashed dinner who can't summon
yet again the appetite to smear
the food about the shrunk face of a woman
weeping for death in her 92nd year.
And of the life she lived remembers little
and stares, like someone playing Kim's Game,
at the tray beneath her nose that fills with spittle
whose bubbles fill with faces with no name.

Lilian, whose love made her decide
to check in with her mate who'd had a stroke,
lost all her spryness once her husband died . . .
He had a beautiful . . . all made of oak . . .
silk inside . . . brass handles . . . tries to find
alternatives . . . *that long thing where you lie*
for words like coffin that have slipped her mind
and forgetting, not the funeral, makes her cry.

And Anne, who treats her roommates to her 'news'
though every day her news is just the same
how she'd just come back from *such a lovely cruise*
to that famous island . . . I forget its name . . .

Born before the Boer War, me, and so
I'm too old to remember I suppose . . .
then tries again . . . the island's called . . . you know . . .
that place, you know . . . where everybody goes . . .

First Gene had one and then a second cane
and then, in weeks, a walker of cold chrome,
now in a wheelchair wails for the Ukraine,
sobbing in soiled pants for what was home.
Is that horror at what's on the TV screen
or just the way the stroke makes Jock's jaw hang?
Though nobody quite knows what his words mean
they hear Scots diphthongs in the New World twang.

And like the Irish Sea on Blackpool Beach,
where Joan was once the pick of bathing belles,
the Lancashire she once had in her speech
seeps into Canadian as she retells,
whose legs now ooze out water, who can't walk,
how she was 'champion at tap', 'the flower'
(she poises the petals on the now frail stalk)
'of the ballet troupe at Blackpool Tower'.

You won't hear Gene, Eugene, Yevgeny speak
to nurses now, or God, in any other tongue
but his Ukrainian, nor your dad Greek,
all that's left to them of being young.
Life comes full circle when we die.
The circumference is finally complete,
so we shouldn't wonder too much why
his speech went back, a stowaway, to Crete.

Dispersal and displacement, willed or not,
from homeland to the room the three share here,
one Ukrainian, one Cretan, and one Scot
grow less Canadian as death draws near.
Jock sees a boozer in a Glasgow street,
and Eugene glittering icons, candles, prayer,
and for your dad a thorn-thick crag in Crete
with oregano and goat smells in the air.

And home? Where is it now? The olive grove
may well be levelled under folds of tar.
The wooden house made joyful with a stove
has gone the way of Tsar and samovar.
The small house with 8 people to a room
with no privacy for quiet thought or sex
bulldozed in the island's tourist boom
to make way for Big Macs and discothèques.

Beribboned hats and bold embroidered sashes
once helped another émigré forget
that Canada was going to get his ashes
and that Estonia's still Soviet.
But now the last of those old-timers
couldn't tell one folk dance from another
and mistakes in the mists of his Alzheimer's
the nurse who wipes his bottom for his mother.

Some hoard memories as some hoard gold
against that rapidly approaching day
that's all they have to live on, being old,
but find their savings spirited away.
What's the point of having lived at all
in the much-snapped duplex in Etobicoke
if it gets swept away beyond recall,
in spite of all the snapshots, at one stroke?

If we *are* what we remember, what are they
who don't have memories as we have ours,
who, when evening falls, have no recall of day,
or who those people were who'd brought them flowers.
The troubled conscience, though, 's glad to forget.
Oblivion for some 's an inner balm.
They've found some peace of mind, not total yet,
as only death itself brings that much calm.

And those white flashes on the TV screen,
as a child, whose dad plunged into genocide,
remembers Dresden and describes the scene,
are they from the firestorm then, or storm outside?

637

Crouching in clown's costume (it was *Fasching*)
aged, 40 years ago, as I was, 9
Eva remembers cellar ceiling crashing
and her mother screaming shrilly: *Swine! Swine! Swine!*

The Tiergarten chief with level voice remembered
a hippo disembowelled on its back,
a mother chimp, her charges all dismembered,
and trees bedaubed with zebra flesh and yak.
Flamingos, flocking from burst cages, fly
in a frenzy with their feathers all alight
from fire on the ground to bomb-crammed sky,
their flames fanned that much fiercer by their flight;

the gibbon with no hands he'd had to shoot
as it came towards him with appealing stumps,
the gutless gorilla still clutching fruit
mashed with its bowels into bloody lumps . . .
I was glad as on and on the keeper went
to the last flayed elephant's fire-frantic screech
that the old folk hadn't followed what was meant
by official footage or survivors' speech.

But then they missed the Semper's restoration,
Dresden's lauded effort to restore
one of the treasures of the now halved nation
exactly as it was before the War.
Billions of marks and years of labour
to reproduce the Semper and they play
what they'd played before the bombs fell, Weber,
Der Freischütz, for their reopening today.

Each bleb of blistered paintwork, every flake
of blast-flayed pigment in that dereliction
they analysed in lab flasks to remake
the colours needed for the redepiction
of Poetic Justice on her cloud surmounting
mortal suffering from opera and play,
repainted tales that seem to bear recounting
more often than the facts that mark today:

the dead Cordelia in the lap of Lear,
Lohengrin who pilots his white swan
at cascading lustres of bright chandelier
above the plush this pantheon shattered on,
with Titania's leashed pards in pastiche Titian,
Faust with Mephisto, Joan, Nathan the Wise,
all were blown, on that Allied bombing mission,
out of their painted clouds into the skies.

Repainted, reupholstered, all in place
just as it had been before that fatal night,
but however devilish the leading bass
his demons are outshadowed on this site.
But that's what Dresden wants and so they play
the same score sung by new uplifting voices
and, as opera synopses often say,
'The curtain falls as everyone rejoices.'

Next more TV, devoted to the trial
of Ernst Zundel, who denies the Jews were gassed,
and academics are supporting his denial,
restoring pride by doctoring the past,
and not just Germans but those people who
can't bear to think such things could ever be,
and by disbelieving horrors to be true
hope to put back hope in history.

A nurse comes in to offer us a cot
considering how bad the blizzard's grown
but you kissed your dad, who, as we left, forgot
he'd been anything all day but on his own.
We needed to escape, weep, laugh, and lie
in each other's arms more privately than there,
weigh in the balance all we're heartened by,
so braved the blizzard back, deep in despair.

Feet of snow went sliding off the bonnet
as we pulled onto the road from where we'd parked.
A snowplough tried to help us to stay on it
but localities nearby, once clearly marked,

those named for northern hometowns close to mine,
the Yorks, the Whitbys, and the Scarboroughs,
all seemed one whited-out recurring sign
that could well be 'Where everybody goes . . .'

His goggles bug-eyed from the driven snow,
the balaclavaed salter goes ahead
with half the sower's, half the sandman's throw,
and follows the groaning plough with wary tread.
We keep on losing the blue revolving light
and the sliding salter, and try to keep on track
by making sure we always have in sight
the yellow Day-glo X marked on his back.

The blizzard made our neighbourhood unknown.
We could neither see behind us nor before.
We felt in that white-out world we were alone
looking for landmarks, lost, until we saw
the unmistakable McDonald's M
with its '60 billion served' hamburger count.
Living, we were numbered among them,
and dead, among an incomputable amount . . .

I woke long after noon with you still sleeping
and the windows blocked where all the snow had blown.
Your pillow was still damp from last night's weeping.
In that silent dark I swore I'd make it known,
while the oil of memory feeds the wick of life
and the flame from it's still constant and still bright,
that, come oblivion or not, I loved my wife
in that long thing where we lay with day like night.

Toronto's at a standstill under snow.
Outside there's not much light and not a sound.
Those lines from Aeschylus! How do they go?
It's almost halfway through *Prometheus Bound*.
I think they're coming back. I'm concentrating . . .
μουσομητορ 'εργανην . . . Damn! I forget,
but remembering your dad, I'm celebrating
being in love, not too forgetful, yet.

Country people used to say today's
the day the birds sense spring and choose their mates,
and trapped exotics in the Dresden blaze
were flung together in their flame-fledged fates.
The snow in the street outside 's at least 6ft.
I look for life, and find the only sign 's,
like words left for, or *by*, someone from Crete,
a bird's tracks, like blurred Greek, for Valentine's.

Toronto, St. Valentine's Day

The title translates the Greek phrase from Aeschylus that Harrison presents himself
as trying to remember at the start of the poem, and which he quotes near the end.
The bombing of Dresden in February 1945 by the RAF and USAF remains one
of the most controversial Allied acts of the Second World War. The Semper Opera
House was destroyed in the bombing and was rebuilt by the Communist govern-
ment of East Germany and re-opened on 13 February 1985, forty years to the day
after its destruction.

1986

liberal

◄◦►

VINCENT O'SULLIVAN

Consider this:
A man who feels for the people.
A friend to the ill-favoured.
Never a word against the bar-
barians assuming Roman dress.

Reconcile this:
A believer in man's potential.
A voice raised against the games
where human flesh is sport.
A man whose eyes fill at music.

You might at least concede:
No man went hungry from my door.
No woman was molested.
No child was imposed on.
Humanitas inevitable as breath.

I who might have, have
never raped, pillaged, extorted;
abused office or position;
concealed; interfered with art;
stood between any man and sunset.

And yet as you say,
I have killed a god. I have made
of impartiality, a farce.
I have dabbled in chaos. I,
Pilate. Who vote as you do.

The poems in the title sequence of O'Sullivan's 1986 collection *The Pilate Tapes* are in the voice of Pontius Pilate, the Roman governor of Judaea who authorised the crucifixion of Jesus Christ.

1986

from The Golden Gate
◄◦►

VIKRAM SETH

7.3

What, after all, is earth's creation?
A virus in the morgue of space.
What's Mozart but a weird vibration
Congenial to a brain-sick race
Rabid with virulence. Why bother
If things like these should maul each other
And, dying, yelp that they have won?
If clouds of dust occlude their sun
From them, it still shines undiminished
In its small galaxy. No change
Of note is likely when this strange
Irradiated beast has finished
Vomiting filth upon its bed
Of inhumanity, and is dead.

7.4

Some disagree. Heroic, silly
– Whichever – they have gathered here
In the pre-dawn, dew-damp and chilly,
On one of two days in the year
When light and night share day's dimension
In equal halves. To ease their tension
(For near them, where a cyclone fence
Delimits the circumference
Of Lungless Labs, police stand sentry,
Guarding a road, checkpost, and gate),
They sing aloud, and celebrate

Fall's somber equinoctial entry
By lighting candles in an arc
Against the encroachment of the dark.

7.5

Dawn rises over Lungless redly.
The pioneers of the blockade
Are joined now by a motley medley;
A marching carnival parade
Starts out from Lungless Park, cavorting
Along to Lungless Labs, supporting
Those who risk prison to defy
The weaponry they all decry.
Young couples, schoolchildren, grandmothers,
Old hippies, punks with hair dyed green,
Staid-suited men who've never seen
Another demonstration, others
Who've been to scores, walk hand in hand
Toward the place where death is planned.

7.6

Those who devise these weapons – decent,
Adjusted, family-minded folk –
Don't think they plan death. Their most recent
Bomb (which, as an engaging joke,
They dubbed 'the cookie cutter') batters
Live cells and yet – this is what matters –
Leaves buildings and machines intact –
This butchering brainspawn is in fact
Soothingly styled a 'radiation
Enhancement device' by these same men.
Blind in their antiseptic den
To the obscene abomination
Of the refined ampoules of hate
Their ingenuity helps create,

7.7

They go to work, attend a meeting,
Write an equation, have a beer,
Hail colleagues with a cheerful greeting,
Are conscientious, sane, sincere,
Rational, able, and fastidious.
Through hardened casings no invidious
Tapeworm of doubt, no guilt, no qualm
Pierces to sabotage their calm.
When something's technically attractive,
You follow the conception through,
That's all. What if you leave a slew
Of living dead, of radioactive
'Collateral damage' in its wake?
It's just a job, for heaven's sake.

7.8

They breed their bombs here; others aim them
– Young targeteers at their controls –
At living souls, to kill and maim them
(Although their unemotive goals
Talk not of 'death' but 'optimizing
Effective yield', while, mobilizing
Uncertain radar, we explore
The skies and prod ourselves to war.
Then, locked inside their lethal closet,
Go codes received, launch keys in place,
Bright crew-cut zombies will efface
All humankind. Too late to posit
What made them fire from the hip.
A flight of geese? A faulty chip?

7.9

Fatigues, down jackets, and bandannas,
Handicapped veterans in wheelchairs,
American flags and rainbow banners,
A band for Sousa, priests for prayers,
A replica of the grim reaper,
Placards – 'I am my brother's keeper,'
'Nice folks don't use nukes,' 'Work for life,
Not death,' and a huge 'Strive with strife' –
Quarreling, waving, wrangling, singing,
The lively ununanimous throng,
Two thousand minds, two thousand strong,
Submerge their disagreements, bringing
Common concern and hope to bear
Against the smithy of 'hardware.'

The words 'I am my brother's keeper' answer those of Cain (Genesis 4:9) – 'Am I my brother's keeper?' – after he has killed Abel.

1986

Albion Market

MICHAEL HOFMANN

Warm air and no sun – the sky was like cardboard,
the same depthless no-colour as the pavements and
   buildings.
It was May, and pink cherry blossoms lay and shoaled
in the gutter, bleeding as after some wedding . . .

Broken glass, corrugated tin and spraygunned plywood
   saying
Arsenal rules the world. Twenty floors up Chantry Point,
the grey diamond panels over two arsoned windows
were scorched like a couple of raised eyebrows.

Tireless and sick, women hunted for bargains.
Gold and silver were half-price. Clothes shops
started up, enjoyed a certain vogue, then
went into a tailspin of permanent sales,

cutting their throats. A window waved *Goodbye, Kilburn,*
and *Everything Must Go.* The *Last Day* was weeks
   ago –
it didn't. The tailor's became *Rock Bottom.*
On the pavement, men were selling shoelaces.

A few streets away, in the renovated precinct,
girls' names and numbers stood on every lamp-post,
phone-booth, parking meter and tree. Felt tip on sticky
   labels,
'rubber', and 'correction' for the incorrigible.

At night, the taxis crawled through Bayswater,
where women dangled their 'most things considered' from
   the kerb.
A man came down the street with the meth-pink eyes
of a white rat, his gait a mortal shuffle.

A British bulldog bowler hat clung to his melting skull.
. . . Game spirits, tat and service industries,
an economy stripped to the skin trade. Sex and security,
Arsenal boot boys, white slaves and the SAS.

Chantry Point was a twenty-two-storey tower block in Westminster, completed
in 1967 (and demolished in 1994). The SAS is the Special Air Service, a special
forces regiment of the British Army.

1986

Waste Land Limericks

WENDY COPE

I

In April one seldom feels cheerful;
Dry stones, sun and dust make me fearful;
Clairvoyantes distress me,
Commuters depress me –
Met Stetson and gave him an earful.

II

She sat on a mighty fine chair,
Sparks flew as she tidied her hair;
She asks many questions,
I make few suggestions –
Bad as Albert and Lil – what a pair!

III

The Thames runs, bones rattle, rats creep;
Tiresias fancies a peep –
A typist is laid,
A record is played –
Wei la la. After this it gets deep.

IV

A Phoenician called Phlebas forgot
About birds and his business – the lot,
Which is no surprise,
Since he'd met his demise
And been left in the ocean to rot.

V

No water. Dry rocks and dry throats,
Then thunder, a shower of quotes
From the Sanskrit and Dante.
Da. Damyata. Shantih.
I hope you'll make sense of the notes.

1987

A Fable

<o>

RICHARD WILBUR

Securely sunning in a forest glade,
    A mild, well-meaning snake
Approved the adaptations he had made
        For safety's sake.

    He liked the skin he had –
Its mottled camouflage, its look of mail,
And was content that he had thought to add
        A rattling tail.

The tail was not for drumming up a fight;
    No, nothing of the sort.
And he would only use his poisoned bite
        As last resort.

    A peasant now drew near,
Collecting wood; the snake, observing this,
Expressed concern by uttering a clear
        But civil hiss.

The simple churl, his nerves at once unstrung,
    Mistook the other's tone
And dashed his brains out with a deftly-flung
        Pre-emptive stone.

Moral

Security, alas, can give
    A threatening impression;
Too much defense-initiative
        Can prompt aggression.

The Strategic Defense Initiative (SDI), a network of ground and space systems
intended to protect the US from missile attack, was established by President
Ronald Reagan in 1983 but quickly criticised as more likely to be understood as
a provocative return to the arms race.

1987

The Quick and the Dead at Pompeii

◄◦►

DAVID CONSTANTINE

I cannot stop thinking about the dead at Pompeii.
It was in the Nagasaki and Hiroshima month.
They did not know they were living under a volcano.
Their augurers watched a desperate flight of birds
And wondered about it in the ensuing silence.

There was sixty feet of ash over Pompeii.
It was seventeen centuries before they found the place.
Nobody woke when the sun began again,
Nobody danced. The dead had left their shapes.
The mud was honeycombed with the deserted forms of
   people.

Fiorelli recovered them by a method the ancients
Invented for statuary. When he cast their bodies
And cracked the crust of mud they were born again
Exactly as they had died. Many were struck
Recumbent, tripped, wincing away, the clothing

Rolled up their backs. They were interrupted:
A visiting woman was compromised for ever,
A beggar hugs his sack, two prisoners are in chains.
Everyone died as they were. A leprous man and wife
Are lying quietly with their children between them.

The works of art at Pompeii were a different matter.
Their statues rose out of mephitic holes bright-eyed.
The fresco people had continued courting and feasting
And playing mythological parts: they had the hues
Of Hermione when Leontes is forgiven.

The Roman city of Pompeii was destroyed and buried when Vesuvius erupted in
AD 79. Giuseppe Fiorelli (1823–96) directed the excavation of Pompeii from 1863
to 1875, and devised the process which bears his name, whereby plaster casts are
used to recreate the forms of bodies. In Shakespeare's *The Winter's Tale*, the statue
of Hermione comes to life in the final act, following Leontes' change of heart.

1987

Cousin Coat

SEAN O'BRIEN

You are my secret coat. You're never dry.
You wear the weight and stink of black canals.
Malodorous companion, we know why
It's taken me so long to see we're pals,
To learn why my acquaintance never sniff
Or send me notes to say I stink of stiff.

But you don't talk, historical bespoke.
You must be worn, be intimate as skin,
And though I never lived what you invoke,
At birth I was already buttoned in.
Your clammy itch became my atmosphere,
An air made half of anger, half of fear.

And what you are is what I tried to shed
In libraries with Donne and Henry James.
You're here to bear a message from the dead
Whose history's dishonoured with their names.
You mean the North, the poor, and troopers sent
To shoot down those who showed their discontent.

No comfort there for comfy meliorists
Grown weepy over Jarrow photographs.
No comfort when the poor the state enlists
Parade before their fathers' cenotaphs.
No comfort when the strikers all go back
To see which twenty thousand get the sack.

Be with me when they cauterise the facts.
Be with me to the bottom of the page,
Insisting on what history exacts.
Be memory, be conscience, will and rage,
And keep me cold and honest, cousin coat,
So if I lie, I'll know you're at my throat.

Jarrow, in the English north-east, entered history in October 1936 when two hundred marchers walked to London (the 'Jarrow crusade') in protest at unemployment and the poverty they were enduring.

1987

Belfast Confetti

Ciaran Carson

Suddenly as the riot squad moved in, it was raining exclamation
marks,
Nuts, bolts, nails, car-keys. A fount of broken type. And the
explosion
Itself – an asterisk on the map. This hyphenated line, a burst of
rapid fire . . .
I was trying to complete a sentence in my head, but it kept
stuttering,
All the alleyways and side-streets blocked with stops and colons.

I know this labyrinth so well – Balaclava, Raglan, Inkerman,
Odessa Street –
Why can't I escape? Every move is punctuated. Crimea Street.
Dead end again.
A Saracen, Kremlin-2 mesh. Makrolon face-shields. Walkie-talkies.
What is
My name? Where am I coming from? Where am I going? A
fusillade of question-marks.

The Belfast street names in the sixth and seventh lines recall the Crimean War of
1953–6 and, by extension, the history of British militarism. The FV603 Saracen
was an armoured personnel carrier used by the British Army. Kremlin-2 mesh
was used as protection against projectiles, and Makrolon face-shields were mili-
tary face-shields made of polycarbon resin.

1987

Looking at My Father

SHARON OLDS

I do not think I am deceived about him.
I know about the drinking, I know he's a tease,
obsessive, rigid, selfish, sentimental,
but I could look at my father all day
and not get enough: the large creased
ball of his forehead, slightly aglitter like the
sheen on a well-oiled baseball glove;
his eyebrows, the hairs two inches long,
black and silver, reaching out in
continual hope and curtailment; and most of
all I could look forever at his eyes,
the way they bulge out as if eager to see and
yet are glazed as if blind, the whites
hard and stained as boiled eggs
boiled in sulphur water, the irises
muddy as the lip of a live volcano, the
pupils glittering pure black,
magician black. Then there is his nose
rounded and pocked and comfy as the bulb of a
horn a clown would toot, and his lips
solid and springy. I even like
to look in his mouth, stained brown with
cigars and bourbon, my eyes sliding down the
long amber roots of his teeth,
right in there where Mother hated, and
up the scorched satins of the sides and
vault, even the knobs on the back
of his tongue. I know he is not perfect but my
body thinks his body is perfect, the
fine stretched coarse pink
skin, the big size of him, the
sour-ball mass, darkness, hair,

sex, legs even longer than mine
lovely feet. What I know I know, what my
body knows it knows, it likes to
slip the leash of my mind and go and
look at him, like an animal
looking at water, then going to it and
drinking until it has had its fill and can
lie down and sleep.

1987

The Missing

◁◦▷

THOM GUNN

Now as I watch the progress of the plague,
The friends surrounding me fall sick, grow thin,
And drop away. Bared, is my shape less vague
– Sharply exposed and with a sculpted skin?

I do not like the statue's chill contour,
Not nowadays. The warmth investing me
Led outward through mind, limb, feeling, and more
In an involved increasing family.

Contact of friend led to another friend,
Supple entwinement through the living mass
Which for all that I knew might have no end,
Image of an unlimited embrace.

I did not just feel ease, though comfortable:
Aggressive as in some ideal of sport,
With ceaseless movement thrilling through the whole,
Their push kept me as firm as their support.

But death – Their deaths have left me less defined:
It was their pulsing presence made me clear.
I borrowed from it, I was unconfined,
Who tonight balance unsupported here,

Eyes glaring from raw marble, in a pose
Langorously part-buried in the block,
Shins perfect and no calves, as if I froze
Between potential and a finished work.

– Abandoned incomplete, shape of a shape,
In which exact detail shows the more strange,
Trapped in unwholeness, I find no escape
Back to the play of constant give and change.

August 1987

1987

Letters to the Winner

LES MURRAY

After the war, and just after marriage and fatherhood
ended in divorce, our neighbour won the special lottery,
an amount then equal to fifteen years of a manager's
salary at the bank, or fifty years' earnings by
a marginal farmer fermenting his clothes in the black
marinade of sweat, up in his mill-logging paddocks.

The district, used to one mailbag, now received two
every mailday. The fat one was for our neighbour.
After a dip or two, he let these bags accumulate
around the plank walls of the kitchen, over the chairs
till on a rainy day, he fed the tail-switching calves,
let the bullocks out of the yard, and pausing at the door
to wash his hands, came inside to read the letters.

Shaken out in a vast mound on the kitchen table
they slid down, slithered to his fingers. *I have 7 children*
I am under the doctor if you could see your way clear
equal Pardners in the Venture God would bless you lovey
assured of our best service for a mere fifteen pounds down
remember you're only lucky I knew you from the paper straightaway

Baksheesh, hissed the pages as he flattened them, baksheesh!
mate if your interested in a fellow diggers problems
old mate a friend in need – the Great Golden Letter
having come, now he was being punished for it.
You sound like a lovely big boy we could have such times
her's my photoe Doll Im wearing my birthday swimsuit
with the right man I would share this infallible system.

When he lifted the stove's iron disc and started feeding in
the pages he'd read, they clutched and streamed up the
   corrugated
black chimney shaft. And yet he went on reading,
holding each page by its points, feeling an obligation
to read each crude rehearsed lie, each come-on, flat truth,
   extremity:
We might visit you the wise investor a loan a bush man like you

remember we met on Roma Street for your delight and mine
a lick of the sultana – the white moraine kept slipping
its messages to him *you will be accursed* he husked them like
   cobs
Mr Nouveau Jack old man my legs are all paralysed up.
Black smuts swirled weightless in the room *some good kind*
   person
like the nausea of a novice free-falling in a deep mine's cage
now I have lost his pension and formed a sticky nimbus round
   him

but he read on, fascinated by a further human range
not even war had taught him, nor literature glossed for him
since he never read literature. Merely the great reject pile
which high style is there to snub and filter, for readers.
That his one day's reading had a strong taste of what he and
   war
had made of his marriage is likely; he was not without
   sympathy,

but his leap had hit a wire through which the human is
   policed.
His head throbbed as if busting with a soundless shout
of immemorial sobbed invective *God-forsaken, God-forsakin*
as he stopped reading, and sat blackened in his riches.

1987

The Reader

<o>

ROBERT BRINGHURST

. . . der da mit seinem Schatten/getränktes liest
Rainer Maria Rilke

Who reads her while she reads? Her eyes slide
under the paper, into another world
while all we hear of it
or see is the slow surf of turning pages.

Her mother might not recognize her,
soaked to the skin as she is in her own shadow.
How could you then? You with your watch and tongue
still running, tell me: how much does she lose

when she looks up? When she lifts
the ladles of her eyes, how much
flows back into the book, and how much
spills down the walls of the overflowing world?

Children, playing alone, will sometimes
come back suddenly, seeing what it is
to be here, and their eyes are altered. Hers too. Words
she's never said reshape her lips forever.

1988

The Moor

—◇—

R.S. THOMAS

It was like a church to me.
I entered it on soft foot,
Breath held like a cap in the hand.
It was quiet.
What God was there made himself felt,
Not listened to, in clean colours
That brought a moistening of the eye,
In movement of the wind over grass.

There were no prayers said. But stillness
Of the heart's passions – that was praise
Enough; and the mind's cession
Of its kingdom. I walked on,
Simple and poor, while the air crumbled
And broke on me generously as bread.

1988

Facing It

‹o›

YUSEF KOMUNYAKAA

My black face fades,
hiding inside the black granite.
I said I wouldn't,
dammit: No tears.
I'm stone. I'm flesh.
My clouded reflection eyes me
like a bird of prey, the profile of night
slanted against morning. I turn
this way — the stone lets me go.
I turn that way — I'm inside
the Vietnam Veterans Memorial
again, depending on the light
to make a difference.
I go down the 58,022 names,
half-expecting to find
my own in letters like smoke.
I touch the name Andrew Johnson;
I see the booby trap's white flash.
Names shimmer on a woman's blouse
but when she walks away
the names stay on the wall.
Brushstrokes flash, a red bird's
wings cutting across my stare.
The sky. A plane in the sky.
A white vet's image floats
closer to me, then his pale eyes

look through mine. I'm a window.
He's lost his right arm
inside the stone. In the black mirror
a woman's trying to erase names:
No, she's brushing a boy's hair.

The Vietnam Veterans Memorial is an American national memorial in Washington,
DC.

1988

After the Deluge

WOLE SOYINKA

Once, for a dare,
He filled his heart-shaped swimming pool
With bank notes, high denomination
And fed a pound of caviar to his dog.
The dog was sick; a chartered plane
Flew in replacement for the Persian rug.

He made a billion yen
Leap from Tokyo to Buenos Aires,
Turn somersaults through Brussels,
New York, Sofia and Johannesburg.
It cracked the bullion market open wide.
Governments fell, coalitions cracked
Insurrection raised its bloody flag
From north to south.

He knew his native land through iron gates,
His sight was radar bowls, his hearing
Electronic beams. For flesh and blood,
Kept company with a brace of Dobermans.
But – yes – the worthy causes never lacked
His widow's mite, discreetly publicized.

He escaped the lynch days. He survives.
I dreamt I saw him on a village
Water line, a parched land where
Water is a god
That doles its favors by the drop,
And waiting is a way of life.

Rebellion gleamed yet faintly in his eye
Traversing chrome-and-platinum retreats. There,
Hubs of commerce smoothly turn without
His bidding, and cities where he lately roosted
Have forgotten him, the preying bird
Of passage.

They let him live, but not from pity
Or human sufferance. He scratches life
From earth, no worse a mortal man than the rest.
Far, far away in dreamland splendor,
Creepers twine his gates of bronze relief.
The jade-lined pool is home
To snakes and lizards; they hunt and mate
On crusted algae.

1988

Down by the Station, Early in the Morning

JOHN ASHBERY

It all wears out. I keep telling myself this, but
I can never believe me, though others do. Even things do.
And the things they do. Like the rasp of silk, or a certain
Glottal stop in your voice as you are telling me how you
Didn't have time to brush your teeth but gargled with
    Listerine
Instead. Each is a base one might wish to touch once more

Before dying. There's the moment years ago in the station in
    Venice,
The dark rainy afternoon in fourth grade, and the shoes then,
Made of a dull crinkled brown leather that no longer exists.
And nothing does, until you name it, remembering, and even
    then
It may not have existed, or existed only as a result
Of the perceptual dysfunction you've been carrying around
    for years.
The result is magic, then terror, then pity at the emptiness,
Then air gradually bathing and filling the emptiness as it
    leaks,
Emoting all over something that is probably mere reportage
But nevertheless likes being emoted on. And so each day
Culminates in merriment as well as a deep shock like an
    electric one,

As the wrecking ball bursts through the wall with the
    bookshelves
Scattering the works of famous authors as well as those
Of more obscure ones, and books with no author, letting in
Space, and an extraneous babble from the street
Confirming the new value the hollow core has again, the
    light
From the lighthouse that protects as it pushes us away.

1988

The Chess Player
◄○►

CHARLES BOYLE

I'm thinking of a famous grandmaster
on the sixteenth floor of a hotel in Bucharest,
kept awake by the gypsy music
of a wedding party downstairs.

I'm seeing him watch from his window
some cleaning women emerge
in the sodium-lit small hours
from the national exhibition centre,
and the rails from the station stretching
towards the vanishing point of asylum.

When at last he falls asleep
to the strains of the last violin,
he dreams fitfully
of a lady with a parasol
stepping out on the first marble square
of a black and white chequered piazza.

His task is to guide her across
to the shade of the colonnade
before history takes over,
before the city lies in ruins.

The light is hot and even
and, like the Pyramids when they were built,
the stones are so perfectly cut
a knife blade couldn't slip between them.

1989–2000
Endgames

I N NOVEMBER 1989 the Berlin Wall was breached and, for the first time in twenty-eight years, citizens of the East were free to cross into West Germany without the risk of being shot by border guards. With unforgettable scenes of ecstatic Germans pulling the wall down with their bare hands beamed around the world, there was global hope for changes few thought they would see in their lifetimes. In Prague, the entire Communist Politburo resigned, leaving the political stage to the playwright and dissident leader, Vaclav Havel. On Christmas Day, Nicolae Ceausescu, the loathed dictator of Rumania, was overthrown and summarily executed with his wife Elena. The freedoms long taken for granted in the Western democracies were becoming available across Europe, and the threat of nuclear annihilation was greatly reduced when the leaders of the two superpowers, George Bush and Mikhail Gorbachev, declared the Cold War over, with a commitment to cutting back conventional and nuclear forces. As Russia made its difficult transition from Soviet state to Federation, with Gorbachev's reforms leading to the unravelling of the USSR and pointing into a future rich in difficult promise, the time was right for worldly-wise debate on whether Perestroika would really effect change, a debate Carol Rumens satirically dramatises in 'A dialogue of Perestroishiks'.

Elsewhere there was fresh cause for hope the following year when Nelson Mandela, the leader and symbol of the black struggle against apartheid in South Africa, was freed from prison after a quarter of a century. In his first statement he said: 'I greet you in the name of peace,

democracy and freedom for all.' Soon afterwards he entered into nego-
tiations with the South African president, F. W. de Klerk, which would
lead to the peaceful holding of a general election in which all citizens
were eligible to vote.

The loss of individual freedom of course takes many forms. Cultural
and religious custom, hardened over centuries, will suffice, as Imtiaz
Dharker's poem 'Purdah I' suggests, while in Northern Ireland similarly
ingrained positions sustained a murderous sectarian antagonism that make
simply going out for a drink so fraught with danger in Ciaran Carson's
'Last Orders'. In America, race hatred, poverty and gender have long
conspired to make the least privileged the most vulnerable, as Toi Derr-
icotte stresses in 'On the Turning Up of Unidentified Black Female
Corpses'. And, casting her net far wider back in time, Eavan Boland
meditates on the unnamed and unnumbered dying in their droves,
unreachable beneath the radar of history.

While the world waited to see how the seismic changes in Europe
and the former Soviet Union would play out, Saddam Hussein's unpro-
voked annexation of Kuwait created mounting tension, and put a UN
alliance of thirty countries, led by the Americans, on a war footing.
When the Allies' invasion, code-named Desert Storm, finally came, it
was exposed to the most detailed television coverage of any conflict in
history, and the massive deployment of firepower not only presented
similarities to violent video games – as John Forbes noted in 'Love Poem'
– but raised complex questions about the relation of television viewers
to the visual material they consume. His speaker's conclusion that 'all
this is being staged for me' simply but eloquently points up the solipsism
in television culture's response to global events. The first Gulf War left
Kuwait liberated but Saddam Hussein still in power – and Denise Levertov
tellingly pondered that weasel phrase, 'the art of war'.

While the Iraqi dictator survived, Britain's most prominent leader
since Churchill had to give way to internal party pressure. Margaret
Thatcher's high-handed style had made her unpopular with her colleagues
and an electoral liability. Riots on the streets of London set the tone
for the Nineties as recession bit deep. And a new wave of poets emerged
to voice the mood of disaffected rethinking which was finally to topple
the Conservative party in 1997. Among them were Simon Armitage,

Glyn Maxwell, Ian Duhig and Don Paterson, in all of whom a formidable blend of formal confidence, sharp attitude, and colloquial brio can be seen. They had benefited from the Thatcherite agenda of promoting national confidence, if only by being forced into an oppositional stance, but at the same time they were having none of the political correctness which made a damp rag of much socio-political talk in the Eighties and Nineties.

As the countdown ran to the end of the millennium, it seemed the dying century was determined to prove it had not kicked its deadly habits. The removal of the authoritarian structures put in place by Marshall Tito to hold the synthetic state of Yugoslavia together resulted in an outbreak of ethnic and religious antagonisms that had been lightly buried for fifty years. With massacres of men, women and children, and policies of 'ethnic cleansing' enforcing not only the separation of Christian and Muslim, of Serb, Croat and Bosnian, but also their murder, the Balkans became a crucible of conflict. The depths to which hatred and fear could drive one ethnic group in its treatment of another were exposed with the upsurge of genocidal terror in Rwanda in 1994. Over half a million people were killed in an orgy of tribal slaughter triggered by the President's death in a plane crash, while the West looked on, horrified but seemingly helpless to intervene. Poems here by Alan Jenkins, Don Paterson, Carol Ann Duffy, Steve Chimombo, Yvette Christianse and Brian McCabe all explore different aspects of the human species' seemingly irresistible pull towards violence, sadism and destruction, collective and individual.

If that were the sum of the poets' diagnosis, it would be a sad day – for humanity, that is – but the same period produced Les Murray's affecting, meticulously tender study of his autistic son, Geoffrey Lehmann's instantly recognisable reflections on parenthood, versions of love told by Vincent O'Sullivan, Hugo Williams and Virginia Hamilton Adair, the tenderness in the face of eternity shown in very different ways by Robert Gray and Don Coles, and the irrepressible humour of Christopher Reid and Glyn Maxwell.

Our long twentieth century, including both 1900 and 2000 to total a hundred and one years, ends where a new millennium begins. Although there was no repeat of the feverish anticipation of the Second Coming that had sent bands of flagellants on pilgrimages in millennial ecstasy across Europe a thousand years earlier, excitement at the second millennium was tempered by misgivings about the future. True, the millennium bug, which was meant to stop all the clocks and more besides, failed to materialise. But our book concludes with two poems in which the profoundly human desire to celebrate beauty and hope is tempered by the grown-up knowledge that that desire may well be disappointed. Kit Wright's 'Hoping It Might Be So' brings us full circle, for it takes its title from the poet with whom this book opened, Thomas Hardy. And in Wright's repeated 'There must be . . .' we hear, deep down under his longing for a place where injustices will be righted and horrors undone, the sad near-certainty that travels in the cadences of Hardy's 'The Oxen' too – that sureness that, alas, there is no such place. With Jeffrey Harrison's 'Pale Blue City', which carries a date precisely a century after our opening poem, we are invited to share an achingly simple vision of beauty: the city of New York, seen from the air, complete with 'the tiny paired towers of the Trade Center'. The human warmth of this poem, and the vision of the 'beautiful pale ash blue' city that can be 'held in your hand', possess a real poignancy for us now, who know what the new century held. 'Here: take it,' writes Harrison, 'before it disappears.' This, before the event, was perhaps the great poem of 9/11.

1989

The Woman on the Dump

———————◄○►———————

ELIZABETH SPIRES

Where was it one first heard of the truth? The the.
                                    Wallace Stevens

She sits on a smoldering couch
reading labels from old tin cans,
the ground ground down
to dirt, hard as poured cement.
A crowd of fat white gulls
take mincing, oblique steps
around the couch, searching for
an orange rind, a crab claw.
Clouds scud backward overhead,
drop quickly over the horizon,
as if weighted with lead sinkers.
The inside's outside here,
her 'sitting room' *en plein air*:
a homey triad of chaise longue,
tilting table, and old floor lamp
from a torn-down whorehouse,
the shade a painted scene
of nymphs in a naked landscape.
The lamp is a beautiful thing,
even if she can't plug it in,
the bare-cheeked, breathless
nymphs part of the eternal
feminine as they rush away
from streaming trees and clouds
that can't be trusted not to change
from man to myth and back again.

The dump's too real. Or not
real enough. It is hot here.
Or cold. When the sun goes down,
she wraps herself in old newspaper,
the newsprint rubbing off,
so that she *is* the news as she
looks for clues and scraps
of things in the refuse. The *the*
is here somewhere, buried
under bulldozed piles of trash.
She picks up a pair of old cymbals
to announce the moon, the pure
symbol, just coming up over there.
Abandoned bathtubs, sinks, and stoves
glow white – abstract forms
in the moonlight – a high tide
of garbage spawns and grows,
throwing long lovely shadows
across unplumbed ravines and gullies.
She'll work through the night,
the woman on the dump,
sifting and sorting and putting
things right, saving everything
that can be saved, rejecting
nothing, piles of tires
in the background unexhaustedly
burning, burning, burning.

The epigraph is the final line of Wallace Stevens' poem 'The Man on the Dump'.

1989

After a Death

ROO BORSON

Seeing that there's no other way,
I turn his absence into a chair.
I can sit in it,
gaze out through the window.
I can do what I do best
and then go out into the world.
And I can return then with my useless love,
to rest,
because the chair is there.

1989

The Forecast for Night

ELIZABETH SMITHER

Showers, though their rhythms may be
Interrupted by wind and gusts
Will not cease in the dark hours
They should continue until first light.

Going to sleep one imagines a dance
With interruptions, a shouldering
A standing to one side, a sweeping
Together and deeper into different arms.

1989

Zoom!

<o>

SIMON ARMITAGE

It begins as a house, an end terrace
in this case
    but it will not stop there. Soon it is
an avenue
    which cambers arrogantly past the Mechanics' Institute,
turns left
    at the main road without even looking
and quickly it is
    a town with all four major clearing banks,
a daily paper
    and a football team pushing for promotion.

On it goes, oblivious of the Planning Acts,
the green belts,
    and before we know it it is out of our hands:
city, nation,
    hemisphere, universe, hammering out in all directions
until suddenly,
    mercifully, it is drawn aside through the eye
of a black hole
    and bulleted into a neighbouring galaxy, emerging
smaller and smoother
    than a billiard ball but weighing more than Saturn.

People stop me in the street, badger me
in the check-out queue
    and ask 'What is this, this that is so small
and so very smooth
    but whose mass is greater than the ringed planet?'
It's just words
    I assure them. But they will not have it.

1989

Last Orders

‹◇›

CIARAN CARSON

Squeeze the buzzer on the steel mesh gate like a trigger, but
It's someone else who has you in their sights. Click. It opens.
 Like electronic
Russian roulette, since you never know for sure who's who, or
 what
You're walking into. I, for instance, could be anybody. Though
 I'm told
Taig's written on my face. See me, would *I* trust appearances?

Inside a sudden lull. The barman lolls his head at us. We order
 Harp –
Seems safe enough, everybody drinks it. As someone looks
 daggers at us
From the *Bushmills* mirror, a penny drops: how simple it would
 be for someone
Like ourselves to walk in and blow the whole place, and
 ourselves, to Kingdom Come.

'Taig' is a derogatory term used for an Irish Catholic by loyalists in Northern
Ireland.

1989

Purdah I

<o>

IMTIAZ DHARKER

One day they said
she was old enough to learn some shame.
She found it came quite naturally.

Purdah is a kind of safety.
The body finds a place to hide.
The cloth fans out against the skin
much like the earth that falls
on coffins after they put the dead men in.

People she has known
stand up, sit down as they have always done.
But they make different angles
in the light, their eyes aslant,
a little sly.

She half-remembers things
from someone else's life,
perhaps from yours, or mine –
carefully carrying what we do not own:
between the thighs, a sense of sin.

We sit still, letting the cloth grow
a little closer to our skin.
A light filters inward
through our bodies' walls.
Voices speak inside us,
echoing in the spaces we have just left.

She stands outside herself,
sometimes in all four corners of a room.
Wherever she goes, she is always
inching past herself,
as if she were a clod of earth,
and the roots as well,
scratching for a hold
between the first and second rib.

Passing constantly out of her own hands
into the corner of someone else's eyes . . .
while doors keep opening
inward and again
inward.

Purdah is the enforced seclusion of women, to prevent their being seen by men.

1989

On the Turning Up of Unidentified Black Female Corpses

TOI DERRICOTTE

Mowing his three acres with a tractor,
a man notices something ahead – a mannequin –
he thinks someone threw it from a car. Closer
he sees it is the body of a black woman.

The medics come and turn her with pitchforks.
Her gaze shoots past him to nothing. Nothing
is explained. How many black women
have been turned up to stare at us blankly,

in weedy fields, off highways,
pushed out in plastic bags,
shot, knifed, unclothed partially, raped,
their wounds sealed with a powdery crust.

Last week on TV, a gruesome face, eyes bloated shut.
No one will say, 'She looks like she's sleeping,' ropes
of blue-black slashes at the mouth. Does anybody
know this woman? Will anyone come forth? Silence

like a backwave rushes into that field
where, just the week before, four other black girls
had been found. The gritty image hangs in the air
just a few seconds, but it strikes me,

a black woman, there is a question being asked
about my life. How can I
protect myself? Even if I lock my doors,
walk only in the light, someone wants me dead.

Am I wrong to think
if five white women had been stripped,
broken, the sirens would wail until
someone was named?

Is it any wonder I walk over these bodies
pretending they are not mine, that I do not know
the killer, that I am just like any woman –
if not wanted, at least tolerated.

Part of me wants to disappear, to pull
the earth on top of me. Then there is this part
that digs me up with this pen
and turns my sad black face to the light.

1989

Breaches

<o>

MATTHEW SWEENEY

For Irmgard Maassen

Glühwein with honey at Potsdamer Platz,
at the breach that drew the biggest cheer
when the pastel-coloured Trabbis drove through.
Slush underfoot, wrecking shoes.
In the darkening distance: the Reichstag.

As we approached the Wall, we heard
a deepening tapping, a chipping that spread
till it was everywhere. Then we saw them:
men and women with masons' hammers and chisels
and bags on the ground; two Frenchmen
attacking the parapet, making sure
nothing fell on the East; cracks widening
to let blue-uniformed *Volkspolizei* peep through,
as they paused in their paired stroll,
while on the West two cops in green
walked up and down, with megaphones,
advising the chippies to leave the wall alone,
at once, or else . . . or else . . .

We took our tiny hammer and whacked chips
from that graffiti-daubed, astoundingly thin,
infamous construction, helping in our way
to make it disappear.

Berlin, November 1989

The Berlin Wall, building of which began on 13 August 1961, was opened on 9 November 1989. A substantial role in its demolition was played by the many who broke out pieces themselves, as souvenirs. The Trabi (usually spelt thus) was an East German car, the Trabant.

1990

A Dialogue of Perestroishiks

‹o›

CAROL RUMENS

Good riddance to that old eyesore, the Engine of Justice

Ah, but the Engine of Justice was theoretically beautiful

Ah, but the Engine of Justice was all bloody theory

Ah, but it went, the good old Engine of Justice

Ah, but it never ran on time, the Engine of Justice

Ah, but the Engine of Justice was greased lightning in its heyday, and it could sing 'How Great is Our Motherland' in four parts

Ah, but the Engine of Justice was ecologically unsound, and it stank to high heaven

Ah, but everyone on board the Engine of Justice had a job

Ah, but the Engine of Justice was a dictatorship

Ah, but the Engine of Justice was a dictatorship of the proletariat

Ah, but the Engine of Justice gave fat hand-outs to the bosses

Ah, but the Engine of Justice put potatoes in all the children

Ah, but the Engine of Justice knew nothing about female orgasm

Ah, but what d'you expect of an Engine of Justice?

Ah, but did you hear the one about the Engine of Justice?

Ah, but there have been some grand stories about the Engine of Justice

Ah, but the Engine of Justice was a fabulous all-time con

Ah, but the Engine of Justice only needed a new oil-can

Ah, but the Engine of Justice only needed a new definition of Justice

Ah, but who will build us a better Engine of Justice?

Ah, but each man should aim to be his own Engine of Justice, and each woman too, of course

Ah, but the Engine of Justice was for everyone

Ah, but was everyone for the Engine of Justice?

Ah, but anyway, I had a soft spot for the dear old Engine of Justice

Ah, but the dear old Engine of Justice eliminated people for

having soft spots
Ah, but, excuse me, what have you got in your hand if it isn't
    the plans for a new Engine of Justice?
Ah, but we're not calling it the Engine of Justice
Ah, but it looks very similar to
Ah, but it's not, so shut up
Ah, but
Ah but ah but?
Ah
Ah!

Perestroika was the movement within the Soviet Communist Party under General Secretary Mikhail Gorbachev that aimed at reforming Soviet politics and economics from within.

1990

Outside History

◄○►

EAVAN BOLAND

There are outsiders, always. These stars —
these iron inklings of an Irish January,
whose light happened

thousands of years before
our pain did: they are, they have always been
outside history.

They keep their distance. Under them remains
a place where you found
you were human, and

a landscape in which you know you are mortal.
And a time to choose between them.
I have chosen:

out of myth into history I move to be
part of that ordeal
whose darkness is

only now reaching me from those fields,
those rivers, those roads clotted as
firmaments with the dead.

How slowly they die
as we kneel beside them, whisper in their ear.
And we are too late. We are always too late.

1990

Shirt

—◦—

ROBERT PINSKY

The back, the yoke, the yardage. Lapped seams,
The nearly invisible stitches along the collar
Turned in a sweatshop by Koreans or Malaysians

Gossiping over tea and noodles on their break
Or talking money or politics while one fitted
This armpiece with its overseam to the band

Of cuff I button at my wrist. The presser, the cutter,
The wringer, the mangle. The needle, the union,
The treadle, the bobbin. The code. The infamous blaze

At the Triangle Factory in nineteen-eleven.
One hundred and forty-six died in the flames
On the ninth floor, no hydrants, no fire escapes –

The witness in a building across the street
Who watched how a young man helped a girl to step
Up to the windowsill, then held her out

Away from the masonry wall and let her drop.
And then another. As if he were helping them up
To enter a streetcar, and not eternity.

A third before he dropped her put her arms
Around his neck and kissed him. Then he held
Her into space, and dropped her. Almost at once

He stepped to the sill himself, his jacket flared
And fluttered up from his shirt as he came down,
Air filling up the legs of his gray trousers –

Like Hart Crane's Bedlamite, 'shrill shirt ballooning.'
Wonderful how the pattern matches perfectly
Across the placket and over the twin bar-tacked

Corners of both pockets, like a strict rhyme
Or a major chord. Prints, plaids, checks,
Houndstooth, Tattersall, Madras. The clan tartans

Invented by mill-owners inspired by the hoax of Ossian,
To control their savage Scottish workers, tamed
By a fabricated heraldry: MacGregor,

Bailey, MacMartin. The kilt, devised for workers
To wear among the dusty clattering looms.
Weavers, carders, spinners. The loader,

The docker, the navvy. The planter, the picker, the sorter
Sweating at her machine in a litter of cotton
As slaves in calico headrags sweated in fields:

George Herbert, your descendant is a Black
Lady in South Carolina, her name is Irma
And she inspected my shirt. Its color and fit

And feel and its clean smell have satisfied
Both her and me. We have culled its cost and quality
Down to the buttons of simulated bone,

The buttonholes, the sizing, the facing, the characters
Printed in black on neckband and tail. The shape,
The label, the labor, the color, the shade. The shirt.

The fire at the Triangle Shirtwaist Factory in New York on 25 March 1911 was one of the deadliest industrial disasters in American history. It has been widely felt that the fifth to eighth tercets uncannily anticipate scenes at the World Trade Center on 11 September 2001. The hoax of Ossian was the publication by James Macpherson (1736–96) of a cycle of rhapsodic texts falsely purporting to be translations from the Gaelic of an author named Ossian.

1990

Parenthood

GEOFFREY LEHMANN

I have held what I hoped would become the best minds of a
   generation
Over the gutter outside an Italian coffee shop watching the small
Warm urine splatter on the asphalt – impatient to rejoin
An almond torta and a capuccino at a formica table.
I have been a single parent with three children at a Chinese
   restaurant
The eldest five years old and each in turn demanding
My company as they fussed in toilets and my pork saté went
   cold.
They rarely went all at once; each child required an individual
Moment of inspiration – and when their toilet pilgrimage was
   ended
I have tried to eat the remnants of my meal with twisting
   children
Beneath the table, screaming and grabbing in a scrimmage.
I have been wiping clean the fold between young buttocks as a
   pizza
I hoped to finish was cleared from a red and white checked
   table cloth.
I have been pouring wine for women I was hoping to impress
When a daughter ran for help through guests urgently holding
   out
Her gift, a potty, which I took with the same courtesy
As she gave it, grateful to dispose of its contents so simply
In a flurry of water released by the pushing of a button.
I have been butted by heads which have told me to go away and
   I have done so,
My mouth has been wrenched by small hands wanting to reach
   down to my tonsils
As I lay in bed on Sunday mornings and the sun shone through
   the slats

Of dusty blinds. I have helpfully carried dilly-dalliers up steps
Who indignantly ran straight down and walked up by
  themselves.
My arms have become exhausted, bouncing young animals until
  they fell asleep
In my lap listening to Buxtehude. 'Too cold,' I have been told,
As I handed a piece of fruit from the refrigerator, and for weeks
  had to warm
Refrigerated apples in the microwave so milk teeth cutting green
Carbohydrate did not chill. I have pleasurably smacked small
  bottoms
Which have climbed up and arched themselves on my lap
  wanting the report
And tingle of my palm. I have known large round heads that
  bumped
And rubbed themselves against my forehead, and affectionate
  noses
That loved to displace inconvenient snot from themselves onto
  me.
The demands of their bodies have taken me to unfamiliar
  geographies.
I have explored the white tiles and stainless steel benches of
  restaurant kitchens
And guided short legs across rinsed floors smelling of detergent
Past men in white with heads lowered and cleavers dissecting
  and assembling
Mounds of sparkling pink flesh – and located the remote dark
  shrine
Of a toilet behind boxes of coarse green vegetables and long
  white radishes.
I have badgered half-asleep children along backstreets at night,
  carrying
Whom I could to my van. I have stumbled with them sleeping
  in my arms
Up concrete steps on winter nights after eating in Greek
  restaurants,
Counting each body, then slamming the door of my van and
  taking

My own body, the last of my tasks, to a cold bed free of
    arguments.
I have lived in the extreme latitudes of child rearing, the blizzard
Of the temper tantrum and my own not always wise or
    honourable response,
The midnight sun of the child calling for attention late at night,
And have longed for the white courtyards and mediterranean
    calm of middle age.
Now these small bodies are becoming civilised people claiming
    they are not
Ashamed of a parent's overgrown garden and unpainted ceilings
Which a new arrival, with an infant's forthrightness, complains
    are 'old'.
And the father of this tribe sleeps in a bed which is warm with
    arguments.
Their bones elongate and put on weight and they draw away
    into space.
Their faces lengthen with responsibility and their own concerns.
I could clutch as they recede and fret for the push of miniature
    persons.
And claim them as children of my flesh – but my own body is
    where I must live.

1990

Bone Scan

◄◦►

GWEN HARWOOD

Thou hast searched me and known me.
Thou knowest my downsitting and mine uprising.

Psalm 139

In the twinkling of an eye,
in a moment, all is changed:
on a small radiant screen
(honeydew melon green)
are my scintillating bones.
Still in my flesh I see
the God who goes with me
glowing with radioactive
isotopes. This is what he
at last allows a mortal
eye to behold: the grand
supporting frame complete
(but for the wisdom teeth),
the friend who lives beneath
appearances, alive
with light. Each glittering bone
assures me: you are known.

1990

When I Grow Up

HUGO WILLIAMS

When I grow up I want to have a bad leg.
I want to limp down the street I live in
Without knowing where I am. I want the disease
where you put your hand on your hip
and lean forward slightly, groaning to yourself.

If a little boy asks me the way
I'll try and touch him between the legs.
What a dirty old man I'm going to be when I grow up!
What shall we do with me?

I promise I'll be good
if you let me fall over in the street
and lie there calling like a baby bird. Please,
nobody come. I'm perfectly all right. I like it here.

I wonder would it be possible
to get me into a National Health Hospice
somewhere in Manchester?
I'll stand in the middle of my cubicle
holding onto a piece of string for safety,
shaking like a leaf at the thought of my suitcase.

I'd certainly like to have a nervous tic
so I can purse my lips up all the time
like Cecil Beaton. Can I be completely bald, please?
I love the smell of old pee.
Why can't I smell like that?

When I grow up I want a thin piece of steel
inserted into my penis for some reason.
Nobody's to tell me why it's there. I want to guess!
Tell me, is that a bottle of old Burgundy
under my bed? I never can tell
if I feel randy any more, can you?

I think it's only fair that I should be allowed
to cough up a bit of blood when I feel like it.
My daughter will bring me a special air cushion
to hold me upright and I'll watch
in baffled admiration as she blows it up for me.

Here's my list: nappies, story books, munchies,
something else. What was the other thing?
I can't remember exactly,
but when I grow up I'll know. When I grow up
I'll pluck at my bedclothes to collect lost thoughts.
I'll roll them into balls and swallow them.

Sir Cecil Beaton (1904–80) was a celebrated photographer and designer.

1991

Living with the Doctor

MICHAEL LASKEY

Once a week I suppose, like a white
wash or my cauliflower bake,
somebody living here dies;

and even if you don't go,
if it's not your day on call
or if you're away, you'll know

in the end: the others will usually
say or someone'll send you a form
if it happens in hospital.

Sometimes you tell me, name names
you think may ring bells for me – Elsie
Fairweather, old Billy Sore –

and sometimes you don't: you come in
bearing dry clothes from the line
which you fold while I'm dishing up lunch.

But on days you need to make sense
of an accident or to relax
the grip of a grief, then we speak

of who and how, what you could do
to help. We've had to develop
a voice that can cope with death

properly, yet fit it in
over our bowls of soup,
before we're summoned to watch

Jack's magic or unsnarl Ben's maths.
Privileged knowledge for me –
a broadening, a warning –

but for you I'm not so sure
this morning, finding your clothes
in a heap on the bathroom floor

and knowing you must have been out
on a call in the night. The jabbing
phone; your questions; our duvet

closing behind you; your footsteps:
I slept through them all, insensible
even to your shivering return.

1991

Mass for the Middle-Aged

PETER GOLDSWORTHY

1. Lacrimosa

Suddenly breakfast is over
and all the years before,
and my dog is dead,
and my children grown old.
It all seems so overnight,
like catching a death of something
or preferring Mozart:
the turning world slips
another ratchet-tooth,
and I awake, alarmed.
For the first time
regrets outnumber dreams.
To have been more useful.
To have fed the hungry
or persuaded the damned.
There was also that night
in the backseat at the Drive-in:
if only I had known.

2. Confutatis

Slowly the future grows cold,
the best water spills
over the edge, displaced,
the fear of death
becomes the longing for death,
the only sure resolution.

3. Libera Me

Deliver me, Lord, from the threat
of heaven, from becoming the angel
who is not me, who smiles
faintly, fondly

before shrugging me off
like some stiff, quaint pupal case:
the battered leather jacket of the flesh,
evidence of misspent youth.

Grant me, Lord, this last request:
to wear bikie colours in heaven,
a grub among the butterflies.
And this: to take all memories with me,

all memories that *are* me,
intact, seized first
like snapshot albums
from a burning house.

Answer, Lord, these prayers,
for I would rather
be nothing
than improved.

4. In Paradisum

With any luck heaven will be much
like here, now, on a good day: pleasant,
but not too, its joys unsaturated, its lusts
remaining, fractionally, lusts.
I see a kind of Swiss Patent Office
with time to think, and skylights.
Somewhere music teases, distant
as Latin, and the volumes on the shelves
are always one page too slim.
As promised, there will be no pain:
each bare nerve-end rewired instead
for tickle. At meal-times I will rise
from my small exquisite portions,
still hungry, just, and mildly restless,
forever.

'Lacrimosa' means 'weeping'; 'Confutatis' usually occurs in the phrase *confutatis maledictis*, or 'when the damned are confounded'; 'Libera me' means 'deliver me'; 'In Paradisum' means 'into paradise'. All four expressions occur in the Latin requiem mass.

1991

Kent
<o>
JOHN FULLER

Old men coming up to bowl remember
Other old men who in their turn remembered
Things that were hardly worth remembering
Through long still nights in Ashford, Faversham,
Sevenoaks and Tunbridge Wells and Westerham
Where even now the fields still smell of beer.

1991

Jalopy: The End of Love

BILL MANHIRE

Do you drive an old car?
Or a jalopy?
Now where could that word come from?

Somewhere in the world
someone you know
must be driving a jalopy.

As for you, one day you are out
on a country road
miles from the sort of place

that might be miles from anywhere
and your car breaks down.
Well, it's an old car.

And somewhere in the world
someone you used to love
has that ancient photograph of you

sitting behind the wheel
high on the Coromandel.
It's a jalopy.

Just at the moment though
it doesn't want to start.
Whatever it is, it's finished.

1991

white lady
a street name for cocaine

LUCILLE CLIFTON

Wants my son
wants my niece
wants josie's daughter
holds them hard
and close as slavery
what will it cost
to keep our children
what will it cost
to buy them back.

white lady
says i want you
whispers
let me be your lover
whispers
run me through your
fingers
feel me smell me taste me
love me
nobody understands you like
white lady

white lady
you have chained our sons
in the basement
of the big house
white lady

you have walked our daughters
out into the streets
white lady
what do we have to pay
to repossess our children
white lady

what do we have to owe
to own our own at last

1991

Cigarettes
◄◦►

JOHN ASH

Problems of translation are, perhaps, not so great
between languages as between different versions
of the same language. Why, for example, does
'fag' mean homosexual in America, when,
in England, it means cigarette? Does this imply
that those who first observed the phenomenon
of smoking in the New World were homosexual?
This would cause some consternation on Columbus Day,
and, in all likelihood, the assumption is unjustified,
since Columbus and his crew were not English-speakers.
Yet, if we dismiss the idea of happy crowds of
homosexual Spanish or Italian mariners
returning to Europe with cigarettes in hand,
eager to introduce this new pleasure to their lovers,
we should perhaps concede that there is some connection
between the two ideas. It was Oscar Wilde, after all,
who described smoking as 'the perfect pleasure, because' –
he opined – 'it always leaves one unsatisfied.'
It is clear from this that he was thinking of sexual pleasure,
of the working-class youths with whom he so recklessly
    dined
in fashionable restaurants of the eighteen-nineties.
A cigarette is like a passion in that it is inhaled deeply
and seems to fill all the empty spaces of the body,
until, of course, it burns down, and is put out amid
the shells of pistachio nuts, or whatever trash
may be at hand, and the passion may leave traces
that in time will grow malignant: he who has taken pleasure
may die many years after in the room of an anonymous
hotel or hospital, under the blank gaze of a washstand,
a bad painting or an empty vase, having forgotten entirely
the moment that announced the commencement

of his dying. And perhaps he will not understand:
it is another false translation, like someone stumbling over
the word for cigarette in a new and intolerable language.

1991

Love Poem

◄○►

JOHN FORBES

Spent tracer flecks Baghdad's
bright video game sky

as I curl up with the war
in lieu of you, whose letter

lets me know my poems show
how unhappy I can be. Perhaps.

But what they don't show, until
now, is how at ease I can be

with military technology: e.g.
matching their *feu d'esprit* I classify

the sounds of the Iraqi AA – the
thump of the 85 mil, the throaty

chatter of the quad ZSU 23.
Our precision guided weapons

make the horizon flash & glow
but nothing I can do makes you

want me. Instead I watch the west
do what the west does best

& know, obscurely, as I go to bed
all this is being staged for me.

The Gulf War of 1991 was triggered by the Iraqi invasion of Kuwait on 2 August 1990 and, after a protracted period of diplomacy and military build-up, began on 17 January with heavy aerial bombardment of Iraq by the United Nations coalition forces. The Iraqi anti-aircraft weaponry referred to in the poem was Soviet-made. The French words *feu d'esprit* translate literally as 'fire of spirit' and pun on the more familiar *'jeu d'esprit'*.

1991

Misnomer

<o>

DENISE LEVERTOV

They speak of the art of war,
but the arts
draw their light from the soul's well,
and warfare
dries up the soul and draws its power
from a dark and burning wasteland.
When Leonardo
set his genius to devising
machines of destruction he was not
acting in the service of art,
he was suspending
the life of art
over an abyss,
as if one were to hold
a living child out of an airplane window
at thirty-thousand feet.

Leonardo is the Italian artist and inventor Leonardo da Vinci (1452–1519).

1991

I'r Hen Iaith A'i Chaneuon
───────◄○►───────
IAN DUHIG

If the tongue spoke only the mind's truth,
there wouldn't be any neighbours
                              The Red Book of Hergest

When I go down to Wales for the long bank holiday
to visit my wife's grandfather, who is teetotal,
who is a non-smoker, who does not approve
of anyone who is not teetotal and a non-smoker,
when I go down to Wales for the long. long bank holiday
with my second wife to visit her grandfather,
who deserted Methodism for the Red Flag,
who won't hear a word against Stalin,
who despite my oft-professed socialism
secretly believes I am still with the Pope's legions,
receiving coded telegrams from the Vatican
specifying the dates, times and positions I should adopt
for political activity and sexual activity,
who in his ninetieth year took against boxing,
which was the only thing I could ever talk to him about,
when I visit my second wife's surviving grandfather,
and when he listens to the football results in Welsh,
I will sometimes slip out to the pub.

I will sometimes slip out to the pub
and drink pint upon pint of that bilious whey
they serve there, where the muzak will invariably be
'The Best of the Rhosllannerchrugog Male Voice Choir'
and I will get trapped by some brain donor from up the
    valley
who will really talk about 'the language so strong and so
    beautiful
that has grown out of the ageless mountains,

that speech of wondrous beauty that our fathers wrought',
who will chant to me in Welsh his epileptic verses
about Gruffydd ap Llywelyn and Dafydd ap Llywelyn,
and who will give me two solid hours of slaver
because I don't speak Irish, and who will then bring up
    religion,
then I will tell him I know one Irish prayer about a Welsh
    king
on that very subject, and I will recite for him as follows:
'Fág uaim do eaglais ghallda
Is do chreideamh gan bonn gan bhrí,
Mar gurb é is cloch bonn dóibh
Magairle Anraoi Rí.' 'Beautiful,
he will say, as they all do, 'It sounds quite beautiful.'

The title is Welsh and means 'To The Old Tongue and its Songs'. The Irish quat-
rain is by Antoine Ó Reachtabhra, translating roughly as "Away with your foreign
religion/ And your baseless, meaningless faith/For the only rock it is built upon/
Is the bollocks of King Henry the Eighth."

1991

£££££

JACKIE KAY

There was no bread so she told a story
until the story told another story
until all the People gathered eating
fiction like hot French bread, melted butter.

This was the decade when people
were given ansamachines for falling into debt,
when between them they owed £47 billion.
Bankers sat counting the numbers
all this gold from plastic –
They sang their tune at the Stock Exchange,

It went Tra la la la la la laughing.

One day when the wind was waltzing
so fast it stole people's hats
and punched dustbins in the gut
the people gathered to burn their plastic.
The smell was so strong it made them collectively faint.
A smart dressed man from Natwest
and another from the Midland
arrived with masks and put new pieces of plastic
in their pockets whilst they slept.

1992

Gooseberry Season

‹◇›

SIMON ARMITAGE

Which reminds me. He appeared
at noon, asking for water. He'd walked from town
after losing his job, leaving a note for his wife and his
    brother
and locking his dog in the coal bunker.
We made him a bed

and he slept till Monday.
A week went by and he hung up his coat.
Then a month, and not a stroke of work, a word of thanks,
a farthing of rent or a sign of him leaving.
One evening he mentioned a recipe

for smooth, seedless gooseberry sorbet
but by then I was tired of him: taking pocket money
from my boy at cards, sucking up to my wife and on his
    last night
sizing up my daughter. He was smoking my pipe
as we stirred his supper.

Where does the hand become the wrist?
Where does the neck become the shoulder. The watershed
and then the weight, whatever turns up and tips us over
    that razor's edge
between something and nothing, between
one and the other.

I could have told him this
but didn't bother. We ran him a bath
and held him under, dried him off and dressed him
and loaded him into the back of the pick-up.
Then we drove without headlights

to the county boundary,
dropped the tailgate, and after my boy
had been through his pockets we dragged him like a
    mattress
across the meadow and on the count of four
threw him over the border.

This is not general knowledge, except
in gooseberry season, which reminds me, and at the table
I have been known to raise an eyebrow, or scoop the
    sorbet
into five equal portions, for the hell of it.
I mention this for a good reason.

1992

Sighting the Slave Ship

PAULINE STAINER

We came to unexpected latitudes –
sighted the slave ship
during divine service
on deck.

In earlier dog-days
we had made landfall
between forests of sandalwood,
taken on salt, falcons and sulphur.

What haunted us later
was not the cool dispensing
of sacrament
in the burnished doldrums

but something more exotic –
that sense
of a slight shift of cargo
while becalmed.

1992

Helene and Heloise

<o>

GLYN MAXWELL

So swim in the embassy pool in a tinkling breeze
The sisters, *mes cousines*, they are blonde-haired
   Helene and Heloise,
One for the fifth time up to the diving board,
The other, in her quiet shut-eye sidestroke
Slowly away from me though I sip and look.

From in the palace of shades, inscrutable, cool,
I watch exactly what I want to watch
   From by this swimming pool,
Helene's shimmer and moss of a costume, each
Soaking pony-tailing of the dark
And light mane of the littler one as they walk;

And the splash that bottles my whole life to today,
The spray fanning to dry on the porous sides,
   What these breathtakers say
In their, which is my, language but their words:
These are the shots the sun could fire and fires,
Is paid and drapes across the stretching years.

Now Heloise will dive, the delicate slimmer,
Calling Helene to turn who turns to see
   One disappearing swimmer
Only and nods, leans languorously away
To prop on the sides before me and cup her wet
Face before me near where I'd pictured it.

I was about to say I barely know them. –
I turn away because and hear of course
   Her push away. I see them
In my rose grotto of thought, and it's not a guess,
How they are, out of the water, out
In the International School they lie about,

What they can buy in the town, or the only quarters
Blondes can be seen alighting in, and only
   As guided shaded daughters
Into an acre of golden shop. 'Lonely?'
Who told me this had told me: 'They have no lives.
They will be children. Then they will be wives.'

Helene shrieks and is sorry – I don't think – my
Ankles cool with the splash of her sister's dive:
   I wave and smile and sigh.
Thus the happiest falling man alive,
And twenty-five, and the wetness and the brown
Hairs of my shin can agree, and I settle down.

'Already the eldest – suddenly – the problems.
The other draws, writes things.' I had heard
   Staccato horrid tantrums
Between earshot and the doorbell, held and read
Heloise's letters in chancery
Script to her dead grandmother, to me,

To nobody. They have a mother and father,
And love the largest pandas in the whole
   World of Toys. The other
Sister rang from Italy and was well,
But wouldn't come this time. 'She'll never come.
She has a home. They do not have a home.'

Stretching out in her shiny gold from the pool,
Heloise swivels, and sits and kicks
   Then reaches back to towel
Her skinny shoulders tanned in a U of lux-
Uriant material. Helene
Goes slowly to the board, and hops again

Into the dazzle and splosh and the quiet. Say,
Two, three miles from here there are heaps of what,
   Living things, decay,
The blind and inoculated dead, and a squad
Of infuriated coldly eyeing sons
Kicking the screaming oath out of anyone's.

Cauchemar. – We will be clear if of course apart,
To London again me, they to their next
   Exotic important spot,
Their chink and pace of Gloucestershire, Surrey, fixed
Into the jungles, ports or the petrol deserts.
I try but don't see another of these visits;

As I see Helene drying, Heloise dry,
The dark unavoidable servant seeming to have
   Some urgency today
And my book blank in my hands. What I can love
I love encircled, trapped and I love free.
That happens to, and happens to be, me,

But this is something else. Outside the fence,
It could – it's the opposite – be a paradise
   Peopled with innocents,
Each endowed with a light inimitable voice,
Fruit abundant, guns like dragons and giants
Disbelieved, sheer tolerance a science –

Still, I'd think of Helene, of Heloise
Moving harmless, shieldless into a dull
   And dangerous hot breeze,
With nothing but hopes to please, delight, fulfil
Some male as desperate and as foul as this is,
Who'd not hurt them for all their limited kisses.

1993

How to Talk

<o>

ANDREW JOHNSTON

It was on the ferris wheel
I was introduced to

the art of conversation.
She was thirteen,

I was fourteen;
many times we passed the point where we'd climbed on.

How high it is, up here, she said
when we were near the top.

I could see my name
on the tip of her tongue.

1993

Timur the Lame

CHARLES BOYLE

A man with a limp came towards me,
begging money for liquor – spoke of cairns
built of skulls, of the wind off the steppes
on the night before battle
and the evils of cholesterol.

Some of this, I thought, he must be making up.
Besides, what was I doing here,
talking with a dead Mongol warrior,
in the middle of the life that was mine?

At the end of the street, some camels
grazing, the air mottled with flies
above ribbons of goat flesh . . .
Even the tourists looked sick.
Even the women, that day, were not untouched.

He said: You think a life
has a beginning, middle and end?
Then he emptied his pockets
and showed me the eyes of Hafiz.

Timur the Lame is also known to us as Tamerlane or Tamburlaine (1336–1405),
the central Asian conqueror who sought to restore the Mongol empire. Hafiz is
the great fourteenth-century Persian poet.

1993

A Game of Bowls

◄◦►

DOUGLAS DUNN

Hard to believe they were children once
Or in certain moods a lyrical triteness
Passes across the mind watching old men
Watching a game of bowls played by younger
Familiars on a day of green breezes.

That man's brother is named on the war memorial.
Two out of five are widowers and one
Went away and came back after forty years.
There were six but last week a man died
Reciting his nine-times table, sticking at

Nine-times-nine in an innumerate
Last few minutes of pillows and pain-killers.
Grandchildren rarely see them like this,
At their loose ends, one with a dog, another
Leaving his bench without a cheerio.

Or in certain moods it feels like half-a-tune
You can't put a name to, a spade's clink
On a stone, when you stand still, listening
To your ears and silence, then unseen children
Shouting from ten yards and many years away.

1993

Untitled

<o>

IMTIAZ DHARKER

I wouldn't say I live in this city.
Every day it comes
and collides with me.
I had begun to see
that this daily accident
had its funny side.
Years after I arrived
and after several attempts to leave
I decided to unpack my bags.

The city and I had both survived.
Or so we thought.

This morning I took a breath
of city air
and smelt our death.

This is not an abstraction.
I am trying to tell the truth
in simple words.
At night I turn out of sleep
into the smoke of reality.
It's not Bombay that burns,
but this specific child
screaming behind a bolted door;
this particular man on fire
trapped inside his locked car.

I wish these were imagined things.
I wish I could put them
safely in another poem,
reconcile them with this
paper and this pen
so I could never smell the burning
or hear the breaking glass again.

On 12 March 1993, thirteen coordinated bomb explosions occurred in Bombay (Mumbai), killing two hundred and fifty-seven people.

1993

The Scale of Intensity

DON PATERSON

1) Not felt. Smoke still rises vertically. In sensitive individuals, déjà vu, mild amnesia. Sea like a mirror.

2) Detected by persons at rest or favourably placed, i.e. in upper floors, hammocks, cathedrals etc. Leaves rustle.

3) Light sleepers wake. Glasses chink. Hairpins, paperclips display slight magnetic properties. Irritability. Vibration like passing of light trucks.

4) Small bells ring. Small increase in surface tension and viscosity of certain liquids. Domestic violence. Furniture overturned.

5) Heavy sleepers wake. Public demonstrations. Large flags fly. Vibration like passing of heavy trucks.

6) Large bells ring. Bookburning. Aurora visible in daylight hours. Unprovoked assaults on strangers. Glassware broken. Loose tiles fly from roof.

7) Weak chimneys broken off at roofline. Waves on small ponds, water turbid with mud. Unprovoked assaults on neighbours. Large static charges built up on windows, mirrors, television screens.

8) Perceptible increase in weight of stationary objects: books, cups, pens heavy to lift. Fall of stucco and some masonry. Systematic rape of women and young girls. Sand craters. Cracks in wet ground.

9) Small trees uprooted. Bathwater drains in reverse vortex. Wholesale slaughter of religious and ethnic minorities. Conspicuous cracks in ground. Damage to reservoirs and underground pipelines.

10) Large trees uprooted. Measurable tide in puddles, teacups, etc. Torture and rape of small children. Irreparable damage to foundations. Rails bend. Sand shifts horizontally on beaches.

11) Standing impossible. Widespread self-mutilation. Corposant visible on pylons, lampposts, metal railings. Most bridges destroyed.

12) Damage total. Movement of hour hand perceptible. Large rock masses displaced. Sea white.

1994

Developments from the Grave
STEVE CHIMOMBO

1

We have come full circle,
it seems: burying our dead
right in the homestead now,
on the sites the living had built.

We no longer bury our corpses
over there and away from us,
overhung by weeping *nkbadzi* trees
just as the missionaries advised us.

We have come full circle,
at last: burying our dead
deep in the soil beneath us;
we climb over the mounds daily.

We no longer hang the cadavers
high in the trees away from scavengers:
hyenas, ants, beaks and talons;
just as the colonials instructed us.

2

We brought the dead to the homestead,
revived them as *ndondocha*,
cut off their tongues and tamed them
to live in our granaries for ever.

Bumper harvests come out of them
and we know who keeps the most,
organizing them into one task force
to labour in the tobacco, tea and cotton estates.

We unearthed the youth for *msendawana*
to skin them for their precious leather
and made purses out of the tender skin
for the most potent charm of them all.

We know who has the largest purse
accumulating wealth, and more.
Out of the mounds of our youth
sprout palaces, fleets and monuments.

3

Development did not catch us
by surprise, asleep or unprepared:
We knew about space exploration;
we had our own flying baskets.

The greenhouse effect is not news;
we know how to heat or cool the land:
Drought comes from a society on heat;
rain comes from a cooled nation.

But development came from the graves,
too full and closely packed to grow any more.
The protective *nkhadzi* trees fenced
each effort to force the grave boundaries.

We have now come full circle,
rightly so: living with our dead,
not only in *nsupa* or spirit houses
but in granaries, purses and coffins.

'*Ndondocha*' are zombies, and '*msendawana*' are purses made of human skin.

1994

Philip Larkin in New Orleans

ANTHONY THWAITE

Suppose he had come here, two days after Mardi Gras,
The wrong time. It would be raining
In sheets up from the Delta, the banquettes awash
And the gutters running with all the festival trash:
Laughing-gas capsules, confetti, a tinsel star,
Cheap beads, purple and golden and green,
Bottle-caps, condoms, masks. Somewhere too far,
Somewhere too foreign. He would be complaining
This wasn't the dream he had had, the dream-place he'd been –
Tapping his feet in a bar in Bourbon or Basin, the moan
Of riverboats drifting through the Vieux Carré
Mingling with a familiar saxophone,
And the girls stepping out on the streets at the end of the day.

His Crescent City is much further off,
A paradise where love and trumpets play
In tune, and out of time, beyond belief
In ordinary days or usual grief,
A place in which all doubt is put away.
Tonight I caught his authentic other note,
Fixed, finite, steady in its monotone,
As I passed an old black with a graveyard cough,
An empty bottle, a funereal hat,
Who muttered something as he cleared his throat,
Trembled, and batted off the rain, and spat
Somewhere between Decatur and Wilk Row,
His hopes expelled with an enormous no.

1994

Early Warning

JOHN LEVETT

If you were a nuclear superpower
And I were a buffer state
I'd cling like dirt to your arable skirt
Where the Cruise proliferate,
And my Early Warning system
Would mesh with the nerve ends of yours
And your arms would keep the peace while I sleep
And colonize the stars;
I would launder inflationary taxes
And absorb your acid rain
Though each river and stream might audibly scream
With the ecological pain.

If you were an overgrown continent
And I were a bit on the side
I would love to explore your coastal floor
And the plains where your prairies ride.
I would hoover your latest missiles
And polish the stainless steel screens
Where titanium fits like silicone tits
On the tops of your submarines;
And at the United Nations,
Alone in the hullabaloo,
Despite the disgrace and the loss of face
I would always vote for you.

Or if I were the dominant planet
And you were my satellite
I would let you pass through my volatile gas
And spin you through the night:
I would catch and recycle your atoms
And cherish your orbit and shape

The darkened half of your crooked path
To speed up your escape,
And then dance you across the heavens
And blister the firmament
And the stars would uncross at whatever the cost
Until our love was spent.

If I were as rich as you're pretty
Or you were as small as I'm poor
Our hands might have stopped the glandular clock
And the hormonal calendar
Where the season was always autumn
And the weather in bad repair,
Trust hung by a thread and the lights went dead
In your eyes and your blinding hair
As I looked for a private conclusion
Or an easier way to choke
On the gorgeous mess of its loveliness
Before the morning broke.

1995

A KISS IN SPACE

◄◦►

MARY JO SALTER

That the picture
in *The Times* is a blur
is itself an accuracy. Where
this has happened is so remote
that clarity would misrepresent
not only distance but our feeling
about distance: just as
the first listeners at the telephone
were somehow reassured to hear
static that interfered with hearing
(funny word, *static*, that conveys
the atom's restlessness), we're
not even now – at the far end
of the century – entirely ready
to look to satellites for mere

resolution. When the *Mir*
invited the first American
astronaut to swim in the pool
of knowledge with Russians, he floated
exactly as he would have in space
stations of our own: no lane
to stay in, no line to determine
the deep end, Norman Thagard
hovered on the ceiling something
like an angel in a painting
(but done without the hard
outlines of Botticelli; more
like a seraph's sonogram),
and turned to Yelena Kondakova
as his cheek received her kiss.

          And in this
        too the blur made sense: a kiss
      so grave but gravity-free, untouched
by Eros but nevertheless
      out of the usual orbit, must
make a heart shift focus. The very
      grounding in culture (they gave him bread
and salt, as Grandmother would a guest
      at her dacha; and hung the Stars
and Stripes in a stiff crumple
      because it would not fall), the very
Russianness of the bear hugs was
      dizzily universal: for who
knows how to signal anything
      new without a ritual?

          Not the kitchen-table
        reader (child of the Cold War,
      of 3 x 5 cards, carbon copies,
and the manila folder), who takes a pair
      of scissors — as we do when the size
of some idea surprises — and clips
      this one into a rectangle
much like her piece of toast. There:
      it's saved, to think of later.
Yet it would be unfair
      to leave her looking smug; barely
a teenager when she watched, on
      her snowy TV screen, a man
seeming to walk on the moon, she's
      learned that some detail —

Virtual Reality or e-mail,
something inexplicable and
unnatural – is always cropping up
for incorporation in what's human.
What ought to make it manageable,
and doesn't quite, is the thought
of humans devising it. She'll
remember Norman Thagard in June,
when the *Mir* (meaning Peace: but how
imagine this without agitation?)
docks with the *Atlantis* (meaning
the island Plato mentioned first
and which, like him, did not disappear
without a splash), to shuttle
the traveler back home – or

to whatever Earth has become.

Mir was the Soviet Russian space station in orbit around the Earth from 1986
to 2001. NASA scientist Norman Thagard (born 1943) was the first American
astronaut to serve aboard a Russian space mission, on *Mir* in 1995. Yelena Konda-
kova (born 1957) was the third Russian woman cosmonaut to serve on a space
mission. The *Atlantis* space shuttle first flew in 1985 and was still operational
when this note was written, though with decommissioning scheduled for 2011.
Plato's references to Atlantis, referred to by Salter in her poem, occur in the
Timaeus and *Critias*. The space shuttle's naming was intended by NASA to recall
an oceanographic research ship that served in the second and third quarters of
the twentieth century.

1995

God's Christ Theory
◄◊►

ANNE CARSON

God had no emotions but wished temporarily
to move in man's mind
as if He did: Christ.

Not passion but compassion.
Com – means 'with.'
What kind of withness would that be?

Translate it.
I have a friend named Jesus
from Mexico.

His father and grandfather are called Jesus too.
They account me a fool with my questions about salvation.
They say they are saving to move to Los Angeles.

1995

A Taste

W. S. MERWIN

When the first summer there was ending more than half
   my life ago Mentières with his strawberry nose
and features to match and his eyes stitched down inside
   them
    in the shade of his black-vizored cap which proclaimed
to the world that he had taken his retirement
    not from the land but from the railroad Mentières with
    his
leer and his vest stretched over his large protuberance
    and his walk like a barrel neither full nor empty
he whom nobody trusted thereabouts laying their
    fingers beside their noses Mentières from elsewhere
the custodian of keys who had no land of his own
    so had been using the garden to grow his potatoes in
and had been picking up the plums from under the trees
    to make his own plum as he put it meaning of course
clear alcohol the water of life but it was
    too hard for him to bend any more in his striped
trousers to hoe the furrows and grope for the plums
    and he would not be doing it another year
so he brought back the big keys and with them a couple
    of
    old corked bottles from the year before and another
already opened for tasting the pure stuff the essence
    of plum to breathe it down your nose
and out like watching your breath on a winter day
    that was what kept them warm in the trenches he told
    me
a drop of that in your coffee he said holding up
    a thick finger and when his wife fell sick everyone
said they were sorry for her and when she died they said
    they were sorry for the daughter who never married

and looked after him he sat on the front step watching
    the road and waving to anyone but when he was gone
nobody seemed to notice the cork is beginning
    to crumble but the taste is the same as it was
the pure plum of the year before that has no color

1995

Her Kiss

◆

KEVIN HART

She said, 'I kissed another boy today.'
Well, that was thirty years ago, and I
Thought then, 'In time it will not hurt at all',

Imagining an afternoon with clouds
Somehow at peace in their high tiers of air,
An older man who goes about his work

Not worried much by silly girls, or who
He was on evenings when thunderstorms
Shook a strange sky until there was no light.

I look outside my office at the clouds
On the first day of summer: endless blue
Parades with white for me, and only me.

So where is 1968 these days?
That older man would know. Fool that I am,
I pick a wound until it starts to bleed.

1995

The Fire in the Forty-four
<o>

JOHN KINSELLA

We're broke this week so my brother
collects aluminium cans and the copper
insides of old hot-water systems –
you need sacks of aluminium
cans to make even a few bucks
but a few kilos of copper or brass knocks
the price right up. It's dusk
as we approach the metalman behind his sooty mask,
storm clouds tinged crimson
and sitting low over his sheet-iron
shed, an almost virulent fire
sparking up in the pit of a forty-four
gallon drum. His sons pour
acetylene into the wounded guts
of a truck, like lightning putting to rights
damage done in some long past storm.
Outside a load of scrap looks almost warm
as it awaits the furnaces of the city.
Our metal is hooked in sacks to scales painfully
close to the fury of the drum.
To the pain of heat the metalman seems numb.
Though as he swings the singed sacks aside
before they burst into flame I note him hide
a softness behind his gauntlets of calluses,
the delicate timing, the dexterity as he tallies
payment rapidly on bone-black fingers.
A flurry of rain hisses deep in the drum
and spits back at the storm.
The metalman speaks in tongues to his vulcan

sons, who, deep in their alchemy, acknowledge only
with jets of flame. Quickly
he pays out and I follow my brother as he turns
away from the shed's darkening outline.

The word 'vulcan', late in the poem, reminds us that the scene we have read bears
a strong resemblance to descriptions and depictions of the smithy of the Roman
god of fire, Vulcan.

1995

Going

AUGUST KLEINZAHLER

The old people are dying,
they're falling apart piece by piece
like vintage Studebakers,
but the docs keep pumping diuretics and Prednisone
into them, doing valve jobs,
so it's slow, terribly slow.

They're talking tumor,
they're talking colon and biopsy
over biscuit tortoni and tea.
                              The doctors
are butchers, and as for the kids –
selfish insensitive little shits.

Look at Sinatra and Reagan,
dewlaps trembling in the wee small hours,
glued to *I Love Lucy* reruns
as the Secret Service men doze.
They own cliffs and enormous stretches
of desert, those two –
shopping centers, distilleries.

Lucy is dead, boys, give it up:
Desi, the Duke and Ava,
dust;
     even little Sammy's
checked out.

All the great ones, the class acts,
taking their bows
or history.

In this all-American vision of the old in a 'home', the options for obsession or even for identification are all afforded by show biz, from Duke Ellington, Ava Gardner and Sammy Davis Jr. to Frank Sinatra and Ronald Reagan and, of course, to Lucille Ball and Desi Arnaz in the Fifties television sitcom *I Love Lucy*, one of the most popular shows ever screened.

1995

Neighbours

ALAN JENKINS

When the rains come in Rwanda in a Tutsi village
and the topsoil's washed away, strange shoots
of fingers, toes, knees and elbows, jawbones,

push up from such wrong, unlikely roots
as have lain there since they were slaughtered –
the cowherd and the teacher and the sawbones

and their women and their children and their neighbours
(for unless you are a hermit in a mountain cavern
or a guru in a temple in the jungle, neighbours

are what you naturally, inevitably have,
to share your sunsets and the fruits of your labours),
all waiting quietly now for when they are watered,

when the rains come, in Rwanda, in a Tutsi village.

For three months, beginning in April 1994, deep tensions and resentments between the Hutu and Tutsi peoples of Rwanda erupted into violence on a genocidal scale. Estimates of the number of Tutsis massacred by organised Hutu killers vary between half a million and a million.

1996

One Ordinary Evening

◄◇►

VIRGINIA HAMILTON ADAIR

Lying entwined with you
on the long sofa

the hi-fi helping
Isolde to her climax

I was clipping
the coarse hairs

from your ears
and ruby nostrils

when you said, 'Music
for cutting nose wires'

and we shook so
the nailscissors nicked

your gentle neck
blood your blood

I cleansed the place
with my tongue

and we clung tight
pelted with Teutonic cries

till the player
lifted its little prick

from the groove
all arias over

leaving us
in post-Wagnerian sadness

later that year
you were dead

by your own hand
blood your blood

I have never understood
I will never understand

1996

A Letter from the Coast

————————◁◦▷————————

MARK DOTY

All afternoon the town readied for storm,
   men in the harbour shallows hauling in small boats
      that rise and fall on the tide. Pleasure,

one by our house is called. I didn't think
   the single man who tugged her in could manage
      alone, though he pushed her up high enough,

he must have hoped, to miss the evening's
   predicted weather: a huge freight of rain
      tumbling up the coast. There's another storm

in town, too, a veritable cyclone
   of gowns and wigs: men in dresses here for a week
      of living the dream of crossing over.

All afternoon they braved the avenue
   fronting the harbour, hats set against the wind,
      veils seedpearled with the first rain,

accessoried to the nines. The wardrobes
   in their rented rooms must glitter,
      opened at twilight when they dress

for the evening, sequin shimmer
   leaping out of the darkness . . . Their secret's
      visible here, public, as so many are,

and in that raw weather I loved
   the flash of red excess, the cocktail dress
      and fur hat, the sheer pleasure

of stockings and gloves.
   I'm writing to tell you this:
      what was left of the hurricane arrived by ten.

All night I heard, under the steep-pitched shallows
　　of our sleep, the shoulders of the sea flashing,
　　　　loaded, silvering with so much broken cargo:

shell and rusted metal, crabclaw and spine,
　　kelp and feathers and the horseshoe carapace,
　　　　and threading through it all the foghorns'

double harmony of warning, one note layered
　　just over and just after the other. *Safety*,
　　　　they said, or *shelter*, two inexact syllables

repeated precisely all night, glinting
　　through my dream the way the estuaries
　　　　shone before sun-up, endless

invitation and promise, till dawn
　　beat the whole harbour to pewter.
　　　　Pleasure was unmoved and burnished a cobalt

the exact shade of a mussel's hinge,
　　and every metal shone in the sea: platinum,
　　　　sterling, tarnished chrome.

The law of the tide is accumulation, *More*,
　　and our days here are layered detail,
　　　　the shore's grand mosaic of detritus:

tumbled beach glass, endless bits
　　of broken china, as if whole nineteenth-century
　　　　　　　　　　　　　　　　　　kitchens
　　went down in the harbour and lie scattered

at our feet, the tesserae of Byzantium.
　　Those syllables sounded all night,
　　　　their meaning neither completed nor exhausted.

What was it I meant to tell you?
　　All I meant to do this storm-rinsed morning,
　　　　which has gone brilliant and uncomplicated

as silk, that same watery sheen?
How the shore's a huge armoire
full of gowns, all its drawers packed

and gleaming? Something about pleasure
and excess: thousands of foamy veils,
a tidal wrack of emerald, glamour

of froth-decked, dashed pearl bits.
A million earrings rinsed in the dawn.
I wish you were here.

1996

What the Gypsies Told My Grandmother
While She Was Still a Young Girl

CHARLES SIMIC

War, illness and famine will make you their favorite
  grandchild.
You'll be like a blind person watching a silent movie.
You'll chop onions and pieces of your heart
  into the same hot skillet.
Your children will sleep in a suitcase tied with a rope.
Your husband will kiss your breasts every night
  as if they were two gravestones.

Already the crows are grooming themselves
  for you and your people.
Your oldest son will lie with flies on his lips
  without smiling or lifting his hand.
You'll envy every ant you meet in your life
  and every roadside weed.
Your body and soul will sit on separate stoops
  chewing the same piece of gum.

Little cutie, are you for sale? the devil will say.
The undertaker will buy a toy for your grandson.
Your mind will be a hornet's nest even on your deathbed.
You will pray to God but God will hang a sign
that He's not to be disturbed.
  Question no further, that's all I know.

1996

Two Dogs on a Pub Roof

◄◌►

CHRISTOPHER REID

There are two dogs on a pub roof.
One's called Garth, the other Rolf.
Both are loud – but don't think they're all mouth.
I've been watching them and it's my belief
that they've been posted there, not quite on earth,
as emissaries of some higher truth
it's our job to get to the bottom of,
if only we can sort out the pith from the guff.
Garth's bark's no ordinary *woof, woof*:
it's a full-throttle affair, like whooping-cough,
a racking hack that shakes him from scruff
to tail in hour-long binges of holding forth
on all manner of obsessive stuff,
from pigeons and planes to not getting enough
to eat and so being ready to bite your head off.
He's whipped up in a perpetual froth
of indignation on his own behalf.
Poof! Dwarf! Oaf! Filth!
These and suchlike are among his chief
forms of salutation – and he means you, guv!
His whole philosophy, his pennyworth,
is 'All's enemy that's not self'
(with the provisional exception of his brother Rolf).
It's no joke and you don't feel inclined to laugh.
Rolf's even more frightening: his *arf! arf!*
seems designed to tear the sky in half,
every utterance an ultimate expletive,
every one a barbed shaft
aimed accurately at your midriff
and transfixing you with impotent wrath.
You and him. It bothers you both.
The thing's reciprocal, a north-south

axis that skewers the two of you like love.
You're David and Goliath, Peter and the Wolf,
Robin Hood and his Sheriff, Mutt and Jeff –
any ding-donging duo from history or myth
that's come to stand as a hieroglyph
for eternal foedom, non-stop strife,
the old Manichean fisticuffs
without which there'd be no story, no life,
and the whole cycle of birth, breath,
scoff, boff, graft, grief and death
would amount to so much waste of puff.
You're spiritual partners, hand in glove,
you and Rolfie, you and Garth,
you and the two of them up on that roof,
barking and hopping, acting tough,
flinging their taunts across the gulf
of the entire neighbourhood: *You lot down beneath!*
You got a diabolical nerve!
Who gave you permission to breathe?
This is our gaff! This is our turf!
Don't even think of crossing our path,
if you happen to value what remains of your health!
One false move and we'll show you teeth . . .
And so on. Of course, that's only a rough
translation, but it will more or less serve,
being at least the gist of the riff
that bores you mad and drives you stiff
all day long. Night, too. Nights, they work shifts.
One sleeps, while the other faces the brave
task of keeping the moon at a safe
distance and making sure the stars behave.
Which is why there are two of them. If
you've begun to wonder. As you no doubt have.
Then sometimes they'll mount an all-night rave,
Garth dancing with Rolf, Rolf with Garth –
though there's nothing queer about these two psychopaths –
and you're the inevitable wallflower, on the shelf,
surplus to requirements. Only you can't stay aloof.

Like it or lump it, you're stuck in their groove.
The joint's jumping in every joist and lath
and nobody, but nobody, is going to leave.
You're as free an agent as the flame-fazed moth
that's in thrall, flamboyantly befuddled, and not fireproof.
You're party to the party, however loth.
You belong along. You're kin. You're kith.
You're living testimony to the preposition 'with'.
You're baby, bathwater and bath.
So don't dash out with your Kalashnikov
and hope to cut a definitive swathe
through the opposition. Don't throw that Molotov
cocktail. Put down that Swiss Army knife.
Stop spitting. Stop sputtering. Don't fluster. Don't faff.
And don't be so daft, naff, duff or uncouth
as to think you're calling anyone's bluff –
let alone that of the powers above –
by threatening to depart in a huff.
They are your world, where you live,
and this is what their telegraph
of yaps and yelps, their salvos of snuff-
sneezes, their one-note arias, oath-
fests and dog-demagoguery, their throes of gruff
throat-flexing and guffaws without mirth,
are meant to signify. And it's all for your behoof!
So thanks be to Garth, and thanks to Rolf –
those two soothsayers with their one sooth,
pontificating on that pub roof –
and thanks to the God who created them both,
for your enlightenment as proof of His ruth.

1996

It Allows a Portrait in Line Scan at Fifteen

Les Murray

He retains a slight 'Martian' accent, from the years of single phrases.

He no longer hugs to disarm. It is gradually allowing him affection.

It does not allow proportion. Distress is absolute, shrieking, and runs him at frantic speed through crashing doors.

He likes cyborgs. Their taciturn power, with his intonation.

It still runs him around the house, alone in the dark, cooing and laughing.

He can read about soils, populations and New Zealand. On neutral topics he's illiterate.

Arnie Schwarzenegger is an actor. He isn't a cyborg really, is he, Dad?

He lives on forty acres, with animals and trees, and used to draw it continually.

He knows the map of Earth's fertile soils, and can draw it freehand.

He can only lie in a panicked shout *SorrySorryIdidn'tdoit!* warding off conflict with others and himself.

When he ran away constantly it was to the greengrocers to worship stacked fruit.

His favourite country was the Ukraine: it is nearly all deep fertile soil.

Giggling, he climbed all over the dim Freudian psychiatrist who told us how autism resulted from 'refrigerator' parents.

When asked to smile, he photographs a rictus-smile on his face.

It long forbade all naturalistic films. They were Adult movies.

If they (that is, he) *are bad the police will put them in hospital.*

He sometimes drew the farm amid Chinese or Balinese rice terraces.

When a runaway, he made uproar in the police station, playing at three times adult speed.

Only animated films were proper. *Who Framed Roger Rabbit*
  then authorised the rest.
Phrases spoken to him he would take as teaching, and repeat,
When he worshipped fruit, he screamed as if poisoned when it
  was fed to him.
A one-word first conversation: *Blane. – Yes! Plane, that's right,*
  baby! – Blane.
He has forgotten nothing, and remembers the precise quality
  of experiences.
It requires rulings: *Is stealing very playing up, as bad as murder?*
He counts at a glance, not looking. And he has never been
  lost.
When he ate only nuts and dried fruit, words were for dire
  emergencies.
He knows all the breeds of fowls, and the counties of Ireland.
He'd begun to talk, then returned to babble, then silence. It
  withdrew speech for years.
Is that very autistic, to play video games in the day?
He is anger's mirror, and magnifies any near him, raging it
  down.
It still won't allow him fresh fruit, or orange juice with bits in
  it.
He swam in the midwinter dam at night. It had no rules about
  cold.
He was terrified of thunder and finally cried as if in
  explanation *It – angry!*
He grilled an egg he'd broken into bread. Exchanges of soil-
  knowledge are called landtalking.
He lives in objectivity. I was sure Bell's palsy would leave my
  face only when he said it had begun to.
Don't say word! when he was eight forbade the word 'autistic'
  in his presence.
Bantering questions about girlfriends cause a terrified look and
  blocked ears.
He sometimes centred the farm in a furrowed American
  midwest.
Eye contact, Mum! means he truly wants attention. It dislikes
  I-contact.

He is equitable and kind, and only ever a little jealous. It was
a relief when that little arrived.

He surfs, bowls, walks for miles. For many years he hasn't
trailed his left arm while running.

I gotta get smart! looking terrified into the years. *I gotta get
smart!*

Who Framed Roger Rabbit? (1988) combined cartoon animation and live action
in a single film.

1997

Legacies
◄◇►
Jamie McKendrick

It was in the cellar of the Edinburgh house
owned by my great great grandfather

that the bodysnatchers, Burke & Hare,
unknown to him, kept their cache of corpses

in cold storage before delivering them
to the School of Human Anatomy.

There was always a skeleton in the closet,
or a skull at least, perched among the army berets,

the Luger, the greatcoat, the Zeiss binoculars
and the fox stole with its red glass eyes

and blackened lips which fastened with a snap.
There was always the skull in the clothes cupboard

with a fidgety script on its fontanel,
saying nothing, its eyes reduced to zeroes.

*

In today's newspaper I read of a Xhosa chief
who believed his great great uncle's skull was kept

somewhere in Scotland. After leaving several
military museums empty-handed,

he had a dream of a field and a white horse
grazing. In the field a barn, in the barn

that skull. And there it seems he found it
– on a shelf among some tarnished bridles –

identified by a bullet hole in the temple
from a British rifle. So some day soon

may we now expect a visit from a man
with or without a leopardskin and flywhisk

who has travelled across two continents to ask
what we've kept all this time in our closet?

William Burke and William Hare murdered seventeen victims in the course of a single twelve-month period in 1827–8 and sold the corpses for dissection purposes. The Xhosa peoples live in today's South Africa, where they make up almost a fifth of the population.

1997

Red Cows

◄◊►

SELIMA HILL

I remember the day we got married.
Very nice.
Prettiness was all I thought about.
It never entered my head to think about *you*.
Who were you?
Were you there?
I can't think why.
I must have told you *Marry*
and you married.
I must have told you
spend the whole week crying.
I gave you food
you didn't know how to eat.
I gave you tears
you didn't know how to shed.
I gave you the moon
like a cold disc on our bed.
We journeyed on,
two white and lonely ships
shifting our consignments
through dull oceans
only crossed
by those who had lost their minds,
who dreamed they sighted herring-gulls
and coconuts;
who when they woke,
a million miles from anywhere,
saw herds of red cows
running down a mountainside
with their tails stuck up in the air
who they thought were their friends.

1998

Seeing You Asked

<o>

VINCENT O'SULLIVAN

There's a dozen things I might tell you.
There is a Chinese poem to begin with
of a woman folding curtains as she leaves
a man, forever. There is a Roman writing
from the edge of ice-fields, a vista
of dull silver beyond clicking reeds,
to a woman who watches a blue smoking
mountain in almost unbearable heat.
There are wartime movies with sad bridges
across morning rivers, the woman pressing
the two wings of her collar together
as a train draws out. There's the story
as well of a woman driving north
towards a lake, a lake that was once fire,
a house by the lake, a life inside the house,
where today's love becomes another fiction
you open when the room is empty,
put down when you hear voices, stand
up, smiling, at life where it happens . . .
There is no ending to certain stories,
the plot has no desperate turns, the vase
on the bedside table burns with azaleas
whatever happens. But love, we say,
love, there are corners on the stairways,
there are fragments in each hour,
when the notes drift back, the ones
scarcely heard – just as the lake is always
beside you, spreading out, and out.
You say you swim, you read, you fish.
There is something like the glint of a hook,
there is something, love, in that shimmering
vault, trolling too fast to speak of.

1998

Deep Sorriness Atonement Song
for missed appointment, BBC North, Manchester

◄◇►

GLYN MAXWELL

The man who sold Manhattan for a halfway decent bangle,
He had talks with Adolf Hitler and could see it from his
    angle,
And he could have signed the Quarrymen but didn't think
    they'd make it
So he bought a cake on Pudding Lane and thought 'Oh well
    I'll bake it'
        But his chances they were slim,
        And his brothers they were Grimm,
        And he's sorry, very sorry,
        But I'm sorrier than him.

And the drunken plastic surgeon who said 'I know, let's
    enlarge 'em!'
And the bloke who told the Light Brigade 'Oh what the hell,
    let's charge 'em,'
The magician with an early evening gig on the *Titanic*,
And the Mayor who told the people of Atlantis not to panic,
        And the Dong about his nose,
        And the Pobble *re* his toes,
        They're all sorry, really sorry,
        But I'm sorrier than those.

And don't forget the Bible, with the Sodomites and Judas,
And Onan who discovered something nothing was as rude as,
And anyone who reckoned it was City's year for Wembley,
And the kid who called Napoleon a shortarse in assembly,
        And the man who always smiles
        'Cause he knows I have his files,
        They're all sorry, truly sorry,
        But I'm sorrier by miles.

And Robert Falcon Scott who lost the race to a Norwegian,
And anyone who's ever spilt the pint of a Glaswegian,
Or told a Finn a joke or spent an hour with a Swiss-
   German,
Or got a mermaid in the sack and found it was a merman,
      Or him who smelt a rat,
      And got curious as a cat,
      They're all sorry, deeply sorry,
      But I'm sorrier than that.

All the people who were rubbish when we needed them to
   do it,
Whose wires crossed, whose spirit failed, who ballsed it up or
   blew it,
All notchers of *nul points* and all who have a problem
   Houston,
At least they weren't in Kensington when they should have
   been at Euston.
      For I didn't build the Wall
      And I didn't cause the Fall
      But I'm sorry, Lord I'm sorry,
      I'm the sorriest of all.

The Quarrymen later called themselves The Beatles. The Great Fire of London (1666) was said to have started in a baker's shop in Pudding Lane. The Dong with a Luminous Nose and The Pobble Who Had No Toes were immortalised in nonsense rhymes by Edward Lear (1812–88).

1999

None of the Blood

◀◇▶

SOPHIE HANNAH

None of the blood that is in your body
　is in my body. None of the blood
　　that is in my body is in your body.
Whatever you are, you are not my blood.

None of the flesh that is on your body
　is on my body. None of the flesh
　　that is on my body is on your body.
Whatever you are, you are not my flesh.

I have shared a bottle of wine with a bigot
　(none of the eggshells, none of the mud
　　in my kitchen and garden, your kitchen and
　　　　　　　　　　　　　　garden).
None of the flesh. None of the blood

that is in my kitchen is in your kitchen.
　(I am being rude. I am not just being rude.)
　　None of your garden is in my garden.
I have shared a picnic bench with a prude.

Furniture, yes, means of transport, yes,
　but no to soul and no to bone
　　(none of your sellotape, none of your glue).
Yes to some stranger. No to you.

1999

Her News

—◇—

HUGO WILLIAMS

You paused for a moment and I heard you smoking
on the other end of the line.
I pictured your expression,
one eye screwed shut against the smoke
as you waited for my reaction.
I was waiting for it myself, a list of my own news
gone suddenly cold in my hand.
Supposing my wife found out, what would happen then?
Would I have to leave her and marry you now?

Perhaps it wouldn't be so bad,
starting again with someone new, finding a new place,
pretending the best was yet to come.
It might even be fun,
playing the family man, walking around in the park
full of righteous indignation.
But no, I couldn't go through all that again,
not without my own wife being there,
not without her getting cross about everything.

Perhaps she wouldn't mind about the baby,
then we could buy a house in the country
and all move in together.
That sounded like a better idea.
Now that I'd been caught at last, a wave of relief
swept over me. I was just considering
a shed in the garden with a radio and a day bed,
when I remembered I hadn't seen you for over a year.
'Congratulations,' I said. 'When's it due?'

1999

The Devil's Wife

CAROL ANN DUFFY

1. DIRT

The Devil was one of the men at work.
Different. Fancied himself. Looked at the girls
in the office as though they were dirt. Didn't flirt.
Didn't speak. Was sarcastic and rude if he did.
I'd stare him out, chewing my gum, insolent, dumb.
I'd lie on my bed at home, on fire for him.

I scowled and pouted and sneered. I gave
as good as I got till he asked me out. In his car
he put two fags in his mouth and lit them both.
He bit my breast. His language was foul. He entered me.
We're the same, he said, That's it. I swooned in my soul.
We drove to the woods and he made me bury a doll.

I went mad for the sex. I won't repeat what we did.
We gave up going to work. It was either the woods
or looking at playgrounds, fairgrounds. Coloured lights
in the rain. I'd walk around on my own. He tailed.
I felt like this: Tongue of stone. Two black slates
for eyes. Thumped wound of a mouth. Nobody's Mam.

2. MEDUSA

I flew in my chains over the wood where we'd buried
the doll. I know it was me who was there.
I know I carried the spade. I know I was covered in mud.
But I cannot remember how or when or precisely where.

Nobody liked my hair. Nobody liked how I spoke.
He held my heart in his fist and he squeezed it dry.
I gave the cameras my Medusa stare.
I heard the judge summing up. I didn't care.

I was left to rot. I was locked up, double-locked.
I know they chucked the key. It was nowt to me.
I wrote to him every day in our private code.
I thought in twelve, fifteen, we'd be out on the open road.

But life, they said, means life. Dying inside.
The Devil was evil, mad, but I was the Devil's wife
which made me worse. I howled in my cell.
If the Devil was gone then how could this be hell?

3. BIBLE

I said No not me I didn't I couldn't I wouldn't.
Can't remember no idea not in the room.
Get me a Bible honestly promise you swear.
I never not in a million years it was him.

I said Send me a lawyer a vicar a priest.
Send me a TV crew send me a journalist.
Can't remember not in the room. Send me
a shrink where's my MP send him to me.

I said Not fair not right not on not true
not like that. Didn't see didn't know didn't hear.
Maybe this maybe that not sure not certain maybe.
Can't remember no idea it was him it was him.

Can't remember no idea not in the room.
No idea can't remember not in the room.

4. NIGHT

In the long fifty-year night,
these are the words that crawl out of the wall:
Suffer. Monster. Burn in Hell.

When morning comes,
I will finally tell.

Amen.

5. Appeal

If I'd been stoned to death
If I'd been hung by the neck
If I'd been shaved and strapped to the Chair
If an injection
If my peroxide head on the block
If my outstretched hands for the chop
If my tongue torn out at the root
If from ear to ear my throat
If a bullet a hammer a knife
If life means life means life means life

But what did I do to us all, to myself
When I was the Devil's wife?

1999

Sunday School

◄◦►

YVETTE CHRISTIANSË

Tell me that old story, the one about
the girl in the schoolyard. The Coloured
girl who was surrounded by boys whose
hair glinted in the late Sunday sun
as if still fresh from a good preaching?

And were they Coloured boys or white
when they found her? I can't remember.
Or were they just men, there in the
late schoolyard where she ran, men
with their bodies erect and driven

to the point of no return, so hard
they broke glass as they passed. And
when they had finished they had one
last joke with a Coke bottle, or was
it a broken broom handle? Do you

remember that story? It has been
running between my legs like blood
for years. My legs are brown. I
keep them covered. I think of her
and how it must have been, giving

birth to broken things – the top
of a bottle or a well-handled broom
long after the men had gone, softly,
back to their mothers and sisters,
wives and daughters. Their stories

of Coloured girls' bodies that
fizz like new Coke, go flat as
piss and taste the same.

1999

Hand

◀◦▶

BRIAN MCCABE

After the floggings the mutilations.
After the mutilations the executions.
In the square the thief waits in line
and he whispers to his hand:

'Forgive me hand I am sorry
for teaching you how to steal.
I misled you my faithful hand.
It was a partnership of a kind.

I will miss you my clever hand.
You will be better without me.
You will just be a hand any hand.
Your duties to me are finished.

The other is no good as you know.
Begging will be more its line.
You were always the talented one.
You are not to blame.

We should not have taken
that star fruit that star fruit
was too colourful and shapely.
What did we want with a star fruit?'

From the parchment is read out
the thief's name, his crime.
People yawn, scratch themselves
and examine their hands.

1999

In Departing Light

ROBERT GRAY

My mother all of ninety has to be tied up
in her wheelchair, but still she leans far out of it sideways;
she juts there brokenly,
able to cut
with the sight of her someone who is close. She is hung
like her hanging mouth
in the dignity
of her bleariness, and says that she is
perfectly all right. It's impossible to get her to complain
or to register anything
for longer than a moment. She has made Stephen Hawking
    look healthy.
It's as though
she is being sucked out of existence sideways through a
    porthole
and we've got hold of her feet.
She's very calm.
If you live long enough it isn't death you fear
but what life can still do. And she appears to know this
somewhere,
even if there's no hope she could speak of it.
Yet she is so remote you think of an immortal – a Tithonus
    withering
forever on the edge
of life,
although with never a moment's grievance. Taken out to air
my mother seems in a motorcycle race, she
the sidecar passenger
who keeps the machine on the road, trying to lie far over
beyond the wheel.
Seriously, concentrated, she gazes ahead
towards the line,

as we go creeping around and around, through the thick
  syrups
of a garden, behind the nursing home.

Her mouth is full of chaos.
My mother revolves her loose dentures like marbles ground
  upon each other,
or idly clatters them,
broken and chipped. Since they won't stay on her gums
she spits them free
with a sudden blurting cough, that seems to have stamped out
  of her
an ultimate breath.
Her teeth fly into her lap or onto the grass,
breaking the hawsers of spittle.
What we see in such age is for us the premature dissolution
  of a body
that slips off the bones
and back to protoplasm
before it can be decently hidden away.
And it's as though the synapses were almost all of them
  broken
between her brain cells
and now they waver about feebly on the draught of my voice
and connect
at random and wrongly
and she has become a surrealist poet.
'How is the sun
on your back?' I ask. 'The sun
is mechanical,' she tells me, matter of fact. Wait
a moment, I think, is she
becoming profound? From nowhere she says, 'The lake gets
  dusty.' There is no lake
here, or in her past. 'You'll have to dust the lake.'
It could be
that she is, but then she says, 'The little boy in the star is
  food,'
or perhaps 'The little boy is the star in food,'

and you think, More likely
this appeals to my kind of superstition – the sleepless, inspiring
     homunculus.
It is all a tangle and interpretation,
a hearing amiss,
all just the slipperiness
of her descent.

We sit and listen to the bird-song, which is like wandering
     lines
of wet paint –
it is like an abstract expressionist at work, his flourishes and
then
the touches
barely there,
and is going on all over the stretched sky.
If I read aloud skimmingly from the newspaper, she
     immediately falls asleep.
I stroke her face and she wakes
and looking at me intently she says something like, 'That was
a nice parcel.' In our sitting about
she has also said, relevant of nothing, 'The desert is a tongue.'
'A red tongue?'
'That's right, it's a
it's a sort of
you know – it's a – it's a long
motor car.'
When I told her I might be in Cambridge for a time, she told
     me, 'Cambridge
is a very old seat of learning. Be sure –'
but it became too much –
'be sure
of the short Christmas flowers.' I get dizzy,
nauseous,
when I try to think about what is happening inside her head.
     I keep her
out there for hours, propping her
straight, as

she dozes, and drifts into waking; away from the stench and
the screams of the ward. The worst
of all this, to me, is that despite such talk, now is the most
    peace
I've known her to have. She reminisces,
momentarily, thinking I am one of her long-dead
brothers. 'Didn't we have some fun
on those horses, when we were kids?' she'll say, giving
her thigh a little slap. Alzheimer's
is nirvana, in her case. She never mentions
anything of what troubled her adult years – God, the evil
    passages
of the Bible, her own mother's
long, hard dying, my father. Nothing
at all of my father,
and nothing
of her obsession with religion, that he drove her to. She says
    the magpie's song,
that goes on and on, like an Irishman
wheedling to himself,
which I have turned her chair towards,
reminds her of
a cup. A broken cup. I think that the chaos in her mind
is bearable to her because it is revolving
so slowly – slowly
as dust motes in an empty room.
The soul? The soul has long been defeated, and is all but
    gone. She's only productive now
of bristles on the chin, of an odour
like old newspapers on a damp concrete floor, of garbled
    mutterings, of
some crackling memories, and of a warmth
(it was always there,
the marsupial devotion), of a warmth that is just in the eyes,
    these days, particularly
when I hold her and rock her for a while, as I lift her
back to bed – a folded
package, such as,

I have seen from photographs, was made of the Ice Man. She
    says,
'I like it
when you – when
when
you . . .'
I say to her, 'My brown-eyed girl.' Although she doesn't
    remember
the record, or me come home
that time, I sing it
to her: 'Sha lala
la la lala . . . And
it's you, it's you,' – she smiles up, into my face – 'it's you, my
    brown-eyed girl.'

My mother will get lost on the roads after death.
Too lonely a figure
to bear thinking of. As she did once,
one time at least, in the new department store
in our town; discovered
hesitant among the aisles; turning around and around,
    becoming
a still place.
Looking too kind
to reject even a wrong direction,
outrightly. And she caught my eye, watching her,
and knew I'd laugh
and grinned. Or else, since many another spirit will be
    arriving over there, whatever
those are – and all of them clamorous
as seabirds, along the walls of death – she will be pushed aside
easily, again. There are hierarchies in Heaven, we remember;
    and we know
of its bungled schemes.
Even if 'the last shall be first,' as we have been told, she
could not be first. It would not be her.
But why become so fearful?
This is all

of your mother, in your arms. She who now, a moment after
   your game, has gone;
who is confused
and would like to ask
why she is hanging here. No – she will be safe. She will be
   safe
in the dry mouth
of this red earth, in the place
she has always been. She
who hasn't survived living, how can we dream that she will
   survive her death?

Physicist Stephen Hawking (born 1942) has a form of muscular dystrophy that
has left him almost completely paralysed and confined to a wheelchair. Tithonus,
in Greek myth (and in Tennyson's re-telling), was granted immortality but not
eternal youth. The Ice Man was the oldest mummified human being found in
Europe, in an Alpine glacier on the Austro-Italian border. The song 'Brown Eyed
Girl' was a hit in 1967 for Northern Irish singer-songwriter Van Morrison.

2000

Bollockshire

<o>

CHRISTOPHER REID

You've zoomed through it often enough
on the long grind north, the grim dash south –
　　why not take a break?
　　Slip off the motorway
at any one of ten tangled junctions
and poke your nose, without compunction,
　　into the unknown.
　　Get systematically lost.
At the first absence of a signpost,
opt for the least promising lane,
　　or cut into the truck traffic
　　along some plain,
perimeter-fence-lined stretch of blacktop
heading nowhere obvious.
　　Open your mind.
　　to the jarring yellow
of that hillside rape crop, the grim Norse green
of that fir plantation, where every tree
　　steps forward to greet you
　　with the same zombie gesture
of exclamation, the last-ditch brown of –
what could it be? Something to do with pigs?
　　Row on row
　　of miniature Nissen huts
laid out like a new speculative estate
in acres of glistening mud, behind an electronic gate . . .
　　But don't stop now.
　　Press on,
undistracted by the lush hedgerows
(of which there are none)
　　or the silence of the songbirds.

Other counties
can match these. It's the essence of Bollockshire
you're after: its secrets, its blessings and bounties.
So keep driving,
past sly-windowed farms,
lying there with hoards of costly machinery
in their arms, like toys they won't share;
past Bald Oak Hill,
down the more shaded side of which
the Bollockshire Hunt has scuffled
many a morning to its kill;
past St Boldric's church,
with the slant steeple,
which Cromwell's lads once briefly visited,
leaving behind them saints re-martyred,
the Virgin without her head;
past Bewlake Manor's
dinky Gothic gatehouse, now the weekend habitat
of London media or money people;
past the isolated
Bulldog pub,
with its choice of scrumpies, microwave grub,
bouncy castle and back-room badger fights –
past all that,
until, if you are lucky,
you hit the famous ring road. Thrown down
decades ago, like a gigantic concrete garland
around the county town,
riddled and plugged
by the random dentistry of maintenance work
and chock-a-block with contraflow,
it must, you feel,
be visible from the moon.
One road sign hides another. There are orange cones
galore. Each cultivated roundabout island
is, if possible, more off-key
than the one before.
But don't stick here all afternoon:

Blokeston itself has to be seen,
   via the brick maze
   of its bygone industrial outskirts.
This is where Shas Balk invented his machine
for putting a true, tight twist in string,
   where they once supplied the world
   with all it needed
of bicycle saddles and cigarette papers,
where cough syrup was king.
   Round the corner,
   just when you least expect,
there's Blokeston FC, home of 'The Blockers',
and Blokeston Prison, by the same no-frills architect.
   Unmissable from any position,
   the Bulwark Brewery
stands up in a haze of its own malty vapours,
which even today's counterwafts of Tandoori
   cannot contest.
   Now, turn east or west,
and you'll find yourself on a traffic-planner's
one-way inward spiral, passing at speed
   through older and older
   parts of town –
the impeccable Georgian manners
of Beauclerc Square, built on slave-trade money;
   bad Bishop Blogg's school;
   the crossroads where
the Billhook Martyrs were tortured and burned –
until you reach the river Bleak.
   Squeeze, if you can,
   over the Black Bridge,
then park and pay – assuming this isn't the week
of the Billycock Fair, or Boiled Egg Day,
   when they elect the Town Fool.
   From here, it's a short step
to the Bailiwick Hall Museum and Arts Centre.
As you enter, ignore the display
   of tankards and manacles, the pickled head

of England's Wisest Woman;
ask, instead, for the Bloke Stone.
Surprisingly small, round, featureless,
   pumice-grey,
   there it sits, dimly lit,
behind toughened glass in a room of its own.
Be sure to see it, if you've a taste
   for this sort of primitive conundrum.
   Most visitors pass
and won't even leave their vehicles,
keen by this time to make haste
   back to the life they know,
   and to put more motorway under them.

2000

Dancing in the Churchill Lounge

ROGER FINCH

To the two-year-old boy in Booth 5,
   the dancers are a garden, slow blooms
beneath showlight, his mother in her red crepe dress
   a hollyhock amidst lighter flowers.
   He stands on the seat to gaze at them,
the satiny turn, turn, and his hair has the gilt
from white, yellow, red in strings above his head.
   And then they are back and he is caught
in red swirls, his mother's breath raspberry sweet
   on his mouth, and cool, from the tall cool pink
   she is sipping. His smile is her smile.
Photographs from those years show them with same
                        cheeks,
   same lips, same eyes. At fourteen, the fit

   is even closer. That Hallowe'en
   I put on the red crepe dress, wore a wig,
reddened my mouth. My mirror showed me, in the realm
   inside the frame, the portrait of one
   from an evening that I only then
remembered. Jewelry was superfluous. On the skin
of the boy I was just outgrowing bloomed
   the beauty of the one I loved the best.
Father was disturbed, but he danced with me, waltzed
   me across beneath the orange-and-black
   of let's pretend. I felt his breath on my ear.
And smiled. Still Mother's smile, but with a hint of my
                     own smile,
   the smile of one far too often kissed.

2000

Kurgan No. 10

‹◇›

DON COLES

Here on this endless steppe the burial mounds seem
slow sails on a flat sea. Keep staring
and you'll know they're stalled. Almost all were
plundered, big surprise, long ago, passing Cossacks or
the local tomb-fanciers have had close on
two thousand years to disturb these peaces –
the only puzzle is how no. 10 escaped them.
But escape them it did, until now. They
must have been tipped off, warned off,
a thin and mephitic smoke wavering forth
from nos. 9 and 11 maybe, deaths of diggers,
a famous malediction. Whatever the reason,
she survived – saving herself for the standard
bright immensities ahead, perhaps –
saving herself, I have improperly, basely,
surmised, for me. When we opened
the square pit of her precocious sleep
the gold about her head startled us. It was
a sort of diadem-cum-headdress, and
the gold-foil stags and birds and trees
rippled in that first air as though
not just stags and birds and trees were
shaking stillness off but she too was
testing her delicate bones – as though
everything we had rudely uncovered here
knew that a long lull was ending.
She was Sarmatian, probably a princess,
and young. About twenty, the consensus was.
Her neck was encircled by a rigid collar
of chiselled gold, ornamented with a series
of unknown magical creatures –
dragons fighting against what seemed to be

monkeys wearing armour and holding clubs.
Towards the front of the collar was, in
the words of our historian/curator, 'one of those
works of art which, once seen, carry out a small
but irreversible coup in the mind' –
in less lapidary terms, a man, cross-legged
and golden-bearded, of serene aspect,
holding a cup in his two hands, certainly
interesting (and shortly thereafter the approved
subject of a doctoral thesis in Rostov and
a less-ambitious work by one of my own
students at the Institute) but 'not quite',
as our Director remarked while gazing
inexactly towards the historian/curator
over lunch, 'Rilke's archaic Apollo'. I'm sure
they'll work it out. As for that coup, I disagreed
only in the detail. That *tableau* so unsparingly
vivant as she lies down, again and again, involuntarily,
on her back, is a loop running incessantly
over my pages, running now as I write this,
lights and shadows over the text, and I have
not the smallest idea how to stop it. I have
walked this plain a hundred times, a thousand,
since I was named to this post, tending
my inconsequential thoughts and staring
at the stalled fleet, the paused convoy –
and all the while 'the poor princess', as they
have begun to call her, was waiting. Waiting
to give me her treasure, waiting to give me
the enigma of her life and especially of her
death (a darkness I may spend the rest
of my own life in close engagement with),
and at the end, when there was nothing else,
waiting to give me what was left of
her twenty-year-old body. What to do
with such *Sehnsucht*? I may have become
irreversibly hers.
        There was a mention

of delicate bones. Not quite all her bones
were there. Some of the very most delicate
fingertip bones, called phalanges, were missing.
Archaeologists are divided on this: some believe
that the phalanges are commonly gnawed off
and removed by mice not long after the burial,
this is the problem, they say, with chambered
graves without coffins. Others maintain
that the fingertips were ritually severed
immediately after death, the purpose of this
being to ensure that the living will not have to
fear the touch of the dead.
    It's this last one I would choose.
I couldn't bear the idea of the mice.

A kurgan, according to the *OED* (compact edition) definition, which Don Coles cites in his 2000 collection *Kurgan*, is 'a prehistoric sepulchral tumulus or barrow in Russia or Tartary', the word being Russian, of Tartar origin. The poet also tells us that his poem is based on a passage in Neal Ascherson's *Black Sea* (1995), and that the German word 'Sehnsucht' means 'longing'. Ancient Sarmatia occupied territory now reaching from Poland to Russia and the Caspian Sea. In saying that the impact of the artwork was not quite that of Rilke's archaic Apollo, the Director in the poem has in mind the closing imperative in Rainer Maria Rilke's poem 'Archaic Torso of Apollo': 'You must change your life.'

2000

Hope for Refugees

<o>

KAREN PRESS

You can go back
you can go back
run backwards
call back the cattle
unstitch the hems
pull the photos out of the fire

you can go back
you can go back
pull down your dress
button your shirt
wipe off the blood
scrub off the blood

you can go back
you can go back
wash the walls
fix the door
remember the step down in the dark
avoid the dark

you can go back
you can go back
dig up the box in the front garden
dig up the box in the yard
dig up the box in your heart
dig up the box in the child's heart

you can go back
you can go back
lay out the skeletons in their beds
hang out the years to air
plant seeds, keep watch at the well
tear up your nightmares, your footprints
lock the door
work hard
give thanks to god

2000

Hoping It Might Be So

<o>

KIT WRIGHT

There must be a place where the whole of it all comes
    right,
Where the little boy buggered and strangled in the wood
Is comforted by his parents, and comforts his parents,
And everything horrible ever is understood.

I say:

For at least six million reasons or else no light,
No light in the day.

There must be somewhere it doesn't happen like this,
Where reparation is made, *à tous compris,*
Where the drowned men rise, walk back from the boats in
    the evening,
And the lost child sings on her new-made father's knee,

I say:

For at least six million reasons or else no reason
And nothing to be.

The title of Wright's poem comes from Hardy's 'The Oxen' (see p. 117). The
figure of six million is the approximate number of Jews killed by the Nazis
during the Second World War.

2000

Pale Blue City
(December 31, 2000)

◄◦►

JEFFREY HARRISON

I've never seen it like this: from up here
the sun sinking fiery on the horizon,
but down there it has already set, and the city,
laid out on its recognizable island,
is a beautiful pale ash blue
because of the snow and the evening.
The streetlights are already lit
but it isn't dark yet, everything is still
visible in the city where we once lived,
but long ago, and now it's all small:
the tiny paired towers of the Trade Center,
midtown stacked up like a digital mountain,
the George Washington Bridge with its festoon
of white Christmas lights, Central Park
an azure band. It's too far away to see
the copper roofs of Morningside Heights,
their green subsumed in the blue
of memory, or covered by the snow
that shut the city down our first year
together, people skiing down Broadway,
everything muffled as we looked down
from our window, already seeing it all
from above, but not from as far away
as this, the lights glittering, as if
through a liquid. I want it all to stay
just like this, I wish I could give you
this pale blue city under the glass
of a plane window like a snowglobe,
all of New York and our time there
held in your hand. But the plane
is moving on, the city slips away . . .

and now it's getting dark, the landscape
turns as black as space, and the orange
lights of other cities slide underneath
in spidery galaxies – as if light-years
separated us from that era. And yet
I try to hold it inside me as the plane
begins its descent toward our present
life together. Here: take it
before it disappears.

Acknowledgments

The authors and publishers have made all reasonable efforts to contact the copyright holders for permission, and apologise for any omissions or errors in the form of credit given. They would like to thank the following for permission to reproduce copyright material:

The Random House Group Ltd. for 'In the Theatre'; and (US) 'In the Theatre' by Dannie Abse from *New and Collected Poems*, Hutchinson, 2003. Copyright © Dannie Abse 2003 is reproduced by kind permission of United Agents (www.unitedagents.co.uk) on behalf of Dannie Abse;

'Vultures' by Chinua Achebe. Copyright © 1971, 1973, 2004, Chinua Achebe, used by permission of The Wylie Agency (UK) Limited; and (US and Canada) Anchor Books, a division of Random House, Inc. for 'Vultures' from *Collected Poems* by Chinua Achebe;

Random House, Inc for 'One Ordinary Evening' from *Ants on the Melon* by Virginia Hamilton Adair;

Bloodaxe Books for 'Zoom!' from *Zoom!* by Simon Armitage;

Carcanet Press for 'Cigarettes' by John Ash;

Carcanet Press for 'Down by the Station, Early in the Morning' from *Collected Poems 1956–1987*; and (US and Canada) 'Down by the Station Early in the Morning' from *A Wave* by John Ashbery. Copyright © 1981, 1982, 1983, 1984 by John Ashbery. Reprinted by permission of Georges Borchardt, Inc., on behalf of the author;

The Estate of W. H. Auden for 'Spain' from *Another Time*, 'Consider', 'In Memory of W. B. Yeats', 'Partition', 'The Shield of Achilles', 'August, 1968', 'Moon Landing' and 'Say this city has ten million souls' from *Collected Works* by W. H. Auden;

'Lord Finchley', 'On a General Election' and 'The Pacifist' by Hilaire Belloc © Hilaire Belloc reproduced by permission of PFD (www.pfd.co.uk) on behalf of the Estate of Hilaire Belloc;

Faber and Faber Ltd for 'Dream Song 41', 'Dream Song 105' and 'Dream

Song 343' all from *The Dream Songs*; 'Sonnet 71' and 'Certainty Before Lunch' both from *Selected Poems* all by John Berryman;

Marion Wood Books, an imprint of G.P. Putnam, a division of Penguin Group (USA) Inc. for 'White Bears: Tolstoy at Astapovo' by Linda Bierds;

Farrar, Straus and Giroux, LLC for 'The Map', 'At the Fishhouses', 'Questions of Travel' and 'One Art' from *The Complete Poems 1927–1979* by Elizabeth Bishop;

Carcanet Press for 'Outside History'; and (US and Canada) W.W. Norton & Company, Inc. for 'Outside History' from *Outside History: Selected Poems 1980–1990* by Eavan Boland;

Roo Borson for 'After a Death' by Roo Borson;

Carcanet Press for 'The Chess Player' and 'Timur the Lame' by Charles Boyle;

Oxford University Press for *from* 'Rites' by Edward Kamau Brathwaite;

The Random House Group Ltd. for 'The Reader' and 'Questions for the Old Woman' from *Selected Poems*; and (US and Canada) Gaspereau Press for 'The Reader' and 'Questions for the Old Woman' all by Robert Bringhurst;

Enitharmon Press for 'Common Sense' from *The Saner Places: Selected Poems* by Alan Brownjohn;

Bloodaxe Books for 'Aus dem Zweiten Reich' and *from* 'Briggflatts' from *Complete Poems* by Basil Bunting;

HarperCollins Publishers, Australia for 'Mothers and Daughters' and 'The Australian Dream' from *Selected Poems* by David Campbell; and (for electronic) 'Mothers and Daughters' and 'The Australian Dream' by David Campbell, reprinted by arrangement with The David Campbell Estate c/o Curtis Brown (Aust) Pty Ltd.;

The Random House Group Ltd.; and (US and Canada) New Directions Publishing Corp for 'God's Christ Theory' from *Glass, Irony and God* by Anne Carson;

Ciaran Carson and The Gallery Press; and (US) Ciaran Carson and Wake Forest University Press for 'Belfast Confetti' and 'Last Orders' from *Collected Poems*;

Pearson Education Ltd. for 'Developments from the Grave' from *Napolo and the Python* by Steve Chimombo;

Duke University Press for 'Sunday School' from *Castaway* by Yvette Christiansë;

R Dardis Clarke, 17 Oscar Square, Dublin 8 for 'Penal Law' from Austin Clarke Collected Poems edited by R Dardis Clarke published by Carcanet/The Bridge Press;

Carcanet Press for 'The Water-Diviner' by Gillian Clarke;

Harry Clifton and The Gallery Press, Ireland for 'Death of Thomas Merton' from *The Desert Route* by Harry Clifton;

Don Coles for *from* 'Landslides' and 'Kurgan no. 10' by Don Coles;

Bloodaxe Books for 'The quick and the dead at Pompeii' from *Collected Poems* by David Constantine;

Faber and Faber Ltd for 'Waste Land Limericks' from *Making Cocoa for Kingsley Amis* by Wendy Cope; and (US) 'Waste Land Limericks' reprinted by permission of United Agents on behalf of Wendy Cope;

Enitharmon Press for 'Autumn Morning in Cambridge' by Frances Cornford;

Liveright Publishing Corp. for 'A Name for All' from *Complete Poems of Hart Crane* by Hart Crane, edited by Marc Simon;

Amistad Research Center for 'Incident' from *On These I Stand* by Countee Cullen;

W. W. Norton & Company for 'may I feel said he' from *Complete Poems 1904–1962* by E.E. Cummings;

Gomer Press Ltd. for 'Cow-parsley and hawthorn blossom' from *Collected Poems of Idris Davies*;

University of Pittsburgh Press for 'On the Turning Up of Unidentified Black Female Corpses' from *Captivity* by Toi Derricotte;

Bloodaxe Books for 'Purdah I' and 'Untitled' from *Postcards from god* by Imtiaz Dharker;

The Random House Group Ltd.; and (US and Canada) HarperCollins Publishers for 'A Letter from the Coast' from *Atlantis* by Mark Doty;

Ian Duhig for 'I'r Hen Iaith A'i Chaneuon' by Ian Duhig;

Faber and Faber Ltd for 'Empty Wardrobes' from *Elegies* and 'A Game of Bowls' from *New Selected Poems 1964–2000* both by Douglas Dunn;

Faber and Faber Ltd for 'Sarajevo' from *Collected Poems 1931–1974* by Lawrence Durrell; and (US) 'Sarajevo' from *Collected Poems of Lawrence Durrell*. Reproduced with permission of Curtis Brown Group Ltd, London, on behalf of The Estate of Lawrence Durrell, © Estate of Lawrence Durrell;

Faber and Faber Ltd for 'The Love Song of J. Alfred Prufrock', *from* 'The Waste Land', 'Journey of the Magi' and 'East Coker' all from *Complete Poems 1909–1962*; and (US) Houghton Mifflin Harcourt Publishing Company for 'Journey of the Magi' from *Collected Poems 1909–1962* and 'East Coker' from *Four Quartets* all by T. S. Eliot;

Allen Lane, The Penguin Press for 'Aubade', 'Missing Dates' and 'Let it go' from *The Complete Poems William Empson*; and (for audio and electronic)

'Aubade', 'Missing Dates' and 'Let it go' reproduced with permission of Curtis Brown Group Ltd, London, on behalf of The Estate of William Empson. *The Complete Poems of William Empson* © Estate of William Empson, 2000;

Watson, Little Ltd for 'Apocalypse' by D. J. Enright;

The Random House Group Ltd. for 'The Lovesleep' from *Selected Poems* by Gavin Ewart;

Oxford University Press India, New Delhi for 'The Double Horror' and *from* 'Very Indian Poems in Indian English' from *Collected Poems* by Nassam Ezekiel;

Enitharmon Press for 'The List' from *New & Collected Poems* by U. A. Fanthorpe;

Reprinted by permission of United Agents on behalf of James Fenton for 'Dead Soldiers';

New Directions Publishing Corp. for 'In Goya's greatest scenes we seem to see' from *A Coney Island of the Mind* by Lawrence Ferlinghetti;

Roger Finch for 'Dancing in the Churchill Lounge' by Roger Finch;

Bloodaxe Books for 'The Entertainment of War' from *The Long & the Short of It: Poems 1955–2005* by Roy Fisher;

HarperCollins Publishers, Australia for 'The Wind at Your Door' from *Forty Years' Poems* by R. D. FitzGerald; and (for electronic) Desmond FitzGerald for 'The Wind at Your Door' by R. D. FitzGerald;

Michael Forbes for 'Love Poem' by John Forbes;

The Random House Group Ltd. for 'Home Burial', 'The Census-Taker', 'Stopping by Woods on a Snowy Evening' and 'Acquainted with the Night' all from *The Poetry of Robert Frost*;

The Random House Group Ltd. for 'Kent' from *Collected Poems*; and (for audio and electronic) 'Kent' © John Fuller by permission of United Agents Ltd (www.unitedagents.co.uk) on behalf of the author;

Enitharmon Press for 'Snow in Europe' from *Selected Poems* by David Gascoyne;

HarperCollins Publishers, Australia for 'Before Action' from *Songs of a Campaign* by Leon Gellert;

'Mass for the Middle-Aged' by Peter Goldsworthy, reprinted by arrangement with Peter Goldsworthy c/o Curtis Brown (Aust) Pty Ltd.;

Carcanet Press for 'History'; and (US and Canada) HarperCollins Publishers for 'History' from *The Errancy* by Jorie Graham;

Michael Snow for 'I Leave this at Your Ear' by W. S. Graham;

Carcanet Press for 'Song: Lift Boy' and 'The Thieves' by Robert Graves;

Carcanet Press for 'Flames and Dangling Wire' and 'In Departing Light' by Robert Gray;

Faber and Faber Ltd for 'The Wound' and 'The Missing' from *Collected Poems* by Thom Gunn;

Ralph Gustafson and McClelland & Stewart Ltd. for 'The Old Moscow Woman' from *The Moment is All: Selected Poems, 1944–83* by Ralph Gustafson;

Carcanet Press for 'Bach and the Sentry' by Ivor Gurney;

Anvil Press Poetry for 'In a Cold Season' from *Collected Poems 1941–1994* by Michael Hamburger;

Carcanet Press for 'None of the Blood' by Sophie Hannah;

Waywiser Press for 'Sketch' from *The Names of Things: New and Selected Poems*; and Four Way Books for 'Pale Blue City' from *Incomplete Knowledge* both by Jeffrey Harrison;

Tony Harrison for 'The Mother of the Muses' from *Collected Poems*;

Bloodaxe Books for 'Her Kiss' from *Flame Tree: Selected Poems* by Kevin Hart;

Penguin Group (Australia) for 'Prize-Giving' and 'Bone Scan' from *Gwen Harwood: Selected Poems* by Gwen Harwood;

Faber and Faber Ltd for 'Punishment', 'Casualty' and 'The Underground' all from *Opened Ground: Poems 1966–1996* by Seamus Heaney;

Alfred A Knopf, a division of Random House, Inc. for '"It out-Herods Herod. Pray you, avoid it."' from *Collected Earlier Poems* by Anthony Hecht;

Penguin Books for *from* 'The Mystery of the Charity of Charles Péguy' and 'Christmas Trees' from *Collected Poems;* and (US) Houghton Mifflin Harcourt Publishing Company for 'Christmas Trees' from *New and Collected Poems, 1952–1992* by Geoffrey Hill;

Bloodaxe Books for 'Red Cows' from *Gloria: Selected Poems* by Selima Hill;

Faber and Faber Ltd for 'Albion Market' from *Acrimony* by Michael Hoffmann;

Carcanet Press for 'On an Engraving by Casserius' by A. D. Hope;

'Cross' and 'The Negro Speaks of Rivers' from *Collected Poems of Langston Hughes* (Alfred A Knopf/Vintage). Reprinted by permission of David Higham Associates; and (US and Canada) Alfred A Knopf, a division of Random House, Inc. for 'Cross' and 'The Negro Speaks of Rivers' from *The Collected Poems of Langston Hughes;*

Faber and Faber Ltd for 'Epiphany', 'Pike' and 'Bride and Groom Lie Hidden for Three Days' from *Collected Poems* by Ted Hughes;

Faber and Faber Ltd for 'A Pilot from the Carrier', 'The Death of the Ball Turret Gunner' and 'The Woman at the Washington Zoo' all from *Complete Poems* by Randall Jarrell; and (US and Canada) Farrar, Straus and Giroux, LLC. for 'A Pilot from the Carrier', 'The Death of the Ball Turret Gunner' and 'The Woman at the Washington Zoo' from *The Complete Poems* by Randall Jarrell;

Carcanet Press for 'The Purse-Seine' and 'The Eye'; and (US) Random House Inc. for 'The Purse-Seine' and 'The Eye' from *Selected Poetry of Robinson Jeffers*;

Carcanet Press for 'My Grandmother' from *New Collected Poems* by Elizabeth Jennings;

Andrew Johnston for 'How to Talk' by Andrew Johnston;

Faber and Faber Ltd for *from* 'In Parenthesis' by David Jones;

Oxford University Press East Africa for 'A Leopard Lives in a Muu Tree' from *An Introduction to East African Poetry* by Jonathan Kariara;

'Epic' by Patrick Kavanagh is reprinted from *Collected Poems*, edited by Antoinette Quinn (Allen Lane, 2004), by kind permission of the Trustees of the Estate of late Katherine B. Kavanagh, through the Jonathan Williams Literary Agency;

Jackie Kay for '£££' from 'Severe Gale 8' in *The Adoption Papers* by Jackie Kay;

Bloodaxe Books for *from* 'The Avenue Bearing the Initial of Christ into the New World' from *Selected Poems*; and (US and Canada) Houghton Mifflin Harcourt Publishing Company for *from* 'The Avenue Bearing the Initial of Christ into the New World' from *What A Kingdom It Was: Poems by Galway Kinnell*;

Faber and Faber Ltd for 'Going' from *Red Sauce, Whiskey and Snow* by August Kleinzahler;

Bloodaxe Books for 'The Priest' from *Collected Poems in English* by Arun Kolatkar;

Wesleyan University Press for 'Facing it' from *Neon Vernacular* by Yusef Komunyakaa;

Faber and Faber Ltd for 'MCMXIV', 'Church Going', 'The Whitsun Weddings' and 'Going, Going' from *Collected Poems* by Philip Larkin;

The Poetry Business for 'Living with the Doctor' by Michael Laskey;

Pollinger Limited and The Estate of Freida Lawrence Ravagl for 'Guards', 'Last Lesson of the Afternoon', 'Piano' and 'Snake' by D. H. Lawrence;

Bloodaxe Books for 'Misnomer' from *New Selected Poems* by Denise Levertov;

Faber and Faber Ltd for *from* 'War Music' by Christopher Logue;

The Random House Group Ltd.; and (US) Michael Longley and Wake Forest University Press for 'Wounds' from *Collected Poems* by Michael Longley;

Farrar, Straus and Giroux, LLC. for 'Skunk Hour', 'Fall 1961', 'For the Union Dead' and 'Walking Early Sunday Morning' from *Collected Poems* by Robert Lowell;

Polygon, an imprint of Birlinn Ltd. for 'Crossing the Border' from *The Poems of Norman MacCaig*;

Carcanet Press for 'The Glen of Silence' by Hugh MacDiarmid;

Carcanet Press for 'Death Valley' by Sorley MacLean;

David Higham Associates for 'Bagpipe Music', *from* 'Autumn Journal, VII', 'Meeting Point' and 'The Taxis' all from *Collected Poems* (Faber and Faber) by Louis MacNeice;

Derek Mahon and The Gallery Press, Ireland for 'A Disused Shed in Co. Wexford' from *New Collected Poems* by Derek Mahon;

Carcanet Press and Bill Manhire for 'Jalopy: the End of Love' by Bill Manhire;

The Society of Authors as the Literary Representative of the Estate of John Masefield for 'Cargoes', 'Sea-Fever' and 'An Epilogue' by John Masefield;

Bloodaxe Books for 'Helene and Heloise' from *Boys at Twylight: Poems 1985–1996* by Glyn Maxwell;

HarperCollins Australia for 'Because' and 'Tabletalk' from *Collected Poems 1936–1970* by James McAuley;

'Let Me Die a Youngman's Death' by Roger McGough © Roger McGough reproduced by permission of PFD (www.pfd.co.uk) on behalf of Roger McGough; 'Let Me Die a Youngman's Death' by Roger McGough from *The Mersey Sound* (© Roger McGough, 1967) is reproduced in electronic and audio editions by permission of United Agents (www.unitedagents.co.uk) on behalf of Roger McGough;

Faber and Faber Ltd for 'Legacies' from *Sky Nails: Poems 1979–1997* by Jamie McKendrick;

Carcanet Press for 'Visitors: Armthorpe, August 1984' by Ian McMillan;

W. S. Merwin for 'For the Anniversary of my Death'; and Alfred A. Knopf, a division of Random House, Inc. for 'A Taste' from *The Vixen* both by W. S. Merwin;

Carcanet Press for 'Dirge without Music' by Edna St. Vincent Millay;

Egmont UK Ltd London; and (US and Canada) Dutton Children's Books, a Division of Penguin Young Readers Group, a member of Penguin Group (USA) Inc. for 'Buckingham Palace' from *When We Were Very Young* by A.A. Milne; and (for audio) text by A.A. Milne copyright © The

Trustees of the Pooh Properties reproduced with permission of Curtis Brown Limited, London;

Faber and Faber Ltd for 'The Steeple-Jack', 'What are years?' and 'The Mind is an Enchanting Thing' from *Collected Poems*; and (US and Canada) Scribner, A Division of Simon & Schuster, Inc for 'What are years?' and 'The Mind is an Enchanting Thing' from *The Collected Poems of Marianne Moore* and Viking Penguin, a division of Penguin Group (USA) Inc. for 'The Steeple-Jack' from *The Poems of Marianne Moore*;

Carcanet Press for 'One Cigarette' by Edwin Morgan;

Faber and Faber Ltd for 'Anne Frank Huis' from *Selected Poems* by Andrew Motion;

Faber and Faber Ltd for 'Cuba' and 'Why Brownlee left' both from *New Selected Poems 1968–1994* by Paul Muldoon;

Carcanet Press for 'The Ballad of Jimmy Governor', 'The Future', 'It Allows a Portrait in Line Scan at Fifteen' and 'Letters to the Winner' all by Les Murray;

Alexander Nemerov for 'August, 1945', 'On Getting Out of Vietnam' and 'On Being Asked for a Peace Poem' by Howard Nemerov;

Carcanet Press for 'The Day Lady Died' and 'Anxiety' by Frank O'Hara;

The Random House Group Ltd. for 'May 1968' from *Selected Poems* and 'Looking at my Father' from *The Sign of Saturn*; and (US and Canada) Alfred A. Knopf, a division of Random House, Inc for 'May 1968' from *The Wellspring* and 'Looking at my Father' from *The Gold Cell* both by Sharon Olds;

Gerald Duckworth & Co Ltd. for 'War Song' by Dorothy Parker; and (US and Canada) Viking Penguin, a division of Penguin Group (USA) Inc. for 'War Song' from *The Portable Dorothy Parker* by Dorothy Parker;

Faber and Faber Ltd for 'The Scale of Intensity' from *God's Gift to Women* by Don Paterson;

Carcanet Press for 'Shirt' by Robert Pinsky;

Faber and Faber Ltd for 'The Bee Meeting' and 'Lady Lazarus' from *Collected Poems* by Sylvia Plath; and (US) HarperCollins Publishers for 'The Bee Meeting' and 'Lady Lazarus' from *Ariel: Poems by Sylvia Plath*;

The Random House Group Ltd. for 'A Walk in Wurzburg' and 'To the Moon and Back' from *Collected Poems* by William Plomer; and (for electronic) The Estate of William Plomer for 'A Walk in Wurzburg' and 'To the Moon and Back';

Faber and Faber Ltd for 'The Gypsy', 'Abu Salammamm – A Song of Empire' and 'E. P. Ode pour l'Election de son Sepulchre' all from *Collected Shorter Poems* and 'Canto XLV' from *The Cantos*; and (US and Canada) New Directions Publishing Corp. for 'Abu Salammam – A Song of Empire', 'E. P. Ode Pour L'election de Son Sepulchre' and 'The Gypsy' from *The Cantos of Ezra Pound* by Ezra Pound;

University of Toronto Press for *from* 'The Titanic' from *E. J. Pratt: Complete Poems* by E. J. Pratt;

Carcanet Press for 'Hope for refugees' by Karen Press;

'To an Anti-Semite' from *Selected Poems* by Carl Rakosi (New Directions Publishing Corp, 1941). Permission granted by Marilyn J Kane, Literary Executor for the Estate of Carl Rakosi (Callman Rawley);

Carcanet Press; and (US and Canada) Alfred A. Knopf, a division of Random House, Inc. for 'Vision by Sweetwater' from *Selected Poems* by John Crowe Ransom;

Bloodaxe Books for 'This is unclean: to eat Turbots on Tuesdays' from *Collected Poems: 1985–1996* by Peter Reading;

'The Curiosity-Shop' from *Dr Faust's Sea-Spiral Spirit and Other Poems* by Peter Redgrove, (Routledge, 1972). By permission of David Higham Associates Ltd;

Carcanet Press for 'Lessons of the War' from *Collected Poems* by Henry Reed;

Black Sparrow Books, an imprint of David R Godine, Publishing, Inc. for *from* 'Jerusalem the Golden' from *The Poems of Charles Reznikoff: 1918–1975;*

Adrienne Rich and W. W. Norton & Company, Inc. for 'The Uncle Speaks in the Drawing Room' from *Collected Early Poems: 1950–1970* by Adrienne Rich;

Carcanet Press for 'Luxury' by Edgell Rickword;

'Escape' from *Poems* (1993) by W. R. Rodgers, reprinted by kind permission of the Estate of W. R. Rodgers and The Gallery Press, Loughcrew, Oldcastle, County Meath, Ireland;

Faber and Faber Ltd for 'Child on Top of a Greenhouse' from *Collected Poems*; and (US and Canada) Doubleday, a division of Random House Inc. for 'Child on Top of a Greenhouse' from *Collected Poems of Theodore Roethke;*

Jane Ross for 'Survivors' by Alan Ross;

Carol Rumens for 'A Dialogue of Perestroishiks' by Carol Rumens;

Houghton Mifflin Harcourt Publishing Company for 'Mohammed Bek

Hadjetlache' and 'Buffalo Dusk' from *Smoke and Steel* and 'Buttons' from *Chicago Poems* all by Carl Sandburg;

The Estate of George Sassoon for 'The Hero', 'They' and 'Reconciliation'; and (US) Viking Penguin, a division of Penguin Group (USA) Inc. for 'The Hero', 'They' and 'Reconciliation' from *Collected Poems of Siegfried Sassoon*;

'All my Pretty Ones' by Anne Sexton. Reprinted by permission of SLL/ Sterling Lord Literistic, Inc. Copyright by Anne Sexton; and (US and Canada) Houghton Mifflin Harcourt Publishing for 'All my Pretty Ones' by Anne Sexton;

Faber and Faber Ltd for 'Prodigy' from *Classic Ballroom Dances*, 'Spoon' from *Dismantling the Silence* and 'What the Gypsies Told my Grandmother while she was still a Young Girl' from *Walking the Black Cat*; and (US) George Braziller for 'Prodigy' and 'Spoon' from *Selected Early Poems* all by Charles Simic;

BOA Editions Ltd for 'Carentan O Carentan' and 'To the Western World' from *The Owner of the House: New Collected Poems 1940–2001* by Louis Simpson;

HarperCollins Australia for 'Five Bells' and 'Beach Burial' from *Selected Poems* by Kenneth Slessor;

Carcanet Press for 'Old Woman' by Iain Crichton Smith;

The Estate of James MacGibbon for 'Not Waving but Drowning' and 'I Remember' from *Selected Poems*; and (US and Canada) New Directions Publishing Corp. for 'Not Waving but Drowning' and 'I Remember' from *Collected Poems of Stevie Smith*;

Auckland University Press for 'The forecast for night' by Elizabeth Smither;

Auckland University Press for 'Waikato Railstop' by Kendrick Smithyman;

The Permissions Company, Inc. on behalf of BOA Editions Ltd for 'Heart's Needle: 4' from *Not for Specialists: New and Selected Poems* by W. D. Snodgrass;

The Estate of Stephen Spender for 'Thoughts during an Air Raid' and 'Port Bou' from *New Collected Poems* by Stephen Spender;

Elizabeth Spires; and (US and Canada) Viking Penguin, a division of Penguin Group (USA) Inc. for 'The Woman on the Dump' from *Acconciade* by Elizabeth Spires;

Bloodaxe Books for 'Sighting the Slave Ship' from *The Lady & the Hare: New & Selected Poems* by Pauline Stainer;

Carcanet Press; and (Aust and NZ) Auckland University Press for 'Dallas, 1963' by C. K. Stead;

Faber and Faber Ltd for 'Sunday Morning', 'The Snow Man' and 'The Idea of Order at Key West' all from *Selected Poems* by Wallace Stevens;

'B Flat' and *from* 'Rutherford' by Arrangement with the Licensor, Estate of Douglas Stewart c/o Curtis Brown (Aust) Pty Ltd in prominently displayed;

The Random House Group Ltd. for 'Breaches' from *Selected Poems* by Matthew Sweeney;

'Fern Hill' and 'Do not go gentle into that good night' from *Collected Poems* by Dylan Thomas (Orion). Reprinted by permission of David Higham Associates Limited; and (US and Canada) New Directions Publishing Corp. for 'Fern Hill' and 'Do not go gentle into that good night' from *The Poems of Dylan Thomas*;

Anthony Thwaite for 'Philip Larkin in New Orleans' by Anthony Thwaite;

Carcanet Press for 'Siena in Sixty-Eight' by Charles Tomlinson;

Yale University for 'Portrait in Georgia' by Jean Toomer;

John Updike for 'Seven New Ways of Looking at the Moon' from *John Updike Collected Poems 1953–1993* (Hamish Hilton 1993) by John Updike;

Faber and Faber Ltd for 'Elegy' and 'Koenig of the River' both from *Collected Poems 1948–1984* by Derek Walcott;

Carcanet Press for 'Mr Gradgrind's Country' by Sylvia Townsend Warner;

Robert Penn Warren for 'Natural History' by Robert Penn Warren;

The Salamander Oasis Trust for 'Day of Liberation, Bergen-Belsen, May 1945' by Phillip Whitfield;

Farrar, Strauss and Giroux, LLC. for 'Tar' from *Collected Poems* by C. K. Williams;

Waywiser Press for 'A Baroque Wall-Fountain in the Villa Sciarra', 'Advice to a Prophet', 'A Miltonic Sonnet for Mr. Johnson on His Refusal of Peter Hurd's Official Portrait' and 'A Fable' all from *Collected Poems 1943–2004* by Richard Wilbur; and (world ex UK/CW) Houghton Mifflin Harcourt Publishing Company for 'A Baroque Wall-Fountain in the Villa Sciarra' from *Things of This World*, 'Advice to a Prophet' from *Advice to a Prophet and Other Poems,* 'A Miltonic Sonnet for Mr. Johnson on His Refusal of Peter Hurd's Official Portrait' from *Walking To Sleep: New Poems and Translations*; and 'A Fable' from *New and Collected Poems* all by Richard Wilbur;

Faber and Faber Ltd for 'Tangerines', 'When I Grow Up' and 'Her News' all from *Collected Poems* by Hugo Williams;

Carcanet Press for 'The Red Wheelbarrow' and 'The Last Words of my English Grandmother'; and (US and Canada) New Directions Publishing Corp for

'The Red Wheelbarrow' and 'The Last Words of my English Grandmother' from *Collected Poems: Volume 1, 1909–1939* by William Carlos Williams;

Wesleyan University Press for 'Eisenhower's Visit to France, 1959' from *The Branch Will Not Break* by James Wright;

ETT Imprint for 'The Hawthorn Hedge', 'The Company of Lovers', 'The Lost Man' and 'At Cooloolah' from *A Human Pattern: Selected Poems* by Judith Wright;

Carcanet Press for 'Walking on the Cliff' by Andrew Young.

Index of poets and titles

SIMON ARMITAGE (1963–)

Armitage was born in Yorkshire and his early poems reflected his regional background, with an exuberant relish for dialect and a talent for story-telling. He has proved a prolific and popular poet, winning wide critical acclaim. He has recently produced a highly-regarded version of *Sir Gawain and the Green Knight*.

JOHN ASH (1948–)

Born in Manchester, Ash moved to New York in the mid-Eighties, and later to Istanbul. His poetry has affinities with that of Ashbery and the New York School, but his subject matter has increasingly been drawn from the eastern Mediterranean.

JOHN ASHBERY (1927–)

Born in Rochester, New York, Ashbery emerged in the Fifties and Sixties as a bizarrely authoritative challenge to received ideas of poetry, and has been a commanding and polarising post-modern presence ever since. 'My poetry is disjunct,' he has conceded, 'but then so is life.' Lauded by some, abhorred by others, he argues: 'I don't think thinking is what it is thought to be.'

W. H. AUDEN (1907–73)

Auden was the leading English poet of his generation from his student days at Oxford, where he naturally attracted followers like Stephen Spender. A committed anti-fascist, Auden's was the defining voice of the Thirties, and his decision in 1939 to move to the United States, where he had met his future partner, Chester Kallman, alienated many in Britain. Auden continued to write prolifically, and although his detractors identified a decline in the quality of his work, he remained a leading literary figure. He was Professor of Poetry at Oxford (1956–60), and returned for the last year of his life to his old college, Christ Church.

Poet and dramatist, Baxter converted to Roman Catholicism in his twenties. Near the end of his relatively short life he began the life of a hermit at Jerusalem, a Maori settlement on the Wanganui River, where he produced his outstanding late work, the *Jerusalem Sonnets* and *Autumn Testament*.

Anglo-French, Catholic, Balliol-educated, Belloc was prolific, robust in his views, and deliciously waspish. His cautionary tales are still widely read, and his tart squibs. 'No man of his time,' said Father Ronald Knox, 'fought so hard for the good things.'

Born in Oklahoma, Berryman studied at Columbia University and taught at Princeton, Harvard and Cincinnati, then at Minnesota from 1955 until his death. The first volume of the *Dream Songs* brought him the Pulitzer Prize.

After failure at Oxford and a brief spell in teaching, Betjeman became a freelance writer and broadcaster, espousing the unfashionable cause of Victorian architecture. He favoured traditional forms in his poetry, and, in the wake of a successful television career, became immensely popular. He became Poet Laureate in 1972 and was also knighted.

Born in Delaware and raised in Alaska, Bierds studied at the University of Washington and later became a professor there. She has received awards from the Ingram Merrill and Guggenheim Memorial Foundations as well as a MacArthur Fellowship.

EARLE BIRNEY (1904–95)

Born in Calgary, Birney studied in Canada, the US and England. A Trotskyist in the Thirties, he travelled from London to Norway to interview Trotsky. In later life he received many awards in Canada, and founded the country's first creative writing department, at the University of British Columbia.

ELIZABETH BISHOP (1911–79)

Brought up by her maternal grandparents in Nova Scotia, Bishop was one of the least rooted of the century's poets, and spent much of her life travelling before settling in Brazil. Her fastidious powers of observation were honed under the tutelage of Marianne Moore, and she had much in common with her contemporary, Robert Lowell.

EAVAN BOLAND (1944–)

In a writing life that has taken her from Dublin to Stanford University in California, Boland has concluded that '20th century poetry took a wrong turning', and the 'ancient trust' that existed between writers and readers was violated by Modernism. Her own work, which has earned several awards, attempts to rebuild that trust.

ROO BORSON (1952–)

Born in Berkeley, California, Roo (Ruth) Borson settled in Canada in her mid-twenties. Her numerous awards include the Governor General's Award and the Griffin Poetry Prize.

CHARLES BOYLE (1951–)

Born in Leeds and educated at Cambridge, Boyle has taught in Egypt and worked in publishing in London. His honours include a Cholmondeley Award and a McKitterick Prize for *24 for 3*, a fiction written under the pseudonym Jennie Walker.

EDWARD KAMAU BRATHWAITE (1930–)

Brathwaite is a poet and historian intent on grounding a Caribbean culture on the West Indies' African origins. His three long poems *Rights of Passage* (1967),

Masks (1968) and *Islands* (1969) were collected as *The Arrivants: a New World Trilogy* in 1973. His many awards include the Griffin Poetry Prize.

CHRISTOPHER BRENNAN (1870–1932)

'I said, This misery must end'	89

Born in Sydney of Irish parents, Brennan absorbed influences of German Romanticism and French Symbolism in his work. A prey to drink and despondency in his later years, he died in poverty.

ROBERT BRIDGES (1844–1930)

'Low Barometer'	189

Bridges met Gerard Manley Hopkins at Oxford and was responsible for editing and publishing the great Victorian's work after his death. Bridges' own poetry was sufficiently well thought-of for him to become Poet Laureate in 1913.

ROBERT BRINGHURST (1946–)

'Questions for the Old Woman'	606
'The Reader'	663

Born in Los Angeles and raised in the northwestern United States, Bringhurst studied at the Massachusetts Institute of Technology before settling in Canada. He has lived in many countries around the world. A many-sided writer, he has translated the fragments of Parmenides, and epic poetry of the Haida people, and has written a standard work on *The Elements of Typographic Style*.

RUPERT BROOKE (1887–1915)

'The Old Vicarage, Grantchester'	73
'The Soldier'	99

Cambridge-educated, handsome and intellectually confident, Brooke seemed destined for a glittering career. He had his moment of national glory when his 'War Sonnets' caught the public mood in 1914, but his own untimely death from septicaemia, far from the trenches, deprived him of the opportunity to revise his early eagerness when hostilities broke out.

GWENDOLYN BROOKS (1917–2000)

'Beverly Hills, Chicago'	353

A black American poet who defined her subject as 'Bronzeville' – i.e. the black ghetto – Gwendolyn Brooks was born in Kansas, but was brought up in Chicago. She published her first book, *A Street in Bronzeville*, in 1945, won a Pulitzer Prize in 1949, and succeeded Carl Sandburg as Poet Laureate of Illinois.

ALAN BROWNJOHN (1931–)

A teacher and lecturer, Alan Brownjohn describes himself as 'quietly, but very seriously, atheist, socialist, and internationalist', but stresses 'the Englishness of what I write'. For many years a presiding presence in the Poetry Society, he records British life in a vein of shrewdly observed satire.

BASIL BUNTING (1900–85)

A friend and disciple of Ezra Pound, whom he sought out in Rapallo, Italy, before the Second World War, Bunting was a leading English Modernist, who achieved wide recognition late in life with the publication of his autobiographical poem, *Briggflatts*.

DAVID CAMPBELL (1915–79)

David Campbell is almost certainly the only eminent Australian poet to have played rugby for England (where he was a student at Cambridge). Raised on a sheep farm in New South Wales, he was a pilot in the Second World War, after which he returned to Australia and to poetry and farming. Encouraged by E. M. W. Tillyard in England and Douglas Stewart in Australia, he was a man who, in Manning Clark's words, 'encouraged everyone in the room to give of their best'.

ROY CAMPBELL (1901–57)

The South African satirist roundly lambasted Georgian poetry in *The Georgiad* (1931) and South African provincialism in *The Wayzgoose* (1924). He went against the liberal literary grain by supporting Franco in the Spanish Civil War, but proved stoutly anti-Fascist during the Second World War.

ANNE CARSON (1950–)

Born in Toronto, Carson has had a distinguished career as a classicist at McGill, Michigan and Princeton universities, and has received a Lannan Award and Guggenheim and MacArthur Fellowships for her poetry.

CIARAN CARSON (1948–)

Carson was born in Belfast, and his poetry provides an intimate portrait of his native city and in particular an unblinking insight into the experience of living through the sectarian violence of the 'Troubles'.

CHARLES CAUSLEY (1917–2003)

A Cornishman, who drew on local folklore for many of his poems, Causley served in the Navy during the Second World War and opted for the quieter life of the classroom when he returned home. He favoured traditional forms, especially the ballad, which brought him a widespread popularity.

G. K. CHESTERTON (1874–1936)

Chesterton was a prolific novelist, poet and journalist, whose aversion to the modern world of big business and centralised political power inspired him both to robust satire and romantic celebrations of an older England. He is best remembered now for his detective stories featuring the canny Catholic priest, Father Brown.

STEVE CHIMOMBO (1945–)

Chimombo was born in Malawi and, after studying at universities in the UK and the US, returned to teach at the University of Malawi, where he is currently Professor of English. In addition to poetry, he has written fiction, drama and a critical study of Malawian oral literature.

YVETTE CHRISTIANSË (1954–)

Christiansë was born in South Africa, but her family left for Australia to escape the apartheid regime. She has taught at universities in the US (Duke, Princeton, and currently African American and postcolonial literatures at Fordham), and in 2006 published a first novel, *Unconfessed*.

AUSTIN CLARKE (1896–1974)

Like James Joyce, Clarke was educated by Jesuits at Belvedere College and at University College, Dublin. Playwright, novelist, poet and autobiographer, he worked for a spell in England as a journalist, but otherwise spent his life in Ireland, concentrating in his work on Irish legend and folk-tales.

GILLIAN CLARKE (1937–)

'The Water-Diviner'	607

Cardiff born and educated, Gillian Clarke's work is rooted in the Welsh experience, urban and rural. Her 1982 collection, *Letter from a Far Country*, brought her a wide readership. In 2008 she became the third National Poet for Wales.

HARRY CLIFTON (1952–)

'Death of Thomas Merton'	502

Clifton brings to his poetry the long and deep perspectives of a man who has lived in many parts of the world. Now back in his native Dublin, he was named Ireland Professor of Poetry in 2010.

LUCILLE CLIFTON (1936–2010)

'white lady'	704

Clifton was born in New York and in a prolific writing life celebrated her African American heritage as well as exploring feminist themes. Her *Blessing the Boats: New and Collected Poems 1988–2000* won the National Book Award for Poetry and she was posthumously awarded the Robert Frost Medal for lifetime achievement by the Poetry Society of America.

DON COLES (1927–)

from 'Landslides'	608
'Kurgan No. 10'	780

Born in Woodstock, Ontario, Coles writes poetry notable for its probing, compassionate openness, and its relaxed familiarity with the high culture of European Modernism. Margaret Atwood wrote that his poetry is 'a joy to follow'. In his late seventies he published a first novel, *Doctor Bloom's Story*, in 2004.

PADRAIC COLUM (1881–1972)

'Roger Casement'	124

Colum was a poet, dramatist and children's writer. In his twenties he associated with Yeats in the development of the Abbey Theatre, but left Ireland in 1914, spending most of the rest of his life in the USA.

DAVID CONSTANTINE (1944–)

'The Quick and the Dead at Pompeii'	652

Lancashire-born, Constantine has spent his professional life as an Oxford don. A highly regarded translator of German and French poetry, he has won wide recognition for his own poetry and short fiction.

Wendy Cope (1945–)

A brilliant parodist and sharply witty observer of the relations between men
and women, Cope became one of the most popular British poets in the closing
years of the century. Ticked off by a reviewer for seeking to entertain, she
riposted: 'Write to amuse? What an appalling suggestion! / I write to make
people anxious and miserable and to worsen their indigestion.'

Frances Cornford (1886–1960)

Granddaughter of Charles Darwin and mother of John Cornford, Frances
Cornford spent most of her life in Cambridge. Her *Collected Poems* were
published in 1954, and she was awarded the Queen's Gold Medal for Poetry
in 1959.

John Cornford (1915–36)

Like his mother, Frances, Cornford wrote poetry from an early age. Educated
at Cambridge, he joined the Communist Party and in 1936 went to fight against
Franco in the Spanish Civil War, where he died on the Córdoba Front.

Noël Coward (1899–1973)

An all-round man of the theatre, Coward was one of the defining figures of
the inter-war years in Britain, writing witty, cynical plays and performing
satirical cabaret lyrics designed to both delight and shock. He also published
poetry and fiction and kept voluminous diaries.

Hart Crane (1899–1932)

Crane was born in Ohio but spent much of his short life in New York. Alco-
holism, an inability to earn a living, and the difficulties of life as a homosexual,
drove him to suicide at the age of thirty-three. His best-known work is his
long poem, *The Bridge*, dominated by the Brooklyn Bridge, which Crane claimed
as a 'symbol of our constructive future'.

Countee Cullen (1903–46)

Cullen was a prominent figure in the Harlem Renaissance and came to prom-
inence with *The Black Christ and Other Poems* (1929), the title poem of which
mourned the victim of a lynching.

E. E. CUMMINGS (1894–1962)

A Harvard graduate, Cummings drove an ambulance in the First World War and stayed on in France to write a novel, *The Enormous Room* (1922). When he turned to poetry, he developed a playfully innovative style which subverted the conventions of punctuation, typography and diction.

ALLEN CURNOW (1911–2001)

Initially intending to follow his father into the Anglican ministry, Curnow turned first to journalism and then, after a spell in London, became an academic at the University of Auckland. With his own cosmopolitan but locally-rooted poetry, and through his work as anthologist, he had a formative influence on the cultural identity of New Zealand.

JOHN DAVIDSON (1857–1909)

Davidson left Scotland and teaching in his thirties, for a writer's career in London. He developed an urban pastoral, which T. S. Eliot admired, and later published a series of 'Testaments' proclaiming a harshly materialistic philosophy, which Eliot found 'uncongenial'. He committed suicide by drowning.

IDRIS DAVIES (1905–53)

A Welsh socialist who insisted on 'the difference between poetry and propaganda', Davies addressed in his own work the social and political concerns of his native South Wales. He wrote a powerful series of poems on the impact of the General Strike of 1926, which was spearheaded by the miners.

W. H. DAVIES (1871–1940)

Monmouthshire-born, Davies spent many years on the road in America before having to come home after losing a leg in an accident. His experiences were recalled in *The Autobiography of a Super Tramp*, which was published (with a preface by George Bernard Shaw) in 1908.

WALTER DE LA MARE (1873–1956)

'The Listeners'   82

Poet, novelist and short story writer (for both adults and children), de la Mare scored a first success with his collection of poems, *The Listeners* (1912). He had a long and successful career, and was awarded the Order of Merit in 1953.

TOI DERRICOTTE (1941–)

'On the Turning Up of Unidentified Black Female Corpses'   683

After a Catholic upbringing in Detroit, Derricotte moved to New York City, where her poetry flourished. She published *The Black Notebooks* in 1997 and is currently Professor of English at Pittsburgh.

IMTIAZ DHARKER (1954–)

'Purdah I'   681
'Untitled'   723

Dharker is an artist, documentary film-maker and poet. She was born in Lahore, brought up in Glasgow, and now divides her time between Bombay and London. Her poetry covers the wide range of her own experience and also speaks powerfully against the oppression of women by religious and political patriarchies.

H.D. (1886–1961)

from 'R.A.F.'   294
from 'The Walls Do Not Fall'   302

The American Hilda Doolittle travelled to Europe in 1911 and became one of the small but influential group of Imagist poets led by Ezra Pound (she signed her early submissions to *Poetry* magazine 'H.D., Imagiste'). She married fellow poet Richard Aldington, helped edit the *Egoist*, and, after some years in Switzerland, returned to London in 1939. There she wrote a powerful trilogy of long poems reflecting the experience of the war, most notably *The Walls Do Not Fall* (1944) about London in the Blitz.

MARK DOTY (1953–)

'A Letter from the Coast'   746

Tennessee-born Doty came to prominence with his collection *Atlantis*, inspired by the AIDS death of his partner Wally Roberts. In 1995 he was the first American poet to win Britain's T. S. Eliot Prize.

KEITH DOUGLAS (1920–44)

Douglas was a young officer in North Africa, and – like Wilfred Owen in the First World War – came to maturity as a writer in time for a short but intense period of creativity before his death in the Normandy campaign of 1944. In addition to his poems, he wrote a powerful memoir of his army experience, *Alamein to Zem Zem* (1946).

CAROL ANN DUFFY (1955–)

Born in Glasgow, Duffy was raised and educated in Stafford, and studied philosophy at Liverpool University. The recipient of numerous awards, she became Poet Laureate in 2009.

IAN DUHIG (1954–)

Duhig, born in London to Irish parents, has proved one of the most original poets of his generation. While contemporary in his concerns and irony, Duhig displays something of an anthropologist's interest in the strange ways of foreign (and forgotten) cultures.

DOUGLAS DUNN (1942–)

Dunn has become one of the foremost Scottish poets of the century, with a succession of books addressing issues of class and national identity. His most successful collection, however, was *Elegies* (1985), written after the death of his first wife.

PAUL DURCAN (1944–)

A brave and outspoken critic of IRA terrorism throughout the Troubles, Durcan has also written with unflinching honesty about his own personal life, in particular about his strained relationship with his father, in *Daddy, Daddy* (1990), which won the Whitbread Poetry Prize.

LAWRENCE DURRELL (1912–90)

Better known as a novelist (*The Alexandria Quartet*, 1957–1960), Durrell was a travel writer as well as a poet. Like his brother, the author and zoologist Gerald,

Lawrence Durrell lived much of his life abroad, initially teaching for the British Council.

BOB DYLAN (1941–)

'Blowin' in the Wind'	438

Born Robert Zimmerman, Dylan took his name from his hero, Dylan Thomas, although he was closer in style and tone to the Beat writers Ginsberg and Kerouac. By far the most influential singer-songwriter of the second half of the century, Dylan provided the soundtrack for the Sixties generation, but effortlessly transcended the 'protest' tag with a wry, satirical and at times surrealist engagement with the American Dream.

T. S. ELIOT (1888–1965)

'The Love Song of J. Alfred Prufrock'	139
from 'The Waste Land'	164
'Journey of the Magi'	195
'East Coker'	284

Poet, playwright, critic and cultural commentator, Eliot was a towering presence in twentieth-century literature, and *The Waste Land* (1922) was unquestionably the single most influential poem of the period. With his fellow American, Ezra Pound, Eliot led the modernist movement, which radically extended the parameters of the possible within poetry in English. In 1927 Eliot took British citizenship and joined the Church of England. This shift to a more conservative perspective disappointed many, but his later masterpiece, *Four Quartets* (1935–1942), proved his creative powers undiminished, and his stature was recognised in 1948 with the Order of Merit and the Nobel Prize for Literature.

KATHLEEN EMERSON (DATES UNKNOWN)

'Oh! who are these in scant array'	68

Little is known about Kathleen Emerson beyond the fact that she was incarcerated in Holloway Prison, London, and contributed to the pamphlet of poems by fellow suffragettes similarly imprisoned for civil disobedience in pursuit of their cause. Emerson's name appears in the roll of honour of Suffragette Prisoners 1905–1914, compiled by the Suffragette Fellowship.

WILLIAM EMPSON (1906–84)

'Aubade'	210
'Missing Dates'	239
'Let it go'	351

Educated at Cambridge, where he studied English under I. A. Richards, Empson showed precocious brilliance with the publication of *Seven Types of Ambiguity* in 1930. His own poetry followed his critical precepts in that it was highly complex and multi-layered. He taught at universities in China and Japan and returned to England to become Professor of English at Sheffield. He was knighted in 1979.

D. J. ENRIGHT (1920–2002)

Like Empson, Enright taught English literature abroad, mainly in the Far East. In addition to poetry, he wrote fiction and criticism, and edited *The Oxford Book of Contemporary Verse 1945–1980*.

GAVIN EWART (1916–95)

After an early start, Ewart wrote virtually no poetry at all for many years, and then produced an unstoppable spate of poems which continued through to the end of his life. Irreverent and unshockable, he displayed a generously open-minded interest in all human foibles, however bizarre.

NISSIM EZEKIEL (1924–2004)

One of India's leading poets writing in English, Ezekiel eschewed the rhetorical heights and reflected the daily life of the sub-continent in a contemporary idiom. A university lecturer, art critic and editor, he also wrote for the stage.

A. R. D. FAIRBURN (1904–57)

Fairburn belonged to the generation that rose to dominate New Zealand poetry in the Thirties. A fourth-generation New Zealander, he was a commanding presence not only in his literary work but in his social gregariousness and his socio-political engagement (like Pound, he was interested in Douglas's Social Credit). After his death, the great short-story writer Frank Sargeson described Fairburn as 'one of the most extraordinary men born in the southern hemisphere'.

U. A. FANTHORPE (1929–2009)

It was while she was working as a hospital receptionist, having given up her job as an English teacher, that Fanthorpe started to publish the poems that made her one of Britain's most popular poets. Her *New and Collected Poems* was published posthumously in 2010.

JAMES FENTON (1949–)

'Dead Soldiers'	597

The Memory of War (1982), which drew on his experiences as a correspondent in Vietnam and Cambodia, established James Fenton as one of the finest poets of his generation. Impressive in its range, both in subject matter and style, his work adheres to his watchword in 'The Manila Manifesto': 'This is no time for people who say: this, this and only this. We say: this, and *this*, and *that* too.'

LAWRENCE FERLINGHETTI (1919–)

'In Goya's greatest scenes we seem to see'	394

Ferlinghetti was a leading light in the Beat movement, and co-founder of City Lights bookshop and publishing house in San Francisco, which promoted the work of Allen Ginsberg, Denise Levertov and Gregory Corso. His own output is extensive, experimental and antithetical to received American values.

ROGER FINCH (1937–)

'Dancing in the Churchill Lounge'	779

Born in Pittsburgh, Finch studied at George Washington University and Harvard before teaching for thirty years at universities in Japan. He now lives in Maine.

ROY FISHER (1930–)

'The Entertainment of War'	280

Fisher's poetry is grounded in Birmingham, where he was born, educated, and worked as a school and college teacher. Strongly influenced by the writing of William Carlos Williams, especially *Paterson*, Fisher remained unmistakably English, and his long poem about his home, 'City' (1962), gradually brought him wider notice and increased critical acclaim. He was elected a Fellow of the Royal Society of Literature in 2005.

R. D. FITZGERALD (1902–87)

'The Wind at Your Door'	399

Fitzgerald's career as a surveyor included ten years working in Fiji, an experience which later fed into his poetry. Like his contemporary Kenneth Slessor, he is credited with lifting Australian poetry to a higher level of intellectual seriousness, and in *The Wind at Your Door* (1959) he revisited the conflicted history of the early convict settlements. He was awarded an OBE in 1951.

JAMES ELROY FLECKER (1884–1915)

'The Ballad of Camden Town'	54

Flecker was a diplomat whose postings to Constantinople and Beirut nourished his fascination with the East, seen most powerfully in his collection of poems, *The Golden Journey to Samarkand* (1913), and his play *Hassan* (published posthumously in 1922). But he was also interested in his own society and in the urban pastoral of the fast-expanding megalopolis that London was becoming.

JOHN FORBES (1950–98)

'Love Poem'	708

Often discussed in connection with Frank O'Hara (on whom he wrote his master's dissertation at Sydney), Forbes was notable for his catholic taste. Alan Wearne reported that Forbes admired Gray and Cowper, Slessor, Manifold and Murray, and in a 1991 interview Forbes sang Tom Lehrer song lyrics. He died of a heart attack in his late forties.

CAROLYN FORCHÉ (1950–)

'The Visitor'	576

A politically engaged poet, translator and editor, Detroit-born Forché worked as a human rights advocate in El Salvador, resulting in her second book of poems, *The Country Between Us* (1981). Her anthology *Against Forgetting: Twentieth-Century Poetry of Witness* was published in 1993.

ROBERT FROST (1874–1963)

'Home Burial'	90
'The Census-Taker'	160
'Stopping by Woods on a Snowy Evening'	181
'Acquainted with the Night'	198

One of the giants of twentieth-century poetry, Robert Frost made a late start but then produced a formidable body of work. In focusing on the ordinary – mainly rural – lives of his fellow Americans, he established a much-loved contemporary voice in America's literature, and his national pre-eminence was reflected in the invitation to read a poem at John F. Kennedy's Inauguration in 1961.

JOHN FULLER (1937–)

'Kent'	702

Fuller shares his father, Roy Fuller's, interest in the varieties of poetic form. An English don at Oxford for most of his working life, he has produced critical works on the sonnet and Auden as well as several well-received works of fiction, for both adults and children. His *Collected Poems* appeared in 1996.

ROY FULLER (1912–91)

'On Seeing the Leni Riefenstahl Film of the 1936 Olympic Games'	224
'Spring 1942'	300

Fuller was a poet and novelist, who worked for most of his life for the Woolwich Building Society. He shrugged off the early influence of Auden to find his own voice and build a substantial reputation. The memorable lectures he gave while Professor of Poetry at Oxford were published in *Owls and Artificers* (1971) and *Professors and Gods* (1974).

DAVID GASCOYNE (1916–2001)

'Snow in Europe'	251

Gascoyne was the foremost English surrealist, displaying in his verse the practices he identified in his *A Short Survey of Surrealism* (1935). His later work made more concessions to the general reader, and a *Collected Poems* was published in 1965.

LEON GELLERT (1892–1977)

'Before Action'	131

Gellert was wounded in the Gallipoli campaign and invalided out of the Australian army in 1916. It was during the First World War that he found time to start writing poetry, and he published his first book in 1917. He had a career in magazines and newspapers as an editor and columnist.

WILFRID WILSON GIBSON (1878–1962)

'Flannan Isle'	15

A friend of Rupert Brooke, Gibson contributed to Edward Marsh's *Georgian Poetry*. In numerous volumes of verse and verse drama he often focused on his native Northumberland.

ALLEN GINSBERG (1926–97)

'America'	378

The leading Beat poet, Ginsberg came to prominence with the publication of *Howl and Other Poems* (1956) and built an international reputation as a charismatic performer and advocate for the peace movement and gay rights.

PETER GOLDSWORTHY (1951–)

'Mass for the Middle-Aged'	699

One of Australia's most acclaimed fiction writers, Goldsworthy is also an accomplished librettist. In 2010 he was honoured with the Order of Australia.

JORIE GRAHAM (1950–)

'History'	609

Born in New York and raised in Rome, Graham studied at the Iowa Writers' Workshop, where she later taught. Her numerous awards include a Pulitzer Prize and a MacArthur Fellowship. In 1999 she succeeded Seamus Heaney as Boylston Professor at Harvard.

W. S. Graham (1918–86)

'I leave this at your ear'	526

Graham was a Scottish poet who moved to St Ives in Cornwall, where he became part of the community of artists that had settled there after the Second World War. Largely neglected during his lifetime, Graham's reputation has grown since his death.

Robert Graves (1895–1985)

'Song: Lift-Boy'	203
'The Thieves'	263

Graves' first love was poetry, but he also wrote highly popular historical novels, including *I, Claudius*, which was turned into a successful television series, and one of the most influential memoirs of the First World War, *Goodbye to All That* (1929). For many years he lived on the island of Majorca, settling there for good after the Second World War. From 1961 to 1966 he was Professor of Poetry at Oxford.

Robert Gray (1945–)

'Flames and Dangling Wire'	569
'In Departing Light'	769

Described by Les Murray as 'one of the contemporary masters of poetry in English', Gray is highly regarded as poet and editor, and in 2008 published a memoir, *The Land I Came Through Last*. His work, often minimal or Imagist in manner, in part reflects his interest in Taoist and Buddhist philosophy, and his conviction that 'things as they are are what is mystical'.

Thom Gunn (1929–2004)

'The Wound'	369
'The Missing'	659

Gunn, like Auden before him, made a reputation in England and then moved to America for a more congenial lifestyle. Living in San Francisco, Gunn was at the epicentre of the AIDS epidemic in the 1980s, responding with his most celebrated collection, *The Man with Night Sweats* in 1992.

Ivor Gurney (1890–1937)

'Bach and the Sentry'	136

Gurney was both a poet and composer. He fought as an infantryman on the Western Front, where he was wounded and gassed. Although he survived, publishing two books of poetry, *Severn and Somme* (1917) and *War's Embers* (1919), he never fully recovered his mental health. He was institutionalised in 1922 and spent the rest of his life in care.

RALPH GUSTAFSON (1909–95)

Born in Quebec, Gustafson was a poet, music critic, academic and anthologist with over twenty volumes of poetry and prose to his credit. He edited the *Penguin Book of Canadian Verse* (1958).

MICHAEL HAMBURGER (1924–2007)

Hamburger's Jewish family moved from Berlin to London in 1933, and he was educated in England and served in the British Army during the Second World War. His own work as poet was accompanied by formidable labours as a translator of German poetry and as a critic.

SOPHIE HANNAH (1971–)

Born in Manchester, Hannah published her acclaimed first book of poems, *The Hero and the Girl Next Door*, when she was twenty-four. She is also a prolific writer of novels, crime fiction and children's books.

THOMAS HARDY (1840–1928)

Trained as an architect, in his thirties Hardy started publishing novels exploring the tragedy of ordinary men and women against a backdrop of indifferent fate. Fame turned to notoriety with the publication of *Jude the Obscure* (1895), after which he gave up fiction and turned to his first love, poetry. His posthumously published *Collected Poems* (1930) included over 900 poems.

JEFFREY HARRISON (1957–)

Born in Cincinatti, Harrison has taught at universities in the US and has received a number of awards, among them a Guggenheim Fellowship. Admirers have included Anthony Hecht and James Merrill.

GEOFFREY HILL (1932–)

Worcestershire-born, Hill brings to poetry a formidable intellect, a rejection of the confessional, and a detached overview of history and human folly. The 'florid grim music broken by grunts and shrieks' he spoke of having attempted in *King Log* (1968) might describe much of his extraordinary achievement as a poet. After spending much of his life in Cambridge and Boston he became Oxford Professor of Poetry in 2010.

SELIMA HILL (1945–)

Born in London, Hill won the 1988 Arvon poetry competition and has developed a highly distinctive, acclaimed fusion of feminism and surrealism. Deryn Rees-Jones has praised her 'dazzling excess'.

MICHAEL HOFMANN (1957–)

Hofmann is the son of the celebrated German novelist, Gert Hofmann (1931–93), and wrote about his relationship with his father in his aptly titled collection *Acrimony* (1986). In addition to being a poet, he is a critic, university teacher, anthologist and award-winning translator.

A. D. HOPE (1907–2000)

Kevin Hart spoke for many when he wrote that Australia had lost 'its greatest living poet' when Hope died. Prized since the Fifties for his exacting poetry, feared and revered for his unsparing critical acumen, Hope spent most of his working life teaching at Australian universities, gaining widespread recognition and many awards and honours.

LAURENCE HOPE (ADELA FLORENCE NICOLSON) (1865–1904)

Adela Florence Nicolson née Cory was the second of three daughters of an Indian Army colonel, and herself married an Indian Army colonel (later general) twice her own age, in 1889. Shortly after his death in 1904, Adela took poison. Two collections of her poems, *The Garden of Kama and Other Love Lyrics from India* (1901) and *Stars of the Desert* (1903), appeared in her lifetime, and quickly brought her a popularity with the reading public that lasted well into the interwar period, with a volume of *Collected Love Lyrics* appearing in 1929. Admirers included Hardy and Flecker.

A. E. Housman (1859–1936)

Housman's first, self-published, collection, *A Shropshire Lad* (1896), initially found few readers, but his poems of longing, loss and resignation became hugely popular during and after the First World War. He published only two further volumes, both in a similar vein.

Langston Hughes (1902–67)

Born in Missouri, Hughes emerged from a turbulent upbringing with an experience of college education (a year at Columbia University) before travelling to Africa, France and England. A lucky encounter with Vachel Lindsay on his return kick-started his career as a poet, and he became a leading figure in the Harlem Renaissance, his blues-based verse proving a popular and successful conduit for the black experience.

Ted Hughes (1930–98)

The raw power of *The Hawk in the Rain* (1957) and following volumes, and his marriage to Sylvia Plath and the tragedy of her suicide, propelled Hughes to early if unenviable prominence. Later he was Poet Laureate, co-edited two very successful anthologies with Seamus Heaney, and wrote a highly personal study of Shakespeare. In the last year of his life he published *Birthday Letters*, a collection of poems he had held back for years about his relationship with Plath.

Randall Jarrell (1914–65)

Born in Nashville and educated at Vanderbilt, Jarrell was an air force navigation trainer, and drew on his wartime experience for some of his best-known poems. A formidable poetry critic as well as poet, he also wrote books for children, and published one novel, *Pictures from an Institution* (1954). 'In works of art,' he observed, 'almost anything stands for more than itself; but this *more*, like Lohengrin, vanishes when it names itself.'

Pittsburgh-born, Jeffers spent most of his life on the Monterey coast of California, in a house and tower he built himself. His poetry revelled in the power of human passion, and the untamed forces of nature. His version of Euripides' *Medea* was a hit on Broadway in 1947.

Jenkins captured the late-century *zeitgeist* with *In the Hot-House* (1988), *Greenheart* (1990) and *Harm* (1994), which won the Forward Prize for the best collection of the year. He has worked at the *Times Literary Supplement* since graduating from Sussex University and is now deputy editor.

Educated at Oxford, Jennings was grouped with the Movement poets, but her Roman Catholicism (and gender) set her apart from Gunn, Larkin and Amis. She survived a period of serious mental illness and crowned her career with an accoladed second *Collected Poems* and a CBE.

Johnston is chief editor of the annual UNESCO report on education worldwide. A New Zealander, he has lived in France since 1997, and till 2010 worked for the *International Herald Tribune*.

Born in Kent to a Welsh father and English mother, Jones served on the Western Front in the Royal Welch Fusiliers. He wrote brilliantly about his experiences of trench warfare in *In Parenthesis* (1937), and his editor at Faber, T. S. Eliot, was among those who hailed him as a modernist master. In later works such as *The Anathemata* (1952) Jones developed his life-long exploration of myth, history and Christianity.

One of the pre-eminent writers of the modernist movement, the author of *Ulysses* and *Portrait of the Artist as a Young Man* started his writing career as a persuasive lyric poet. Rejecting the stranglehold of the Catholic Church over Irish life and culture, he left Dublin for a life of exile in various parts of Europe.

JONATHAN KARIARA (1935–93)

'A Leopard Lives in a Muu Tree'   528

Celebrated in Kenya as a poet, publisher and teacher, Kariara also wrote a highly-regarded play, *The Green Bean Patch*, and a book of *Stories from Kenya's History* for children.

SHIRLEY KAUFMAN (1923–)

'Stones'   621

Born in Seattle to immigrant Polish parents, Kaufman has lived in Jerusalem since 1973. 'I've felt all along that I'm living between two cultures, two languages, two identities,' she told the *Jerusalem Post* in 1997.

PATRICK KAVANAGH (1904–67)

'Epic'   346

A statue now shows Kavanagh sitting by the Grand Canal in Dublin, a location associated with the poet's joyful attainment of 'simplicity' in the Fifties. A novelist too, Kavanagh was praised by Seamus Heaney for 'the purity, authority and authenticity of his voice'.

JACKIE KAY (1961–)

'*££££*'   713

Born in Edinburgh to a Scottish mother and Nigerian father, Kay was adopted at birth by a white couple and raised in Glasgow. The experience inspired the poetry collection that made her name, *The Adoption Papers* (1991). Since then her fiction and poetry have brought her wide recognition.

WELDON KEES (1914–55)

'The View of the Castle'   345

Trotskyist, jazz pianist and journalist, Nebraska-born Kees published just three books of poems during his lifetime. He disappeared near the Golden Gate Bridge in San Francisco and is presumed to have committed suicide.

GALWAY KINNELL (1927–)

from 'The Avenue Bearing the Initial of Christ into the New World'   415

Born in Providence, Rhode Island, Kinnell has won numerous awards, including a MacArthur Fellowship. Troubled by 'a sense that so many things lovely and precious in our world seem to be dying out', in his poetry he seems to strive for a spiritual oneness with things. 'Nobody would write poetry if the world seemed perfect,' he has remarked.

JOHN KINSELLA (1963–)

'The Fire in the Forty-four'	739

Born in Western Australia, Kinsella has written in various genres at the inter-section of several core interests: in radical politics, environmentalism, vegan ethics, re-imagined pastoral, and avant-garde poetics. His admirers include Harold Bloom.

RUDYARD KIPLING (1865–1936)

'Bridge-Guard in the Karroo'	25
'Mesopotamia'	137
from 'Epitaphs of the War'	150

One of the most popular writers of his day, winning a huge readership with poetry and fiction alike, Kipling's stock fell as the generation after the First World War turned against the perceived causes of the slaughter, including the imperialism with which he was so strongly associated. He was the first British writer to be awarded the Nobel Prize (1907).

AUGUST KLEINZAHLER (1949–)

'Going'	741

Born in New Jersey, Kleinzahler has made his home in San Francisco, where he was a close friend of Thom Gunn. He has published a number of collect-ions on both sides of the Atlantic, and enjoys a reputation as a combative critic. Awards include a Guggenheim Fellowship (1989) and the Berlin Prize (2000).

KENNETH KOCH (1925–2002)

'You were wearing'	439

Koch was born in Cincinnati, educated at Harvard, and became one of the New York School of poets along with Frank O'Hara and John Ashbery. Influ-enced by the French surrealist Jacques Prévert, his work relishes the kaleidoscope of modern urban life.

INGRID DE KOK (1951–)

'Our Sharpeville'	423

Born and raised in South Africa, de Kok emigrated to Canada in her twenties, but returned in 1984 to take up a career as a university teacher. She is now a Fellow of Cape Town University. She writes in English, but some of her poems have been translated into Afrikaans.

ARUN KOLATKAR (1932–2004)

'The Priest'	555

A significant Indian poet in both English and Marathi, Kolatkar won the Commonwealth Poetry Prize for *Jejuri*. After his death, when that collection was reissued by New York Review Books in 2006, Amit Chaudhuri described

Kolatkar's influence as 'no less far-reaching, potentially, than that of *Midnight's Children*'.

YUSEF KOMUNYAKAA (1947–)

'Facing It'	665

Komunyakaa was born and brought up in Louisiana, and served in Vietnam. He started writing after he returned to the US and twenty years later, in 1994, won the Pulitzer Prize for Poetry. He has taught at several universities, among them Princeton and New York.

EVE LANGLEY (1908–74)

'Native-born'	282

Born in New South Wales, Langley spent twenty midlife years in New Zealand before returning to a reclusive life in a shack in the Blue Mountains. She claimed Oscar Wilde as her alter ego and took his name by deed poll in 1954. As well as poetry, she wrote numerous novels, most of which remain unpublished.

PHILIP LARKIN (1922–85)

'MCMXIV'	102
'Church Going'	367
'The Whitsun Weddings'	396
'Going, Going'	533

Coventry-born, Oxford-educated, Larkin had more success initially as a novelist, but from the appearance of his second book of poems, *The Less Deceived*, in 1955, his rise was rapid and assured. Living in Hull, where he was the university's librarian, Larkin wrote slowly, but his two remaining books, *The Whitsun Weddings* (1964) and *High Windows* (1974), were both highly successful, establishing him as the major English poet in the second half of the century.

MICHAEL LASKEY (1944–)

'Living with the Doctor'	697

Founder of the Aldeburgh Poetry Festival and of the poetry magazine *Smiths Knoll*, Laskey was born in Lichfield, studied at Cambridge, and after teaching in Spain settled in Suffolk.

D. H. LAWRENCE (1885–1930)

'Guards'	53
'Last Lesson of the Afternoon'	57
'Piano'	149
'Snake'	176

A miner's son, Lawrence soon abandoned his early life as a teacher and embraced the writer's life with messianic enthusiasm. One of the most controversial novelists of the century, he also produced large quantities of poetry, travel writing, criticism, correspondence and drama. For most of the Twenties he lived in the US, Mexico, Australia and Italy.

GEOFFREY LEHMANN (1940–)

'Parenthood'   691

Co-author of a standard work on Australian tax law, Lehmann is notable for the range of his subjects and the versatility of his tones, with poems voiced for the Emperor Nero and for his farmer father-in-law.

DENISE LEVERTOV (1923–97)

'Misnomer'   710

Born in Essex, Levertov emigrated to the US in 1948, where her poetry developed under the influence of William Carlos Williams and Charles Olson. She was of a dissident disposition and wrote poems opposing armed conflict throughout her life.

JOHN LEVETT (1950–)

'Early Warning'   730

Like Larkin, Levett pursued a career as a librarian. Peter Porter was among those who admired his 'considerable virtuosity' with traditional form.

ALUN LEWIS (1915–44)

'All Day it has Rained . . .'   276

Lewis was born in Wales and after joining the army went to India, and died in Burma under ambiguous circumstances. A selection of his work from India, *Ha! Ha! Among the Trumpets*, was published in 1945.

NICHOLAS VACHEL LINDSAY (1879–1931)

'The Leaden-Eyed'   180

Born in Springfield, Illinois, Vachel Lindsay took to the road and bartered poems for food and lodging. *General William Booth Enters Into Heaven and Other Poems* (1913) made his name, and the follow-up volume, *The Congo and Other Poems*, gave him a platform for increasingly popular readings. Dogged by financial worries and depression, he committed suicide by poison in 1931.

DOUGLAS LIVINGSTONE (1932–96)

'Bad Run at King's Rest'   592

Born in Kuala Lumpur, Livingstone was moved to South Africa with his family when the Japanese invaded Malaya. Considered by some to have been 'South Africa's most important poet of the late twentieth century', he also wrote plays and translations, and was a marine biologist by profession.

CHRISTOPHER LOGUE (1926–)

from 'War Music'	593

Logue has written for theatre and television, has himself had small parts in movies, and has contributed to *Private Eye*. His acclaimed project for half a century, though, despite his lack of ancient Greek, has been a strikingly original reworking of Homer's *Iliad* in a modern idiom.

MICHAEL LONGLEY (1939–)

'Wounds'	611

Longley was born in Belfast and read classics at Trinity College, Dublin. Among the foremost Ulster poets of his generation, with Heaney and Mahon, Longley made his career in arts administration. Awards include the T. S. Eliot Prize and the Queen's Gold Medal for Poetry.

ROBERT LOWELL (1917–77)

'Skunk Hour'	411
'Fall 1961'	434
'For the Union Dead'	454
'Waking Early Sunday Morning'	473

Born into one of New England's leading families, Lowell cut a Byronic figure in rejecting his ancestral values. He was imprisoned as a conscientious objector in the Second World War. Publication of *Life Studies* in 1959 gave him the presiding role in a new poetry of intimate revelation that came to be termed 'confessional', and from that time till his death he dominated American poetry.

NORMAN MacCAIG (1910–96)

'Crossing the Border'	500

MacCaig was born and brought up in Edinburgh, and taught at schools and universities in Scotland. He declared himself a born atheist and a born pacifist, and his poetry is wry, dry, witty and non-conformist.

HUGH MacDIARMID (1892–1978)

'The Glen of Silence'	248

'Hugh MacDiarmid' was the pseudonym chosen by Christopher Murray Grieve, a Scottish journalist, when he started to publish in Scots. With his new identity, he gradually became established as a modernist giant in Scottish poetry, with nationalist and communist convictions, and *A Drunk Man Looks at a Thistle* (1926) remains the most important poem in twentieth-century Scottish poetry.

SORLEY MacLEAN (1911–96)

'Death Valley'	304

Educated at Edinburgh University, MacLean was the leading Gaelic poet of the century, combining ancient and modern to breathe new life into the poetry of a beleaguered language. He served with the British Army in North Africa during the Second World War.

LOUIS MacNEICE (1907–63)

from 'Autumn Journal'	225
'Bagpipe Music'	237
'Meeting Point'	264
'The Taxis'	431

MacNeice was born in Belfast and educated in England, where his left-leaning, anti-fascist views drew him into the Auden camp. It was with Auden that he co-authored *Letters from Iceland* (1937), and his *Autumn Journal* (1939) captured the nervous atmosphere of the pre-war years. He made a career in radio, and wrote an autobiography, *The Strings Are False*, published posthumously in 1965.

JOHN MAGEE (1922–41)

'High Flight'	293

Born in Shanghai to an American father and a British mother, Magee was schooled in England, and then, having won a scholarship to Yale, chose instead to join the Royal Canadian Air Force. He was killed in a mid-air collision over Lincolnshire.

JAYANTA MAHAPATRA (1928–)

'The Abandoned British Cemetery at Balasore'	557

A teacher of physics until his retirement, Mahapatra has enjoyed steadily growing recognition for the firm-minded tranquillity of his meditative poems. Recent awards include India's Padma Shri Award and a SAARC Literary Award.

DEREK MAHON (1941–)

'A Disused Shed in Co. Wexford'	548

Born in Belfast and educated at Trinity College, Dublin and the Sorbonne, Mahon has long been celebrated for the music and muscle of his voice and the vigour of his conceptual imagination. Numerous distinctions include a Lannan Award and the David Cohen Prize.

DAVID MALOUF (1934–)

'Reading Horace outside Sydney, 1970'	520

Malouf's writing has brought him many international awards, among them the Neustadt International Prize. Born in Brisbane to a Lebanese father and an Anglo-Portuguese mother, he brings to both his poetry and his fiction a unique lyrical economy.

BILL MANHIRE (1946–)

'Jalopy: the End of Love'	703

In the late Nineties, Manhire was New Zealand's first poet laureate. A prolific poet, he works at the understated, whimsical end of the post-modern spectrum, with subject matter ranging from Antarctica to Billy Graham. 'If poets aren't exploring their way forward into mystery,' he has said, 'they might as well give up completely.'

JOHN MANIFOLD (1915–85)

'Fife Tune'	315

Born in Melbourne in 1915, Manifold was educated locally and at Cambridge, where he read modern languages. A recruit to the Communist cause, he fought against Franco in Spain, and during the Second World War was in British army intelligence. Afterwards, in Australia, he devoted his energy to working for the Communist Party and researching Australian bush music.

KATHERINE MANSFIELD (1888–1923)

'To God the Father'	72
'To L. H. B. (1894–1915)'	110

Compared as a short-story writer with Chekhov and Joyce, Mansfield was born in New Zealand and lived much of her short life in England and continental Europe. Authentic utterance was an abiding concern. In a letter of 1919 she followed admiration of Emily Brontë's poetry with the remark, 'one of the chief reasons for one's dissatisfaction with modern poetry is one can't be sure that it really does belong to the man who writes it.'

DON MARQUIS (1878–1937)

'mehitabel s morals'	214

Don Marquis was a versatile American writer of journalism, fiction, drama and poetry. He is best known for Archy, a cockroach reincarnation of a free-verse poet whose work was supposedly tapped out on Marquis's typewriter, and which satirised American mores through reporting the scandalous life of Mehitable, the alley cat. Don Marquis was so popular that he had a US Navy vessel named after him in 1943, the USS Don Marquis (IX-215).

JOHN MASEFIELD (1878–1967)

'Sea-Fever'	30
'Cargoes'	34
'An Epilogue'	192

Masefield trained for the merchant navy at thirteen, and at seventeen jumped ship and adopted the life of a vagrant in America. When he returned to England, he became a prolific writer – of prose and verse – and gained a great popular following. He became Poet Laureate in 1930 and received the Order of Merit in 1935.

R. A. K. MASON (1905–71)

'Lugete o veneres'	215
'Sonnet to MacArthur's Eyes'	352

With Curnow, Fairburn and Denis Glover, Mason belonged to the generation of New Zealand poets that came to maturity in the Thirties and gave the country – despite solitary earlier voices – its first authoritative poetry. Described by Curnow as New Zealand's 'first wholly original, unmistakably gifted poet', Mason was deeply involved with left-wing politics in the Thirties and worked for the Auckland General Labourers' Union after the Second World War.

EDGAR LEE MASTERS (1868–1950)

'Mrs Kessler'	112

Poet, playwright, biographer, Masters is chiefly remembered today for his *Spoon River Anthology* (1915), a collection of more than two hundred epitaphs and short verse tales, adding up to a deft collective portrait of a fictional community.

GLYN MAXWELL (1962–)

'Helene and Heloise'	717
'Deep Sorriness Atonement Song'	760

Maxwell's first book, *Tale of the Mayor's Son* (1990), was impressively assured, and his work as poet, dramatist and librettist has remained striking for its technical poise and wide-ranging subject matter. Born in Welwyn Garden City, Maxwell has lived in Amherst and New York and is currently based in London.

JAMES McAULEY (1917–76)

'Because'	517
'Tabletalk'	519

Even before he published his own first collection of poems, McAuley was notorious as co-perpetrator of the Ern Malley hoax. Founder editor of the Australian cultural monthly *Quadrant*, McAuley was anti-Communist in politics, Catholic by religion, spiritual in aesthetics, and often tart in his critical views. His poetry mellowed towards the end of his writing life.

BRIAN McCABE (1951–)

'Hand'	768

McCabe is an award-winning Scottish writer of novels, short stories and poems. He has been a freelance writer since 1980, and has held various residencies and writer's fellowships.

Carol Ann Duffy for 'the range of his inventiveness, the generosity of his imagination, the moral alertness of his social observation'.

ANDREW MOTION (1952–)

'Anne Frank Huis'	590

Poet Laureate from 1999 to 2009, Motion was knighted for services to literature in 2009. He is celebrated not only for his poetry but also for his biographies of Keats and Larkin and a memoir of his mother. While Laureate he established The Poetry Archive, an important online poetry resource.

EDWIN MUIR (1887–1959)

'The Castle'	328
'The Horses'	376

Born on the Orkney Islands, Muir was a Scot of international convictions, at odds with Hugh MacDiarmid's understanding of Scottish nationalism. He translated Franz Kafka, Heinrich Mann and Hermann Broch, and in his poetry pursued archetypal and visionary motifs fundamental to all human experience.

PAUL MULDOON (1951–)

'Cuba'	435
'Why Brownlee left'	586

Muldoon was educated at Queen's University, Belfast, where he was taught by Seamus Heaney. His dazzling technical virtuosity has always been carried easily, and his riddling wit and ready wordplay enhance his engagement with serious themes and subjects. Now a professor at Princeton, his awards include the T. S. Eliot Prize, the Pulitzer Prize and the Griffin Prize.

LES MURRAY (1938–)

'The Ballad of Jimmy Governor'	19
'The Future'	559
'Letters to the Winner'	661
'It Allows a Portrait in Line Scan at Fifteen'	753

Seen not only as Australia's leading living poet but as a writer of global stature, Murray has famously said he is 'only interested in everything'. The generous range, geographical, historical, philosophical, and even botanical, of his work is exhilarating. In addition to a stream of poetry collections, he has published the verse novels *The Boys Who Stole the Funeral* (1979) and *Fredy Neptune* (1999), and highly original and illuminating criticism.

Shaw Neilson (1872–1942)

Born in South Australia to Scottish parents, Neilson was brought up in rural parts, with very little formal education. His first full collection, *Heart of Spring*, was delayed by the First World War until 1919. Neilson scraped a living as an ill-paid labourer, and even as he rose to prominence as a poet, he was afflicted with failing eyesight, which made it hard for his supporters to find him gainful employment. Despite the odds against him, his *Collected Poems* appeared in 1934.

Howard Nemerov (1920–91)

A formalist of the generation of Wilbur and Hecht, Nemerov was born in New York and served as a pilot in the Second World War. His 1977 *Collected Poems* took the Pulitzer and Bollingen Prizes and a National Book Award.

Arthur Nortje (1942–70)

Born in Oudtshoorn, South Africa, Nortje spent much of his short life in England and Canada, and died of a drug overdose. His poetry, published posthumously in the Seventies, was gathered as *Anatomy of Dark: Collected Poems* in 2000.

Sean O'Brien (1952–)

O'Brien's poetry has brought him a Cholmondeley Award, the T. S. Eliot Prize and the Forward Poetry Prize, and a chair at Newcastle University. He is also a highly-regarded broadcaster, stage writer and critic.

Frank O'Hara (1926–66)

Born in Baltimore, O'Hara studied at Harvard on a war veterans' grant, having seen service in the US Navy in the South Pacific. In his years working for the Museum of Modern Art in New York he came to epitomise the New Yorker of the Sixties, witty, well-connected, warm. His tongue-in-cheek manifesto 'Personism' required among other things that poetry be written as if addressed to one other person.

SHARON OLDS (1942–)

Raised as a 'hellfire Calvinist', Olds was born in San Francisco and educated at Stanford and Columbia. The intensity of her fixation on the body, sexuality, and parents, has brought her wide recognition, and – with sales exceeding fifty thousand – *The Dead and the Living* (1984) is among the best-selling poetry collections of recent decades.

MICHAEL ONDAATJE (1943–)

Born in Ceylon (Sri Lanka), Ondaatje spent eight teenage years in England before becoming a Canadian citizen in the Sixties. As well as poetry, he has written acclaimed memoirs (*Running in the Family*, 1982) and fiction, notably *The English Patient* (1992).

VINCENT O'SULLIVAN (1937–)

Born in Auckland but long associated with Wellington, O'Sullivan has enjoyed equal acclaim as poet, dramatist, and fiction writer. He has also been a highly influential anthologist and editor. 'With his trenchant mix of philosophical erudition and vernacular ease,' Andrew Johnston has observed, 'he comes across as the defrocked priest of New Zealand literature.'

WILFRED OWEN (1893–1918)

Unquestionably the finest poet of the First World War, Wilfred Owen enlisted in 1915 and served as an infantryman on the Somme before being diagnosed as 'shell-shocked' and sent to Craiglockhart Hospital, Edinburgh in May 1917. There he met Siegfried Sassoon, who proved an inspirational friend and mentor. In the few months after his discharge from Craiglockhart, Owen worked on the poems that would elegise a generation slaughtered in the trenches. He also made the momentous decision to return to his regiment, and he was killed on 4 November 1918 on the Sambre Canal, just a week before the Armistice was signed.

DOROTHY PARKER (1893–1967)

'War Song'	314

The most celebrated wise-cracker of the inter-war years, Parker was a leading wit at *The New Yorker* from its founding in 1925. Twice nominated for an Academy Award, she was blacklisted in Hollywood during the McCarthyist witch-hunt.

GEOFFREY PARSONS (1910–)

'Lorca'	230

A politically committed poet in the 1930s, Parsons later turned to satire with his Byronic account of a public schoolboy drawn to poetry, *Peter's Progress*, published in 1953.

DON PATERSON (1963–)

'The Scale of Intensity'	725

Paterson is a Scottish poet, critic and musician. His first collection, *Nil Nil* won the Forward Poetry Prize in 1993, and *God's Gift to Women* (1997) took the T. S. Eliot Prize and Geoffrey Faber Memorial Prize. He was awarded the Queen's Gold Medal for Poetry in 2010.

STEPHEN PHILLIPS (1864–1915)

from 'The Apparition'	42

Phillips shot to prominence with his first acclaimed books of poetry in the 1890s, but after the turn of the century gave more of his attention to writing blank verse dramas on classical and biblical subjects, several of which were produced by Sir Herbert Beerbohm Tree. Symons, Gosse, William Watson and William Archer all admired his work, but it is now mostly forgotten.

ROBERT PINSKY (1940–)

'Shirt'	689

Born at Long Branch, New Jersey, Pinsky studied under Yvor Winters at Stanford. The recipient of numerous awards, he served as US Poet Laureate from 1997 to 2000.

SYLVIA PLATH (1932–63)

'The Bee Meeting'	444
'Lady Lazarus'	446

Plath won a Fulbright to Cambridge University, where she met and married Ted Hughes. Before the breakdown of the marriage and her tragic suicide in 1963, she published *The Colossus and Other Poems* (1960). Her growing reputation was confirmed by the shocking power of her posthumous collection, *Ariel* (1965). Further selections of her poetry, letters and journals have been published since her death, as has her one novel, *The Bell Jar* (1963).

CRAIG RAINE (1944–)

'In Modern Dress'	622

Raine's first collections, *The Onion, Memory* (1978) and *A Martian Sends a Post-card Home* (1979), established him as a highly inventive image-maker. He has worked in publishing and has taught at Oxford, and has published further books of poetry and criticism, and a book of prose fiction, *Heartbreak* (2010).

CARL RAKOSI (1903–2004)

'To an Anti-Semite'	299

Born in Berlin, Rakosi came to the US as a child. Associated with the loose grouping of Objectivist poets (he admired Reznikoff's work), for many years he abandoned poetry altogether. Australian poet John Tranter, who chanced to call on Rakosi on his hundredth birthday, described him as 'kind, thoughtful, bright and alert, and as sharp as a pin'.

JOHN CROWE RANSOM (1888–1974)

'Vision by Sweetwater'	194

Born in Tennessee, Ransom studied at Oxford and later taught for many years at Kenyon College in Ohio, where he founded the influential literary magazine *The Kenyon Review*. His influence as critic was as great as his impact as poet, which was mainly confined to the 1920s, but his slender output is memorable for its formal elegance and his subtle air of being on speaking terms with the uncanny.

H. D. RAWNSLEY (1851–1920)

'To the Mikado, Portsmouth, USA'	41

The Reverend Hardwicke Drummond Rawnsley, canon of Carlisle, a graduate of Balliol and later a founder of the National Trust, wrote large quantities of verse as well as guides to the Lake District and to Switzerland.

PETER READING (1946–)

'This is unclean . . .'	632

Misanthropic, mordant and almost as reclusive as Larkin, Reading has been described as Britain's unacknowledged poet laureate. His subject matter has often been cheerless – *H. sap*'s inhumanity to *H. sap* – but despite the air of despair and radical doubt he is among the most prolific contemporary poets.

PETER REDGROVE (1932–2003)

'The Curiosity-Shop'	532

Redgrove's visionary poetry explored the spiritual and sensual parameters of the human. Born in Surrey and educated at Cambridge, he published several novels, some in collaboration with his wife, the poet Penelope Shuttle, with whom he also co-wrote two studies of the female cycle.

Robinson was a popular and prolific American poet, to whom Theodore Roosevelt gave encouragement early in his career. He won the Pulitzer Prize three times, and one of his early poems, 'Richard Cory', was adapted decades after his death for a song by Simon and Garfunkel.

Rodgers was born in Belfast, attended Queen's University and trained for the ministry. After some years as a Presbyterian pastor, he moved to post-war London and worked at the BBC with fellow poets Louis MacNeice and Dylan Thomas. He was elected to the Irish Academy of Letters in 1951 – to fill the vacancy caused by the death of George Bernard Shaw.

Despite his openness to experience – 'I could say hello to things,' he said – Roethke was not a happy man, and was prone to depression and heavy drinking. He taught at American universities, where he was generally loved by his students, if not by the authorities, and his collected poems, *Words for the Wind*, won several awards when it appeared in 1959.

Rosenberg's parents had fled anti-Jewish pogroms in Lithuania, and he was born in Bristol. In 1911 he began studies at the Slade School of Fine Art, but in 1914 moved to South Africa for reasons of health. He returned to join the army, and was killed during the German spring offensive of 1918 on 1 April.

Born in Calcutta, Ross served in the Royal Navy before making a London-based career in sports journalism and publishing. As well as poetry he published highly-regarded memoirs and books on cricket, and for forty years edited the key literary and arts periodical *London Magazine*.

Born in London, Rumens has taught at universities in the UK, Ireland and Sweden. A prolific poet, she has written plays and a novel, is highly regarded as an editor, and has translated Russian poetry (in collaboration with Yuri Drobyshev).

VICTORIA SACKVILLE-WEST (1892–1962)

'Full Moon'	163

Better known as novelist, biographer, gardener – and wife of the diplomat and diarist Harold Nicolson – Victoria Sackville-West published several volumes of poetry, achieving greatest acclaim for her long poem, *The Land* (1926).

MARY JO SALTER (1954–)

'A Kiss in Space'	732

Born in Michigan, educated at Harvard and Cambridge, Salter is an editor of *The Norton Anthology of Poetry* and a professor at Johns Hopkins University, Baltimore.

CARL SANDBURG (1878–1967)

'Buttons'	111
'Mohammed Bek Hadjetlache'	155
'Buffalo Dusk'	156

Sandburg made his breakthrough with *Chicago Poems* in 1916. He was soon the unofficial laureate of the Midwest, with a growing national reputation, and went on to win three Pulitzer Prizes, one for his *Complete Poems* (1950) and one for his biography of Abraham Lincoln.

SIEGFRIED SASSOON (1886–1967)

'The Hero'	129
'They'	130
'Reconciliation'	148

Educated at Marlborough and Cambridge, Sassoon served in France during the First World War, an experience which transformed his understanding of writing and brought him important friendships with Graves and Owen. In the Twenties and Thirties he published three acclaimed volumes of fictionalised autobiography.

E. J. SCOVELL (1907–99)

'A Refugee'	313

Born in Sheffield and educated at Oxford, Edith Joy Scovell married a biologist and acted as his field assistant in South America. Her first collection, published in 1944, gave an insight into the war on the Home Front. Her *Collected Poems* appeared in 1988.

KENNETH SLESSOR (1901–71)

'Five Bells'	257
'Beach Burial'	306

Slessor was first a reporter, then literary editor on the Sydney *Sun*. He built up a reputation as one of Australia's leading poets of the mid-century, and a fine selection of his critical writings appeared in *Bread and Wine* (1970).

DAVE SMITH (1942-)

'Cumberland Station'	587

Virginia-born, Smith has been an editor and university professor, and has published fiction, but he is best known for his poetry. His many honours include Guggenheim and National Endowment for the Arts fellowships.

IAIN CRICHTON SMITH (1928–98)

'Old Woman'	464

Born in Glasgow, raised on the island of Lewis, and educated at Aberdeen, Smith was devoted to his Scottish heritage, and helped to preserve it by writing much of his poetry in Gaelic. His most powerful novel is *Consider the Lilies* (1968), set during the Highland Clearances, and he also wrote plays, short stories and translations from Gaelic.

STEVIE SMITH (1902–71)

'Not Waving but Drowning'	390
'I Remember'	391

Smith embodied the notion of English eccentricity. She worked all her life in magazine publishing, and produced a steady stream of poetry, often illustrated with childlike cartoons. Her *Collected Poems* appeared posthumously in 1975.

ELIZABETH SMITHER (1941–)

'The Forecast for Night'	678

Smither was born in New Plymouth, on the north island of New Zealand, where she still lives. Highly regarded for her fiction too, she has served as New Zealand Poet Laureate.

KENDRICK SMITHYMAN (1922–95)

'Waikato Railstop'	392

From a logging community in the far north of New Zealand, Smithyman taught children with special needs for many years before moving into university teaching. At his death he had completed a remarkable long poem about a nineteenth-century Ngapuhi religious leader, published to posthumous acclaim as *Atua Wera* (1997).

W. D. Snodgrass (1926–2009)

Born in Pennsylvania, Snodgrass studied at the Iowa Writers' Workshop and himself had a distinguished university teaching career. The first of his four marriages ended in divorce in 1953 and produced the poems in *Heart's Needle* (1959), which won a Pulitzer Prize and is widely seen as sharing with Lowell's *Life Studies* the honour of having ushered in 'confessional' poetry (a term Snodgrass himself disliked).

Wole Soyinka (1934–)

Born in Nigeria, Soyinka was the first African writer to be awarded the Nobel Prize for literature, in 1986. Celebrated as poet, playwright and memoirist, he has been a consistent and vocal opponent of oppressive regimes in Africa, and was condemned to death in absentia by the Nigerian regime of General Sani Abacha in the Nineties.

Stephen Spender (1909–95)

A friend and disciple of Auden, Spender visited Germany in the early days of the Nazi party and Spain during the Spanish Civil War. In his later work he turned to more personal themes, and extended his self-exploration through autobiography and journals. He co-edited *Encounter*, worked for UNESCO and International PEN, held university posts, and was knighted in 1983 for services to literature.

Elizabeth Spires (1952–)

Born in Ohio and educated at Vassar and Johns Hopkins, Spires is herself a professor at Groucher College in Baltimore. Brought up as a Catholic, she exhibits a mildly-stated moral sense in her poetry, which goes hand in hand with an understated affinity with Elizabeth Bishop.

Pauline Stainer (1941–)

Born in Stoke-on-Trent, Stainer published her first book of poems in her late forties. Her ability to create an idiosyncratically-balanced, newly-unfamiliar lyric world out of familiar materials has been widely admired.

C. K. STEAD (1932–)

A prolific novelist and distinguished critic, Stead is one of the most substantial writers to have come out of New Zealand. His poetry and fiction have won every accolade his country can bestow, and his numerous international successes include, most recently, the *Sunday Times* Short Story Award and the Hippocrates Prize.

WALLACE STEVENS (1879–1955)

Harvard-educated, Stevens joined the legal department of the Hartford Accident and Indemnity Company, where he became vice-president in 1934. *Harmonium* (1923) sold fewer than one hundred copies, and Stevens did not publish another collection until 1936. Technically adroit, rhythmically seductive, with a tone that 'ranged from the chuckling-oblique to the mellifluous-sublime' (Ian Hamilton), Stevens's poetry has been immensely influential on other poets.

DOUGLAS STEWART (1913–85)

Born in New Zealand, Stewart moved to Australia in his mid-twenties, and through the Forties and Fifties exerted an important influence as literary editor of *The Bulletin*. As well as poetry he wrote several verse plays and biographies.

MATTHEW SWEENEY (1952–)

Donegal-born, Sweeney has lived in London, Berlin, and other parts of Europe, and in much of his poetry reflects a sense that the real is in fact unsettlingly fantastical. He also writes fiction and poetry for children.

J. M. SYNGE (1871–1909)

In his relatively short life (he died of Hodgkin's disease before he was forty), Synge established himself as the first great playwright of the Irish Literary Theatre. Encouraged by W. B. Yeats, he made five trips to the Aran Islands, whose hardy and independent communities provided him with material for a succession of plays, culminating in *The Playboy of the Western World*, which caused a riot when first presented in 1907 for its supposed subversion of the Catholic Church.

Stoke-on-Trent, he has embraced the world's poetry, through friendship (with Octavio Paz) and through translation (of Machado, Vallejo and Bertolucci). He edited *The Oxford Book of Verse in English Translation* (1980).

JEAN TOOMER (1894–1967)

'Portrait in Georgia'	179

Born in Washington, D.C., Toomer was an important figure in the Harlem Renaissance, and his *Cane* (1923) – a blend of poetry and prose – was an important contribution to the re-evaluation and celebration of black culture. He published *Essentials*, a book of philosophical aphorisms, in 1931.

JOHN TRANTER (1943–)

from 'Crying in Early Infancy'	561

Twice winner of the Kenneth Slessor Prize, Tranter is the most highly-regarded of Australia's avant-garde poets. He was the founder and long-time editor of the online poetry journal *Jacket*.

JOHN UPDIKE (1932–2009)

'Seven New Ways of Looking at the Moon'	511

In an extremely productive writing life, Updike won many awards, some more than once, for his fiction, poetry and criticism. His own professed aim in writing was 'to give the mundane its beautiful due'.

DEREK WALCOTT (1930–)

'Elegy'	490
'Koenig of the River'	572

Born at Castries on the Caribbean island of St Lucia, Walcott has been prolific as poet and playwright for sixty years, and is also a gifted painter. Landmark works include *Another Life* (1973), *The Star-Apple Kingdom* (1980) and *Omeros* (1990). The recipient of a MacArthur Fellowship and the Queen's Gold Medal for Poetry, Walcott was awarded the Nobel Prize in 1992.

SYLVIA TOWNSEND WARNER (1893–1978)

'Mr Gradgrind's Country'	343

Poet and novelist, Warner devoted ten years of her life to working on a ten-volume compilation of Tudor church music. She and her partner, Valentine Ackland, joined the Communist Party in 1935. Warner published a biography of T. H. White and several collections of short stories.

ROBERT PENN WARREN (1905–89)

'Natural History'	535

Penn Warren was born in Kentucky, and attended Vanderbilt, Berkeley, Yale and Oxford. Heaped with honours, and appointed the first US Poet Laureate in

1983, he is still the only writer to have won the Pulitzer Prize for both fiction and poetry.

WILLIAM WATSON (1858–1935)

'Rome and Another'	35
from 'Sonnets to Miranda'	48

A once-popular and prolific poet, heavily under the influence of Tennyson and the great Victorians, Watson has long been ignored. A patriot with a conscience, he opposed the Boer War, and showed an independence of mind that probably cost him the Laureateship.

PHYLLIS WEBB (1927–)

'My loves are dying'	626

Born in Victoria, British Columbia, Webb is a Canadian poet and critic, and worked for many years as a CBC radio producer. She has also taught in Canadian universities. She lives on Salt Spring Island.

LANDEG WHITE (1940–)

'Raid'	613

Welsh-born, White taught at universities in Trinidad, Malawi, Sierra Leone, Zambia and England before settling in Portugal. Co-editor of an anthology of African oral poetry, he is also widely praised for his translations of Camões.

PHILLIP WHITFIELD (1918–96)

'Day of Liberation, Bergen-Belsen, May 1945'	324

Whitfield was a Captain in the Royal Army Medical Corps and was the first doctor present when British soldiers liberated Belsen concentration camp. Trained at University College, London, he worked as a specialist in community medicine and paediatrics, and as an active member of Amnesty International helped create the Medical Foundation for the Care of Victims of Torture. His selected poems, *A Dram of Time*, were published in 1987.

JOHN WHITWORTH (1945–)

'These Boys'	614

Described by Les Murray as 'Kent's rococo rhymer and hyperbolist', Whitworth was born in India, educated at Oxford, and lives in Canterbury. Asked by an interviewer what he dislikes, Whitworth replied: 'Free verse. Walt Whitman. The whole *Guardian* thing.'

ANNA WICKHAM (1884–1947)

'The Fired Pot'	126

Born in Wimbledon, but educated in New South Wales, Edith Harper returned to England in 1905, and later started writing under the name Anna Wickham.

Her feminism was fuelled by an unhappy marriage to a solicitor who actively opposed her career as a poet.

Wilbur's first four collections, starting with *The Beautiful Changes* (1947) and culminating in *Things of This World* (1956), which won the Pulitzer Prize and a National Book Award, made him the leading American poet of the Fifties. He has written poetry, criticism, and acclaimed translations of French theatre, to an exhilarating standard for more than sixty years. In 1987 he was appointed second US Poet Laureate.

Williams, who divides his time between his native US and France, has won the Pulitzer Prize and numerous other awards. Admirers have included Anne Sexton, Paul Muldoon and Dan Chiasson.

Born in Windsor, Williams is a poet, travel writer and journalist, and has written a regular column for the *Times Literary Supplement* for many years. His collection *Billy's Rain* won the T. S. Eliot Prize, and in 2004 he was awarded the Queen's Medal for Poetry.

Born in Rutherford, New Jersey, to an English father and Puerto Rican mother, Williams strove to be identified with the 'American grain' in poetry, rather than with the new poetics of Pound and Eliot. Though his views on 'measure' and the 'variable foot' may be tenuous, he re-created the spoken vernacular for poetry, and in *Spring and All* (1923) and the huge and ambitious *Paterson* (1963) he made sustained inquiries into the nature of language and of life in a modern American city.

JAMES WRIGHT (1927–80)

Wright was educated at Kenyon College, Yale and the University of Washington, and then taught at Hunter College in New York for the rest of his life. His *Collected Poems* won the Pulitzer Prize in 1971.

JUDITH WRIGHT (1915–2000)

Born in New South Wales, Wright became a leading figure in Australian poetry, as well as an active environmentalist and supporter of Aboriginal land rights. She was awarded the Queen's Gold Medal for Poetry in 1992. Her *Preoccupations in Australian Poetry* (1965) remains one of the shrewdest critical studies in the field.

KIT WRIGHT (1944–)

The son of a schoolmaster, Wright was brought up in Kent and educated at Oxford. A traditionalist in matters of form – 'it don't mean a thing if it ain't got that swing,' he likes to quote – he writes for adults and children with a rare rhythmical zest, and everything he writes is grounded in a deep human empathy.

W. B. YEATS (1865–1939)

A principal in the Irish Literary Revival, and a co-founder of the Abbey Theatre in Dublin, Yeats served as a senator when Ireland gained its independence from British rule. The Nobel Prize was awarded him in 1923 in recognition of his expression of 'the spirit of a whole nation'. Inspired by his wife's automatic writing, he produced *A Vision* in 1925, a study of the occult and an account of the symbols which dominated his poetry. Yeats died in France in January 1939 and was re-interred at Drumcliffe in County Sligo after the Second World War.

ANDREW YOUNG (1885–1971)

Born in Scotland, Young was an Anglican vicar and later a canon of Chichester Cathedral. He wrote exquisite pastoral lyrics underpinned by an understated spiritual enquiry, and a prose account of his botanical interests, *A Prospect of Flowers* (1944).

Index of First Lines